A Handbook of
MANAGEMENT
TECHNIQUES

A Handbook of
MANAGEMENT
TECHNIQUES

A COMPREHENSIVE GUIDE TO
ACHIEVING MANAGERIAL EXCELLENCE
AND IMPROVED DECISION MAKING

REVISED 3RD EDITION

Michael Armstrong

**KOGAN
PAGE**

OCM 65468491

London and Philadelphia

Publisher's note
Every possible effort has been made to ensure that the information contained in this book is accurate at the time of going to press, and the publishers and author cannot accept responsibility for any errors or omissions, however caused. No responsibility for loss or damage occasioned to any person acting, or refraining from action, as a result of the material in this publication can be accepted by the editor, the publisher or any of the authors.

First published in Great Britain and the United States in 1986 by Kogan Page Limited
Second edition 1993
Third edition 2001
Revised third edition 2006

120 Pentonville Road
London N1 9JN
United Kingdom
www.kogan-page.co.uk

525 South 4th Street, #241
Philadelphia PA 19147
USA

ISBN 0 7494 4766 4

British Library Cataloguing-in-Publication Data

A CIP record for this book is available from the British Library.

Library of Congress Cataloging-in-Publication Data

Armstrong, Michael, 1928-
    A handbook of management techniques : a comprehensive guide to achieving managerial excellence and improved decision making / Michael Armstrong – Rev. 3rd ed.
        p. cm.
    ISBN 0-7494-4766-4
    1. Management. I. Title.
    HD31.A72 2006
    658–dc22

                                           2006017490

Typeset by Saxon Graphics Ltd, Derby
Printed and bound in Great Britain by Bell & Bain, Glasgow

Contents

Contents

List of Figures

List of Tables

Preface to the Revised Third Edition

This edition of *A Handbook of Management Techniques* revises and updates the techniques described in the previous editions to take account of the considerable developments that have taken place over the past 20 years.

The book includes completely new sections covering Human Capital Measurement, Role Analysis, Grade and Pay Structures and Contingent Pay. These sections greatly reflect the changes brought about by new technology and its impact on modern management practices.

1

Introduction: Management Techniques

DEFINITION

Management techniques are the systematic and analytical methods used by managers to assist in decision making, the improvement of efficiency and effectiveness and, in particular, the conduct of the two key managerial activities of planning and control. Areas of management such as corporate planning, marketing, management accounting and operation research, which make considerable use of related techniques, may be termed disciplines.

Techniques, used singly or grouped into disciplines, should be distinguished from:

- *managerial skills*, such as coordinating, delegating, communicating, negotiating or interviewing, which rely on personal expertise developed by experience and training;
- *procedures*, which consist of the various administrative tasks, systems and guidelines needed to get work done – the way in which sales orders are processed is a procedure;
- *activities or functions*, in which various administrative tasks are carried out and skills and procedures used in order to achieve a desired result; for example, advertising, recruitment and selection or purchasing.

In each of these areas of skills, procedures and activities, however, management techniques play an important part, either generally in helping to solve problems, or particularly by enabling things to be done more effectively. For example, the technique of media planning is used in advertising, selection testing in recruitment and make or buy analysis in purchasing.

CHARACTERISTICS OF MANAGEMENT TECHNIQUES

All management techniques are systematic and, in one sense or another, analytical. Quantification plays an important part in many techniques, and all techniques attempt to be objective or at least try to minimize the amount of subjectivity in decision making. These characteristics are discussed below.

Systematic

All techniques are systematic in that they consist of specified and often sequential methods of tackling a problem, providing information for decision making or improving operational efficiency. Because they are systematic, techniques ensure that each step required to deal with a situation is carried out in a prescribed manner. The systematic approach encouraged by the use of management techniques provides a framework within which managers can exercise their skills in a more orderly and purposeful manner.

Analytical

Techniques are analytical in two senses. First, the techniques themselves have been developed by considering what systematic and possibly quantitative methods are required to deal with every aspect of a situation and to achieve an end result.

Second, and most importantly, techniques are usually analytical in the sense that they subject complex situations to close and systematic examination, and resolve them into their key elements. This process of identification and dissection facilitates the orderly arrangement of a mass of data, which may be present in a confused state, into logical patterns, thus promoting understanding and pointing the way to an appropriate decision.

Analysis concentrates on facts rather than opinions and provides a precise structure and terminology which serves as a means of communication, enabling managers to make their judgements within a clearly defined framework and in a concrete context.

Quantitative

Wherever relevant, management techniques measure in numerical or financial terms what is happening, and quantify forecasts of future trends. Most management decisions involve financial considerations, so management techniques place monetary values on performance reports, forecasts, plans and the control information needed to assess results against budgets or targets.

Statistical and mathematical methods are used to analyse data, evaluate alternative courses of action and indicate the optimum decision – ie the decision which will produce the best results for the organization, bearing in mind any limiting factors or constraints arising from a lack of resources.

Mathematical models are created which provide a simplified representation of the real world which abstracts the features of the situation relevant to the questions being studied. Such models, and simulations of operational situations, assist managers to deal with uncertainty. The right or optimum choice is seldom obvious. Quantitative techniques help managers to understand the probable consequences in financial and numerical terms of taking alternative courses of action. They therefore focus attention on what is likely to be the best course of action among the competing alternatives which are available.

Objective

By concentrating on facts, by subjecting these facts to systematic analysis, and by quantifying this analysis wherever possible, management techniques help managers to be objective. Techniques such as market research, forecasting, and job evaluation will use subjective methods to a degree. But subjectivity will be exercised within these bounds. The analytical framework provided by techniques in these areas will at least ensure that any subjective element in the decision-making process is channelled and subjected to the rigorous analysis which is characteristic of any properly administered technique.

APPLICATIONS

Management techniques have applications in all aspects of planning, organizing, directing and controlling the affairs of an enterprise or a public sector organization. The particular areas in which they are applied, as described in this handbook, are:

1. *General management*, which covers the overall planning and control of the organization. General management as such is not a technique, but it

is a discipline which largely relies on management techniques to ensure its success. The particular techniques or disciplines most relevant to general management are corporate and organization planning.

2. *Marketing management,* which, as the crucial business generation function in any company, relies heavily on techniques such as market research, forecasting, product analysis and planning, pricing, and marketing and sales planning and control.

3. *Operations management,* which, with the help of computers, uses planning, scheduling and production control techniques extensively and ensures that resources are allocated and used effectively by means of resource allocation and inventory control systems.

4. *Financial management,* where analytical, planning, budgeting and control techniques play a vital part in ensuring that the organization has the resources it needs and can afford, and that it uses them effectively.

5. *Human resource management,* which uses various techniques such as human resource planning, salary administration, performance appraisal, training and management development to ensure that the organization has the number of qualified, competent and motivated people it needs.

6. *Information technology,* which provides for computers and telecommunication systems to give the information, data-processing capacities and facilities required in complex and fast-moving organizations.

7. *Management science,* which makes available the quantitative techniques used in operation research to provide guidance on planning, problem solving and decision making.

8. *Planning and resource allocation,* where the analytical techniques of network planning and line of balance are used to plan projects and calculate the resources required.

9. *Efficiency and effectiveness,* where investigation techniques such as the management audit are used to monitor the performance of the organization in association with ratio analysis, and remedial techniques such as cost reduction, profit improvement, productivity planning and work study are available to improve performance and results.

BENEFITS

Management techniques provide a foundation for improved managerial performance. Their main strengths lie in their systematic, analytical and, in many cases, quantified base. They operate by means of a continuous cycle of gathering and analysing factual data, formulating problems, selecting objectives, identifying alternative courses of action, building new models, weighing costs against performance and benefits, and monitoring performance to point the way to corrective action and improvements.

Their value in all these respects is undeniable, but a word of caution is necessary. Techniques are only as good as the people who use them. Quantification is fine, but if it is based on doubtful assumptions, it can result in ponderous edifices being built on sand and collapsing when the sand shifts and can no longer bear their weight. Techniques such as investment appraisal and risk analysis will put executives into the best position possible to determine where they are going, but judgement is still required. Management techniques can help managers to make better decisions, but can never replace good judgement, which is the hallmark of the successful executive.

Part 1

Marketing Management

2

Marketing Management: An Overview

DEFINITION

Marketing is 'the management process responsible for identifying, antici- pating and satisfying customer requirements profitably' (Chartered Institute of Marketing).

OBJECTIVES

The overall objective of marketing is to ensure that the company obtains the revenues it needs to achieve its profit targets.

As defined by Kotler,[1] marketing management is: 'The analysis, planning, implementation, and control of programs designed to create, build, and maintain beneficial exchanges and relationships with target markets for the purpose of achieving organisational objectives.' According to Theodore Levitt:[2] 'The purpose of a business is to get and keep a customer.' Marketing aims to decide what companies should do to achieve that purpose and then to ensure that it is done.

THE MARKETING CONCEPT

'The marketing concept holds that the key to achieving organisational goals consists in determining the needs and wants of target markets and delivering the desired satisfactions more effectively and efficiently than competitors' (Kotler). The target market is defined as the set of actual and potential buyers of a product.

Kotler distinguishes the marketing concept from the following:

- *The product concept,* which holds that consumers will favour those products that are available and highly affordable, and therefore management should concentrate on improving production and distribution efficiency.
- *The product concept,* which holds that consumers will favour those products that offer the most quality, performance and features, and therefore the organization should devote its energy to making continuous product improvements.
- *The selling concept,* which holds that consumers will not buy enough of the organization's products unless the organization undertakes a substantial selling and promotional effort.

The limitations of these concepts are obvious. While not dismissing the importance of production quality and product innovation, the danger of being production orientated is that products are handed over to the sales force to sell without any consideration being given to these fundamental truths: 'Consumption is the sole end purpose of all production; and the interest of the producer ought to be attended to only in so far as it may be necessary for promoting that of the consumer' (Adam Smith, *The Wealth of Nations*, 1776). 'The customer is the only arbiter of quality – and an improvement the customer cannot understand or doesn't want is no kind of improvement at all' (Willsmer).[3] However desirable the merits of the product, they are never desirable at any price (Heller).[4] The danger of being sales orientated is the pursuit of volume rather than profit. And, as Levitt[5] wrote: 'Selling focuses on the needs of the seller: marketing on the needs of the buyer. Selling is preoccupied with the seller's need to convert his product into cash; marketing with the idea of satisfying the needs of the customer by means of the product and the whole cluster of things associated with creating, delivering and finally consuming it.'

THE MARKETING MIX

The main elements that a company can manage to its advantage for marketing purposes comprise the 'marketing mix'. The four Ps in the marketing mix are:

- *Product* – what is sold.
- *Place* – the medium through which goods or services reach customers.
- *Price* – what goods or services are sold for. (See Chapter 4.)
- *Promotion* – how goods and services are promoted to customers through communication and by other means. (See Chapter 8.)

The other key marketing elements associated with the concept of marketing mix are:

- *Target marketing* – the process of aiming marketing efforts to meet more precisely the needs and wants of customers.
- *Segmentation* – the breakdown of customers into segments that will respond to more precisely targeted marketing mixes.
- *Positioning* – distinguishing a brand from its competitors so that it becomes the preferred brand in defined market segments.

These three elements are discussed more fully in Chapters 5, 6 and 7.

ANALYSIS, RESEARCH AND PLANNING

Marketing is an analytical process based on product life cycle analysis (Chapter 3), the use of marketing information (Chapter 10), buyer behaviour analysis (Chapter 11) and various forms of market research (Chapters 12–14), and leading to systematic planning (see Chapters 17–19). The analysis will rely on information from marketing research and also from the data in marketing information systems (see Chapter 10). It will also be concerned generally with the external environment, using techniques such as 'PEST' analysis covering:

- *Political* factors that might impinge on the operation of a business. Typical factors are: privatization, international events, trading practices, monopolies and mergers legislation, levels of public spending and controls on advertising. Marketing has to be aware of these macro-environmental factors even though it has little control over them.
- *Economic* factors, including economic growth, income levels, interest rates, exchange rates, balance of payment levels, employment percentages, credit policies, income distribution, savings/debt, personal and corporate taxation and indirect taxation like value added tax. A company must monitor these economic factors at both domestic and international levels so that it can be in a better position to capitalize upon any opportunities and be aware of any threats in sufficient time to take remedial action.
- *Socio-cultural* factors concerning matters like the changing age structure of the population, trends in the size of families, changes in the amount

and nature of leisure time, changes in attitude towards health and lifestyles, improvement in education, changes in attitudes towards family roles, changing patterns of work and equal opportunities. In some countries, the religious environment might also be a source of opportunities or threats to companies doing business there.

■ *Technological* factors concerning such matters as the Internet, automation, new methods of travel, computer-assisted telephone interviewing, electronic point of sale, new materials and more powerful computing methods. All of these can have a direct influence on the marketing firm, particularly if its own methods of production, or the products/services that it produces, are directly affected by, or actually form, an integral part of the products that it offers to customers. This may be extended to PESTLE, which also covers legal, environmental and ecological factors.

BENEFITS

The potential benefits of marketing are that the company will:

■ adopt a systematic approach to assessing and exploiting marketing opportunities;
■ view and organize its marketing activities from the consumer's point of view;
■ identify, serve and satisfy a defined set of needs of a defined set of customers;
■ continually seek product improvements;
■ continually develop and improve the way in which products are presented and distributed to customers;
■ operate on the basis of clearly defined plans and targets; and
■ exercise control to ensure that the required results are achieved.

REFERENCES

1. Kotler, P, *Marketing Management* (12th edition), Prentice-Hall, Englewood Cliffs, NJ, 2005.
2. Levitt, T, *The Marketing Imagination,* Free Press, New York 1983.
3. Willsmer, R L, *The Basic Arts of Marketing,* Business Books, London 1984.
4. Heller, R, *The Naked Market,* Sidgwick & Jackson, London 1984
5. Levitt, T, 'Marketing myopia', *Harvard Business Review,* July–August 1960.

3

Product Life-cycle Analysis

DEFINITION

The product life cycle is the sales pattern of growth and decline of a product over a period of time. This period may be the whole life of the product from its launch until it is withdrawn because it is no longer profitable or because it has been replaced.

Product life-cycle analysis is the process of describing and forecasting the pattern of sales for a product for a period of time or the whole of its life.

THE PRODUCT LIFE-CYCLE CONCEPT

The typical cycle

The typical product life cycle is S-shaped (Figure 3.1) and consists of four distinct stages:

Stage 1: Introduction. This is the period immediately following the launch when, if all goes according to plan, sales will grow slowly but steadily as the product is progressively introduced to the market. Profits are probably non-existent during this stage because of the costs of introducing the product; promotional costs are high in proportion to sales, and costs per unit of output are high because of low volume.

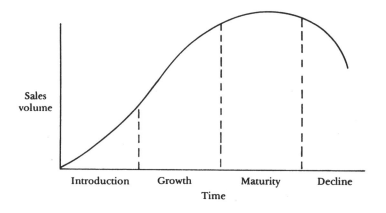

Figure 3.1 *A typical S-shaped product life cycle*

Stage 2: Growth. This is the period when market penetration increases rapidly. If the new product is successful, the rate of sales growth gains momentum as consumer/user demand expands following increased knowledge and acceptance of the product because of advertising, sales promotion and field sales effort. This growth in customer awareness and satisfaction is exploited progressively during this period by segmentation and differentiation and by expanding into new markets. Profits increase steadily during this period.

Stage 3: Maturity. When this stage is reached, the basic product concept has gained considerable consumer acceptance. However, although the demand for it may continue to rise slightly, the rate of increase has diminished considerably and may eventually 'plateau out' or even decline. The reduced rate of growth is partly caused by increased competition from other companies either entering the market with new versions of the product or attacking the market share achieved by the product through more aggressive advertising, promotion, selling or pricing policies. The slowdown in sales growth may also be caused by the market becoming saturated for the product as it exists. During this stage profits stabilize or decline because of increased marketing outlays to defend the product against competition.

Stage 4: Decline. The sales of most product forms and brands eventually dip because of consumer shifts in tastes, increased competition, technological advances and the availability of substitute products. The market may be saturated and, unless action is taken, sales and profits will decline to zero or petrify at a low level. Purchases will tend to be of the replacement type, but brand loyalties will progressively diminish if nothing is done about it.

Other forms of product life cycle

1. *The recycle* (Figure 3.2). Sales begin to fall off, as in the typical cycle, but are then regenerated as new applications, new product characteristics or new users emerge. This process can be repeated, resulting in a succession of life cycles.
2. *The humpback* (Figure 3.3). After the product life cycle apparently enters the decline stage, sales recover again. This may occur when buyers take some time to test and evaluate the product after their initial purchase. When they approve, they place repeat orders.
3. *The plateau* (Figure 3.4). Sales may plateau out when there is no better alternative available. The product is still in demand until a substitute appears, when sales may decline dramatically. The plateau may incline slightly upwards, however, if sales increase at a rate in line with growth in the economy.

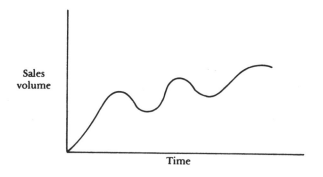

Figure 3.2 *Recycle pattern*

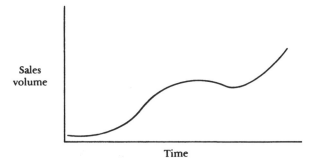

Figure 3.3 *The humpback cycle*

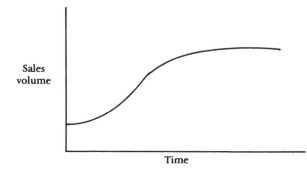

Figure 3.4 *The plateau cycle*

PRODUCT LIFE-CYCLE ANALYSIS

Product life-cycle analysis is the process of assessing the type of life cycle which is applicable to the product, the point in the life cycle where the product is, and the reasons why it is in this position. For existing company products, the analysis provides a basis for forecasts of future sales and for deciding on recycling actions. But the analysis of the stage in the life cycle which products already marketed by other companies have reached helps in decisions on whether to develop and launch new or substitute products.

The analysis of the company's own products covers:

■ trends in sales volume;
■ trends in profit;
■ trends in market share – rate of market penetration;
■ economic trends (which may explain a growth or decline in sales);
■ the pattern of sales – who buys, where they buy, to what extent they are first-time or repeat buyers;
■ consumer opinions about the product derived from consumer surveys, media comment or test-marketing; and
■ the features of the product compared with what is available elsewhere or is becoming available.

The analysis of competitive products also measures sales volume, market share and the pattern of sales. In addition, it assesses the reasons why the products are more or less competitive: price, advertising, promotion, sales, distribution and servicing effectiveness, product features which are uniquely attractive or increase the perceived value of the product.

ACTION

As a result of the analysis the following are actions that can be taken to ensure that a favourable trend continues or to arrest a decline by recycling.

Introduction stage

- Increase advertising and promotional expenditure to accelerate growth.
- Adjust prices to increase penetration.
- Adjust promotional message and sales approaches in response to analysis of consumer reactions.
- Improve product features in response to initial consumer reaction.

Growth stage

- Improve quality.
- Modify product characteristics.
- Extend market into new segments.
- Develop new distribution channels.
- Reduce prices to attract the next layer of price-sensitive buyers.

Maturity stage

- Find new market segments and customers.
- Reposition brand to appeal to a larger or faster-growing segment.
- Encourage increased usage among existing customers.
- Modify product characteristics – new features, style improvements.
- Modify marketing mix, eg cut prices, advertise or promote more aggressively, move into higher-volume market channels.

Decline stage

- Maintain brand in the hope that competitors will withdraw their products.
- Harvest brand, ie maximize profits by reducing costs but keeping up sales pressure.
- Terminate and withdraw the product.

BENEFITS

The main benefit of product life-cycle analysis is that it forces the company to recognize what is happening to its product in the marketplace over time. Forecasts can be made of future trends and the likely impact of competition. The strengths and weaknesses of the company's product are identified so that the former can be exploited and the latter overcome. Life-cycle analysis is a continuous process which enables the company to review its marketing mix on the basis of a better understanding of the performance of its product.

4

Pricing

DEFINITION

Pricing is the method used by a company to fix or change its price with regard to costs, sales and profit targets, the pricing policies of competitors and the perceived value of the product by customers.

APPROACHES TO PRICING

The four basic approaches to pricing are:

- *The economist's*, which suggests that price is the medium through which supply and demand are brought into equilibrium.
- *The accountant's*, commonly used in manufacturing, which states that the aim of pricing is to recover costs and make a profit.
- *Market-based*, which adopts a customer/demand focus.
- *Competitor-related*, which fixes prices by reference to those charged by competitors.

The economist's approach is of purely theoretical interest. In practice it is the accountant's or the market-based approaches as described below that are the ones used.

THE ACCOUNTANT'S APPROACH

The aim of the accountant's approach is to seek a targeted rate of return on investment for a specific level of sales. The main techniques used are:

- cost-plus pricing;
- standard cost pricing;
- marginal pricing;
- break-even analysis.

Cost-plus pricing

Cost-plus pricing (called mark-up pricing in retailing) means adding a standard mark-up to the total cost of the product. Thus, if a retailer pays a manufacturer £10 for a product and marks it up to sell at £15, there is a 50 per cent mark-up on the product and the retailer's gross margin is £5. If the operating costs of the store are £4 per unit sold, the retailer's profit margin will be £1 or 10 per cent.

This is a production-orientated approach commonly used in manufacturing and it is at odds with market-based approaches, which take account of customer preferences and the pricing policies of competitors. However, prices should cover costs, so all pricing systems are, to that degree, cost-related. Cost-plus or mark-up pricing systems do this, and have the additional virtue of being based on ascertainable facts rather than on suppositions about demand. Demand and the perceived value of the product cannot be ignored, however. There is a danger of overpricing if too much attention is paid simply to obtaining an acceptable profit margin over total costs, and of underpricing if the perceived value is underestimated.

Standard cost pricing

Standard cost pricing is based on the cost standards developed in management accounting systems.

The standard variable cost per unit is calculated by adding the total variable costs of production, namely the cost of materials and direct labour, and the cost of bought-in components, and dividing this sum by the number of units produced.

The steps taken to establish a standard cost price are as follows:

1. Calculate the standard variable cost per unit.
2. Calculate the fixed cost per unit (the running expenses, including administration and selling expenses of the business over a period of time divided by the number of units to be sold in that period.

Again, this approach is also used in manufacturing and takes no account of demand.

Marginal pricing

Marginal pricing fixes the selling price of additional units by reference to the marginal cost of manufacturing each unit.

The theory of marginal pricing is that, after a company's total fixed and variable costs have been covered by the existing volume of production, the cost of producing an extra unit – of marginal production – will only be the total variable cost of producing and selling it. In such circumstances, the selling price of additional goods can be reduced, if necessary, to match the total variable cost without any loss to the company. Any amount by which the selling price exceeds the variable cost of marginal outputs is then an extra or marginal contribution to the company's net profits and fixed costs. Again, this is a manufacturing approach.

Break-even analysis

Break-even analysis uses the concept of a break-even chart to develop a system of target pricing in which the company tries to determine the price that will produce the profit it is seeking. Although profit related, this form of pricing is based on an analysis of total costs, upon which is superimposed an assessment of total revenue.

Break-even analysis determines fixed and variable costs and enables the price-setter to investigate the profit implications of alternative price–volume strategies. As illustrated in Figure 4.1, a break-even chart represents the following elements of costs and revenue:

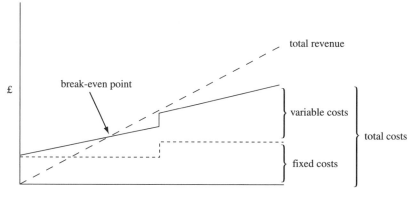

Figure 4.1 *Break-even chart*

- *Fixed costs* – the costs of production that will not vary in the short term, though at a certain level of output it may be necessary, for example, to install an extra production line, in which case there will be an increase in fixed costs, known as a step cost.
- *Variable costs* of labour and materials, etc, which increase in proportion to volume.
- *Total costs* – the sum of fixed and variable costs.
- *Total revenue* – the sales made to customers, which increase with output, although as output increases, a company may have to trim its margins, and revenue may then decline.
- *Break-even point* – this is reached when total revenue exceeds total costs. Sales above this point will be profitable; below this point a loss will be incurred. Break-even analysis concentrates attention on the likely profit or loss that may be incurred by alternative pricing strategies. It is therefore an essential technique for selecting the best policy, as long as sufficient attention is paid to the demand curve. Unless the elasticity of demand (the impact of price changes on sales) is taken into account, break-even analysis can be misleading.

Target pricing

Target pricing techniques are based on break-even analysis. They involve:

- estimating demand at different price levels;
- drawing up total revenue curves at different price levels;
- referring to the break-even chart and assessing the profit implications of setting different price levels;
- making a final decision on price levels and profit targets by considering the profit implications in relation to estimates of sales volumes and then selecting the optimum alternative.

MARKET-BASED PRICING

Market-based pricing emphasizes price as a variable element of the marketing mix. Its concern is how it can affect the company's position in the marketplace. Value is included in this notion of price, and the underlying marketing theme is to set prices at 'what the market will bear'.

Profit maximization is natural in marketing, but it is not feasible to do this on all products/services amongst all customer groups. Companies can employ many pricing tactics that might promote sales yet reduce margins in the short term. The general objective might be profit maximization, but the company's product mix should be examined in terms of individual items, and price tactics applied individually, rather than singular pricing decisions applying to the complete range. Prices should adopt a customer focus, and this will determine whether the product is bought or not.

Although the assumption behind market-based pricing techniques is that prices are a major factor in achieving competitiveness, this can also be attained through non-price competition. Market share can be improved through customer care, the delivery of value for money, quality and high levels of service (response, delivery and after-sales service).

The main market-based pricing techniques are described below.

Penetration pricing

Penetration pricing involves setting prices at a sufficiently low level to make them attractive to the mass market. The aim is to achieve high initial sales, which are maintained during the life cycle of the product. An associated aim is to deter competitors. Penetration pricing is particularly appropriate for products where unit cost reductions can be achieved through initial mass production.

Setting-up costs are usually high and initial development costs are recovered over a long period. The task of marketing is to ensure that customers retain interest during the life of the product.

Skimming

A skimming approach adopts a high-price strategy, charging what the market will bear. The aim is to 'skim the cream off the market'. This policy is particularly attractive to a company with a new and unique product. When the cream has been skimmed, prices can be progressively reduced.

Perceived value pricing

Perceived value pricing determines prices from assumptions made about the beliefs that consumers have of the value of the product to them. These assumptions may be founded on market research aimed at establishing in buyers' minds values about the basic product and the various special features in the product that appeal to them.

If the company charges more than the buyer-recognized value, sales will suffer. Revenue may also fall below attainable levels if prices are lower than the perceived value.

Psychological pricing

Many consumers use price as an indicator of quality. Prestige pricing uses higher prices to promote the idea of value and status.

Price levels can be set just below a round figure, for example £9.99 rather than £10.00. These pricing points, as they are called, persuade people to think that the price is in a lower range than they expected.

Value for money can be emphasized by the effective presentation of discounts and free offers. The perceived value of offering one item free if four items are purchased may have a greater impact than a 20 per cent discount offered over the whole five purchases.

Promotional pricing

Promotional pricing is a method of clearing excess stocks or generating high-volume sales by offering large discounts. Retailers buy in special stocks to benefit from extra sales over limited periods.

COMPETITOR-RELATED PRICING SYSTEMS

Competitor-related pricing systems fix prices by reference to the going rate – the level of competitors' prices. Less attention is paid to demand and, while the aim is to cover costs, they are not the main determinant of prices.

The market is divided according to the levels of quality, service or prestige provided by suppliers of the produce or service. Each sector has a price leader who determines the going rate. The price leader is the market leader with, usually, but not always, the highest sales in the sector. The market leader makes the first move on prices, up or down, and his or her competitors tend to follow.

When using this approach, the company has to decide on its pricing policy. It may go for market leadership, bearing in mind John Winkler's[1] advice that 'Market leaders make most money. On average their price is better, their volume is greater and their unit costs are lower… [if] you want to outsell everyone then get your price about 7 per cent above the average.' Or the company may decide to maintain its prices in line with the average or broadly in the middle segment of the range. It may then follow a policy of parallel pricing by aligning its price increases with those of its competitors. If oligopolistic conditions prevail, in other words if the market consists of a few powerful suppliers, prices may be closely aligned throughout the market and parallel pricing will be the general rule. Two variants of this approach are described below – competitive pricing and discount pricing.

Competitive pricing

Competitive pricing means tackling the price leader in the market segment in which the company is operating. Where possible, the aim would be to set a slightly higher price than the price leader's (say 7 per cent) and then launch a marketing campaign to demonstrate that what Winkler calls a 'discernible product difference' exists. This means demonstrating that the company's product offers a distinct improvement over its competitor's.

If the firm cannot compete on quality it may have to set slightly lower prices or offer higher discounts of at least 10 per cent but not more than 15 per cent or so.

Discount pricing

Discount pricing is a technique that sets artificially high prices but then offers large discounts to attract customers. It is advisable not to offer discounts on a permanent basis. Flexibility is important.

Considerations affecting pricing strategy

Product costs set a floor to the price but are not the only consideration. A ceiling may be set by the unique features that the company offers, although this level will also be influenced by the company's strength and prestige in the marketplace. Competitors' prices and the prices of substitutes provide an intermediate point that the company has to consider in setting its price. Finally, demand has to be taken into account. The relative elasticity of demand will influence the extent to which the company can maintain the volume of unit sales after a price increase, or can increase sales by means of a cut in prices.

REFERENCE

1. Winkler, J, *Pricing for Results,* Heinemann, London 1983.

5

Positioning

DEFINITION

Positioning is the process of reaching market segments. It distinguishes a branded product or service from its competitors so that it becomes the preferred brand in defined segments of the market. Positioning can focus on new brands but may also involve repositioning existing brands.

THE POSITIONING PROCESS

The five sequential steps in the process of positioning are:

- Carry out market research to gain understanding of consumer wants and needs and to identify gaps (gap analysis) which existing, modified or new company products or services could fill.
- Develop segmentation and targeting strategies.
- Establish the relevant attributes that are used by customers in the segment evaluating and choosing between brands in this market.
- Analyse these attributes by 'brand mapping' to assess the current perceived position of existing brands in the market.
- Determine the positioning strategy.

Relevant attributes

The initial step is to establish the attributes – the characteristics and features of the product or service that are relevant to customers in each market segment. Attributes can be objective (for example colour or taste) or subjective (for example brand name, 'value for money'). The aim is to establish key differentiating attributes that will attract customers to the particular product or service. This is sometimes referred to as the unique sales proposition (USP).

Brand mapping

Brand mapping, sometimes called perceptual mapping, is a method of identifying market gaps (gap analysis) and thereby developing a positioning strategy. The process involves:

- identifying criteria, for example price and other attributes such as colour and taste;
- identifying existing brands and analysing them by reference to the criteria;
- mapping the brands;
- identifying any area in which existing brands are not placed – the market gap.

Positioning strategy

The positioning strategy will be derived from the processes described above: research, the segmentation and targeting strategies, attribute analysis and brand mapping. The strategy will determine where and how the product or service will be positioned and leads to the development of an overall marketing mix strategy. The latter would concentrate on ensuing that the various elements of the marketing mix integrate successfully to produce the right kind of product suggested by appropriate policies relating to the other three Ps, namely price, promotion and place.

BENEFITS

Positioning is a means of achieving marketing objectives by ensuring that the right product is developed at the right price in the right segment of the market.

6

Segmentation

DEFINITION

A market segment is a group of customers sharing particular wants or needs. Market segmentation divides the total market available to the company into segments that can be targeted with specially developed and marketed products and that can form the basis for positioning the product in the market.

BASES FOR SEGMENTATION

The main bases for segmentation are as follows:

- *Consumer preferences* – for specific product attributes.
- *Benefits sought by customers* – for example, quality, prestige, durability and economy.
- *Demographic variables* – the market can be segmented according to demographic variables such as age, sex or social class. The following socio-economic group classification system is often used:
  - A Upper middle class – higher managerial, administrative or professional people.
  - B Middle class – intermediate managerial, administrative or professional people.
  - C1 Lower middle class – supervising, clerical and lower managerial administrative or professional people.
  - C2 Skilled working class – skilled manual workers.

- – D Working class – service and unskilled manual workers.
  - – E Pensioners, widows and casual or lowest-grade workers.
- ■ *Buying behaviour* – where people buy, their readiness to buy (degree of awareness of the product), the amount they buy (light, medium and heavy users) and their loyalty to the brand (hard core, shifting, switchers).
- ■ *Lifestyle* – a person's lifestyle is his or her pattern of living in the world. Lifestyles are assessed by psychographics, which list variables under three dimensions: activities, interests and opinions. These are analysed to reveal lifestyle groups.

SEGMENTATION BASES IN ORGANIZATIONAL MARKETS

The term 'organizational markets' refers principally to organizational buying behaviour. It covers the following subdivisions:

- ■ *Industrial markets* – where the major criterion is keeping production satisfied in order that materials and components are available for incorporation in production processes. The ultimate objective is to satisfy the needs of the company's customers, be they intermediate manufacturers further down the production chain or end customers.
- ■ *Institutional markets* – relates to purchasing for public institutions like the police force, the fire service, local and central government establishments and educational establishments. Here, the principal criterion is to keep spending within predetermined budget limits that have been set as part of previously agreed operational spending limits.
- ■ *Resale markets* – where the main criterion is the mark-up percentage that can be added to goods purchased from manufacturers and wholesalers in bulk and then resold to individual customers.

BENEFITS

Segmentation concentrates the minds of those responsible for marketing policies and plans to look for specific marketing opportunities and to develop an appropriate marketing mix that fits in with the requirements of identified market segments and the resources and skills of the company.

7

Target Marketing

DEFINITION

Target marketing is the process of formulating market coverage policies –
which segments of the market provide the best opportunities for the
company.

PROCESS

The process of target marketing (note that the terms 'target marketing' and
'market targeting' are interchangeable) is the manipulation of the marketing
mix such that a distinctive product is made available for each chosen market
segment. It involves formulating market coverage policies that determine
the segments of the market that present the best opportunities.

When the segmentation process has taken place, each identified
segment must be assessed in order to decide whether or not it is worth
while serving as a profitable target market with its own distinctive
marketing mix. If a company decides *not* to operate a 'blanket' strategy (no
segmentation), then it is engaging in what is called a 'concentrated' or
'differentiated' market targeting strategy. The company then has to decide
which potential segments to serve.

Favourable attributes of a target market will include segments where
there is good sales and profit potential, where competition is not too
intense and where the segment might have some previously unidentified
requirements that the company is able to serve. It is this latter notion that
we explore in the next section.

Method

A decision is required about which of the following market coverage strategies will produce the best results:

- Undifferentiated marketing – ignoring segments and attacking the whole market, aiming to satisfy the common needs of customers.
- Differentiated marketing – operating in several segments of the market and designing separate offers for each.
- Concentrated marketing – aiming for a large share in one or a few segments.

The decision will be influenced by the following factors:

- Company resources, which will determine the extent of coverage that is achievable.
- Product and market homogeneity – the more homogeneous the product or market, the greater the pressure for undifferentiated targeting.
- Product stage in the lifestyle – it might be appropriate to go for wide coverage in the initial stages and to target specific segments as the product matures.
- Competitors' segmentation strategies – the company may wish to target market segments neglected by competitors.

Target marketing strategies

The following strategies can be adopted for target marketing:

- *Differentiated*, where there are multiple marketing mixes for different market segments.
- *Undifferentiated*, where there is a single marketing mix for all customers.
- *Concentrated*, which has one marketing mix for a segment of the entire market.
- *Custom*, which attempts to satisfy each customer's needs with an individual marketing mix.

BENEFITS

Target marketing processes identify the particular direction the company wants to follow in accordance with its understanding of market segmentation. It leads to the development of market positioning strategies.

8

Promotion

DEFINITION

Promotion activities are a key component of the marketing mix. Their aim is to present products and services in an attractive light to customers to encourage them to buy. They consist of:

- *Selling*, which is concerned with direct contact with customers.
- *Advertising*, which is non-personal mass communication, paid for by a sponsor. It is sometimes referred to as *above the line*, which is an advertising term that refers to the line above which the agency receives a commission for placing the sponsor's advertising.
- *Sales promotion*, which refers to short-term activities like free samples and competitions that encourage quick action by buyers. This is referred to as *below the line*, as agencies do not receive commission here, and a direct charge is made to the sponsor for the work performed.
- *Public relations (PR)*, which also covers publicity, and is not promotion that is paid for directly by a company to the media. It relies for its coverage on news or editorial about a company's products/services and obtaining such coverage is the province of PR.

SELLING

The role of selling is to gain new customers, but also, importantly, to retain existing customers (customer care).

Selling involves identifying customers (proprietors) and then going through a sales sequence to obtain an order. The sequence is illustrated below.

1. Prospecting.
2. Preparation.
3. Opening.
4. Requirement identification.
5. Presentation/demonstration.
6. Handling objectives.
7. Negotiation.
8. Close.
9. Follow-up.

ADVERTISING (ABOVE-THE-LINE PROMOTION)

Media advertising to potential or existing customers is about the products or services on offer to them. The aims are to impart information, to develop favourable attitudes to the product or service, and to generate sales.

Media scheduling

Media scheduling is the process of deciding what type of media to adopt (TV, radio, cinema advertising, press, internet). When deciding on the optimum media schedule, four factors should be considered:

- Coverage (or reach), which is the percentage of the target market that will see the campaign at least once.
- Frequency, which is the number of times each person will have an opportunity to see (OTS) or opportunity to hear (OTH).
- Cost per thousand (CTH), which is the cost of reaching 1,000 of the target audience whether these be men, housewives with children, homeowners, and so forth.
- Television rating points (TVRs), which is the percentage of the target viewing (or at least having the set on during a particular spot).

When considering these factors, the aim is to obtain as high a coverage as the media budget allows. Budgets for media plans are prepared on the basis of next year's expectations of sales turnover as a result of the implementation of the marketing plan. The budget is expressed as a percentage of potential sales and the amount allocated will depend on the market position and the results of product life-cycle analysis (for example, developing a new product or boosting a declining one). Budgeting procedures will be very different in the case of direct-response advertising, where sales of the product depend entirely on a response directly from the consumer to advertisements (termed 'off the page') or direct mail shots. A key ratio in such instances will be cost per order (CPO).

Media planning

The media planning process consists of the following steps:

1. *Appraisal of:*
   - sales trend data;
   - brand share data;
   - market seasonality;
   - competitive advertising patterns;
   - purchasing or usage profile by demographic group; and
   - results achieved from other campaigns.
2. *Budgeting,* which will take into account the appraisal and other factors mentioned earlier.
3. *Planning,* which may follow the budgeting process and simply be concerned with deciding on the best method of allocating funds. But the planning process may indicate changes in direction or emphasis that could result in modifications to the budget. The plan will take into account answers to the following questions:
   - Is national coverage required or can a regional policy be adopted?
   - Does advertising need to be more or less continuous, or can a burst strategy be effective within the peak sales seasons?
   - Which target group or groups need to be covered?
   - Is heavyweight activity required at the beginning of the campaign to either launch or relaunch the product or the advertising idea?
   - Which medium or media mix is required to ensure optimum communication of the advertising?
   - What is the weight of advertising required in each medium from both a communication and a competitive point of view?
4. *Buying* – using negotiating skill, research backup and 'muscle' to negotiate the best terms with the media.
5. *Evaluating.* There is no simple method of measuring the effectiveness of an advertising campaign except, of course, indirect response where coupons and orders can be counted. In this field, 'split-run' tests can be run in certain media where different offers or styles are tested in alternate (A or B) copies and the results can be compared directly.

In more conventional advertising the most commonly used methods include market research and sales analysis. *Market research* involves general research into consumer attitudes and responses, or particular research into the reaction to an advertisement (reactions to proposed campaigns can be pre-tested by qualitative research). *Sales analysis* is used especially when area tests are conducted for new products or new advertising treatments. The problem is to isolate those factors other than advertising that have affected sales. The area marketing test evaluation system (AMTES) developed by Beecham attempts to do this by isolating the measurable factors that affect sales.

The media planner's task is to assess the results of the evaluations and, in so far as he or she considers them valid and reliable, to adjust the media mix.

SALES PROMOTION (BELOW-THE-LINE PROMOTION)

Sales promotion involves providing customers with an incentive to purchase expressed in cash or in kind. The promotion is usually over a limited period not normally lasting longer than six months, with the majority lasting for a much shorter period.

Competitive advantage can be gained by companies through creating an unusual and innovative promotion, of which there are many varieties. Using the same type too frequently can diminish its impact.

PUBLIC RELATIONS (PR)

Public relations is defined by the Institute of Public Relations as 'The deliberate, planned and sustained effort to establish and maintain mutual understanding between the organization and its public'. Public relations relies on editorial for its coverage, and this is based on press releases. Public relations activity also aims to establish and promote the corporate identity – through visible signs such as logos, which indicate how the company wants to present itself to its public.

BENEFITS

Promotion is a key element in the marketing mix. Products do not sell themselves; they have to be promoted.

9

Distribution

DEFINITION

Distribution is the 'P for place' in the 'four Ps' of the marketing mix. It covers the channels through which goods are sold – wholesalers, retailers, agents and so forth – as well as physical distribution (logistics).

DISTRIBUTION STRATEGY

The amount of market exposure required by companies formulates channel policy and the choice of channel strategy will depend on:

- the nature of the product or service;
- the technical complexity of the product;
- its servicing arrangements;
- the image the company wishes to portray to consumers.

Three distribution strategies can be identified:

- *Intensive distribution* is used by fast-moving consumer goods (FMCG) manufacturers and convenience goods manufacturers, some raw materials producers and sometimes 'white' (for example, refrigerators) and 'brown' (for example, furniture) goods manufacturers, whose aim is to stock their products in the maximum number of outlets. The idea is that maximum exposure at point of sale is the most important criterion.
- *Selective distribution* comes next and instead of spreading marketing effort over a wide range of outlets, manufacturers concentrate on the

most promising of profitable outlets. It is also used where retail facilities, resources or image might have an impact on consumer impressions (for example, expensive perfumes being sold in higher-class stores). Certain products may require special storage and facilities like refrigeration or regular servicing, so retailers will have to be adequately equipped.

■ *Exclusive distribution* to a limited number of retailers might be designed to enhance the brand image of a product (for example, motor car distribution, whereby the retailer only distributes a single brand).

SELECTING AND COORDINATING CHANNELS

It is necessary to take the following steps to select and coordinate channels:

1. Determine the service output levels needed by customers.
2. Look at the duties that channel members must perform to ensure adequate delivery to end customers.
3. Use economic or other measures to motivate channel members to carry out their duties.
4. Look for mechanisms for dealing with conflicts that might arise between channel members.

The choice includes obvious channels such as retail outlets and wholesalers, but it may also include such approaches as business format franchising and mail order, as summarized below. The internet is being increasingly used.

Business format franchising

Business format franchising is a system of selling and distribution organized through a contract between a principal seller (franchiser) and distributive outlets (owned by franchisees). This depends on the franchiser having an idea, a powerful brand name, and a 'secret process' or specialized equipment or goodwill that can attract customers. If this is the case, then the franchiser can grant the franchisee a licence, for a commercial consideration. The franchisee then exploits that name, idea or product and the commercial process is beneficial to both parties.

Mail order

Mail order relies on catalogues to obtain sales, often using agents to administer orders and collect payment for a commission. There are also specialist mail-order houses that deal with a limited range of lines that are difficult to access in shops (such as specialist garden care materials). Non-catalogue mail order depends on magazine and television advertising and is normally used to sell a restricted or specialist range of products.

LOGISTICS MANAGEMENT

Logistics management, also known as physical distribution management, is concerned with obtaining materials from suppliers and storing, processing, retrieving and delivering products to the customer.

Elements

The main elements of 'total business logistics' are:

- order processing;
- stock levels/inventory;
- warehousing;
- transportation;
- service levels.

This is sometimes termed 'the systems approach' to distribution management.

Aim

The aim is to ensure that goods ordered are made available in the right place at the right time. The period of time between the placing of the order and receipt of the goods is known as the 'lead time', and this varies for different types of products and types of markets and industry. The lean manufacturing/JIT concept aims to eliminate lead time.

BENEFITS

It is not enough to have the right product or to promote it effectively. Effective distribution in the form of getting the product to customers in good time and in good shape is a vital component of the marketing mix.

10

Marketing Information Systems

DEFINITION

A marketing information system provides the basis for marketing planning. It includes data on economic and business trends, consumer-buying behaviour, market developments, competitive products and prices as well as data generated by market research.

THE MARKETING INFORMATION SYSTEM

A marketing information system collects and analyses information to assist marketing decision makers. It is an integral part of the company's overall management information system.

The marketing information system operates as a decision support system to the following four systems:

- The *internal accounting system,* which generates data as part of the process of everyday business. This includes not only financial and cost-accounting information but all information received and generated by the firm. This information can be used to measure efficiency ratios like sales to selling expenses. It can also provide information on seasonal and cyclical demand patterns for planning, monitoring and control purposes. If this system is to be of use in planning, monitoring and control, marketing management needs to know how to use it effectively.

- The *marketing intelligence system,* which produces internal information through the process of managing and administering the business. The type of information to which this refers is collected less formally than marketing research, often in an ad hoc fashion. It can be described as procedures and information sources used by managers to obtain daily information about developments in the marketing environment. Marketing and other company staff come across information that may seem inconsequential but that might be of use in marketing planning. This includes reports of sales visits from members of the field sales force, which can include such matters as market developments, competitive products, prices and concessions and future customer purchasing plans. Marketing intelligence is the formal process that marshals such information together and feeds it into the information system. Sales personnel attend conferences, conventions and trade exhibitions, as well as courses and sponsored events, and assist with hospitality. It is their business to network effectively with people within the industry, be they customers or competitors. The use of sales personnel in gathering marketing intelligence is invaluable.
- The *marketing research system,* which makes use of both secondary data (already in existence) and primary data (collected for a specific research purpose) through desk and field research.
- The *analytical marketing system,* which is the final part of the overall marketing information system. It does not produce new data, but takes data from the other three component parts and enhances its value. Users of the system do this by applying 'management science' to the data, thereby transforming it into a more easily understood form for the marketing decision maker. The techniques applied to the data are usually statistical in nature. It is from this that marketing plans are made.

Information collected from marketing research, marketing intelligence and internally generated data can be used as inputs to sales forecasting. An external marketing audit, described below, also provides general information on the marketing environment.

THE EXTERNAL MARKETING AUDIT

The external marketing audit is conducted by a process called environmental scanning. This assesses the external/environmental factors that are affecting or may affect in the future the company's marketing efforts. The basic approach is known as 'PEST', which covers political, economic, socio-cultural and technological factors. The addition of legal and environmental factors produces the acronym PESTLE, the components of which were defined in Chapter 2.

BENEFITS

A marketing information system provides invaluable inputs to the marketing planning process. It acts as a control mechanism as customer reactions are also fed into it from market intelligence, the field sales force or marketing research. Information on sales analysis is fed into the system so decisions can be made as to whether or not forecast sales are being achieved.

11

Buying Behaviour Analysis

DEFINITION

Buying behaviour analysis aims to determine the factors affecting the behaviour of customers with regard to the purchase of existing or proposed products or services. The analysis has to be based on an understanding of the influences on buyer behaviour (individual or organizational) and uses various models.

INFLUENCES ON INDIVIDUAL BUYING BEHAVIOUR

The psychological concepts explaining individual buying behaviour are:

- *Motivation* – goal-directed behaviour: the emotional and rational motives that affect buying decisions and involve a reaction to a stimulus.
- *Self-concept* – consumers tend to make purchases that confirm their self-image so that they can safeguard and boost it.
- *Personality* – this strongly influences buying behaviour and an aim of buyer behaviour analysis will be to identify what sort of products or services might appeal to different personality types.
- *Perception* – the analysis that identifies the meanings that buyers attach to stimuli, how they distinguish between products and services, and how these satisfy their needs.
- *Attitudes* – the set of perceptions that an individual has, leading to beliefs that a buyer might have regarding a possible purchase. Potential

positive or negative attitudes need to be identified so that marketing action such as repositioning can be taken.

MODELS OF CONSUMER BUYING BEHAVIOUR

The simplest model means responding to immediate needs in the following 'AIDA' sequence: awareness, interest, desire, action.

An alternative model is the buyer/decision sequence:

- problem recognition – establishing a need;
- information search – seeking ways of satisfying the need that can be influenced by marketing;
- evaluation of alternatives – this can be influenced by promoting the product or service;
- purchase decision – to purchase or not to purchase, based upon the evaluation;
- post-purchase behaviour – the degree of satisfaction or dissatisfaction will affect future purchasing decisions and sales tactics will aim to produce a positive reaction.

ORGANIZATIONAL BUYING BEHAVIOUR

Organizational buying, which includes industrial and institutional (local government, hospitals) buying behaviour involves people carrying out different roles, which need to be understood by marketeers. The roles consist of:

- *Users* – people who work with, or use, the product. They include supervisors. In some buying circumstances they help to mould the product specification and in others their input is minimal.
- *Influencers* – those who might influence the product specification or who can affect the buying decision in other ways (for example, accountants might influence purchasing budgets).
- *Deciders* – people with authority to make the purchasing decision. In most cases this will be the buyer, but high-value items might involve a team decision.
- *Gatekeepers* – personnel who control the flow of information to and from buyers (for example, technical staff, secretarial staff who may arrange appointments for buyers, junior purchasing personnel with whom potential suppliers might have to liaise prior to contacting other members of the decision-making unit (DMU)).

■ *Buyers* – people with responsibility for signing orders, administering and progressing the order through to its final delivery. They sometimes assist in shaping the specification, but their main role is in supplier liaison and selection.

BENEFITS

Marketing strategies and tactics are more likely to be successful if they are based on a thorough analysis of the factors that will affect buying behaviour.

12

Marketing Research

DEFINITION

Marketing research provides (1) information for management about the company's actual or potential markets and (2) information on the existing or potential users of the goods or services marketed by the company. This information assists in marketing, product and sales planning, and in the planning of advertising and promotional campaigns.

Marketing research provides answers to the following typical questions put by manufacturers, distributors, wholesalers or retailers:

- How many people buy my product?
- How much do they buy?
- Who are my competitors?
- How strong are they?
- Are we/they gaining or losing?
- What sort of people buy our/their products?
- How responsive is my/their brand to promotion?
- Has my product any particular strengths or weaknesses in different regions or outlets or for different socio-economic groups?

This information is used to formulate plans and measure performance.

WHAT IS INVOLVED?

Marketing research deals with the following areas:

Market research

- The size and nature of the market – in terms of the age, sex, income, occupation and social status of consumers (consumer market research).
- The nature, distribution and requirements of the industrial, commercial, government or local government users of the goods, equipment or services markets by the company (industrial market research).
- The geographical location of actual or potential customers and users.
- The market shares of major competitors.
- The nature of the distributive channels serving the market.
- The nature of economic and other environmental trends affecting the market.

Product research

- Product concept testing.
- Product testing.
- Analysis of the competitive strengths or weaknesses of the company's products vis-à-vis those marketed by competitors.
- Investigation of alternative uses for existing products.
- Gap analysis – the identification of any areas in the market which the company can exploit.

Motivational research

- Attitudes and reactions to product attributes.
- The consumer values that influence and motivate customers.

Advertising research

- Media research.
- Measurement of advertising effectiveness.

Marketing research techniques

The basic techniques used in marketing research are:

1. Desk research.
2. Field research.
3. Qualitative research.

A marketing research study will normally contain two or more of these elements.

BENEFITS

Marketing research produces the data essential for strategic and product planning. It will identify opportunities and gaps, reveal weaknesses and provide a basis for effective segmentation and differentiation. It will provide guidelines on where the company should be going and a means of evaluating whether or not the right methods are being used to get there.

FURTHER READING

Birn, R, *The Effective Use of Market Research* (4th edition), Kogan Page, London 2004.

Birn, R, Hague, P and Vangelder, P (eds), *A Handbook of International Market Research Techniques*, Kogan Page, London 2002.

Hague, P and Jackson, P, *Do Your Own Market Research* (3rd edition), Kogan Page, London 1998.

13

Desk Research

DEFINITION

Desk research is the assembly, collation and analysis of marketing information which is already published or in existence.

APPLICATIONS

According to Newson-Smith,[1] research has three clear applications:

1. To provide a background for a field study or other marketing activity.
2. As a substitute for a field study.
3. As a technique in its own right.

Background research

Desk research can provide the basic information about a market on which further field studies or a product or market development plan can be based. It will indicate whether it is worthwhile proceeding with a project and, if it is, the broad direction in which it should go. Desk research will also provide the information necessary to decide on the size of the market, rates of growth or decline, the types of product being supplied, who the customers are and where they may be found.

Substitute for a field study

It may seem essential to get in direct touch with consumers to find out about buying motivations and to obtain their reactions to the company's products, but a detailed desk study coupled, perhaps, with re-analysis of existing research data, can provide valid conclusions about the market.

Desk analysis of, for example, the results of a retail audit (ie, analysis of samples of retail outlets to measure the sales of different product brands) or a product test (ie tests of consumer reactions to sample products) can reveal much of what a marketing planner needs to know about the consuming public's reaction to a product.

As a technique in its own right

Desk research can be used without recourse to any fieldwork where the two key questions to be answered are: 'How big is the market?' and 'At what rate is it growing?' This applies particularly in industrial research.

But desk research on its own can also be relevant in consumer marketing where the market is diffuse and difficult to define and an unacceptable level of sampling error may occur in the results obtained from consumer surveys and test panels as in the food market.

'Hard' data about market dimensions and trends can be retrieved from government or trade association statistics, trade periodicals and published market research results.

Input and output analysis can be used to set out purchases and sales between industries so that management can more easily identify markets to be attacked. Input–output tables (as published in the UK by The Stationery Office) present a picture of multi-trading between industries which enables the market analyst to trace indirect demand for a product as well as the more straightforward direct demand.

BENEFITS

Desk research is:

1. a fast and relatively inexpensive method of obtaining basic data about the size of a market and market trends;
2. an essential tool in industrial marketing, where good statistics are usually available and the scope for field research is more limited; and
3. usually a necessary complement to field research in that it can obtain a comprehensive picture of the market, free of sampling error (although desk research will, of course, provide no information on consumer motivation or reactions to the company's products).

REFERENCE

1. Newson-Smith, N, 'Desk Research', in *Consumer Research Handbook*, Worcester, R M and Downham, J (eds), Van Nostrand Reinhold, Wokingham 1978.

14

Field Research

DEFINITION

Field research is the conducting of investigations by direct contact or observation to collect fresh information about the attitudes and behaviour of consumers and industrial buyers. It deals especially with:

1. the factors underlying choice and preference;
2. reactions to new product concepts and offerings; and
3. user and non-user profiles.

It also assists in evaluating the effectiveness of alternative channels of distribution. It is to be distinguished from desk research, which simply uses published or otherwise available information.

TECHNIQUES

The principal techniques used in field research are:

1. Sampling.
2. Observation.
3. Questionnaires.
4. Interviewing.
5. Panels.
6. Attitude scaling.

Sampling

Sampling involves the collection of attitudes, opinions and facts from a representative number of people in the total population. It is used in consumer market research because it is impracticable to get information from all existing or potential customers, and even if it were, it would be too costly.

The basic technique is random sampling, which means picking the people from whom information is to be obtained on the basis that every individual has an equal chance of being selected.

But sampling investigations are subject to experimental error and the outcome of a study has to be expressed in terms of probability and the confidence with which its findings can be treated by management in planning a launch or repositioning a product. Confidence limits can be stated in percentage terms, eg a 90 per cent confidence limit indicates a range of values within which there is 90 per cent confidence that the true population lies.

Bias can also creep in if the sampling method does not allow each member of the population an equal chance of contributing to the sample.

Error can be reduced by increasing the size of the random sample, but this could be expensive. The technique most commonly used to overcome the costs of a very large random sample is quota sampling, in which interviewers are given a quota of informants in particular classes, such as socio-economic status (a classification of heads of households into social grades A, B, C, D and E), age or sex.

Observation

Data on customer buying habits and reactions can be collected by observing their behaviour when shopping or looking at promotional displays. Behaviour patterns can be established as a guide to the best way to present or package a product. But the results of observational studies can be difficult to interpret accurately.

Interviewing

Interviewing is the key field-research technique because it establishes direct contact with users or potential users.

The basic approach is the face-to-face interview, usually structured (ie the interviewer has to cover predetermined areas), which collects information on behaviour, attitudes or opinions. Unstructured or depth interviews are sometimes used to obtain impressions of feelings or attitudes.

Other techniques include:

■ group interviewing – in which the attitudes and beliefs of a group of people are explored, usually in a fairly unstructured manner;

- telephone interviewing;
- postal interviewing; and
- shop audits to measure sales volume and purchasing rates.

Research based on interviewing has to ensure by planning and control that a representative sample of respondents is seen and that, where a structured interview is used, the subject areas are covered comprehensively.

When questionnaires are used, the questions must be clear and unambiguous. They should not 'lead' respondents by, in effect, answering themselves. And the questionnaire design should facilitate interpretation and data processing.

Panels

Panels measure the consumer behaviour of a representative sample of individuals or households over extended periods. The two basic methods are:

1. *the home audit* – panel members allow an auditor into their homes to check levels of household stocks in a product field; and
2. *diaries* – panel members record in a preprinted diary all purchases made in a product field.

Attitude scaling

Besides measuring behaviour – what consumers actually do – market research also attempts to assess attitudes to the product. Consumer attitudes are clearly important when assessing the likely impact of a new product or the reasons for the success or failure of an existing product.

To measure attitudes it is necessary to have a scale. The most frequently used scales are as follows:

1. *Thurston's comparative judgement technique.* A scale is drawn up of a number of statements about a subject which range from very favourable to very unfavourable expressions of attitude towards it. Respondents are asked to select the statement which most accurately reflects their attitude. A score is given to each statement to produce an overall summary.
2. *Likert scales.* These present respondents with a series of statements and ask them to indicate their degree of agreement/disagreement with each. Respondents are often offered five categories: strongly agree, agree, uncertain, disagree, strongly disagree.
3. *The semantic differential technique.* A concept about a brand or product is set out. Respondents are then asked to rate it by ticking a point on a

five-point scale on which end points are defined by pairs of adjectives, eg strong–weak, good–bad. Numerical values are then assigned to the scale positions so that comparisons can be made between various brands or between users and non-users of a brand. This is one of the most popular methods because the scale is fairly easy to construct and analyse.

BENEFITS

The benefits of a properly conducted field survey are:

1. specific information is obtained about the dynamics of consumer behaviour;
2. attitudes to new and existing products can be measured; and
3. from this factual information on behaviour and attitudes, conclusions can be reached on shaping marketing strategies or solving marketing problems.

15

Qualitative Research

DEFINITION

Qualitative research obtains information about attitudes by impression-istic means.

USES

Typical examples of the uses of qualitative research are to:

1. identify relevant or 'salient' (ie significant) consumer behaviour patterns, beliefs, opinions and attitudes;
2. explore consumer motivation, ie the broad consumer values that influence buying habits;
3. obtain background information about consumer attitudes or behaviour patterns;
4. explore attitudes to product or marketing concepts; and
5. conduct post-research investigations to amplify or explain points emerging from a major desk or field study.

TECHNIQUES

The three most commonly used qualitative research techniques are as follows:

1. *The individual interview,* which may take the form of a 'depth' or non-directive interview which is largely unstructured and attempts to get to the heart of an individual's motivation. This approach may be modified a little to allow more structure in the form of a checklist of points to be covered, although respondents will be allowed to reply freely about each topic.
2. *Group discussions,* in which a reference group, ie a group of people with certain common characteristics, is gathered together. The group leader guides the discussion, encouraging members to express their views and exchange them with one another. This interaction between group members is an important feature of the technique.
3. *The Kelly repertory grid,* which obtains the opinions of respondents on competing products and their brand images. The interviewer presents informants with the names of products in groups of three for them to select the product that is different from the other two and to describe how it is different. There is then a final sifting through all the products in the test to check out the characteristics attributed to them.

BENEFITS

Qualitative market research provides information on consumer tastes, preference, attitudes and buying habits which, although subjective, can yield significant insights which complement the more factual data obtained from desk and field research.

16

Sales Forecasting

DEFINITION

Sales forecasting assesses the sales potential and market trends for individual products and product groups. It is used for setting individual sales staff targets at a tactical level, and makes a major contribution to the corporate planning and budgeting system. The operational approach to forecasting and its links to sales forecasting is covered in Chapter 34.

SALES FORECASTING TECHNIQUES

The main techniques are summarized below:

- *Derived demand* includes lead/lag indicators in which an analysis is made of trends or economic indicators that are known to be related to the data being forecast. Sales data are then applied to this, but lagged by a year. Consequently the indicator should predict the future trend. The tied indicator method is where the sales performance of one product is known to be related to the future performance of another product.
- *Time series analysis* is based on extrapolation (the process of projecting a past trend or relationship into the future in the belief that history will repeat itself), the components of which are trends, cycle, seasonality and erratic events.
- *Trend fitting* is a projective technique that is best made from a long series of data. This includes linear trends, exponential trends that increase by the same percentage each year and 'S' shaped curves that illustrate how

sales build up slowly after a product launch, accelerate as the product takes off and then ease off as maturity is achieved. This pattern corresponds broadly with the stages of the product life cycle.

■ *Smoothing* is used where sales fluctuate during the year and it may be desirable to smooth out the peaks and troughs to produce a recognizable pattern for projection purposes. The two most commonly used smoothing techniques are:

  – moving averages, calculated by taking a period of time (say, one year) and then totalling these quarterly figures and dividing by four to produce the average per quarter. When the next quarter's figures are available they are added to the previous total and the sales for the first quarter are deducted. The residual figure is divided by four to produce the moving average. The process continues until a trend is established;

  – exponential smoothing, which is a technique that takes into account the greater significance of recent trends by progressively weighting them more heavily and this produces an exponential curve.

■ *Decomposition* analysis smoothes a trend to remove seasonal variations that are not reproduced in the projection. When a company has to take account of such variations in its trading pattern when making sales plans, it is useful to restore them by this technique. It involves:

  – taking the seasonal element out of past trends;
  – projecting the de-seasonalized trends for the period of the forecast;
  – projecting the seasonal variations for the same period;
  – adjusting the de-seasonalized projection to take account of forecast seasonal movements.

■ *Statistical demand analysis* treats sales as a dependent variable and it is a function of a number of independent variables that can affect sales, namely price, income, promotion and population. Multiple regression analysis is used to investigate the relationships between the dependent and the independent variables and to obtain a regression equation for predicting the former in terms of the latter. This technique takes account of the various factors that are likely to affect sales, rather than relying on relatively crude projections of past sales.

■ *Marketing models* can be constructed that provide abstract representations of how markets and consumers behave in different situations. They are used to explain how and why customers buy and gain understanding of the effects of different courses of action. They can thus help in the development of marketing strategies and in predicting the effects of marketing decisions. Marketing models provide answers to what the company needs to do to the product to improve sales, the features of promotion that might affect customers and new brand issues. Such models have a conceptual base that generally comes from the behavioural sciences including:

- consumer motivation;
- influences on buying intentions;
- information theory that deals with how consumers think and make purchasing decisions.
■ *Subjective methods of forecasting* depend on judgement and intuition using:
  - subjective probability assessment that gets managers to rate the likelihood of something happening in percentage terms;
  - the Delphi technique, whereby a panel of experts is assembled and each makes an intuitive forecast. The different forecasts are then analysed and assembled in a combined report that is sent to members of the panel for them to make their separate assessments of the levels of probability of the forecasts;
  - sales force composite forecasts, which are made when field sales staff are asked to assess separately how they believe that sales will move; the distribution of forecasts is analysed and a view is taken on the extent to which predictions need to be modified.

Subjective methods are not normally used exclusively. The usual approach is to combine objective and subjective predictions. They can each then serve as a check on the validity of the forecasts made by the other method.

BENEFITS

Sales forecasting provides the essential input to financial budgeting, manufacturing and distribution planning, and sales planning.

17

Marketing Planning

DEFINITION

Marketing planning decides on the basis of marketing analysis and assessment in the context of the overall company plan:

1. The marketing objectives, policies and strategies of the company in terms of its product range, market position and penetration, pricing and distribution systems.
2. The action plans required to implement strategies in terms of research, product development, promotion, advertising, selling and distribution.
3. The results to be achieved in terms of sales revenue and profit targets, and budgeted marketing and selling expenditure.

THE MARKETING PLANNING PROCESS

Marketing planning involves the following:

- *Diagnosis* – where is the company now and why?
- *Prognosis* – where is the company heading?
- *Objectives* – where should the company be heading?
- *Strategy* – what is the best way to get there?
- *Tactics* – what specific actions should be undertaken, by whom and when?
- *Control* – what measures should be watched to indicate whether the company is succeeding?

The process of marketing planning is also described in a model called APACS (Adaptive Planning and Control Sequence) developed by the Marketing Science Institute which sets out the following stages:

Step 1. Define problem and set objectives.
Step 2. Appraisal using SWOT analysis.
Step 3. Determine the tasks to be accomplished and identify the means to achieve these aims.
Step 4. Identify alternative plans and mixes.
Step 5. Estimate the expected results arising from implementation of the alternative plans.
Step 6. Managerial review and decision.
Step 7. Feedback of results and post audit.
Step 8. Adapt programme if required.

The sequence of activities required by these processes is illustrated in Figure 17.1.

ANALYSIS

The analytical stage of marketing planning requires an appraisal of:

1. the current situation: strengths and weaknesses;
2. marketing threats and opportunities; and
3. future trends.

The current situation

This is analysed under the following headings:

1. *Corporate position*:

   ■ The business the company is in and the salient features of that business.
   ■ The company's overall objectives, explicit or implied.
   ■ The company's resources – productive, technical, financial and marketing, and their strengths and weaknesses.
   ■ The policies of that company, explicit or otherwise, with regard to the use and development of these resources.
   ■ The special skills or competences possessed by the company.

2. *Marketing description*:

   ■ Definition of the market and each of its segments.
   ■ Current size of the market in units and sales revenue for the whole market and each segment.

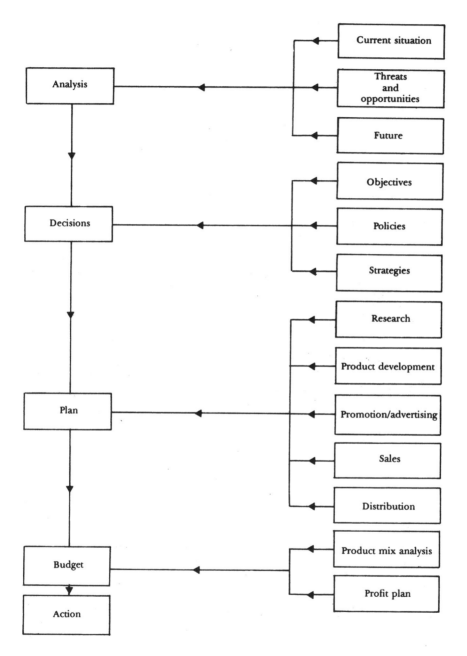

Figure 17.1 *The marketing planning process*

- Sales trends over the past few years for the whole market and each segment.
- Environmental factors in the market that may affect customer purchasing.

3. *Product review*:

- The sales, prices and gross margins for each product in the product line.

4. *Competition*:

- Market shares held by the company and each competitor.
- Description of the strategies adopted by major competitors in terms of product range and quality, promotion, pricing and distribution.

5. *Distribution*:

- Analysis of sales trends and developments in the major distribution channels.

Marketing threats and opportunities

An assessment of existing *and* potential threats and opportunities is made. As defined by Kotler:[1]

- *A marketing threat* is a challenge posed by an unfavourable trend or specific event that would lead, in the absence of purposeful marketing action, to product stagnation or demise.
- *A marketing opportunity* is an attractive arena for company marketing action in which the particular company would enjoy a competitive advantage. The assessment of marketing opportunities includes gap analysis, ie the identification of gaps in the product range or segments of the market not covered by the company or its competitors and which can profitably be developed or penetrated by the company using its existing or potential resources.

Threats and opportunities can be categorized by using the grids in Figure 17.2. Immediate action is required for any threat or opportunity which is placed in the top left-hand high/high cell. No immediate action is needed for one placed in the low/low cell. Any threats or opportunities put into the high/low category will need to be monitored and outline longer-term or contingency plans will have to be prepared.

Future trends

The analysis of future trends takes the form of a summary of the results of market and sales forecasts and market research activity as follows:

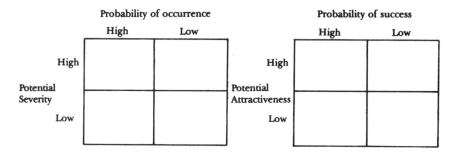

Figure 17.2 *Threat and opportunity grids*

- Economic data and forecasts.
- Industry data and forecasts.
- Competitor data – trends in market share.
- Factors influencing purchasing/using decisions such as quality, price, design, image, perceived market position, after-sales service.
- Objective forecasts of sales in the market generally, for product groups and for specific products.
- Subjective forecasts of likely trends in the market giving most optimistic, pessimistic and best estimate values.

MARKETING PLAN DECISIONS

The decisions incorporated into the marketing plan cover:

1. objectives;
2. policies;
3. strategies.

Marketing objectives

Marketing objectives are set out under the following headings:

- Market share – the degree to which the market is saturated.
- Market penetration – increase in sales to existing customers.
- Sales revenue for period of the plan.
- Contribution or profit on sales for the period of the plan. (Contribution is the difference between the sales revenue for a product and the marginal or variable costs directly attributed to it, which include variable manufacturing, selling and administrative costs. It thus indicates the contribution made by the product to profit and to covering fixed costs.)

Marketing policies

Marketing policies provide guidelines on the approach the company will adopt to market its products. The headings to be covered are as follows:

- *Market position.* Does the company want to maintain its position as market leader? Or does it want to become market leader?
- *Product development.* Is the company interested in achieving technological breakthroughs and introducing radically different products to the market or is it content to maintain and develop the present product range without making substantial changes?
- *Product quality.* What is the level of quality of the product or service that the company wishes to provide and what image does it want to present to its customers?
- *Pricing.* What price levels should be adopted for each product?
- *Promotional/advertising.* How much promotional or advertising effort will be put behind the product?
- *Packaging.* To what extent is the company going to rely on improved packaging to increase sales?

Marketing strategies

Marketing strategies are the broad approaches the company intends to adopt in the longer term to achieve its marketing objectives in accordance with its marketing policies. Strategies are developed for the following:

- *Target markets* – the market segments in which the company will concentrate and the marketing position it proposes to adopt in each segment (ie the extent to which it positions itself close to a competitor but establishes differentiation through product features and price/ quality difference, or the extent to which it attacks holes in the market established by gap analysis).
- *Marketing mix* – the blend of controllable marketing variables required to produce the response wanted in the target market. The mix includes new products, prices, promotion, packaging, advertising, field sales and distribution.
- *Marketing expenditure* – how much will have to be spent to implement the various marketing strategies.

PLANS

Plans deal with the specific areas, as set out below, where action has to be taken to implement strategies and thus achieve objectives. They specify not only what has to be done but also who does it and when it has to be accomplished:

1. *Research* – programmes of marketing research to obtain data on consumer behaviour and reactions.
2. *Product development* – plans to develop and launch new products or to reposition existing products.
3. *Sales promotion and advertising* – details of the promotional and advertising campaigns required to assist product launches or to increase market penetration.
4. *Sales* – plans for redeploying or expanding the sales force and for increasing its effectiveness.
5. *Distribution* – plans for improving the effectiveness of existing distribution channels or for opening up new channels.

MARKETING BUDGET

The marketing budget sets out for the whole company and each product group and product:

1. the targets for sales volume, sales revenue, gross margin (the amount by which sales revenue exceeds the factory cost of goods sold) or contribution (sales revenue less variable costs), and net profit; and
2. the marketing expenditure budgets for advertising promotion, research, field sales, distribution and the costs of the marketing department itself.

The budget will be strongly influenced by the processes of product-mix analysis and profit planning.

Product-mix analysis

Product-mix analysis aims to optimize profits by selling products in the most profitable ratio to one another.

Profit planning

Profit planning is carried out as follows:

1. Preliminary profit targets are set in line with corporate planning objectives.
2. Projections are made of sales revenue on the basis of the sales plans and the pricing policies which it is believed will achieve the desired profit target.

3. Estimates are made of fixed and variable costs in relation to projected activity levels.
4. The projected contribution to profits and fixed costs (sales revenue minus variable costs) is calculated.
5. Estimated fixed costs are deducted from the contribution to show the residual profit level.
6. Adjustments are then made as required and as possible either:

   ■ to sales plans, pricing policies or cost budgets to achieve the profit target – these adjustments may increase marketing expenditure if it is felt that the consequential increase in the 'bottom-line' profit figure would provide an acceptable return on that expenditure; or
   ■ to the profit target, on the basis of the assessment of what can realistically be achieved in terms of an increase in sales revenue or a reduction in costs.

REFERENCE

1. Kotler, P, *Marketing Management* (12th edition), Prentice-Hall, Englewood Cliffs, NJ 2005.

FURTHER READING

Baker, M, *Marketing Strategic Management* (2nd edition), Macmillan, London 1992.

Westwood, J, *The Marketing Plan* (3rd edition), Kogan Page, London 2002.

18

Product Planning

DEFINITION

Product planning is the process of developing and maintaining a portfolio of products which will satisfy defined customer needs and wants, maximize profitability and make the best use of the skills and resources of the company. In this chapter, product planning is examined from the viewpoint of marketing. The operational aspects of product planning are covered in Chapters 29 and 30.

REASONS FOR PRODUCT PLANNING

- The best consumer marketers have long known that safety lies not in products but in portfolios of products (Robert Heller).[1]
- A truly marketing-minded firm tries to create value-satisfying goods and services that customers will want to buy. What it offers for sale includes not only the genetic product or service but also how it is made available to the customer, in what form, when, under what conditions and what terms of trade. Most important, what it offers for sale is determined not by the seller but by the buyer. The seller takes his or her cues from the buyer in such a way that the product becomes a consequence of the marketing effort, not vice versa (Theodore Levitt).[2]
- (1) The form of a product is a variable, not given in developing market strategy. Products are planned and developed to serve markets. (2) The 'product' is what the product does; it is the total package of benefits the customer receives where he or she buys... Even though a product

might, in its narrow sense, be indifferentiable, an individual supplier may differentiate his or her product from competitive offerings through service, product availability, and brand image, and differentiation in one respect or another is the basis for developing a market franchise (E Raymond Corey).[3]

■ The main job of distribution is not to get rid of what production makes; it is to tell production what it ought to make (Lyndall F Urwick).[4]

■ A product is, to the potential buyer, a complex cluster of value satisfactions... a product has meaning only from the viewpoint of the buyer or the ultimate user. Only the buyer or user can assign value, because value can reside only in the benefits he or she wants or perceives (Theodore Levitt).[5]

THE COMPONENTS OF PRODUCT PLANNING

Product planning requires decisions followed by action on:

1. the product line;
2. the product mix;
3. branding;
4. packaging;
5. new product development.

PRODUCT LINE ANALYSIS

A product line is a group of products that are closely related, either because they have similar characteristics or because they are sold to the same type of customer. Cars would be one product line in a vehicle manufacturing company.

Product line analysis involves looking at, first, the viability of each individual product using *product life-cycle analysis* techniques. Second, product line analysis considers the length of the line. The line is too short if profits can be increased by lengthening it; too long if profits can be increased by shortening it.

Product line analysis will lead to decisions on the extent to which the company wants to:

■ extend the product line into the higher or lower end of the market; or
■ concentrate in the higher, middle or lower end of the market.

It will also determine policy on the extent to which it is necessary to increase the differentiation of products in the line to increase or maintain sales.

PRODUCT-MIX ANALYSIS

The product mix is the set of all product lines and the numbers of models, sizes and other significant product variations within each line that a company offers for sale.

Product-mix analysis leads to decisions on whether the company should add new product lines to the mix or remove existing ones. The decisions will be affected by market research on potential demand, gap analysis and by obtaining answers to the basic corporate planning questions, namely:

1. What business is the company in?
2. What are the strengths and weaknesses of the company?
3. What are the opportunities and threats facing the company?

The product mix will be widened if the analysis shows that the new line is potentially profitable, not only because it meets consumer needs but also because it capitalizes on the company's reputation in its other lines and uses the skills and resources available to the company.

Decisions to remove non-profitable lines will be influenced by variety reduction techniques, as described in Chapter 128.

BRANDING

A brand is the name or design which identifies the products or services of a manufacturer and distinguishes them from those of competitors. Brand names may be given to individual products or to a complete product line. Branding is the process of deciding what brands the company should offer.

Branding differentiates the product, thus bringing it to the attention of buyers. It provides information on quality and can be used to attract a loyal and profitable set of customers, thus creating brand loyalty. Branding also helps to segment the market – a basic product can be differentiated into several brands, each appealing to a different group of buyers.

Branding decisions are based on market assessment and research. They will be affected by the answers obtained to such questions as the following:

1. Is a brand name necessary?
2. How much quality should be built into the brand?
3. Should products be individually or family branded?
4. Should other products be given the same brand name?
5. To what extent can or should the market be segmented?
6. Should additional brands be developed in existing product categories to exploit different market segments?

7. Should the brand be repositioned to increase market share or to re-establish itself?

PACKAGING

Packaging is the process of designing the container or wrapper for a product and is an essential element in product and brand development. The packaging concept is what the package should basically be or do for a product. The basic purposes of the package are to protect the goods in storage or in transit and to help the customer use the product. But packages also sell the product by conveying brand image – ie the benefits promised by the brand to the consumer – and by facilitating the instant recognition of the brand in shops and advertisements.

NEW PRODUCT DEVELOPMENT

New product development is the process of:

1. identifying and evaluating new product opportunities and developing them to meet market and consumer wants and needs; and
2. testing the marketability of new products.

Identifying new product opportunities

The process of identifying new product opportunities starts by establishing search criteria. These are as follows:

- The special skills or competences of the company.
- Its experience in particular fields of development, marketing and selling.
- The experience available to it in the shape of research, development and manufacturing facilities, finance for development, the availability of means of access to customers through retail outlets, wholesalers, distributors or dealer networks, agents, mailing lists, and the number or quality of people required in each of the areas of research and development, manufacturing, marketing, sales and distribution.

Ideas for new products are generated from research and development projects, market research activities and *technological forecasting*.

Evaluation and screening

New product ideas are evaluated and screened by obtaining answers to the following questions:

1. Does it meet a well-defined consumer need?
2. In which segment(s) of the market can this product be sold?
3. Can it be differentiated adequately from alternative products in the appropriate segment(s)?
4. How well does it fit in with the existing product range?
5. Does it exploit the company's existing skills and resources?
6. What investment is required in developing and introducing the new product?
7. What is the likely return on that investment?

Concept development and testing

Following screening, new product ideas are developed into product concepts which define the potential market for the product, the benefits the product will provide to consumers and its positioning, ie how it stands in relation to alternatives and how its distinctiveness can be established and maintained in the minds of purchasers.

Concepts are tested by means of consumer research, for example, by presenting members of the public with a prototype and getting them to answer questions which will assess their reactions to what is being offered.

Test marketing

New products can be tested by launching them on a limited scale in a representative market. The aims are to obtain information on consumer reaction, to provide a basis for forecasting future sales and to pre-test advertising, promotional and merchandising approaches.

In a typical market test, the company selects a small number of representative towns in which the sales force will persuade shops to carry the product and give it good shelf exposure. An advertising and promotional campaign will be mounted in these markets similar to the one planned for use in national marketing.

REFERENCES

1. Heller, R, *The Naked Market*, Sidgwick & Jackson, London 1984.
2. Levitt, T, 'Marketing Myopia', *Harvard Business Review*, July–August 1960.

3. Corey, E R, *Industrial Marketing: Cases and Concepts*, Prentice-Hall, Englewood Cliffs, NJ 1976.
4. Urwick, L, *The Elements of Administration*, Pitman, London 1947.
5. Levitt, T, *The Marketing Imagination*, Free Press, New York 1983.

19

Sales Planning

DEFINITION

Sales planning decides how sales targets are to be reached and sets standards for their achievement. It ensures that the objectives set in the marketing planning process are achieved.

THE SALES PLANNING PROCESS

Sales planning is related to the marketing plans and uses research and control data on potential and actual sales. It is carried out in the following stages:

1. Set overall sales targets – for the year and for each sales period or month.
2. Decide on an acceptable level of selling costs in relation to sales, prepare cost budgets and set an overall target for the ratio of selling costs to sales. Sales costs include not only the cost of the sales force but also the cost of price concessions, service to accounts and the adjustment of complaints.
3. Evaluate existing sales resources by region and area to establish from recent performance what sales results can be achieved, given effective training and motivation.
4. Analyse the sales results achieved in each region and area to decide whether additional sales resources or effort will produce better results.

5. Analyse product profitability so that effort can be directed through call planning or incentives to where the best return will be obtained on selling costs, thus achieving a more profitable product mix.
6. Analyse the sales obtained from individual accounts to establish where the best results can be obtained in relation to sales effort.
7. On the basis of the evaluation and analysis carried out by stages (2) to (5) above:

   ■ decide how many sales staff are ideally required;
   ■ calculate the total cost of the field sales force and assume that these costs are within budget and that the target ratio of costs to sales will be achieved, if necessary modifying the number of sales staff and, therefore, sales costs to the required level;
   ■ decide how the field sales force is to be deployed by region and area; and
   ■ ensure through sales management that call schedules are prepared for each sales representative so that the best use is made of his or her time and important accounts are handled properly.

8. Set sales targets for each region, area and territory.
9. Set targets for the acquisition of new accounts and the sales to be achieved from those accounts.
10. Set quantitative standards for:

    ■ call rates – the number of calls made by a sales representative per day, week or month;
    ■ the proportion of calls that result in an order; and
    ■ the average sales per call – these targets will be varied according to the classification of accounts within the sales representative's territory into, say, large, medium or small.

11. Set qualitative standards for sales calls in terms of:

    ■ the information content of the call – the extent to which the sales representative is aware of the qualities of the products sold and of the customer's needs;
    ■ the effectiveness of the call as an act of communication – the extent to which the message is delivered in an understandable and convincing manner; and
    ■ the interpersonal aspects of the call – the extent to which the sales representative establishes and maintains a good relationship with the customer.

12. Devise training programmes for sales management and sales representatives to improve performance.
13. Design incentive schemes which will channel greater effort in the right direction.
14. Set up programmes for communicating to the sales force through sales management in order to inspire greater effort and to ensure that

everyone is aware of the targets and standards they have to meet and how they are expected to achieve them.

BENEFITS

Sales planning along the lines described above ensures that:

- the resources needed are deployed properly;
- the targets and standards required at all levels are set and communicated clearly;
- sales effort is directed where it will achieve the most profitable results;
- the return on sales effort and the costs thereof are maximized; and
- a sound basis is provided for the control of sales performance.

20

Web Marketing

DEFINITION

Web marketing is the process of promoting business and selling to customers through the use of the internet. It is commonly referred to as e-commerce.

THE WEB MARKETING PROCESS

The internet marketing process, as described by Judy Davis,[1] is summarized in Figure 20.1.

OBJECTIVES

The marketing objectives of using the internet are defined by Davis as follows:

- *Increasing brand and/or company awareness* – the web can raise awareness but its reach may still be smaller than traditional media. The web can supplement or complement other campaigns; it is unlikely to replace them.
- *Build brand image* – the web can extend brand definition. It is particularly appropriate, by association, for creating and monitoring the credibility of high-tech companies and their products or services.

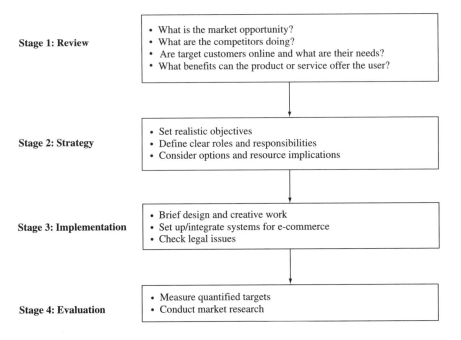

Figure 20.1 *Summary of the internet marketing process*

■ *Increase sales* – the web can provide extensive and vivid information about a product. It can be used to attract sales enquiries (which may be followed up by traditional means) and to link potential buyers to a site where products can be bought online. The site provides the basis for 'one-to-one' marketing and corporate promotional offers.
■ *Generate loyalty* – customers who actively decide to visit a website are likely to be attracted by the brand offer. Many of them will have bought the product already and can be rewarded accordingly with special offers.
■ *Reduce costs* – websites provide automatic ordering, invoicing and customer services and cut down on time and paperwork. A web catalogue is cheaper to update and distribute than a printed one.

SPECIFIC AIMS OF A WEBSITE

To achieve the objectives described above, the specific aims of a website are to:

■ attract interest – providing a reason to visit the site (the 'hook');
■ generate traffic (hits);
■ encourage return visits.

DEVELOPING A WEBSITE

The stages of developing a website are:

1. *Create interest* – the aim is to attract interest (to provide a 'hook') that will generate visits and sales.
2. *Design* – the design of the site should be attractive, but it is equally, if not more, important to ensure that it is easy to navigate. Users must be able to register easily, to find what they want to know quickly, and to place orders or ask for information without getting lost in a complex sequence of actions. Care should be taken over the design of site maps that guide users from one part of the site to another.
3. *Develop content* – the language should be informal and the text needs to be broken down into easily assimilated chunks. The patience of website visitors is limited and if there is too much indigestible prose, they will move on.
4. *Programme* – the site needs to be programmed to enable a web browser to use animation, video and, possibly, audio files. Multimedia effects can be added and web pages can be programmed to be interactive. It is important to minimize downloading time in order to be user-friendly, however, and the simplest approach may sometimes be the best. Systems need to be set up for handling transactions.
5. *Maximize traffic* – the site should be indexed and cross-referenced so that it is flagged up by the major search engines used by potential customers.
6. *Financing* – finance has to be obtained to fund the development of the website. Static pages (with no interactive elements) are cheaper. The costs will include the design of the site, expenses incurred in inputting material and agency fees.

BENEFITS

The benefits of web marketing are clearly the ability to gain access to many more customers, to enhance brand or company image and to generate interest and sales.

REFERENCE

1. Davis, J, *A Guide to Web Marketing*, Kogan Page, London 2000.

21

Relationship Marketing

DEFINITION

Relationship marketing is an approach to marketing which emphasizes the continuing relationships which should exist between the organization and its customers, with the emphasis on customer service and quality. Relationship marketing is therefore primarily a concept which adds customer service and quality to the traditional marketing mix of product, price, promotion and place.

DEFINITION OF THE CONCEPT

The term 'relationship marketing' was first formulated by Theodore Levitt in *The Marketing Imagination*.[1] He suggested that the relationship between a seller and a buyer seldom ends when the sale is made: 'In a great and increasing proportion of transactions, the relationship actually intensifies subsequent to the sale. This becomes the central factor in the buyer's choice of the seller the next time around.' According to Levitt the relationship between the buyer and the seller is 'inextricable, inescapable and profound'.

OBJECTIVES

The objectives of relationship marketing are to:

- achieve competitive advantage by creating value for the firm's customers;
- ensure that enough value is created in the sale to bring customers back for more; and
- build and maintain mutually satisfying relationships with customers.

ESSENCE OF RELATIONSHIP MARKETING

The essence of relationship marketing is contained within the concepts of:

- the value chain;
- the basic dimensions of quality and service support;
- specific quality solutions; and
- service support activities.

The value chain

The concept of the value chain was developed by Michael Porter[2] as a tool to identify those of the firm's activities which are strategically relevant. Service and the value provided to the customer are integral and key parts of this chain, leading to competitive advantage.

Quality solutions

The basic dimensions for the provision of quality solutions in relationship marketing as set out by Berry *et al*[3] are as follows:

- *Reliability* – the ability to perform the promised service dependably, accurately and consistently. This means doing it right, over a period of time.
- *Responsiveness* – prompt service and willingness to help customers, which requires both speed and flexibility.
- *Assurance* – knowledge and courtesy of staff and their ability to inspire trust and confidence.
- *Empathy* – caring and individualized attention to customers.
- *Tangibles* – physical facilities, equipment and staff appearance.

Service support activities

Service support activities as defined by Christopher *et al*[4] are designed to be perceived by customers as being of unique value, thus extending the offer beyond the customer's expectations and contributing to a shift in the customer's perceptions of the firm and its products. Service support includes such activities as pre-sale information, objective advice, care and attention during the sales negotiation, financing options, and after-sales support in the form of warranties, accessories and repair services.

DEVELOPING A RELATIONSHIP MARKETING APPROACH

The development of a relationship marketing approach requires the alignment of the three functions of marketing, customer service and quality. This involves the following:

■ Charting the service delivery system and setting standards for each part of the system, especially the 'encounter points' – the critical events in the system when the customer comes face to face with the service process.
■ Identifying critical service issues by research and analysis of customer needs and reactions.
■ Setting service standards for all aspects of service delivery.
■ Developing customer communication systems which define service standards and how the company is achieving them.
■ Developing programmes for contacting and maintaining good and continuing relationships with customers with the aim of retaining their loyalty.
■ Instituting intensive training courses for staff on their responsibility for building and maintaining good relationships with customers.
■ Monitoring service standards and rewarding staff for exceeding service levels while taking corrective action if service levels are persistently substandard.
■ Ensuring that all staff in all functions (operations, distribution and support services as well as sales and marketing) are fully aware at all times that customer service and qualities are key elements in the marketing mix, and that it is their responsibility to achieve the high levels of performance required.

BENEFITS

The benefits of relationship marketing are:

■ focus on providing value to customers;
■ emphasis on customer retention;

- the integrated approach to marketing, service and quality provides a firmer basis for achieving sustainable competitive advantage; and
- the importance of quality and service support is made absolutely clear to *all* staff.

REFERENCES

1. Levitt, T, *The Marketing Imagination*, Free Press, New York 1983.
2. Porter, M E, *Competitive Advantage*, Free Press, New York 1984.
3. Berry, L, Shostack, G and Upah, G, *Emerging Perspectives in Services Marketing*, American Marketing Association, Chicago 1983.
4. Christopher, M, Payne, A and Ballantyne, D, *Relationship Marketing*, Butterworth-Heinemann, Oxford 1991.

22

Database Marketing

DEFINITION

Database marketing uses information held on a computer database about existing or potential customers in such a way as to improve the effectiveness of the marketing and selling activities of the business.

A database is a set of data entries which is held on a computer and organized by a software package. It enables users to relate, collate, summarize and reproduce the data entries in accordance with defined parameters and criteria.

OBJECTIVE

The objective of database marketing is to exploit information held about customers in a way which maximizes the value of such information as a means of targeting them in accordance with their needs and buying habits.

APPLICATIONS

Database marketing is associated primarily with direct mail, which is a method of selling goods or services by means of communication to individuals through the post. Database techniques also offer a means of defining and refining markets.

More specifically, database marketing enables business to:

- target advertising and mail shots on the basis of a better understanding of the buying habits and wants of individual customers;
- plan the deployment of sales representatives to concentrate their efforts on more likely prospects;
- manage telesales by providing the telesales team with immediate access to customer information;
- plan the location of retail outlets in accordance with an understanding of potential demand;
- handle queries and complaints more easily, especially if an online database exists (ie if information from the database is instantly available);
- enhance loyalty by providing a personalized service; and
- obtain direct customer feedback on the degree to which they are satisfied and why.

DEVELOPING A DATABASE

The steps required to set up a database are to:

1. decide on the information required;
2. decide on the sources of that information; and
3. set up the software systems required to operate the database.

Information requirements

Information requirements will depend entirely on the type of business, its marketing strategies, how it carries out marketing and selling activities and the target population of existing customers or prospects (the 'audience' in mail-order operations). The headings under which information may be gathered or stored comprise the following:

- *Customer data* – names and addresses and information on all sales transactions: products bought, number of purchases, total and average value of payments, date of last order, response to promotions, method of payment and speed of payment.
- *Demographic data* – statistical information about population groups covering such areas as numbers by age and marital status, type of housing and socio-economic conditions such as numbers in certain types of occupation, levels of car ownership, etc. The aim is to obtain information which describes groups of people so that it is possible to differentiate one group from another. The assumption is then made that differences in the demographic make-up of groups will be reflected in differences in purchasing behaviour. The demographic profile is then

attached to individual households in the district and sales can be targeted to those who, on the balance of probabilities, are potentially the most responsive customers.

- *Psychographic data* – information about the personal characteristics of customers covering such items as their household, their possessions, their interests and their buying behaviour.

Information sources

The main information sources are as follows:

- *Customer data*. Obviously, this is collected from records of sales transactions. When designing the database it will be necessary to specify precisely what data is required and modify the data-processing systems accordingly. It will be essential to provide precise postcodes (this can be done through a specialized computer bureau).
- *Demographic data*. This can be obtained from the census. It is necessary to analyse each enumeration district (the smallest available building block of census data) to establish its demographic profile – the characteristics of residents in the district. This profile will not accurately describe every household but will probably apply to a sufficiently large proportion of them to justify targeting sales to all residents in accordance with the overall profile. Organizations such as Acorn can provide demographic profiles of their clients' customers.
- *Psychographic data*. This can be provided by organizations such as Behaviour Bank and Lifestyle Selector. They obtain their information through surveys which involve the completion of questionnaires by people and their subsequent analysis.

Setting up software systems

A database marketing system is often founded on some form of DBMS (database management system) upon which is built whatever application software is required. This software can be obtained from a software house as a package, or it can be custom-built by a software consultancy.

BENEFITS

The benefits of database marketing are:

- the ability to generate business at a lower cost per order;
- an increase in the productivity of sales representatives and assistants; and
- the capacity to respond more accurately to customer needs and wants.

FURTHER READING

Fairlie, R, *The Marketing Person's Guide to Database Marketing*, Exley Publications, Watford 1990.

23

Marketing Control

DEFINITION

Marketing control measures performance against plans so that swift action can be taken to correct adverse variances and amendments can be made as required to marketing plans.

THE CONTROL PROCESS

The basis of control is measurement, so that what has been achieved can be compared with what should have been achieved. The control process consists of:

1. planning what is to be achieved;
2. measuring regularly what has been achieved;
3. comparing actual achievements with the plan; and
4. taking action to exploit opportunities revealed by this information or to correct deviations from the plan.

THE ELEMENTS OF MARKETING CONTROL

The headings under which marketing control is exercised are the same as those used for setting targets and budgets in the marketing plan:

- sales volume and revenue;
- gross margin or contribution;
- net profits;
- market share;
- marketing expense.

Under each heading, any variances between the plan and performance are identified. The reasons for the variance are then established, which should indicate the corrective action to be taken.

SALES ANALYSIS

Performance data

Total sales and sales by product or product group are measured in unit and revenue terms for each month or four-week period. These results are compared with the forecast and the positive or negative variance recorded.

Sales are also measured on a cumulative year-to-date basis and compared with the forecast. Information is recorded for comparative purposes on the sales achieved in the corresponding period in the previous year and for the corresponding year-to-date figure for the previous year. An example of this type of analysis is given in Table 23.1.

Table 23.1 *Marketing control data*

	This month			Year-to-date		
	Actual	*Forecast*	*Previous year*	*Actual*	*Forecast*	*Previous year*
Sales £000	2,856	2,888	2,710	18,414	17,310	16,500

Charting sales data

Actual sales are displayed and compared with the forecast by use of the Z chart (see Figure 23.1). The name arises because the pattern on such a graph forms a rough letter Z. The chart records four items of information:

1. Actual sales for the month or period.
2. Cumulative total actual sales for the year to date.
3. The moving annual average of actual sales.
4. The forecast cumulative sales.

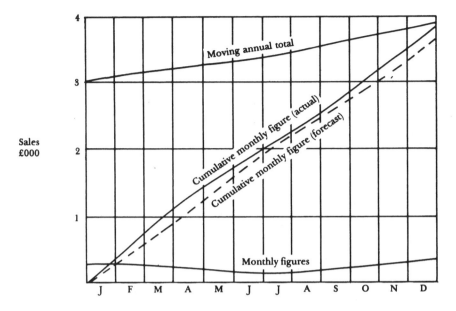

Figure 23.1 *Z chart used for marketing control*

Variance analysis

Variances are analysed to find out why they have happened. Corrective action should follow where necessary. Variances can be caused by one or a combination of any of the following three factors and should be assessed accordingly:

1. *Sales price variance* – differences between the budget price and actual price.
2. *Sales volume variance* – differences between forecast and actual sales.
3. *Product mix variance* – variations in the mix of products where the pattern of products actually sold differs from the pattern upon which the forecast was based.

Variance analysis may reveal inadequacies in performance, but it could indicate unrealistic (ie over-optimistic or unduly pessimistic targets or budgets).

CONTRIBUTION ANALYSIS

The analysis of contribution is made on the same lines as for sales, ie actuals are compared with budget and with the previous year on a monthly or period and year-to-date basis.

Variances in contribution are attributable to differences between forecast and actual sales or between budgeted and actual variable costs. As sales variances will have been separately analysed, the assessment of contribution variances concentrates on variable costs, ie the unit cost of the product sold plus the variable selling costs specifically incurred in selling more of the product. Variances can be caused by differences between actual and budgeted costs or by variations in the product mix.

MARKETING COSTS

Marketing costs are those directly incurred by the marketing and sales departments, ie market research, sales promotion, advertising, distribution and the costs of running the marketing department and the field sales organization.

Marketing costs are analysed in the same way as sales and contribution – the analysis of variances should not only establish why they have happened but also what results have been obtained from any extra expenditure incurred, eg an estimate of the impact on sales of spending more on promotion or advertising.

NET PROFITS

Net profit is sales revenue minus marginal costs (equals contribution) minus fixed costs (fixed factory overheads, marketing, distribution, research and development, financial and administrative costs) and minus tax. This is the 'bottom line' from the marketing point of view. The only additional factor subject to marketing control which may contribute to variances is that of marketing and distribution costs, which are analysed separately. But the marketing function has a key responsibility for achieving the net profit budget and must regard this as the ultimate measure of its performance.

MARKET SHARE

The forecast and actual market shares are compared under two headings:

1. *Market saturation* – the relationship between actual market volume of sales and market potential. A market segment is saturated when actual volume equals market potential (100 per cent) and degrees of saturation are expressed as percentages. The degree of saturation achieved against

budget indicates the extent to which marketing opportunities have been seized or are still available for further exploitation.

2. *Market penetration* – the relationship between actual market share in terms of sales and the actual market volume. Degrees of market penetration are expressed as percentages, and the overall effectiveness of marketing strategies and plans are assessed by comparing targets for increasing market penetration with the results achieved.

BENEFITS

Monitoring control information is the best way to ensure that what was intended has been done. More importantly, the analysis of variances points the way to future action. In addition, this analysis highlights any faults in the forecasting and budgeting process which can be corrected in the future.

24

Sales Control

DEFINITION

Sales control monitors sales performance in the field against the plan and initiates corrective action where targets or standards are not being achieved.

THE PROCESS OF SALES CONTROL

Sales control is exercised by comparing the results achieved with the targets, standards and budgets contained in the plan. It is directed towards the inputs and outputs of the sales force (field or internal) and the overall result they achieved.

This section concentrates on field sales control as the most important element in most companies. The process of field sales control is illustrated in Figure 24.1.

CONTROLLING SALES EFFORT IN THE FIELD

The control of sales effort in the field is effected by measuring achievements under the three input variables shown in Figure 24.1:

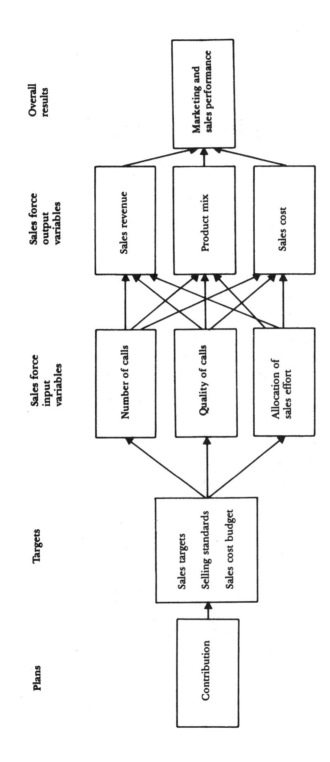

Figure 24.1 *The field sales control process*

1. The number of calls made by representatives against targets.
2. The quality of those calls against the quantitative targets for success and sales per call and the qualitative standards for the effectiveness of the sales representative during the calls.
3. The allocation of sales effort by sales management to achieve economy and effectiveness in the deployment of sales representatives. The objective is to obtain the optimum frequency of calls on large, medium and small customers, and on large, medium and small prospects, that will maximize the profit return per unit of sales effort expended.

The quantitative information is obtained by returns and reports originally from the individual sales representatives for their territories and analysed by area and region. The qualitative information is obtained by regular performance reports on sales representatives from sales management.

CONTROLLING SALES PERFORMANCE IN THE FIELD

Sales performance in the field is controlled under three headings:

1. Sales revenue against targets, for the company as a whole, for each region, area, territory and major outlet, and for each product line.
2. Product mix – the extent to which sales effort is being directed to the products producing higher profits, so that a more profitable product mix is achieved (the tendency for sales representatives to sell volume rather than optimize profitability must be controlled).
3. Selling costs expressed as actual against budget and as an actual ratio of costs to sales against the target ratio.

OVERALL CONTROL

The best overall measure of sales performance in the field is the contribution. The sales force sells the products at a margin, and this margin, minus all costs of the selling operation – sales representatives' salaries and commission, sales management and supervision costs, travel expenses, special discounts and interest on accounts receivable – represents the contribution of the sales department to corporate net profits and fixed costs.

BENEFITS

Managing a sales force consisting of independent-minded people scattered far and wide is never easy. It becomes impossible if the systems for monitoring sales performance are inadequate. Information not only on sales but also on what the sales force is actually doing and how well they are doing it is essential to maintain a sense of direction towards achieving corporate sales targets.

FURTHER READING

Henry, P, 'Manage your sales force as a system', *Harvard Business Review*, March–April 1975.

Part 2

Operational Management

25

Operations and Products

DEFINITION

Operations management is responsible for all the activities that are directly concerned with making an organization's products. It organizes the process of taking raw materials and turning them into products that satisfy customer demand.

GOODS AND SERVICES

Operations managers see every organization as making a product. This product can be the tangible goods made by a manufacturer, or the intangible services given by a service company. From an operations viewpoint, the intangible services given by an insurance company are their products, in exactly the same way as washing machines are the products of other companies.

In reality, almost every product is a combination of goods and services. Ford is clearly a manufacturer of cars, but its products include warranties, finance options and a range of other services; the BBC clearly provides a service, but its products include books, videos and a range of other goods. It is more realistic to describe a spectrum of products, ranging from those that are almost entirely goods through to those that are almost entirely services (as shown in Figure 25.1).

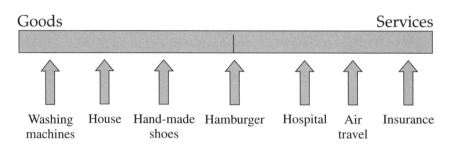

Figure 25.1 *Spectrum of products from largely goods to largely services*

OPERATIONS AND PRODUCTS

At the heart of every organization are the activities that make its products. These activities are the operations. To put it simply, the operations describe what the organization does. Operations at Dell make computers; operations at Lufthansa fly passengers; at The Wall Street Journal they publish a newspaper; at Dyson they make vacuum cleaners.

A common view of operations is that they take a number of inputs, and transform them into products (see Figure 25.2). The inputs include raw materials, money, people, machines, time and other resources. Operations include activities such as manufacturing, serving, training and distributing. The outputs are goods, services, waste material and so on.

Everything that you own, use, buy or borrow is a product of some organization – and it has been made by the operations. These operations manufacture, serve, transport, sell and do everything needed to supply

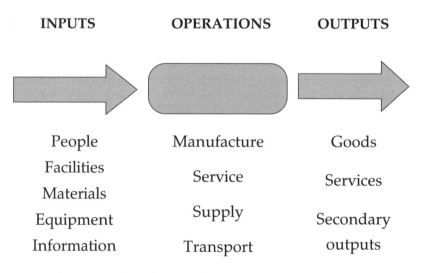

Figure 25.2 *Operations transform a range of inputs into outputs*

the products. Not surprisingly, the people who are responsible for these operations are the operations managers. In practice, organizations give their operations managers a range of different titles, but this does not change their basic function of making products.

When taken together, all the operations that make a particular product form its process. The process starts with the collection of inputs from initial suppliers, and ends with the delivery of finished products to customers. (See Figure 25.3.)

The aim of every organization is to make a product that satisfies customer demand. To be successful, a product must have features that customers prefer so that they buy this product in preference to others. The features of a product depend on the process used to make it, so this process must be appropriate, effective and efficient.

We can summarize this view of operations management as follows:

- a product is any combination of goods and services that an organization supplies;
- the aim of the product is to satisfy customer demand;
- taken together, the operations form a process that makes the product;
- operations managers are responsible for all aspects of this process;
- operations managers organize resources so that the process is as effective and efficient as possible.

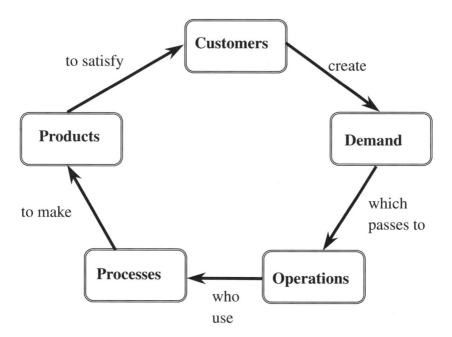

Figure 25.3 *Operations in the supply cycle*

QUESTIONS IN OPERATIONS MANAGEMENT

There are so many different types of operations that it may seem difficult to develop general ideas about their operations. The operations in British Steel (or Corus), for example, do not seem to have much in common with the operations of a local charity shop. Some of the main differences include their:

■ objectives;
■ volume of sales and size of operations;
■ type and variety of products;
■ balance between goods and services;
■ amount of variation in demand;
■ customer contact;
■ technology used.

Despite these apparent differences, most organizations actually face a range of similar problems. They have to design products that customers want, forecast demand for these products, plan their capacity, control stocks, distribute products, and so on. Typical questions faced by operations managers include:

■ What products do we make?
■ What type of process do we use to make them?
■ How can we best organize our resources in the process?
■ How can we forecast demand and set production levels?
■ How do we guarantee high quality?
■ Where do we locate the operations?
■ How do we organize the flow of materials through the process?
■ Who do we employ and what skills do they need?
■ Who are the best suppliers for materials?
■ How do we organize distribution to customers?

The aim of operations managers is to find the best answers to these and a range of related questions.

ACTIVITIES IN OPERATIONS MANAGEMENT

The next set of chapters cover some of the core questions in any organization. They start by showing how the operations fit into the broader business strategies. In essence, an operations strategy shows how the business strategy is translated into general concepts for products and processes. These concepts set the overall direction of operations and give the context for other decisions. Chapter 26 shows how the operations strategy forms a link between the rather vague higher strategies and more tangible ideas about products.

Operations managers look for the best way of organizing their resources and making products. They develop the strengths of the organization into a distinctive competence that allows them to compete effectively against other organizations. Ways of using operations management to gain a competitive advantage are discussed in Chapter 27.

An organization depends entirely upon its products. Chapter 28 looks at some aspects of product design and the following two chapters look in more detail at product planning and new product development. In recent years organizations have been putting a lot more emphasis on product quality. This theme is introduced in Chapter 31, and extended with descriptions of total quality management in Chapter 32 and quality control in Chapter 33.

Perhaps the key element for all operations is the overall demand for a product. This is not known with certainty in advance, but must be forecast. Chapter 34 describes some aspects of demand forecasting. These forecast demands can be used to find the best process. There are several different types of process and these are discussed in Chapters 35 and 36. A key question for a process concerns the best level of automation, and this is discussed in Chapters 37 and 38. Chapter 39 then describes some alternative policies for the physical layout of the process.

Every organization must measure its performance. The measures often concentrate on financial performance, but it is important to consider the core functions and use direct measures of the operations. There are many alternatives to this, some of which are described in Chapters 40 and 41. Chapter 42 looks at ways of improving performance.

The next chapters look at different aspects of planning. Chapter 43 starts by giving the context of planning, and describing a general approach. Chapter 44 shows how this is applied to capacity planning, and Chapters 45 and 46 look at tactical aggregate plans and master schedules. Chapter 47 moves down to the operational details of short-term schedules, and Chapter 48 finishes this theme by outlining the control of schedules.

The next two chapters introduce alternative approaches to planning. Chapter 49 shows how material requirements planning coordinates the supply of materials needed for production. This approach to 'dependent demand' systems is expanded in Chapter 50. An alternative approach pulls materials through the supply chain to give just-in-time operations, as discussed in Chapter 51. These special approaches are grouped together in Chapter 52 under the topic of 'project management'. Chapter 53 shows how planned maintenance and replacement is needed for smooth operations.

The last group of chapters in this section discusses supply chain management. Chapter 54 introduces the subject and shows its scope and importance. Then Chapters 55 to 57 look at procurement, inventory control and facility location.

Taken together, the techniques described in this section cover some of the most important areas in any organization. They show how the operations set about making the organization's products – and hence satisfying customers and achieving long-term objectives.

FURTHER READING

Krajewski, L J and Ritzman, L P, *Operations Management* (5th edition), Addison-Wesley, Reading 1998.

Slack, N, Chambers, S, Harland, C, Harrison, A and Johnston, R, *Operations Management* (2nd edition), Pitman Publishing, London 1998.

Waters, D, *Operations Management*, Kogan Page, London 1999.

26

Operations Strategy

DEFINITION

The *operations strategy* of an organization consists of all the long-term decisions, policies and plans made for operations management. It shows the overall direction of operations and gives the context for lower-level decisions.

CONTEXT OF THE OPERATIONS STRATEGY

Senior managers make the long-term strategic decisions that set the overall direction of an organization. Their strategic decisions include:

- *the mission* – a short statement which summarizes the overall aims of the organization;
- *corporate strategy* – which shows how a diversified organization will achieve its mission;
- *business strategy* – which gives the direction for each separate business within the diversified corporation and shows how each will contribute to the corporate strategy;
- *functional strategies* – which show how each function, including operations, will contribute to the business strategy.

ROLE OF THE OPERATIONS STRATEGY

An operations strategy is one of the key functional strategies. It describes the general features of an organization's products and processes, as well as long-term policies for location, capacity, quality, employees, relations with customers, etc.

The operations strategy gives the context for all other decisions in operations management. It shows how the organization is going to make products that satisfy customer demand – matching what the organization is good at with what the customers want. It is the link between the more abstract corporate and business strategies and real products and processes.

The operations strategy defines the ways the organization can achieve a long-term – and sustainable – competitive advantage. If a company's strength is making high-quality products, while its competitors are aiming for lower quality, it can get a clear advantage by making the highest quality products. The best strategies can usually be found from comparisons with competitors. These comparisons are formalized in a *SWOT analysis* – which lists the organization's strengths, weaknesses, opportunities and threats:

- *Strengths* show what the organization does well – features on which it should build.
- *Weaknesses* are problems the organization has – areas that it should improve.
- *Opportunities* can help the organization – openings that it should seize.
- *Threats* can damage the organization – hazards that it should avoid.

Strengths and weaknesses describe the organization's internal features, and typically include people, products, structure, finances, reputation, processes, assets, innovation and knowledge. Opportunities and threats describe external features and typically include the economy, competitors, markets, technology, new controls, laws, external relations, society, the environment and expectations of stakeholders.

DESIGNING THE OPERATIONS STRATEGY

The operations strategy shows how an organization plans to build its strengths into a *distinctive competence* that will give it a competitive advantage. If customers' priority is a low price, a good operations strategy is based on low costs; if customers want fast delivery, the operations strategy should emphasize speed; if customers demand high quality, the operations strategy should aim at guaranteeing perfect quality.

The operations strategy is framed in general terms and describes the features of products – processes rather than the details. It might, for example, include a strategy of low-cost, mass production. This gives the general concept, which leads to a series of related, more detailed decisions.

Unfortunately, there is no single best way of designing an operations strategy. Managers approach this in many different ways, usually involving a mixture of analysis, reasoning, experience and intuition. There are, however, some common principles and a reasonable approach includes the following steps:

1. Analyse the business strategy – and other strategies – from an operations viewpoint. This gives the context and overall aims for the operations strategy.
2. Use this analysis to set goals to show what the operations strategy must achieve.
3. Look at the existing operations strategy, find its aims, see how well it achieves these and look for improvements.
4. Understand the environment in which the operations strategy works. This identifies the market, customers, competitors, their performance, products, changes, and so on.
5. Find the factors that will lead to success in this market, and the importance of each one. This includes the general features that products must have to meet customer expectations.
6. Describe the general features of the process that can best deliver these products. This includes factors such as capacity, quality, flexibility and level of technology.
7. Design the best organizational structure, controls and functions to support the process.
8. Define measures to compare actual performance with planned, optimal and competitors' performance.
9. Implement the plans, setting the aims and conditions for other levels of decisions.
10. Monitor actual performance and continuously look for improvements.

At the end of this planning, the organization should have a coherent set of policies that show what the operations are going to achieve and how they will achieve it. These policies concentrate on the type of customers to be served, the type of products to be made, the types of processes to be used and the associated organization of resources.

PROBLEMS WITH IMPLEMENTATION

One of the main difficulties with operations strategies – and with all other strategies – is that they are designed by senior managers, but are implemented by more junior managers. Even with the best intentions and communications, senior managers can become too remote from operations: they see the financial ratios, but have little idea how the operations are really done. On the other hand, people working with the details of day-to-day operations have little time for vague corporate generalizations and ideals. Some common problems with strategies are:

- they are badly designed;
- they are not implemented properly;
- they are not related to actual operations;
- they are not realistic;
- they ignore key factors;
- people only give the appearance of supporting the strategies;
- enthusiasm for the strategies declines over time.

OTHER LEVELS OF OPERATIONS DECISIONS

Designing the operations strategy is the first step of a long and complicated planning process. At the end of this, managers have answered questions about all aspects of the operations. Table 26.1 shows some examples of these questions.

The distinctions between strategic, tactical and operational decisions are not really as clear as Table 26.1 suggests. Quality, for example, is a strategic issue when a company plans its competitive strategy, but it becomes a tactical issue when the company decides how to measure quality and set targets for performance, and then it becomes an operational decision when testing production to see if quality targets are being met.

FURTHER READING

Johnson, G and Scholes, K, *Exploring Corporate Strategy* (4th edition), Prentice-Hall, London 1997.

Wheelin, T L and Hunger, J D, *Strategic Management and Business Policy*, Addison Wesley, Reading 1998.

Table 26.1 *Typical operations decisions*

Decision area	Typical operations decisions
Strategic decisions	
Business	What business are we in?
Product	What type of products do we make?
Process	How do we make the products?
Location	Where do we make the products?
Capacity	How big should facilities be?
Quality management	How good are the products?
Other organizations	What are our relations with other organizations?
Tactical decisions	
Layout	How should we physically arrange operations?
Product planning	When should we introduce a new product?
Structure	What structure do we give the organization and the process?
Quality assurance	How do we achieve planned quality?
Logistics	How should we distribute the products?
Maintenance	How often should we maintain equipment and when should we replace it?
Staffing	How many people should we employ and what skills do they need?
Technology	What level is best for planned production?
Procurement	How do we organize purchasing?
Make/buy	Is it better to make or buy components?
Operational decisions	
Scheduling	In what order should we make the products?
Inventory	How much should we order and when should we place orders?
Reliability	How often does equipment break down: what can we do to improve this?
Maintenance	When can we schedule maintenance periods?
Quality control	Are products reaching designed quality?
Job design	What is the best way to do an operation?
Work measurement	How long will operations take?

27

Using Operations to Gain a Competitive Advantage

DEFINITION

Almost every organization faces competition from other organizations that make – or could start to make – similar products. To be successful, an organization has to develop its strengths into a distinctive competence that gives it a sustainable competitive advantage.

COMPETITION AND PRODUCTS

Organizations remain competitive by supplying products that customers buy in preference to any alternatives. The operations strategy gives the general concepts for these products and the processes used to make them. The next stage is to add some details to the concepts.

Unfortunately, when we begin to move beyond the general concepts, we quickly meet problems. The first is the obvious difference in the viewpoint of customers and the organization. Customers would like to buy high-quality products with lots of features at very low prices – but organizations would like to make standard products, with few features and higher prices. This is a common theme for operations managers, who are constantly searching for the best compromise between conflicting goals.

Not only do customers and producers want different features in their products but each customer frequently wants a different product. Some people want clothes that are very fashionable, others want them to be sensible and hard wearing, others want them to send out a particular image. Again the operations managers have to find a compromise between the wide range of products that customers would like to buy, and the narrow range that the organization would like to produce. The best place for this compromise is largely set by the balance of power within the supply chain. If there are many suppliers offering similar products, the customers may have more power and their demands become more important. On the other hand, if there are fewer suppliers dominating the market, they may have more control.

An important point for operations is the way that customers approach their purchases. The decision to buy something usually comes in two stages. The first stage finds a shortlist of products that have the qualifying factors. These are the factors that a product must have before a customer will even consider buying it. The second stage looks at order-winning factors. These are the additional factors that make a customer choose the best product – in their view – from the shortlist.

Operations managers have to make sure that their products have all the important qualifying factors, and as many of the order-winning factors as possible. Two ways of achieving this are cost leadership and product differentiation – both of which have important implications for operations.

Cost leaders make the same, or comparable, products more cheaply. They lower unit costs by having efficient operations, perhaps by improving the process, simplifying designs, reducing waste, using higher technology, getting economies of scale, locating near to customers, focusing on target products and/or reducing the length of the supply chain.

Product differentiation makes products that customers cannot find anywhere else. There are many ways of differentiating products, typically based on cost, quality, performance, technology, reliability, availability, amount of customization, delivery speed, innovation, reputation, associated services and/or location.

TOWARDS PRODUCT DESIGN

A traditional view of marketing says that an organization can compete by concentrating on the 'four Ps':

- *Product* – developing the right products that customers want.
- *Place* – efficiently delivering the products to customers.
- *Price* – setting a price that is acceptable to customers.
- *Promotion* – telling potential customers about the product.

A broader view says that an organization can compete by building on the strengths of its operations. Then it can design operations that emphasize cost, quality, timing, flexibility, technology, service, reliability, availability, flexibility, delivery speed, location and a range of other factors. Some of the most important of these, from an operations point of view, are listed below:

- *Cost.* Some organizations adopt a positive strategy of minimizing costs and supplying products at the lowest possible prices. Such organizations typically aim at high sales, lowering unit costs by automation, eliminating waste, reducing stocks, cutting overheads, and so on.
- *Quality.* Few customers are willing to accept poor quality, even at a low price. Many organizations use guaranteed high quality to gain a competitive advantage.
- *Timing.* Some organizations compete by supplying products at exactly the time that customers want them. This might mean that products are delivered at specified times, or with short development times for new products. Usually, it means that customers want products delivered as soon as possible, with short lead times.
- *Flexibility.* This is the ability of an organization to meet changing customer requirements. There are two important aspects to flexibility: product flexibility, which makes products that are customized to individual customer needs; and volume flexibility, which allows an organization to respond quickly to changing levels of demand.
- *Technology.* Some organizations, such as computer manufacturers or mobile telephone operators, remain competitive by using the latest available technology. These companies are usually strong in research and development, or they may exploit ideas from other companies.

There are many ways for operations managers to develop a competitive advantage. The important point is that organizations can only remain competitive if they organize their operations properly.

FURTHER READING

Stacey, R D, *Strategic Management and Organisational Dynamics* (2nd edition), Pitman, London 1996.
Worley, C G, Hutchin, D E and Ross, W L, *Integrated Strategic Change*, Addison Wesley, Reading, MA 1996.

28

Product Design

DEFINITION

Product design describes the features of product. It shows how the general characteristics outlined in the operations strategy are translated into actual products.

MATCHING PRODUCT DESIGN TO DEMAND

An operations strategy sets the general features of an organization's products and the processes used to make them. For the next stages of planning, the organization has to add details to these general concepts and show what the products actually look like – in other words, it has to consider their design.

Many people think that designers are only interested in the appearance of the finished product. Product design is much more complicated than this and describes all the details of the product package, as well as the process used to make it. Designers at McDonald's are not only interested in how its Big Mac looks, but also how it tastes, how customers like it, how to cook it, the design of the restaurant and kitchen, staff uniforms, where the materials come from, and all the other parts of the product package. The design concerns every part of this package, and typically includes:

- items supplied – goods that are bought;
- environment – the surroundings in which customers buy the product;
- associated items – items that support the main product;
- items changed – customers' goods that change with the product;
- explicit services – associated services that come with the goods and are part of the product specifications;
- implicit services – services which are not part of the product specifications, but are still given to customers.

FEATURES OF THE DESIGN

There is such a wide range of products – and so many different factors to consider – that it is almost impossible to describe specific features that make a good design. We can, however, mention the general requirements that a product be functional, attractive and easy to make.

Functional

Being functional means that the product can do the job for which it is designed – it must be 'of merchantable quality and fit for the purpose intended'. The best way of ensuring that a design is functional is to ask customers exactly what they want the product to do, have designers make sure their designs actually do this, and then test the product widely to make sure it really works. This is the idea behind prototypes and test marketing. Another tool that can help is quality function deployment. This essentially forms a table with the customer demands listed down one side, the proposed design features listed across the top, and an indication of how well the two are matched in the body.

Attractiveness to customers

This has something to do with appearance and aesthetics, but customers judge products in many different ways, including:

- style – that it is pleasant to look at and use;
- price – generally low price is an advantage, but there are many examples ranging from perfumes to luxury cars where it seems better to charge higher prices;
- availability – which usually means short lead times;
- designed quality – which shows how good a product is meant to be;
- reliability – which is often a measure of achieved quality;
- customization – flexible organizations customize products so that they match individual customer demands;

- durability – with long-lasting products generally being preferred;
- service – which includes aspects of before, during and after-sales service.

Easy to make

From an operations point of view, the best products are fast, cheap and easy to make. Features that operations managers do not like – as they cause problems and increase costs – include designs that:

- need a lot of work in a long or complicated process;
- have steps that must be done manually;
- use non-standard procedures, parts or components;
- use too many materials, or materials that are too expensive;
- have designed quality that is too high;
- have poor achieved quality – perhaps from using poor materials – especially if the cost of defects is high;
- have many variations or different products;
- interfere with the production of other items.

SIMPLIFIED AND STANDARD PRODUCTS

Operations managers like to simplify and standardize product designs. Simplifying means reducing the number of parts and removing unnecessary features so that the product is easier to make.

Standardizing uses common parts and materials in a range of different products. This leads to easier ordering of materials, discounts for larger orders, smaller stocks of parts, and longer production runs for components. Standardization does not necessarily reduce the choice of products, as the same parts can be used in a variety of ways.

These ideas have been extended by manufacturers into design for manufacture. This makes sure that the design is as easy to make as possible, typically suggesting designs that are simple, have a small number of operations, use as few parts as possible, use modular designs, have common parts across the product range, use inexpensive materials, do not interfere with other operations, use high-quality materials to reduce defects, and so on.

A related view of product design comes with value analysis. This asks whether customers see a product as giving good value – which means that the amount they are asked to pay is low in relation to the benefits they get. Value analysis can be seen as a way of reducing costs, with a special team looking at product designs and seeing how they can be altered to reduce costs or improve value.

FURTHER READING

Baxter, M, *Product Design*, Chapman & Hall, London 1995.

Boothroyd, G, Dewhurst, P and Knight, P, *Product Design for Manufacturing*, Marcel Dekker, New York 1994.

Hollins, B and Pugh, S, *Successful Product Design*, Butterworths, London 1990.

29

Product Planning

DEFINITION

Product planning is concerned with all decisions about the introduction of new products, changes to existing products and withdrawal of old products. The aim of product planning is to ensure that an organization continues over the long term to supply products that customers want.

PRODUCT LIFE CYCLE

An obvious problem with making products that satisfy customer demand is that their demands keep on changing. A product that is very popular this week might have no demand next week. The demand for most products follows a standard life cycle (also referred to in Chapter 3 as a key marketing management concept), which has the five stages shown in Figure 29.1:

1. *Introduction* – a new product appears on the market and demand is low while people learn about it, try it and see if they like it.
2. *Growth* – new customers buy the product and demand rises quickly.
3. *Maturity* – demand stabilizes when most potential customers know about the product and are buying it in steady numbers.
4. *Decline* – sales fall as customers start buying new, alternative products.
5. *Withdrawal* – demand declines to the point where it is no longer worth making the product.

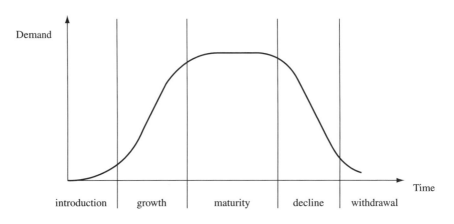

Figure 29.1 *Stages in a typical product life cycle*

This life cycle is found both in general categories of products, such as beer, microwave ovens and running shoes, and in specific brands.

Product life cycles have five important consequences for operations managers:

- Organizations emphasize different types of operations at each stage of the life cycle.
- Costs, revenues and profits vary considerably at each stage.
- Organizations with different expertise start (and later stop) making products at different points in the life cycle.
- Organizations usually make a range of products to smooth overall production.
- Organizations need to continually develop new products to replace older ones.

We will outline the first four of these in this chapter, and look at the development of new products in more detail in Chapter 30.

EMPHASIS OF OPERATIONS DURING THE LIFE CYCLE

The life cycle of every product has unique features, but we can describe a general, if somewhat simplified, view of the operations.

Early in the life cycle, operations centre around research and development. At the end of this, the product is launched and moves into the introduction stage. Initial demand is low, and this is met by small-scale operations – perhaps making units for specific orders. The initial design of the product is adjusted as customers give their reaction, so the operations must be flexible enough to deal with changes in both demand and specifications.

Demand increases as the product moves into the growth stage. The product design becomes more stable, and operations managers look for improvements in the process, typically changing to a more automated one. The aim is to increase capacity to meet the growing demand, and to discourage competition by keeping quality high and unit costs low. Units are no longer made for specific orders, but are put into a stock of finished goods, from which customer demands are met with short lead times. This makes forecasting of demand more important, with emphasis on planning and scheduling of resources.

Eventually, the product reaches its mature stage, when demand stabilizes. Forecasting and production planning are now easier. Some early competitors have stopped production, leaving the market to a few larger companies, who are competing on price. Operations now emphasize cost reduction and improved productivity, so the process may change to use more automation for standard products.

Eventually demand will decline, and competitors will drop out of the market. There is still likely to be excess capacity, and organizations might change the product design and process to try to extend its life. When this is no longer worthwhile, they will design termination procedures to stop production.

Most of the product development is done in the early stages of the life cycle, but most of the process development is done in later stages, as shown in Figure 29.2.

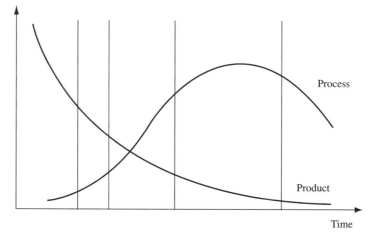

Figure 29.2 *Amount of innovation during a product life cycle*

COSTS, REVENUE AND PROFITS DURING THE LIFE CYCLE

Before a new product is introduced, the organization spends money on research, development, design, planning, testing, setting up new facilities and so on. These costs have to be recouped from later income.

In the early stages of the life cycle the unit costs are high. This is mainly because low-volume processes are expensive – but the organization may also try to recover some of the development costs by assigning them as overheads on early sales. At this stage the profit on each unit may also be high, as customers are willing to pay a premium to get a new or novel product. Total revenue is limited by small sales, as shown in Figure 29.3.

Revenue begins to rise when the product moves from introduction to the growth stage. At this point the development costs are recovered and the product starts to make an overall profit. The profit per unit can be high, as customers still view the product as new and are willing to pay a reasonably high price, there is little competition, and new production equipment is working efficiently.

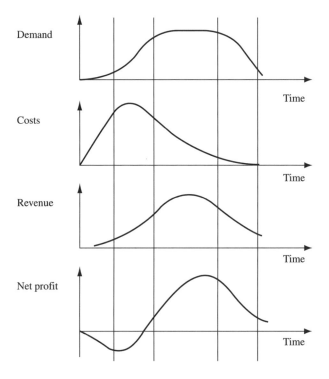

Figure 29.3 *Cost, revenue and profit during a product life cycle*

Revenue will rise until the product is somewhere in the mature stage. By this time competitors start to make similar products and demand slackens, so both the unit price and revenue begin to fall.

Beyond the mature stage profit falls as excess capacity leads to competition for the smaller demand. Sometimes, improved production methods, experience and higher productivity can offset the decline, but profits will inevitably fall. At some stage demand and profit fall to an unacceptable level and the organization withdraws the product.

ENTRY AND EXIT STRATEGIES

Some companies spend a lot of money on research and development to find new products. Pharmaceutical manufacturers, for example, do basic research to develop entirely new drugs. These companies look for the high profits that come from new products, but they have to bear the high cost of research and development.

Such companies might follow a product for its entire life cycle. Most organizations, however, do not start with basic research to develop entirely new products; nor do they continue making a product through its entire life. Instead, they start product planning by looking at existing products – normally those made by competitors. Then they try to find an existing product which would fit into their own range, and which they could modify to create their own 'new' product. In other words, they start supplying a product that is already some way through its life cycle. The time when an organization starts – and later stops – making a product defines its *entry and exit strategy.*

An organization's entry and exit strategy depends on its expertise and overall objectives. We can describe three common strategies as follows:

Research driven

- do basic research to give the ideas and technology for new developments, but they do not exploit them;
- work in the introduction stage and leave the market before the growth stage – as they lack the resources and production skills to manage a growing demand;
- are good at research, design and development;
- are innovative with constant changes in product;
- are characterized by high quality and high cost;
- are characterized by low sales volumes;
- are characterized by slow delivery.

New product exploiters

- look for research that has commercial potential and then exploit it during the growth stage;
- aim for the high prices available during growth, and exit when profit margins begin to fall;
- identify new products with wide appeal;
- are good at developing new processes for production;
- are strong in marketing to create demand;
- are characterized by high quality with reducing cost;
- move to high volume.

Cost reducers

- design very efficient operations, so they enter the market at the mature stage and produce large quantities efficiently enough to compete with organizations already in the market;
- exit when the product declines and the volume is too low to maintain high production levels;
- are characterized by high-volume, low-cost production;
- are characterized by low innovation, concentrating on established products;
- are characterized by low price and fast delivery;
- are often automated with production or assembly lines.

There are, of course, other types of entry and exit strategies. Some companies, for example, specialize in entering declining markets and extending product lives.

RANGE OF PRODUCTS OFFERED

Ideally, organizations would like to supply a single product, as this makes their operations very simple and efficient, but the overall demand for any product is made up of a large number of individual demands, each of which is slightly different. Organizations allow for these differences by supplying a range of similar or related products.

Most organizations concentrate on one kind of product in which they develop knowledge, skills and experience. When they look for new products, they want products that are similar to those they already make but are different enough to create new demands. There are, of course, conglomerates that make completely unrelated products, but these usually organize each business as an independent entity.

An obvious question is 'how wide should the range of products be?' Customers want a wide range of products, so they can choose one that gives a close fit to their individual needs – but producers want a narrow range so they can benefit from:

- giving long production runs that reduce equipment set-up times;
- using specialized equipment that has high productivity;
- making production routine and well practised;
- increasing experience and expertise with the product;
- encouraging long-term improvements to the product;
- making purchasing, inspections and handling routine;
- reducing staff training time;
- reducing stocks of parts and materials.

An organization must find a balance between its own operations and customer satisfaction. If its range is too narrow, the organization can use standard operations, but it loses customers to competitors who offer more products, or different ones. If its range is too wide, the organization can satisfy varied customer demands, but it loses the efficiency that comes from standardization.

However wide the range, organizations try to have products at different stages in their life cycles. This allows long-term stability, with new products being phased in while older ones are declining and being withdrawn. The overall production is smoothed as shown in Figure 29.4.

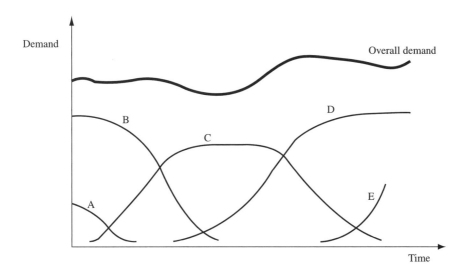

Figure 29.4 *Timing products to give a stable overall demand*

FURTHER READING

Crawford, C M, *New Products Management* (5th edition), Irwin, Chicago 1997.

Kuczmarski, T D, *Managing New Products* (2nd edition), Prentice-Hall, Englewood Cliffs, NJ 1992.

30

Developing New Products

DEFINITION

Organizations need a continuous supply of new products to replace old ones that are reaching the end of their life cycle. Product development includes all the work needed to ensure this supply of new products, starting with the generation of ideas, and finishing with the introduction of new products.

STAGES IN PRODUCT DEVELOPMENT

When the demand for an old product falls, an organization must have a new product ready to replace it. The planning for this new product has several stages, which start with the generation of ideas, and end when the product is actually sold to customers. Details of this planning vary, but a common approach has six stages.

Stage 1: generation of ideas

Most organizations continuously search for new ideas they can exploit. These initial ideas come from many sources, including:

- work in research and development;
- operations people suggesting changes to an existing product, perhaps to make the process more efficient;

- marketing reports of changes in customer demand;
- other internal sources;
- customers contacting the organization with demands for new products;
- focus groups organized to collect ideas from customers;
- competitors' products that can be adapted;
- changing laws or regulations that create demand for new products;
- other external sources.

New ideas are surprisingly easy to find – the difficulty is looking at these ideas, choosing the best and turning them into viable products that customers will buy.

Stage 2: initial screening of ideas

All ideas must go through an initial screening to reject those that have obvious flaws. This screening can quickly reject products that:

- are impossible to produce, or are technically too difficult;
- have been tried before and were unsuccessful;
- duplicate an existing product;
- need expertise or skills that the organization does not have;
- do not fit into current operations;
- would obviously not sell;
- would obviously not make a profit;
- are too risky.

This screening might remove 80 per cent of the original ideas, leaving 20 per cent that have no obvious flaws and can move to the next stages of development (see Figure 30.1).

Stage 3: technical evaluation – initial design, development and testing

At this point the initial ideas seem feasible, so details are added to take them from a general concept through to the initial designs. This stage gives a technical evaluation of ideas. It considers whether the product could be made by the organization and typically asks two types of questions.

General questions about the concept:

- Can the product be made?
- Is the idea based on sound principles?
- Is it safe and legal?
- Is it entirely new, or a variation on old ideas?

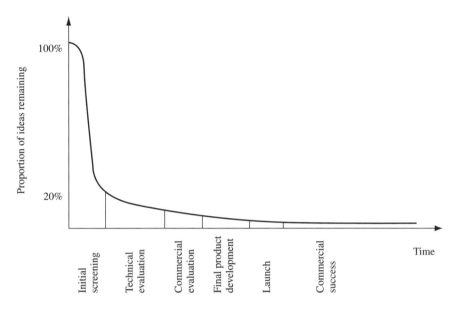

Figure 30.1 *Percentage of original ideas remaining*

- If it is an old idea, why has the organization not made it before?
- Are there problems with patents or competitors?
- Are developments likely to overtake the product?

More specific questions about the product:

- Is the proposed design technically feasible?
- Can it be made with available technology?
- Would it fit into current operations?
- Does the organization have the necessary skills and experience?
- Is there enough capacity in operations?

Prototypes and trials help with these decisions and suggest modifications to the initial designs. At this point, the initial designs for the process are also considered.

Stage 4: commercial evaluation – market and financial analysis

If the product passes the technical evaluation, it moves on to a commercial evaluation to see whether it will make a profit. This stage removes products that:

- customers will not buy;
- are too similar to existing products;
- are so different from existing products that customers will not accept them;
- are in a rapidly declining market;
- do not fit into existing strategies;
- will not make enough profit, or have margins that are too small;
- need too much capital, or have poor returns on investment;
- have too high production or operating costs.

This stage builds a commercial case for continuing development of the product. If this case is sound, the product moves forward to full development.

Stage 5: final product development

Products that pass the feasibility study move on to final design and testing. This is where all the lessons learnt from previous stages, together with the results from customer surveys and any other relevant information, are used in the final designs. The product changes from a prototype or concept model to the final form that customers will see. This design describes the overall package, including the design of any goods, the services offered, materials used, quality measures, and everything else that forms the final product package. This stage also finalizes the details of the process used to make the product.

Stage 6: launch of product

After the development, production starts and the organization offers its new product to customers. This is the first chance to see if the planning has worked and the product will actually be a success. Many products are not successful and are quickly withdrawn. Very few of the initial ideas – perhaps one or two per cent – go through all the stages of development to the point where they are launched on the market. Even fewer become successful products.

CONCURRENT DEVELOPMENT

The six stages described above are carried out roughly in order, but there can be a lot of cycling and repetition. If, for example, the results of the commercial evaluation are unclear, the organization might adjust the designs and initiate a new technical evaluation.

There are obvious benefits of doing the development as quickly as possible. Faster development can make an organization the first to market a new product and so gain the price premium of new products, gain a dominant position in the market, and set the standards for later competitors. Fast development also frees up resources quickly and speeds up the income that is needed to recover development costs.

An obvious way of reducing the development time is to use concurrent development. This happens when there is no need to wait until one stage is completely finished before starting the next, and the stages overlap each other. The initial screening of ideas, for example, need not wait until all ideas have been generated; it can quickly remove obvious non-starters while other ideas are still being generated. The more overlap that can be achieved, the shorter is the overall development time. Companies using concurrent development in different industries have reduced the time to bring new products to market by up to 70 per cent.

FURTHER READING

Ulrich, K T and Eppinger, S D, *Product Design and Development*, McGraw-Hill, New York 1995.

Urban, G and Hauser, J R, *Design and Marketing of New Products* (2nd edition), Prentice-Hall, Englewood Cliffs, NJ 1993.

Wheelwright, S C and Clark, K B, *Revolutionising Product Development*, Free Press, New York 1992.

31

Quality Management

DEFINITION

Quality management is concerned with the plans, decisions, tests, design, performance and all other aspects of a product's quality.

DEFINING QUALITY

Everyone is concerned with product quality, whether they are organizations supplying products, or customers buying them. This is fairly clear, but we hit a major obstacle when trying to define exactly what we mean by 'quality'. If someone asks you to judge the quality of, say, a novel, you can say whether you enjoyed reading it, but would find it difficult to describe its quality in objective terms, let alone measure it. Sometimes there are agreed measures for quality, such as the industry standards for concrete, but these are very specific and cannot be used for other products.

As a starting point, we can say that a product has high quality if it does the job it was designed for. This gives one view of quality, which is that quality is the ability of a product to meet – and preferably exceed – customer expectations. This definition shows why quality is so important: the only way an organization can remain competitive is by making products with the high quality that customers demand and expect.

This still gives a rather vague idea of quality, especially as different customers have different expectations. Quality depends on many factors, and producers and customers typically think in terms of:

- innate excellence;
- fitness for intended use;
- performance;
- reliability;
- durability;
- specific features – perhaps for safety or convenience;
- level of technology;
- conformance to design specifications;
- uniformity, with small variability;
- perceived high quality;
- convenience of use;
- attractive appearance and style;
- value, or the ratio of performance to cost;
- customer service before and during sales;
- on-time deliveries;
- after-sales service.

This list identifies two specific views of product quality: an *internal* view, from the producer, who defines quality as the closeness of a product's performance to its designed specifications, and an *external* view, from the customer, who defines quality by how well a product does the job it was bought for.

In the past, organizations tended to emphasize the internal view, suggesting that a product that meets their standards should be acceptable to customers. More recently, organizations have taken more notice of customers' views, and have recognized the obvious point that it is customers who decide when a product meets their expectations. This does not mean that customers always demand products with the highest technical quality. They want some balance of features that gives an acceptable overall picture. A Rolls-Royce car has the highest possible quality of engineering, but most people include price in their judgement and buy a cheaper make. This leads to another two aspects of quality: *designed* quality – which sets the quality that a product is designed to have; and *achieved* quality – which shows how closely a product comes to meeting the designed quality.

BENEFITS OF HIGH QUALITY

In recent years there has been an enormous growth of interest in quality management. This has happened for four main reasons:

- improved processes can make products with guaranteed high quality;
- high quality gives a competitive advantage;

- consumers have become accustomed to high-quality products and will not accept anything less;
- high quality reduces costs.

This list shows why organizations *must* make high-quality products. If they make poor-quality products, customers will simply move to a competitor who is better at meeting their expectations. Although high quality will not guarantee a product's success, low quality will certainly guarantee its failure.

Long-term survival, coming from satisfied customers, is the major benefit of high quality. Other benefits include:

- higher customer satisfaction;
- less waste and increased productivity;
- lower costs and improved profitability;
- reduced warranty costs;
- elimination of procedures for correcting defects;
- reduced administration costs for dealing with customer complaints;
- reduced liability for defects;
- competitive advantage coming from an enhanced reputation;
- larger market share with less effort in marketing;
- enhanced motivation and morale of employees;
- removal of hassle and irritants for managers.

COSTS OF QUALITY

One interesting point from the list above is that higher quality reduces costs. At first this seems to go against the traditional view that increasing quality can only be bought at increasing cost. If you look at the wider costs, however, you see that some actually go down with increasing quality. Suppose, for example, you buy a washing machine with a faulty part. You complain, and the manufacturer arranges for the machine to be repaired. The manufacturer could have saved money by finding the fault before the machine left the factory – and it could have saved even more by making a machine that did not have a fault in the first place.

At this point we should look at the costs of quality in a little more detail. There are four components to the costs of quality – for prevention, appraisal, internal failure and external failure.

Prevention costs are the costs incurred to prevent defects occurring. The quality of a product is largely set at the design stage, so the best way to guarantee high quality is not by inspections during the process but by designing a good product in the first place. Prevention costs cover all aspects of quality that are designed into a product. They include direct costs for the product itself, such as the use of better materials, inclusion of features to ensure good quality, and extra time to make the product. They also include indirect costs related to the ease of production, type of process, amount of automation, procurement needed, skills needed by employees, and the amount of training they need. All things being equal, prevention costs rise with the quality of the product.

Appraisal cost is the cost of ensuring that the designed quality is actually achieved. As units move through the process, they are inspected to make sure that they actually reach the quality specified in the design. Related costs include sampling, inspecting, testing and all the other elements of quality control (which is discussed in Chapter 33). Generally, the more effort that is put into quality control, the higher will be the end quality of the product and the higher will be the cost of achieving it.

Internal failure cost. As a product moves through its process, it will be inspected several times, and any unit that does not meet a specified standard will be scrapped, returned to an earlier point in the process, or repaired. This involves extra work and higher costs. These costs form part of the internal failure cost, which is the total cost of making defective products that are detected somewhere within the process.

The further a product goes through the process, the more money is spent on it and the more expensive it will be to scrap or rework. Ideally, then, defects should be found as early in the process as possible.

Part of the internal failure costs come directly from the loss of material, wasted labour effort, wasted machine time in making the defective item and so on. Another part comes from the indirect costs of higher stock levels, longer lead times and extra capacity needed to allow for scrap and rejections.

External failure cost. Producers are normally held legally responsible for the quality of their products and they often give a written guarantee. If a unit that goes through the entire process is delivered to a customer and is then found to be defective, the producer must bring the defective unit back from the customer and replace, rework or repair it as necessary. The cost of this work is part of the external failure cost, which is the total cost of making defective units that are not detected within the process but are recognized as faulty by customers.

External failure faults are often the highest costs of quality management and are the ones that should be avoided. External failure costs, like internal failure costs, decline with higher quality.

MINIMIZING THE TOTAL COST OF QUALITY

The total cost of quality comes from adding these four separate components. The result is often surprisingly high – sometimes amounting to 25

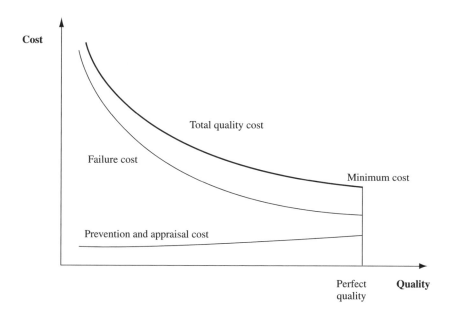

Figure 31.1 *Minimum costs come with perfect quality*

per cent of sales – with the failure costs being highest. Plotting these components gives the results shown in Figure 31.1. The failure costs are so high that organizations clearly want to avoid them, and the best way of doing this is to make products without defects – in other words, to make products of 'perfect quality', where every unit is guaranteed to be free of any faults. This is the idea of *total quality management,* which is described in the next chapter.

FURTHER READING

Ho, S, *Operations and Quality Management*, International Thomson Business Press, London 1999.

Kehoe, D F, *The Fundamentals of Quality Management*, Chapman & Hall, London 1996.

Whitford, B and Bird, R, *The Pursuit of Quality*, Prentice-Hall, London 1996.

32

Total Quality Management

DEFINITION

Total quality management (TQM) has the whole organization working together to give products with guaranteed high quality. It aims at systematically improving the quality of products until the organization makes products of perfect quality.

AIMING FOR PERFECT QUALITY

The last chapter showed how organizations could minimize their costs by aiming for perfect quality or zero defects in their products. An obvious way of improving quality is to use more rigorous inspections – but there is an old saying that 'you can't inspect quality into a product'. A better alternative is not to inspect units and discard defective ones but to make sure that no defective units are made in the first place. This is the basis of TQM.

The key idea behind TQM is that quality management is not a separate function to be treated in isolation, but is an integral part of all operations. Everybody in the organization is concerned with quality. Suppose you go to a tailor and order a suit. You will only be satisfied if the suit is well designed, if it is well made, if there are no faults in the material used, if the price is reasonable, if the salesperson is helpful, if the shop is pleasant and so on. This means that everyone in the tailor's shop – from the person who designs the suit to the person who sells it, and from the person who owns the organization to the person who keeps it clean – is directly involved in the quality of their product.

ORGANIZING FOR TQM

Total quality management involves a change of emphasis from inspections at the end of a process to a focus on operations during the process itself, to make sure no defects are produced, and on the planning stages, to ensure that the design allows high quality.

During the process, operations departments take responsibility for their own quality. Each person is responsible for only passing on units that are of perfect quality. This is quality at source, with job enlargement for each person who is now responsible for both their previous job and an inherent quality management function.

With quality at source, anyone who finds a fault realizes that something has gone wrong and has the authority to stop the process and investigate. They find the cause of the fault and suggest ways of avoiding more faults in the future. Total quality management also affects the way people are paid. Traditionally people were paid to make high volumes – often using 'piece work' – with little regard for quality. Total quality management requires that people should also be paid for quality, so they become interested in how well they make the product and are willing to suggest improvements. These might be collected at quality circles, which are informal groups of about 10 people who work on a process. They typically meet for an hour once or twice a month to discuss ways of improving their operations, perhaps discussing problems, looking at alternatives for improvements, examining suggestions, modifying designs, and so on. Their aim is simply to discuss the operation and try to find improvements.

Many companies who use quality circles have immense benefits, but they can only be used with:

- a well-educated workforce capable of recognizing, analysing and solving problems;
- people who are able and willing to exchange ideas;
- people who see themselves as working for the good of the organization;
- a management that is willing to share information about costs and operations.

Table 32.1 summarizes the main difference in attitudes brought about by TQM.

IMPLEMENTING TOTAL QUALITY MANAGEMENT

Total quality management needs major changes within an organization. Edwards Deming spent 40 years looking at way of introducing these

Table 32.1 *Different attitudes introduced by TQM*

Criteria	Traditional attitude	New attitude with TQM
Importance:	quality is a technical issue	quality is a strategic issue
Cost:	high quality costs money	high quality saves money
Responsibility:	quality assurance department	everyone in the organization
Target:	meet specifications	continuous improvement
Measured by:	average quality level	zero defects
Emphasis:	detecting defects	preventing defects
Attitude:	inspect quality	build quality
Defined by:	organization	customers

changes and developing his ideas of TQM. During this time he compiled a list of '14 principles'.

Deming's 14 principles

1. Create constancy of purpose towards product quality.
2. Refuse to accept customary levels of mistakes, delays, defects and errors.
3. Stop depending on mass inspection, but build quality into the product in the first place.
4. Stop awarding business on the basis of price only – reduce the number of suppliers and insist on meaningful measures of quality.
5. Develop programmes for continuous improvement of costs, quality, productivity and service.
6. Institute training for all employees.
7. Focus supervision on helping employees to do a better job.
8. Drive out fear by encouraging two-way communication.
9. Break down barriers between departments and encourage problem-solving through teamwork.
10. Eliminate numerical goals, posters and slogans that demand improvements without saying how these should be achieved.
11. Eliminate arbitrary quotas that interfere with quality.
12. Remove barriers that stop people having pride in their work.
13. Institute vigorous programmes of lifelong education, training and self-improvement.
14. Put everyone to work on implementing these 14 points.

Deming's 14 points suggest a new way of thinking in organizations. They emphasize the fact that managers are in control of the organization, and are responsible for its performance. The process is really in two parts: the *system* over which managers have control, and which contributes 85 per cent of the variation in quality; and the *workers* who are under their own control, and who contribute 15 per cent of the variation in quality.

Major improvements in quality come from managers improving the system rather than workers improving their own performance.

STEPS FOR IMPLEMENTATION

Now we have seen what is involved with TQM, we can describe the steps that are needed for its implementation. A useful approach has the following seven steps:

1. *Get top management commitment.* This is a key point for TQM. Managers have control of the organization, and they must realize that TQM is not another fad that will disappear in a few months but is a way of thinking that improves long-term performance.
2. *Find out what customers really want.* Without knowing exactly what customers want it is impossible to design products that satisfy them. This goes beyond simply asking for opinions, and gets customers involved in the process, perhaps discussing designs in focus groups.
3. *Design products with quality in mind.* Organizations must design their products carefully so that they are robust and satisfy both internal and external demands.
4. *Design the process with quality in mind.* The quality of the product depends on the process used to make it, so this must work effectively and efficiently to achieve perfect quality.
5. *Build teams of empowered employees.* Quality depends on everyone in the organization, so they should be recognized as the most valuable asset, with appropriate training and motivation.
6. *Keep track of results.* TQM looks for continuous improvement, with the adjustments to products and processes having a cumulative effect over time.
7. *Extend these ideas to suppliers and distributors.* Organizations do not work in isolation, but are part of a supply chain, with the quality of the final product depending on every link of this chain.

It can take years of continuous effort to implement TQM, so it is not surprising that many organizations fail somewhere on this road. There are a lot of reasons for these failures. Perhaps suppliers cannot guarantee the quality of their materials; or managers only gave TQM lip service without becoming really involved; or administration got out of hand; or the process could not reduce the variability enough; or TQM simply was not implemented properly. Many organizations have found considerable benefits from TQM, but few say that the implementation was easy.

ISO 9000 STANDARDS

The International Standards Organization (ISO) has designed a family of standards for quality management. If an organization can show that it consistently achieves certain quality standards, it can apply for ISO 9000 certification. There are actually five separate standards:

- ISO 9000, which defines quality and gives a series of quality standards for which an organization might aim, with guidelines for their use;
- ISO 9001, which is used by organizations that design and make products – it is the most comprehensive of the standards and deals with the whole range of TQM, from initial product design and development, through to standards for inspecting and testing final products;
- ISO 9002, which is used by organizations that make standard products and has less involvement in the design – it concentrates on the actual process, and how to document quality;
- ISO 9003, which deals with final product inspection and testing procedures; and
- ISO 9004, which is a guide to overall quality management and related systems, and says how operations can develop and maintain quality.

ISO 9000 and 9004 are guides to be used within the organization for setting up quality management programmes. ISO 9001, 9002 and 9003 describe what a quality management system must achieve to be certified. The standards are administered by independent third parties who check that an organization:

- says what it is going to do to ensure high quality, describing its procedures, operations and inspections;
- actually does the work in the ways described;
- proves that the work has been done properly by doing audits and keeping records.

FURTHER READING

Bounds, G, Yorks, L, Adams, M and Ranney, G, *Beyond Total Quality Management*, McGraw-Hill, New York 1994.

Evans, J R and Lindsay, W M, *The Management and Control of Quality* (3rd edition), West Publishing, St Paul, MN 1996.

Oakland, J S, *Total Quality Management* (2nd edition), Heinemann, London 1992.

33

Quality Control

DEFINITION

Quality control uses a series of independent inspections and tests to make sure that designed quality is actually being achieved.

PRODUCT VARIABILITY

No matter how good the operations are, there will always be some variation in the units made. Differences in materials, weather, tools, employees, moods, time, stress and a whole range of other things combine to give apparently random variations. Provided these variations are small, the performance of each unit remains within acceptable limits. If the variation is too large, it is impossible to guarantee that every unit actually reaches designed specifications.

The way to improve quality, therefore, is to reduce variability between units, and get the performance of each as close to the target as possible. Genichi Taguchi formalized this in a loss function that gives a notional cost of missing the target. The further a unit is away from the target, the higher is this cost.

Organizations should try to minimize the value of this loss function, but the only way they can monitor performance is to inspect units and test the variation. This is the purpose of quality control. Quality control gives independent evidence that the process is working properly and that no defects are being made. It ensures that designed quality is actually being achieved.

CAUSES OF FAULTS

If the quality control inspections find a defective unit, it means that something has gone wrong with the process. Then the organization should find the cause of the problem and correct it before any more defects are made. Typical causes of faults are:

- human errors of various kinds;
- machine faults, perhaps caused by poor maintenance;
- poor materials;
- faults in operations, such as speed or temperature changes;
- changes in the environment, such as humidity, dust or temperature;
- errors in the monitoring equipment, such as errors in measuring tools.

It is often difficult to find the real cause of a fault, but two simple diagrams help with this. First, there are cause-and-effect diagrams, which show the possible causes of a problem in the form of 'fish-bone diagrams'. Suppose a customer complains at a hamburger restaurant. The fault may be caused by the raw materials, the cooking, the staff or the facilities. Problems with the raw materials may, in turn, be caused by suppliers, storage or costs. A cause-and-effect diagram draws these relationships as coming from spines, like a fish bone, as shown in Figure 33.1.

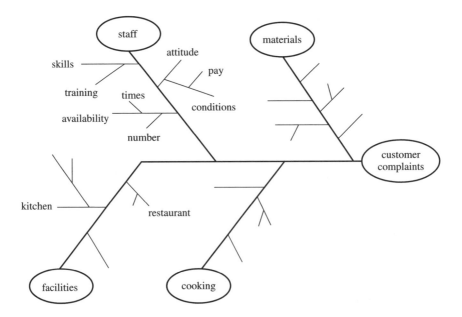

Figure 33.1 *Part of a cause-and-effect diagram*

Pareto charts are based on the observation that 80 per cent of the problems come from 20 per cent of the causes. A Pareto chart lists the possible causes of problems, counts the number of faults that come from each, and shows the results on a bar chart. Typically, a few causes will be responsible for most of the problems. So the chart identifies the areas that need special attention (as shown in Figure 33.2).

TIMING OF INSPECTIONS

The longer a unit is in a process, the more time and money will be spent on it, so it is best to find faults as soon as possible. The main effort in quality control should be early in the process, with tests on materials when they arrive from suppliers or before they leave the suppliers. Then a series of inspections should continue all the way through the process, from the production of raw materials to the completion of the final product and its delivery to customers. If the main effort of inspection is started early enough, there should be very few defects in the later stages, and the product reaching the customer should be as nearly free from errors as possible. There are some specific points in a process where inspections are most useful.

For raw materials:

- during suppliers' operations;
- on arrival at the organization.

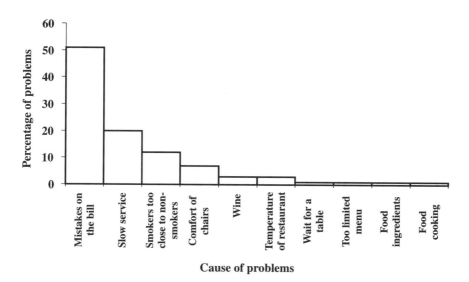

Figure 33.2 *Example of a Pareto chart*

During the process:

■ at regular intervals during the process;
■ before high-cost operations;
■ before irreversible operations, like firing pottery;
■ before operations that might hide defects, like painting.

For finished products:

■ when production is complete;
■ before shipping to customers.

It is, of course, possible to have too many inspections. Each one has costs, and there comes a point where the benefit from an inspection is less than the cost involved.

SAMPLING

It is often impossible to test every unit as it moves through its process. Then quality control relies on samples – usually random – of units from the output. Reasons for using samples rather than the whole output include:

■ *expense* – it may be too expensive to test each unit;
■ *time needed* – some tests are so long or complicated that they cannot be fitted into normal operations;
■ *destructive testing* – sometimes tests are destructive;
■ *reliability* – no test is completely reliable, so testing all the units does not necessarily give better results than a sample;
■ *feasibility* – sometimes, as when testing new medicines, there is an infinite number of tests that could be done.

If the samples perform well, it is assumed that the whole production reaches the designed quality, but if the sample performs badly, something has gone wrong and the operations have to be checked. This gives a general approach to sampling, with the following steps:

1. Choose the features to be measured.
2. Define acceptable quality – or the tolerance – for each measure.
3. Design a sampling plan, setting the sample size and the number that must reach acceptable standards.
4. Take a sample – usually random – of units.
5. Measure the features for each unit and see how much of the sample meets the standards for acceptable quality.

6. Say that production is satisfactory if the predetermined number of units from the sample reaches the acceptable standard.
7. Say that production is unsatisfactory and there are problems with the process if fewer than the predetermined number reach the acceptable standard.

The sample size and number which must be satisfactory are largely a matter of policy – managers set the quality levels they want to reach and standard sampling plans give the details of samples. Remember, however, that organizations should aim for perfect quality, and this means that a single defect often renders production unacceptable. Alternatively, the organization can work to a higher standard than customers will accept, so that if a 'defect' fails the organization's criterion, it is still acceptable to customers.

No sampling can ever be completely accurate – and a test might reject good products because the sample has an unexpectedly large number of defects, or it might accept bad products because the sample has an unexpectedly small number of defects. The way to get more accurate samples is to make them bigger – the larger the sample, the more reliable the results. Unfortunately, bigger samples also have higher costs, and a compromise is needed between reliability and cost.

ACCEPTANCE SAMPLING

There are two types of statistical quality control. *Acceptance sampling* tests the quality of a batch of products. It takes a sample of units from the batch at the beginning or end of an operation, and tests to see whether the whole batch should be accepted or rejected.

Process control tests the performance of the process. It takes a sample during the operations to see if the process is working within acceptable limits or if it needs adjusting. (See Figure 33.3.)

Acceptance sampling emphasizes the detection of faults – it investigates whether a batch of products reaches its designed quality. There are two main types of acceptance sampling. With *sampling by variables*, performance is measured by some continuous property, such as the weight, length, strength or power output. Then the performance of this property in the batch is compared with the designed performance. *Sampling by attributes* has some criterion of quality that allows a unit to be described as either 'acceptable' or 'defective'. A light bulb, for example, either works or it does not; a box either contains 1 kg of soap powder or it does not; a piece of furniture made with polished wood may look good to an experienced inspector, or it may not.

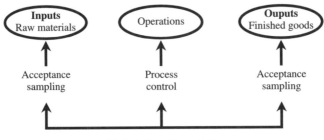

Figure 33.3 *Types of statistical testing*

PROCESS CONTROL

Process control emphasizes the prevention of defects – it investigates whether the process is working as planned. There is always some random variation in a process, and process control makes sure that this variation stays within acceptable limits. It does this by taking samples over time to see if there are any noticeable trends. If there is a clear trend – or poor individual performances – the process needs adjusting.

Patterns can best be seen on a process control chart, which shows the results from samples over time. A p-chart, for example, plots the proportion of defective units in each batch over time. Provided this does not vary too far from a mean value, the process is working normally. If there is a sudden jump in the proportion of defects, however, or a trend away from the mean, the process is out of control and needs adjusting. This can be checked using two limits – an upper control limit and a lower control limit. If the proportion of defects moves outside these limits, the process is out of control (as shown in Figure 33.4).

A common approach to process control adds a second control chart, which measures the range of observations (where the range is the difference between the biggest observation and the smallest).

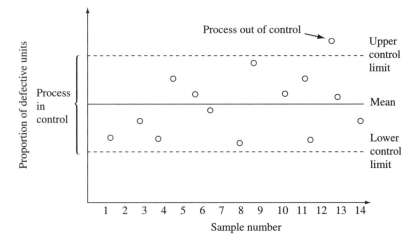

Figure 33.4 *A typical process chart*

FURTHER READING

Banks, J, *Principles of Quality Control*, John Wiley, New York 1989.

Evans, J R and Lindsay, W M, *The Management and Control of Quality* (3rd edition), West Publishing, St Paul, MN 1996.

Montgomery, D, *Introduction to Statistical Quality Control* (3rd edition), John Wiley, New York 1996.

34

Forecasting

DEFINITION

Managers have to plan all their operations some time in advance, and their decisions take effect at some point in the future. These decisions should not be based on current circumstances but on circumstances when the decisions become effective. Nobody knows exactly what will happen in the future, so the best we can do is make forecasts. These forecasts are our best estimates of what is going to happen in the future. This chapter examines forecasting from the operational perspective. Sales forecasting techniques are covered in Chapter 16.

APPROACH TO FORECASTING

All the planning and decisions of managers are based on forecasts of future conditions. Forecasts are used throughout an organization wherever decisions are made and they should be integrated into the decision making. Forecasting is continuous and is never finished. As time moves on, actual circumstances are compared with forecasts, original forecasts are updated, plans are modified, decisions are revised and so on.

Good forecasts should give an accurate view of some feature – typically product demand – in the future. Some of the characteristics of a good forecast are that it is:

- unbiased (does not always underestimate or overestimate demand);
- unaffected by the odd unusual figure;

- in time for its purpose;
- cost effective;
- easy to understand.

Unfortunately, there is no single 'best' method of forecasting, and we have to use different approaches in different circumstances. The choice of methods depends on factors like:

- the time covered by the forecast;
- availability of historical data;
- relevance of historical data to the future;
- type of product, particularly the balance between goods and services;
- variability of demand;
- accuracy needed and cost of errors;
- benefits expected from the forecasts;
- amount of money and time available for the forecast.

DIFFERENT METHODS OF FORECASTING

One classification of forecasting methods considers the time in the future covered by the forecasts. *Long-term forecasts* look ahead several years – the time needed to build a new factory or organize major resources. *Medium-term forecasts* typically look ahead between three months and a year – the time needed to replace an old product by a new one, or organize less demanding resources. *Short-term forecasts* cover the next few weeks – describing the continuing demand for a product, or short-term schedules for resources.

There is a clear link between the time covered by the forecast and the levels of decision. In general, long-term forecasts are used for strategic decisions, medium-term forecasts for tactical decisions, and short-term forecasts for operational decisions.

Another classification of forecasting methods shows the difference between qualitative and quantitative approaches (see Figure 34.1).

If an organization is already making a product, it has records of past demand and knows the factors that affect this. Then it can use a quantitative method for forecasting future demand. There are two ways of doing this: projective methods, which look at the pattern of past demand and extend this into the future, and causal methods, which analyse the effects of outside influences and use these to forecast.

Often organizations do not have the accurate numerical data needed by quantitative forecasts – sometimes these data do not exist and at other times any historical data is irrelevant to the future. Then the only alternative is a qualitative or judgemental forecasting method.

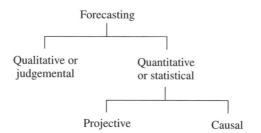

Figure 34.1 *Classification of forecasting methods*

JUDGEMENTAL FORECASTING

Judgemental forecasting uses the opinions of experts in the field. There are five widely used methods.

Personal insight. This has a single person, who is familiar with the situation, using his or her own judgement to forecast. This is fast, cheap and convenient, but it relies entirely on one person's judgement – as well as his or her opinions, prejudices, ignorance and mood. It can give good forecasts, but often gives very bad ones.

Panel consensus or focus group. One person can easily make a mistake, but collecting together a group of people should give a consensus that is more reliable. If there is no secrecy and the group talks freely and openly, a genuine consensus can be found. On the other hand, there may be difficulties in combining the views of different people when a consensus cannot be found; even groups of experts make mistakes; everyone is tempted to agree with the boss; some people do not speak well in groups; 'he who shouts loudest gets his way', and so on. Overall, panel consensus is an improvement on personal insight, but you should be cautious about the results from either method.

Market surveys. Sometimes, even groups of experts do not have enough knowledge to give a reasonable forecast and it is more useful to talk directly to, say, potential customers. Market surveys collect data from a sample of customers, analyse their views and make inferences about the population at large.

Historical analogy. An organization that is introducing a new product may have a similar product that was launched recently, and may assume that demand for the new product will follow the same pattern. A publisher, for example, who is selling a new book could forecast demand for this book from the actual demand for a similar book it published earlier.

Delphi method. A number of experts are contacted by post and each is given a questionnaire to complete. The replies from these questionnaires are analysed and summaries are passed back to the experts. Each reply is anonymous to avoid the influences of factors such as status. The experts are then asked to reconsider their original replies in the light of the summarized replies from others. They may be convinced by the arguments in other replies, and adjust their answers for a second round of opinions. This process of modifying responses in the light of replies made by the rest of the group is repeated several times – usually between three and six. By this time, the range of opinions should be narrow enough to help with decisions.

NOISE IN TIME SERIES

Quantitative forecasts often look at time series, which give a series of observations taken at regular intervals, such as daily cost figures, weekly production, or annual sales. These time series often have an underlying pattern, such as: 1) a *constant series,* where values stay roughly the same over time; 2) *a trend,* which either rises or falls steadily; and 3) a *seasonal series,* which has regular cycles.

If demand followed such simple patterns there would be no problems with forecasting. Unfortunately, there are almost always differences between actual observations and the underlying pattern. These differences form random noise, which is superimposed on the underlying pattern (as shown in Figure 34.2). The noise is a completely random effect that is caused by many factors, such as variations in demand from customers, hours worked by employees, speed of working, weather conditions, rejection rates at inspections, and so on. It is the noise that makes forecasting difficult. If the noise is small, actual demand is close to the underlying pattern and we can make good forecasts; if there is a lot of noise it hides the underlying pattern and forecasting becomes difficult.

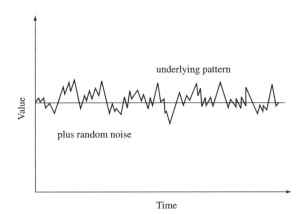

Figure 34.2 *Noise on an underlying stable demand*

CAUSAL FORECASTING

Causal forecasting looks for a cause or relationship that can be used to forecast. The sales of a product, for example, might depend on the price being charged. If we can find the relationship between the price and sales, we can use a proposed price to forecast expected sales.

The most widely used form of causal forecasting is linear regression, which finds the line of best fit relating two variables. Then a typical result is:

$$\text{Forecast sales} = (125 + 12) \times \text{advertising costs}$$

The calculations for this are fairly straightforward, and Figure 34.3 shows a typical spreadsheet of results.

Inspection	Defect	Forecast		Summary output			
0	92	95.9					
1	86	88.0		*Regression Statistics*			
2	81	80.1		Multiple R	0.9938		
3	72	72.2		R Square	0.9877		
4	67	64.3		Adjusted R Square	0.9863		
5	59	56.5		Standard Error	3.0766		
6	53	48.6		Observations	11		
7	43	40.7					
8	32	32.8					
9	24	24.9			*Coefficients*		
10	12	17.0		Intercept	95.8636		
				X Variable 1	−7.8818		
	Coefficient	*Standard Error*	*t Stat*	*P-value*		*Lower 95%*	*Upper 95%*
Intercept	95.864	1.735454	55.23837	1.05068E−12		91.9377642	99.78951
X Variable 1	−7.8818	0.293345	−26.8687	6.63179E−10		−8.5454117	−7.21822

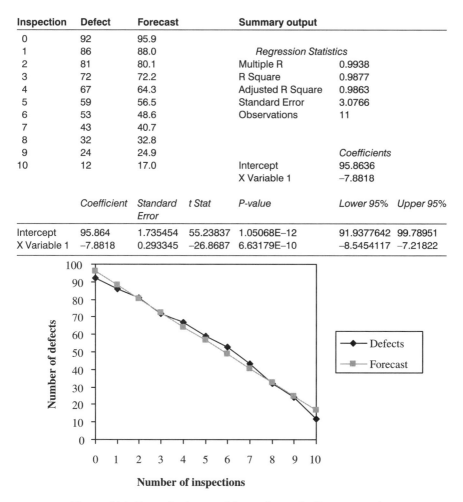

Figure 34.3 *Example of a spreadsheet printout for linear regression*

There are several extensions to simple linear regression, including multiple regression and non-linear regression.

PROJECTIVE FORECASTING

Projective forecasting examines historical values for demand and uses them to forecast the future. Some simple methods include the following:

- *Simple averages.* This simply takes the average of past values as the forecast for the future. The average number of people attending a conference in the past, for example, might give a reasonable figure for next year's attendance.
- *Moving averages.* Usually only a certain amount of historical data is relevant to future forecasts, and all observations older than some specified age can be ignored. A moving average uses this reasoning to take the average demand over the past few periods as a forecast, and ignores any older data.
- *Exponential smoothing.* Exponential smoothing is based on the idea that as data become older they become less relevant and should be given less weight. We can get this declining weight using only the latest demand figure and the previous forecast. To be specific, a new forecast is calculated from:

$$\text{New forecast} = (\alpha \times \text{latest demand}) + [(1 - \alpha) \times \text{last forecast}]$$

where α is a smoothing constant that takes a value of around 0.1.

These three methods can give good results when demand is fairly stable, but they need adjusting for more complicated patterns, such as seasonality or trend. There are several ways of doing this, and the most common:

- separates the overall demand into different components such as underlying demand, trend, seasonality, and cyclical factors;
- forecasts each of these separately;
- recombines the separate results to give the final forecast.

FURTHER READING

Jarrett, J, *Business Forecasting Methods*, Blackwell, Oxford 1991.
Pecar, B, *Business Forecasting for Management*, McGraw-Hill, London 1994.

35

Defining the Process

DEFINITION

The process consists of all the operations used to make a product. It is the set of related activities that combine to give a specific result that customers want. The structure of the process describes the relations between different operations.

IMPORTANCE OF THE PROCESS

The process includes all the operations used to make a specific product. In different circumstances, a process might be centred around:

- *manufacturing* – when changing a product's physical form;
- *chemical processing* – such as processing crude oil into chemicals;
- *information processing* – with clerical or managerial processes;
- *supply* – when changing a product's ownership;
- *transport* – when changing a product's location;
- *warehousing* – storing a product until it is needed;
- *other service* – changing a product's condition in some other way.

There are usually several different ways to make a product – in other words, there is a choice between different types of process. As the design of the process affects costs, quality, productivity, etc, it is important to find the best match between the product and the process used to make it. We can summarize this reasoning by saying:

- the object of all organizations is to make a product that satisfies customer demand;
- the product must, in some way, be better than competitors' products;
- the process consists of all the operations used to make the product;
- the link between the product and the process is so close that sometimes, particularly with services, it is impossible to draw a clear distinction between the two;
- to make better products, an organization needs a better process.

PROCESS-CENTRED ORGANIZATIONS

Some organizations place so much emphasis on the process that they have become process centred. They argue that even the best product currently available will soon be overtaken by improved technology, competitors' designs or changing demands. So they should not concentrate on the short term and current product designs, but on the longer term and the process that can deliver a stream of products for the future.

With a process-centred organization everyone works as a team, with:

- the single purpose of satisfying customer demand;
- concentration on the whole process of delivering products that customers want;
- expansion of traditional jobs, with employees making decisions and dealing with all types of customer issues;
- access to all types of information throughout the organization;
- a matrix or cross-functional management structure.

PROCESS STRUCTURE

The process is often seen as a 'black box' with inputs of materials and outputs of products. Within this black box are all the details designed by process planning. These include:

- the type of operations involved;
- how the operations are organized;
- details of tasks involved in the operations;
- type of equipment and other resources used;
- people working on the process, their skills and jobs;
- material movement through the process.

We can start to add some details to the process by giving it some structure. In its simplest form, a process might consist of a series of operations, separated by stocks of work in progress, as shown in Figure 35.1. If the process is a service, then the customer becomes involved earlier and we have the system structure shown in Figure 35.2.

WORK STATIONS

Operations along the process are divided into a series of stages, each of which uses resources, such as the machines in a production line, to add value to the product. These stages are known by different names, but are commonly called work stations. Each work station might consist of a single machine, but more often has a cluster of equipment and resources that

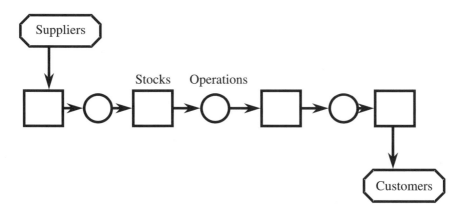

Figure 35.1 *Typical structure of a manufacturing process*

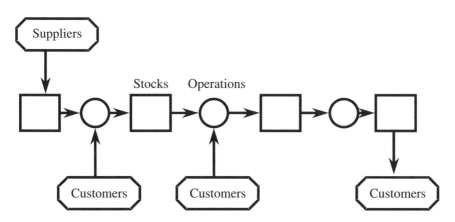

Figure 35.2 *Customers are more involved in service processes*

work together on one aspect of the product. Effectively, each work station is the smallest grouping of resources that can work as an autonomous unit.

The benefits of organizing the process in work stations include:

- it simplifies the organization of operations;
- it allows a smooth, balanced flow of products through a process;
- it reduces stocks of work in progress;
- it reduces handling of parts.

GROUP TECHNOLOGY

Usually each work station concentrates on a particular type of operation, but there is a problem with low-volume production. Organizations prefer to use more specialized equipment, which generally gives higher productivity (as discussed in Chapters 37 and 38), but they cannot justify this with low production levels. One way of getting around this problem is to combine similar jobs into larger batches. These jobs are different, but have some similar feature, which allows them to be combined for a specific work station. To take a simple example, a range of different products may each need a 5 cm hole drilled in a plate. Although these are different products, they can be combined into a single batch for drilling the hole. This is the basis of group technology, which has the advantages of:

- larger batches and reduced set-up times;
- higher utilization of equipment;
- less duplication of effort;
- drawing attention to the similarities of products and common operations;
- encouraging standardized design features;
- improving quality because the variety of products is reduced.

FURTHER READING

Ramaswamy, R, *Design and Management of Service Processes*, Addison Wesley Longman, Harlow 1996.

Wu, B, *Manufacturing Systems Design and Analysis* (2nd edition), Chapman & Hall, New York 1994.

36

Process Planning

DEFINITIONS

The process consists of all the operations needed to make a specific product. Process planning ensures that the best process is used, and that it is organized as effectively and efficiently as possible.

TYPES OF PROCESS

Two key factors for the choice of process are the total number of units made and the amount of variation in the final product. In general, higher volumes mean that there is less room for variation in the product.

There are five basic types of process that are suited to different combinations of volume and variety. At one extreme are continuous flows like an oil refinery that continually makes large volumes of the same product without any changes or interruptions. At the other extreme are projects like those of satellite manufacturers, who rarely make the same product twice. In between these extremes are jobbing, batch and mass processes. Although some of these terms seem to refer to manufacturing, they can be used equally well for services.

A *project* makes a single unit, usually tailored to customer specifications, such as building a Formula 1 racing car or writing a management consultant's report. The product from each project is essentially unique, so there is a lot of variety with little standardization.

Jobbing makes small numbers of a wide variety of products. Organizations usually tender for work, so that details of future work are uncertain and there can be variability in overall demand. Each product uses a different mix of resources, so there are short-term mismatches between capacity and workload, with time lost as equipment is set up between products. As a result, jobbing processes have relatively low capital costs, but high unit costs. The mix of different products makes scheduling and keeping track of work difficult.

Batch processes make larger batches of similar products on the same equipment. This reduces the time spent setting up equipment between different products, and any units not used to meet current orders are put into a stock of finished goods. This type of process is used for medium volumes of products, where there is less product variety and customizing.

Mass process is typical of an assembly or production line that makes large numbers of a single product. There is very little variety in the product, except small changes to the basic model introduced in the finishing. Specialized equipment can be used, with no disruptions to the process and few problems with control. There is, for example, no need to schedule individual pieces of equipment, or check the progress of individual units through the process. Once the process is set up it needs a small workforce to keep it functioning and in extreme cases may be completely automated. Although capital costs for specialized equipment can be high, mass processes give low unit costs.

Continuous process is used for very high volumes of a single product or small group of related products, such as bulk chemicals, oil and paper. The process is different from assembly lines as the product effectively emerges as a continuous flow rather than discrete units. Such processes use highly specialized equipment that can work for 24 hours a day with virtually no changes or interruptions.

Figure 36.1 shows the type of process that is best suited to different combinations of volume and product variety. There is a diagonal across the table, and any process not on this diagonal has problems. If a process works in area A, making high volumes of a highly variable product, it would be better to move towards the diagonal and reduce the variability of the product or reduce the volume made. If a process works in area B, making small numbers of the same product, it would be better to increase the volume of a standard product, or allow more customization.

FACTORS IN CHOOSING A PROCESS

So far, we have emphasized two important factors in the choice of process – volume and variability. Some other considerations include the following:

- overall demand;
- point in the product life cycle;
- variability in product range;

		Very low	Low	Medium	Very high	Continuous
				Volume		
	None	None – unit costs are too high	B			**Continuous**
	Little				**Mass**	
Product variation	Medium			**Batch**		
	High		**Jobbing**		A	
	Very high	**Project**				None – capital costs are too high

Figure 36.1 *Types of process and their product variation and quantities*

- product design;
- changes in demand;
- product flexibility;
- human resources;
- automation;
- customer involvement;
- product quality;
- finances;
- amount of vertical integration.

LEVELS OF TECHNOLOGY

One obvious feature of a process is the level of technology that it uses, which can be described as manual, mechanized or automated.

- *Manual process.* People have full control over operations that need their constant attention. Manual systems have the benefits of flexibility, low capital costs and low risk. Their disadvantages are high unit cost, need for a skilled workforce, variable quality and low output.
- *Mechanized process.* A typical mechanized process has an operator loading a piece of equipment, which can work without further intervention until the task is finished, when the operator unloads it. Mechanized processes have the advantages of producing high volumes of uniform products at low unit cost, but the disadvantages of high capital cost and inflexibility.
- *Automated process.* This is a broad category, in which equipment performs a series of operations without any operator involvement.

The level of automation is clearly linked to the type of process, with higher volumes of output using higher levels of automation. In general projects and jobs shops use manual processes, batches are made with mechanized processes, and mass and continuous processes use automation.

Higher levels of automation reduce the flexibility and variability in a process. They also create barriers between customers and the final product, which is why people walk around information machines in tourist offices to talk to someone behind the counter. Perhaps the major criticism of automated processes, however, is that they ignore the skills that people can bring, including:

■ giving a personal service;
■ drawing upon varied experiences;
■ intelligent use of all available information;
■ use of subjectivity and judgement;
■ ability to adapt to new and unusual circumstances;
■ generating entirely new solutions;
■ recognizing patterns;
■ using creativity;
■ flexibility.

On the other hand, automation has the advantages of:

■ working continuously without tiring;
■ giving consistent precision and products;
■ giving higher quality;
■ being very fast and powerful;
■ doing many jobs at the same time;
■ storing large amounts of information;
■ analysing data very quickly;
■ doing boring and dangerous jobs;
■ allowing tighter control with short lead times and lower stocks;
■ being good at monitoring and reacting to signals;
■ reducing labour costs.

People and machines are better at different jobs and because automation is better in some circumstances you should not assume that it is better for everything. We will expand this discussion of technology in the next two chapters.

FURTHER READING

Armistead, C and Roland, P, *Managing Business Processes: BPR and beyond*, John Wiley, Chichester 1996.
Ould, M A, *Business Processes*, John Wiley, Chichester 1995.

37

Automation in Manufacturing

DEFINITION

Organizations can often improve their performance by using a more automated process. Some types of automation, such as industrial robots, are clearly more common in manufacturing than services. This chapter describes some types of automation for manufacturing, and the next chapter looks at the automation of services.

COMPUTER-AIDED MANUFACTURING

Many people think of automation in terms of assembly lines making cars. These are examples of fixed or hard automation, where specialized equipment is dedicated to making a single product. The process typically has a conveyor moving units along a fixed path between single-purpose, highly specialized machines. The result is an efficient process with little flexibility, of the type that is suited to high-volume production.

A lot of work has been done trying to make high-technology processes more flexible, so that they can be used for lower volumes. The aim is to combine versatility with efficiency to give flexible or programmable automation.

NUMERICALLY CONTROLLED MACHINES

Flexible automation for intermittent processes became possible in the 1950s with numerically controlled (NC) machines. These were originally general-purpose machines that could do a series of tasks without any intervention by an operator. Paper tapes or cards controlled the machines and they could be reprogrammed quickly by simply replacing the tape.

Magnetic tapes replaced paper tapes for the control of NC machines, and these, in turn, were replaced by microprocessors. Each of these computerized numerically controlled (CNC) machines is controlled by a dedicated computer, and can do a long series of operations without interruption. These standard machine tools are the most widely used form of automation in manufacturing. They have the advantages of being fast, flexible, giving consistent quality, low unit costs, and being able to do a variety of complicated work. Operators do not do any of the actual work, but they still have to load and unload the machine, check units, make adjustments, change the programme, and so on.

COMPUTER-AIDED MANUFACTURING

Systems where computers assist in the actual manufacturing are called computer-aided manufacturing (CAM). Computerized numerically controlled machines were the first step in this direction, and the next step came in the 1960s with industrial robots. These are usually stationary machines that have programmable arms (or manipulators) with a hand (or effector) at the end. They were first used for welding and paint spraying in car assembly lines, but their costs fell and they have become common for a variety of simple jobs. They are particularly useful for reaching places that are difficult for humans to get at, and for handling dangerous substances, such as explosives, poisons, hot metal ingots or radioactive materials.

FLEXIBLE MANUFACTURING SYSTEMS

The next type of automated production is flexible manufacturing systems (FMS). These combine the computers that control each piece of equipment (CNC machine or robot) so that a number of separate machines are under the control of a central computer. This computer finds the best production schedule, and coordinates operations to achieve this. It also controls the flow of materials, typically using wire-guided vehicles to move products, components, materials and tools between machines. Automatic loading and unloading stations transfer the materials between the transport system and manufacturing equipment. The essential parts of FMS are:

- a central computer to schedule, route, load and control operations;
- a number of machines working under the control of the central computer;
- a computer-controlled transport system for moving materials between the machines;
- computer-controlled loading and unloading equipment.

Once an FMS is programmed, the system can work with very little human intervention, and has the following advantages:

- it allows fast, easy changes between different products;
- low operating costs;
- the computer takes over the difficult jobs of scheduling and routing;
- utilization of equipment can be very high;
- the computer can control inventories, reducing stocks of raw materials and work in progress;
- the output has consistently high quality, without the variation found in less automated processes.

On the other hand, there are some disadvantages of FMS:

- the equipment is expensive to buy and set up;
- although the systems can be programmed to make many different products, there are limitations and they lack the flexibility of some other processes;
- FMS is designed for current production, so there may be problems with major changes to products in the future;
- the technology is still being developed and there are often teething troubles;
- FMS works best with families of similar products that need small changes, rather than radically different products;
- the machines still have fixed capacities, tolerances and so forth, so they cannot deal with unusual products.

COMPUTER-AIDED DESIGN

As well as its direct use in production, automation can also be used in associated functions, such as product design. With computer-assisted design (CAD), designers use computers to build up designs, check for obvious faults, do related calculations, generate bills of materials, transmit designs to distant sites, and so on. Design time is cut by having computer libraries of designs rather than designing from scratch; similar designs are recovered and modified as necessary. The benefits of CAD are that it:

- reduces the time needed to produce designs;
- allows quick changes to existing designs;
- enhances basic drawings, showing how the actual product will look, rotating it, showing different perspectives, changing scales, and so on;
- does calculations about stresses, strengths and any other engineering factors;
- produces all necessary drawings and blueprints from the master set;
- stores a library of designs;
- estimates costs for products as they are being designed;
- generates bills of material (the list of parts needed to make a product);
- communicates with other computer systems.

Organizations found that they were using computers to design products (with CAD) and to control production (with CAM), so it made sense to join these two parts into a single CAD/CAM system. The designs are prepared using the CAD part, and these are automatically transferred to the CAM part, which controls the machines and actually makes the products. This lays the foundations for computer-integrated manufacturing.

COMPUTER-INTEGRATED MANUFACTURING

Flexible manufacturing systems combine the systems actually involved in manufacturing, but computer-integrated manufacturing (CIM) goes a step further and combines the systems that support these operations. Many separate systems support production, including product design, engineering, production planning, production control, materials handling, inventory control, procurement, maintenance, logistics, accounting and all the related management systems. Computer-integrated manufacturing aims to combine these separate systems into a single integrated unit.

Ultimately, a CIM could integrate all the systems of a factory and work with virtually no human intervention. At this point there seems little to stop the next step towards an automated factory. This would generate the design for a product and have a completely automated process for making and delivering it.

FURTHER READING

Cohen, M A and Apte, U M, *Manufacturing Automation*, Irwin, Chicago 1997.

Harrison, M, *Advanced Manufacturing Technology Management*, Pitman, London 1990.

38

Automation in Services

DEFINITION

Services provide the intangible parts of products – the parts that are not goods, but that still give benefit to customers. In recent years many services – particularly communications and information processing – have undergone a major transformation as they moved from manual to automated processes.

BACKGROUND

Improvements in electronic communications and information processing have allowed many services to move from manual processes to automated ones. Banking, for example, has become more efficient and cheaper as its automated systems evolved. Unfortunately, many services – like those given by dentists, lawyers, accountants, hairdressers and taxis – are highly customized and are made either singly or in very small batches. These inevitably have high costs. Organizations have tried many ways of reducing these costs by standardizing products and introducing mass processes. The result is that people receive services that are less personal but are a lot cheaper. Once the mass processes are in place, they can introduce automation to work on:

- customers themselves;
- customers' goods;
- information;
- some other aspect of the service.

Unfortunately, services are so varied that it is difficult to describe automation in the same general terms we used in the last chapter for manufacturing. Perhaps we can best illustrate the principles by some specific examples:

- *Offices.* Clerical jobs in offices prepare, store, analyse, copy and distribute documents and information. Most of these are now computerized as we move relentlessly towards paperless offices.
- *Debit cards.* Debit cards transfer money directly from a customer's bank to a supplier's. Technology has opened many new ways of paying bills, including Switch cards, telephone banking, electronic fund transfer, internet services and so on. At some point in the future, presumably all coins and notes will be replaced by machine-readable cards.
- *Supermarkets.* Supermarkets are reducing their operating costs in many ways, including self-scanning by customers, computer-readable shopping lists, automatic materials handling equipment to fetch and deliver goods, virtual shopping via the internet, telephone shopping and sensors that automatically transmit an order when something is used from the pantry.
- *Post Office.* Post codes and high-speed scanners allow automated sorting of mail. The need to send letters is declining with expanding computer networks and various types of electronic mail.
- *Warehousing.* Automated warehouses have computers recording stock movements, allocating locations and controlling all the physical handling of goods.
- *Reservation systems.* Airlines started using online reservation systems in the 1960s. They are now essential, and similar systems are used by buses and trains, theatres, sporting events, taxis and so on.

There are, of course, many other examples of services becoming more automated. As with manufacturing, the aim is to bring the efficiency of mass production processes to smaller batches. As the average productivity of service industries is relatively low, this is an area with considerable potential.

INFORMATION TECHNOLOGY

Information technology has obviously had a dramatic effect on operations. Sometimes it can improve the performance of operations and at other times it can allow new operations that were previously impossible. The following list gives some of the developments in information technology that have had direct consequences for operations. The first of these are concerned with the way that information is moved around an organization:

- *Distributed processing.* Distributed processing has information stored in machines near to its source and use. This has benefits over centralized data as it is maintained by those most closely involved, and can be accessed quickly. But there may be problems with creating distinct sets of data that cannot be accessed by remote users. This problem may be overcome by communications that allow physically separate computers to share data.
- *Local area networks.* A local area network (LAN) is a communications system that connects a series of computers in a physical area – typically within a building, site or organization. All computers connected to a LAN can share common databases, peripherals and other facilities. The direct links between different parts of an organization allow, for example, an inventory system to be linked to a procurement system, so that removing an item from stores triggers a message to buy a replacement.
- *Electronic data interchange.* The benefits of LANs are so obvious that organizations moved to the next stage and linked their computers to systems in other organizations. Instead of linking the inventory system to a purchasing system, they could link directly to the supplier. Then removing an item from stores sends a message to the supplier who automatically delivers a replacement. This is the basis of electronic data interchange (EDI), which allows documents and information to move directly between organizations.
- *The Internet.* There are obvious benefits of moving information between, say, customers and suppliers, but it may also be useful to move information between organizations that are not so closely connected. Research departments in universities, for example, do not necessarily have close links, but it is useful to see what problems each is working on and to share results. This became possible with the internet, which gave a standard format for communicating between LANs.
- *World wide web (WWW).* The WWW gives a standard way of organizing data for the internet. A hypertext markup language (HTML) allows any organization to create pages on its website that can be read by any other user. This allowed a variety of new services, such as virtual shopping, home banking and virtual organizations.

These developments have allowed information to flow more easily through a process. The next type of development shows how this information is used by operations managers:

- *Management information system (MIS).* Improved communications mean that managers can access virtually limitless amounts of information from anywhere in the world. In practice, they rely far more on information that comes from within the organization itself. A management information system ensures a smooth flow of data into and within the organization. It collects, analyses, distributes and presents data to managers so that they can make informed decisions.

■ *Decision support system (DSS)*. A decision support system goes one step further than a management information system. Rather than just presenting information, a DSS gives more positive assistance in a decision. It can analyse the consequences of various decisions, do a series of 'what-if' calculations, suggest new alternatives, recommend the best options, and so on.

■ *Expert systems*. These go one step further than DSS and take a more active role in the actual decision. An expert system records the skills of experts in a knowledge base, and when faced with a decision it uses an 'inference engine' to select and use these rules to duplicate the decision-making process of a human expert.

■ *Artificial intelligence (AI)*. This attempts to give computers the ability to understand language, reason, make assumptions, learn and solve problems. It tries to create computers that can make reasoned decisions in the same way as humans.

Information technology is changing many aspects of operations. Unfortunately, there has been so much overselling of the benefits that the reality often does not live up to expectations. Introducing new IT does not automatically improve an organization's performance or give it a sustained competitive advantage; it does not necessarily give better products or even a better process. This leads to the 'IT productivity paradox', which describes how organizations can spend money to improve information technology, but not achieve any apparent increase in performance.

FURTHER READING

Gunton, T, *Inside Information Technology: A practical guide to management issues*, Prentice-Hall, Englewood Cliffs, NJ 1990.

Ramaswamy, R, *Design and Management of Service Processes*, Addison Wesley Longman, Harlow 1996.

39

Facility Layout

DEFINITION

Facility layout is the physical arrangement of equipment, offices, rooms and other resources within an organization. It describes the location of resources and their relationship to each other. Layout planning aims to organize the physical arrangement of facilities so that operations run as efficiently as possible.

TYPES OF LAYOUT

Every organization has to consider the layout of its operations, whether it is a shop, manufacturer, warehouse, office or government debating chamber. Well-laid-out facilities are efficient and allow products to flow easily and smoothly through the process: poorly laid-out facilities disrupt operations and reduce efficiency. The purpose of layout planning is to arrange the facilities so that the process can run as smoothly as possible.

There are five general types of layout:

- *process layout* – which puts similar resources together;
- *product layout* – which puts resources for a particular product together;
- *hybrid layout* – which is some mixture of these two;
- *fixed-position layout* – where everything is done in the same place;
- a series of *specialized layouts*, such as retail shops, offices and warehouses.

The choice of layout depends on the objectives and constraints on the process. Typical objectives are to use a minimum amount of resources, or to achieve the maximum possible output. Other objectives minimize the cost of movement, minimize the amount of handling, minimize the area used, maximize visibility, give secure operations, give attractive appearance, increase customer access, and so on.

There can be many types of constraint on the layout, including the planned capacity, total space available, building used, material handling equipment, capital available, need for service areas, safety needs, and so on. The best type of layout is clearly related to the type of process, and Table 39.1 gives some guidelines about this.

PROCESS LAYOUTS

In a process layout all similar equipment and other facilities are grouped together. Offices use a process layout when they put all accountants in one area, all purchasing people in another, all reference books in another, and so on. This layout works best when different products use the same resources, and every product follows a different route through them. Each product uses the facilities in a different sequence, as shown in Figure 39.1.

Advantages of process layouts include:

- A variety of products can be made on the same facilities.
- Operations continue if some equipment cannot be used because of breakdown or planned maintenance.
- It is suitable for low volumes and variable demand.
- People work in cohesive groups and generally enjoy the environment.

Disadvantages of process layouts include:

- Small batches give lower utilization of equipment and unit costs can be high.
- Movement of jobs between operations is complicated, with larger stocks of work in progress.

Table 39.1 *Relating the layout to the process*

Type of process	Usual type of layout	Example
project	fixed position	road resurfacing
jobbing	process	hospital kitchens
batch	hybrid	airport terminals
mass	product	assembly line
continuous	product	oil refinery

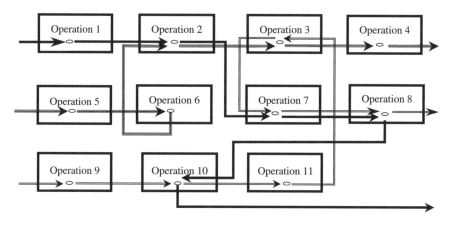

Figure 39.1 *Process layout with similar operations grouped together and products following different paths*

- Scheduling work on equipment is complicated and must be done continuously.
- Controlling the work is difficult.
- There is a lot of handling of products and materials.

Movements between operations

Process layouts often involve a lot of movement between operations, and a common objective is to minimize the total distance travelled. There is a lot of standard software for this and many specialists who can offer advice.

Often it is not only the amount of movement that is important, but also the relationships between areas. Systematic layout planning allows subjective views of how close areas should be to each other. In a warehouse, for example, it may be best to have the security group near the main gate. Systematic layout planning describes such relationships in six ways:

A – Absolutely essential that areas are close to each other.
E – Especially important that they are close.
I – Important.
O – Ordinary importance.
U – Unimportant.
X – Undesirable and areas should be separated.

PRODUCT LAYOUTS

A product layout groups together all the facilities and equipment used to make a particular product. A common form of product layout is a production line in manufacturing (as shown in Figure 39.2).

This layout is obviously related to mass processes, so it works best with stable, high demand for a standard product, with established supplies of raw materials, and so on.

Advantages of product layouts include:

■ they can achieve a high rate of output;
■ high equipment use gives low unit costs;
■ materials handling is easy with low stocks of work in progress;
■ scheduling and controlling operations is easy.

Disadvantages of product layouts include:

■ operations are inflexible and it is difficult to change the output rate, product or process;
■ equipment failure and routine maintenance can disrupt the whole process;
■ equipment may be specialized and expensive, needing a high initial investment;
■ people often do not like working in process layouts as the repetitive work can be boring.

Line balancing

Product layouts essentially consist of a series of facilities through which units of the product move. In principle, they should be easy to design, but getting a smooth flow through the process can be difficult. As we saw in Chapter 35, the process is usually divided into a number of distinct work stations, so the time spent in each must be about the same. The line is then balanced. With an unbalanced line, some work stations finish products

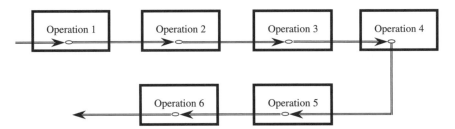

Figure 39.2 *Product layout with all operations taken in order*

quickly and build up stocks of work in progress in front of the next work station, which is working more slowly.

There is a straightforward procedure balancing product layouts, which has three steps:

■ Step 1. Find the cycle time, which is the maximum time any workstation can work on a unit. This is found by dividing the planned output by the time available. If the operations at any stage take longer than this, there is a bottleneck and the planned output cannot be achieved.
■ Step 2. Calculate the theoretical minimum number of workstations needed for the entire process. This is found by dividing the total time needed to make a unit by the cycle time. Usually fractional values and scheduling constraints mean that a process needs more than this minimum number of stations.
■ Step 3. Do the actual line balancing, which allocates operations to each station, so that the total time taken for operations in each station is as close as possible to the cycle time.

HYBRID LAYOUTS

Often the best layout for a process is a combination of product and process layouts. Most of an airport terminal, for example, has a process layout with different areas for checking in, eating, shopping, arrivals and so forth, but some parts have a product layout, such as passport control and customs clearance. Arrangements of this kind are called hybrid layouts.

One common hybrid arrangement is a work cell. This is an arrangement with a dominant process layout, but with some operations set aside in a product layout. A factory, for example, might have most machines laid out in a process layout, but a certain sequence of operations is repeated so often that a special area, or work cell, is set aside to deal with them on an assembly line. These work cells form islands of product layout in a sea of process layout.

Some people suggest that there is an important difference between a work cell, which is a temporary arrangement, and a focused work centre, which is a permanent arrangement. The idea of a permanent focused work centre can be extended to focused factories, where the process is moved to another building, which concentrates on developing a very efficient process for making a single component.

FIXED-POSITION LAYOUTS

In fixed-position layouts the product stays still and operations are all done on the same site. This usually happens when a product is too big or heavy to move around, like ships or construction sites. Fixed layouts might also be useful when special environments, such as dust-free rooms, are needed.

Fixed layouts have several disadvantages, including:

- all people, materials and components have to move to the site;
- there is often limited space at the site;
- there must be a reliable schedule of activities;
- disruptions to this schedule might cause delays in completion;
- external factors, such as weather conditions, may affect operations.

Because of these disadvantages, fixed-position layouts are only used when it is impossible or very difficult to move the product. One way of partially avoiding these disadvantages is to do as much of the work as possible off site. A road bridge, for example, may be prefabricated off site and moved to the site for erection.

SPECIALIZED LAYOUT

Many operations need specialized layouts, with typical examples including:

- warehouses – which store goods on their journey between suppliers and customers;
- offices – which are organized around a flow of information;
- retail shops – which try to encourage customers to buy goods;
- schools – which have to consider the movement of large numbers of pupils;
- shopping centres – which find the best arrangements for different kinds of shops.

FURTHER READING

Francis, R L, McGinnis, L F and White, J A, *Facility Layout and Location: An analytical approach* (2nd edition), Prentice-Hall, Englewood Cliffs, NJ 1992.

Luggen, W, *Flexible Manufacturing Cells and Systems*, Prentice-Hall, Englewood Cliffs, NJ 1991.

40

Measuring Performance

DEFINITION

Measures of performance show how well the operations in an organization are working. They show whether the organization is achieving its aims, or whether performance needs to be improved.

DIFFERENT MEASURES

Every organization measures its performance. There are many possible measures of performance, including:

- flexibility;
- quality;
- profitability;
- return on investment;
- gross profit;
- stock turnover;
- conformance to standards;
- number of customer complaints;
- innovation;
- sales per square metre;
- throughput time;
- amount of scrap;
- percentage of lost orders;
- lead time;

- return on value added;
- number of customers;
- ratio of sales to stock;
- use of equipment;
- number of returns;
- staff morale;
- absenteeism;
- machine breakdowns;
- production rate;
- and a whole host of others.

Many of these measures look at the finances, largely because an organization is judged on its financial performance but also because they are fairly easy to calculate. Unfortunately, the financial measures tend to emphasize what has happened in the past, are slow to respond to changes, and often do not record important aspects of operations. Financial measures give a surrogate view of operations, but there are several more direct measures.

MEASURING THE OPERATIONS

From an operations point of view, a basic measure of performance is capacity. This sets the maximum amount of a product that can be made in a specified time. There is a difference between: *designed capacity*, which is a largely theoretical value that gives the maximum output in ideal circumstances, and *effective capacity*, which shows the output that can actually be achieved over the long term, in normal circumstances.

Actual production is generally less than the effective capacity and it varies quite widely depending on how hard people are working, the number of disruptions, the quality being made, how efficiently equipment is working, and a wide range of other factors. This leads to the related measure of *utilization*, which shows the proportion of designed capacity that is actually used.

$$\text{Utilization} = \frac{\text{amount of capacity used}}{\text{designed capacity}}$$

There are many other measures for the performance of operations, but perhaps the most widely used is *productivity*. This measures the amount of output that is achieved for each unit of resource used. This is so important that many organizations have a strategic goal of improving productivity.

Unfortunately, people often use these terms rather loosely and mistake production (which is the total output from a process) with the productivity (which is the output achieved for each unit of a resource). Many people assume that productivity is the number of units made by each person working on the process, but this is only one aspect of productivity.

Another term that causes confusion is *efficiency*. Efficiency describes the percentage of possible output that is actually achieved. This is often confused with effectiveness, which measures how well an organization sets and achieves its goals.

To summarize these measures:

- Designed capacity is the maximum amount of a product that can be made in a given time, under ideal conditions.
- Effective capacity is the maximum amount that can realistically be made in a given time, under normal conditions.
- Utilization measures the proportion of designed capacity that is actually used.
- Production is the total amount of a product that is made.
- Productivity is the amount produced in relation to one or more of the resources used.
- Efficiency is the ratio of actual output to possible output.
- Effectiveness shows how well an organization sets and achieves its goals.

Example

A machine is designed to produce 100 units in a 10-hour shift. During one shift, the machine actually worked for eight hours and produced 70 units.

- *Designed capacity* is the maximum amount that can be produced in a given time, which is 100 units a shift, or 10 units an hour.
- *Effective capacity* depends on details of operations, but is less than the designed capacity.
- *Utilization* is the proportion of designed capacity actually used, which is 70/100 or 70 per cent.
- *Production* is the amount actually made, which is 70 units.
- *Productivity* is the amount produced in relation to resources used, so a reasonable measure is 70/8 = 8.75 units a machine hour.
- *Efficiency* is the ratio of actual output to possible output, which is 70/(8/10) or 87.5 per cent.

PRODUCTIVITY

Productivity is the most widely used measure of operations, and most managers assume that increasing productivity is always beneficial. The main incentive to increase productivity is competition. Competitors are always trying to gain an advantage by increasing their own productivity, so an organization must match this improvement simply to stay in business. The benefits of higher productivity include:

- long-term survival;
- lower costs;
- less waste of resources;
- increased profits, wages, real income, and so forth;
- giving realistic targets for improving operations;
- allowing realistic comparisons between operations;
- measuring management competence.

There are really only four ways of improving productivity:

- improve effectiveness with better decisions;
- improve efficiency so that the existing resources are used better, giving more outputs with the same inputs;
- improve the process in some other way – designing changes to the process, perhaps increasing automation or putting more emphasis on quality;
- improve morale – to give more cooperation and incentives.

The old-fashioned idea of 'getting people to work harder' has very little to do with productivity. A hard-working person with a spade is far less productive than a lazy person with a bulldozer. In general, 85 per cent of productivity is set by the system that is designed by management, and only 15 per cent is under the control of the individual worker. More importantly, productivity does not necessarily measure the production per person.

Different types of productivity

Total productivity is defined as:

$$\text{Total productivity} = \frac{\text{total output}}{\text{total input}}$$

Unfortunately, this definition has a number of drawbacks that limit its use. The input and output must be in consistent units and this normally means that they are translated into units of currency. Then the amounts depend on the accounting conventions used and they no longer give an objective measure. Another problem is finding and evaluating all the inputs and outputs – including natural resources, waste, pollution and so on.

A more widely used measure is partial productivity, which is defined as:

$$\text{Partial productivity} = \frac{\text{total output}}{\text{single output}}$$

In practice, organizations are only concerned with primary outputs, so the 'total output' is taken as the production and does not include secondary outputs, like waste and scrap. Then typical measures of partial productivity are the amount produced per machine-hour, or the amount produced per kilowatt-hour of electricity. In practice, partial productivity is related to four types of resource:

■ *equipment productivity*, such as units made per machine hour;
■ *labour productivity*, such as units made per person;
■ *capital productivity*, such as units made for each pound of investment;
■ *energy productivity*, such as units of output per kilowatt-hour of electricity.

Whichever measure of productivity is used, it should give a reliable view of the performance of the organization. It would, for example, make little sense to measure the productivity of automatic telephone exchanges by measuring the number of calls per employee, or the productivity of a bank by measuring the number of transactions per kilowatt-hour of electricity used. This seems obvious, but you can find many examples of organizations that ignore this simple advice.

CHOOSING THE MEASURE

The measures used by managers must relate to the operations and aims of the organization. It would, for example, make no sense to aim for high productivity if the quality of products becomes too low, or if the finished products then sit in a warehouse because there is no demand for them. The measures must give information that shows how well the organization is doing its operations and achieving its goals. Then a reasonable measure must:

■ relate to the organization's objectives;
■ focus on significant factors;
■ be measurable;
■ be reasonably objective;
■ be understood by people working on the operations;
■ be agreed by everyone concerned;
■ be linked to the reward and recognition system of employees;
■ use consistent units;
■ be difficult to manipulate.

One warning is that a measure should not be used simply because it is easy to find, or because it shows the organization in a good light. On the other hand, an organization should not ignore important aspects of performance such as staff morale because they are difficult to measure.

FURTHER READING

Belcher, J G, *Productivity Plus*, Gulf Publishing, Houston 1988.
Kaplan, R S, *Measures for Performance Excellence*, Harvard Business School Press, Boston, MA 1990.

41

Comparing Performance

DEFINITION

Absolute measures of performance give little useful information. It is usually much better to use the measures in some form of comparison. There are several standard methods of comparison, of which the most popular is benchmarking.

COMPARING PERFORMANCE

The last chapter showed how measures of performance should give a reasonable view of an organization's operations. These measures can be used to:

- see how well objectives are being achieved;
- compare the current performance of the organization with its performance in the past;
- make comparisons with other organizations that have similar operations;
- compare the performance of different parts of the organization;
- help with decisions about investments and proposed changes to the process;
- measure the effects of changes to operations;
- help with other internal functions, such as wage negotiations;
- highlight areas whose performance should be improved.

It is clear from this list that measures of performance are normally used for some kind of comparison. Absolute measures often have little real meaning – you may be interested to hear that a shop has annual sales of $1,700 per square metre, but you cannot say how well it is doing until you compare this with figures from other shops.

Most measures are used to compare the organization's actual performance with some agreed standard measures. There are four sources for these standards:

■ *Absolute standards* – which give the best performance that could ever be achieved. This is a target performance for which an organization would ideally aim, such as zero defects.
■ *Target performance* – which is a more realistic target that is agreed by managers, who want to set a tough but attainable level of performance.
■ *Historical standards* – which look at performance that has actually been achieved in the past. Historical standards show the performance that is achieved if there is no improvement; as organizations are always looking for improvements this is the lowest level of performance that can be accepted.
■ *Competitors' standards* – which show the performance actually being achieved by competitors. This is the lowest level of performance that an organization must achieve to remain competitive.

These comparisons can be done in many ways. Some of these are very informal, such as pub managers visiting other pubs to get ideas for improving their own operations, or football managers watching other teams play. Usually it is better to have a more formal procedure for comparing performance, and the most popular method is benchmarking.

BENCHMARKING

Benchmarking compares an organization's performance with the best operations in the industry. There are several steps in benchmarking, which are shown in Figure 41.1. These start when an organization recognizes the need to improve a process. Then it has to define the most appropriate measures of performance for the process, find the competitor that achieves the best performance, examine the competitor's operations to see how it achieves this performance, and look for ideas that it can adopt.

To be blunt, organizations use benchmarking to find ideas and ways of doing operations that they can copy or adapt. Benchmarking allows an organization to set realistic performance targets, and it shows how these targets can be met.

Sometimes it is difficult to find a direct competitor that can be used for benchmarking, or to collect enough information about its operations.

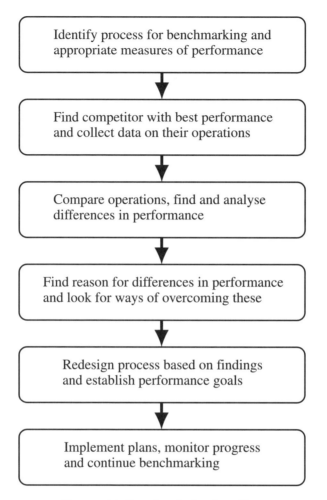

Figure 41.1 *Procedure for benchmarking*

Then organizations can use several variations on the basic theme. They can, for example, use an organization that is not a direct competitor. British Petroleum is not a direct competitor of Tate & Lyle, but they both run fleets of tankers and might learn from each other's transport operations. Sometimes it is possible to learn from completely different types of organization. So a train operator might look at the operations of an airline, or other companies that give high customer service, like supermarkets. Perhaps the easiest benchmarking to organize is internal, so that one division of an organization compares its operations with another division.

ANALYSING A PROCESS

Wherever an organization looks for its comparisons, it needs some way of analysing a process – in other words, it needs a clear description of the operations and the relationships between them. The best way of describing these often uses a simple diagram.

Process charts

There are several types of process chart but they all start by breaking down the process into separate operations. Suppose, for example, you want to describe the process that a patient goes through when visiting a doctor's surgery. A simple chart of this is given in Figure 41.2.

This informal chart gives a general view of the process but it does not give many details. A more useful approach describes each operation as:

- *operation* – where something is actually done;
- *movement* – where products are moved;

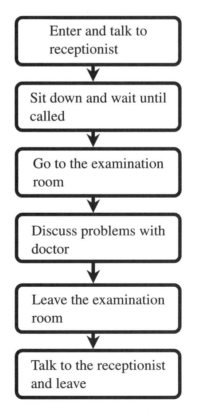

Figure 41.2 *Informal process chart for visit to doctor*

- *storage* – where products are put away until they are needed;
- *delay* – where products are held up;
- *inspection* – which tests the quality of the product.

Then a standard analysis of the process involves six steps. The first three of these describe the current process, while the last three look for improvements:

1. Look at the process and list all the operations in their proper sequence.
2. Classify each step according to operation, movement, storage, delay and inspection. Find the time taken and distance moved in each step.
3. Summarize the process by adding the number of each type of operation, the total time for the process, the rate at which each operation is carried out, and any other relevant information.

These three steps give a detailed description of a process, and an example of the resulting chart is shown in Figure 41.3. The next part of the analysis looks for improvements to the process.

Process chart	- Part 421/302								
Step number	Description	Operation	Movement	Inspection	Delay	Storage	Time (mins)	Distance (metres)	Comments
1	Fetch component		X				2.5	50	
2	Put components on machine	X					2		
3	Start machine	X					1.2		
4	Fetch sub-assembly		X				3	40	
5	Wait for machine to stop				X		5.2		
6	Unload machine	X					2		
7	Inspect result			X			1.5		
8	Join sub-assembly	X					5		
9	Move unit to machine		X				2.5	25	
10	Load machine to start	X					2		
11	Wait for machine to stop				X		5		
12	Unload machine	X					1.4		
13	Carry unit to inspection area		X				2	25	
14	Inspect and test			X			5.2		
15	Carry unit to finish area		X				1.4	20	
16	Finish unit	X					5.5		
17	Final inspection			X			3.5		
18	Carry unit to store		X				5.3	45	
Summary:		#							
	Operations	7					19.1		
	Movements	6					16.7	205	
	Inspections	3					10.2		
	Delays	2					10.2		
	Storage	0					0		
Totals:		18					56.2	205	

Figure 41.3 *Example of a process chart*

4. Critically analyse each operation. Ask questions like: 'Can we eliminate this activity?', 'How can we improve this operation?', 'Can we combine operations?'
5. Based on this analysis, revise the process. This should give fewer operations, shorter times, less distance travelled and so on.
6. Check the new process, prepare the organization for changes, train staff and so forth, and implement the changes.

The maximum output from the process is limited by the longest operation. In Figure 41.3 finishing takes 5.5 minutes, so the product cannot be made at a rate faster than 60/5.5 = 10.9 units an hour.

In operations 5 and 11 the machine operator has to wait a total of 10.2 minutes. Better planning might reduce this. In operations 1, 4, 9, 13, 15 and 18 the product is moved a total of 660 feet, taking 16.7 minutes. This might be reduced by better layouts.

Multiple-activity charts

Process charts do not show what each participant in the process is doing at any time. We can show this using a multiple-activity chart, as illustrated in Figure 41.4. The blocked off areas show at a glance what each participant is doing at any time.

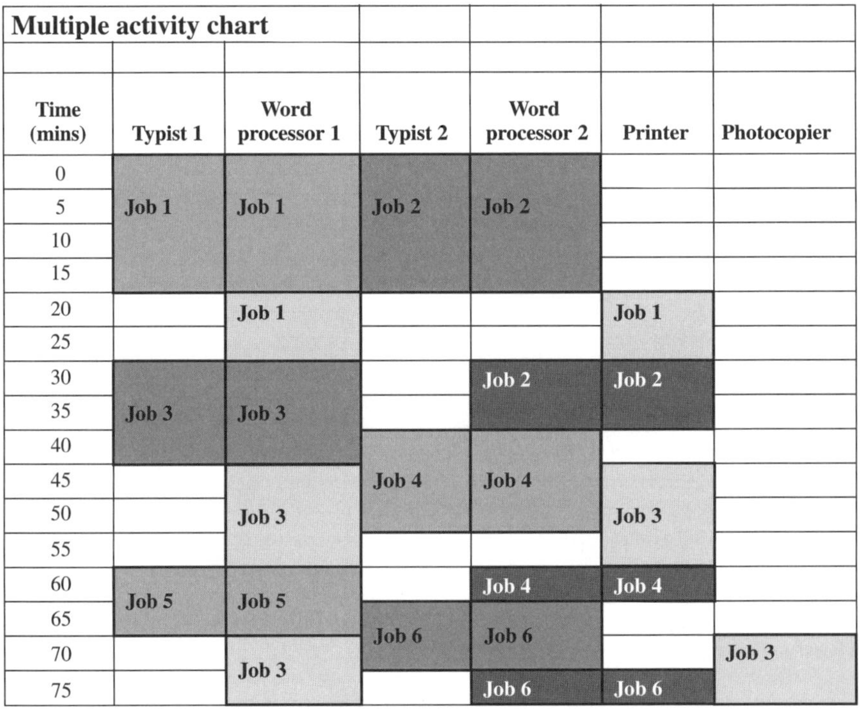

Multiple activity chart						
Time (mins)	Typist 1	Word processor 1	Typist 2	Word processor 2	Printer	Photocopier
0						
5	Job 1	Job 1	Job 2	Job 2		
10						
15						
20		Job 1			Job 1	
25						
30				Job 2	Job 2	
35	Job 3	Job 3				
40						
45			Job 4	Job 4		
50		Job 3			Job 3	
55						
60	Job 5	Job 5		Job 4	Job 4	
65			Job 6	Job 6		
70		Job 3				Job 3
75				Job 6	Job 6	

Figure 41.4 *Example of a multiple-activity chart*

FURTHER READING

Leibfried, K H J and McNair, C J, *Benchmarking: A tool for continuous improvement*, HarperCollins, New York 1992.

Sink, D S, *Productivity Management: Planning, evaluation, control and improvement*, John Wiley, New York 1985.

42

Improving the Process

DEFINITION

Organizations work with continual change. Products change, as do competitors, costs, markets, locations, customers, the economy, the business environment, company objectives, technology, shareholders, employees, and just about everything else. Any organization that does not continually update and improve its operations will be left behind by its more flexible and innovative competitors. The way that operations change has to be carefully managed.

IMPORTANCE OF CHANGE

Successful organizations must continually change their operations – and those that do not get left behind by more innovative competitors. Some signs that an organization is not managing change well include:

- old products that are being overtaken by competitors;
- low sales volume and falling market share;
- problems with product quality and delivery dates;
- large numbers of customer complaints;
- reliance on a few customers, especially with long-term, fixed-price contracts;
- an old-fashioned process;
- low employee morale and high staff turnover;
- poor industrial relations;

- poor communications;
- too much inflexible top management;
- inward looking managers who are out of touch with operations or customers;
- heavy debts.

Most people do not like changes, as they force them to abandon old and familiar practices, to learn new skills, new ways of doing things, new procedures, and to form new relationships. Change is essential for an organization's survival, however. The organization should, therefore, positively welcome change as a necessary step towards improvement. This constructive attitude involves:

- commitment to change, accepting that continual change is inevitable, necessary and beneficial;
- an organizational culture and environment that welcomes change;
- an experimental approach, encouraging new ideas and practices;
- products and operations based on innovation and new ideas;
- keeping abreast of new developments and likely changes in the industry;
- acceptance that not all new ideas will be successful, and willingness to learn from failures;
- easy communications, so that everyone knows about the changes, why they are needed, their effects, new practices, and so forth;
- reassurance, guidance and protection for people most affected by the changes;
- managers who enjoy change.

CONTINUOUS IMPROVEMENT

Anyone familiar with a process can usually suggest improvements. This principle is used in TQM, which looks for continuous improvement (described in Chapter 32). Most of these improvements are small, can be absorbed by the process without disruption, and cause no major problems if things go wrong. Over time the accumulated effects of these small changes can give dramatic improvements in performance. In TQM, this is called *kaizen*, which is Japanese for 'improvement'.

The management of small changes can be quite informal, with someone working on a process finding a better way of doing things and simply changing the operations. Sometimes there is a more formal approach, when organizations positively look for improvements. One approach for this uses a plan-do-check-act cycle, which has a team of people who:

- *Plan*: look at the current operations, collecting data and designing improvements.
- *Do*: implement the improvements.
- *Check*: see if the new operations actually bring the improvements that were expected.
- *Act*: confirm the changes if they were successful, and make adjustments if they were not.

As this is a cycle that aims to bring a continual stream of improvements, the next stage is to go back to the start and plan the next changes.

RATE OF IMPROVEMENT

Critics of *kaizen* and its incremental approach to change say that continually tinkering with a process gives an impression of uncertainty and lack of leadership. It might also move the process in the wrong direction, as an attractive small change might block the way for much bigger gains in another direction. The major criticism, however, is that incremental changes do not get to the root of problems and look for dramatic improvements. If you have a fundamentally bad process, then making small adjustments will still leave you with a bad process. What you should do is stop tinkering with the current process, and start designing a new, ideal one. This would give a fundamental, sudden and dramatic change in operations, typical of the breakthrough that comes when introducing new technology (see Figure 42.1). The best known approach of this kind is business process re-engineering (BPR). 'Business process reengineering is the fundamental rethinking and radical redesign of business processes to achieve dramatic improvements in critical, contemporary measures of performance, such as cost, quality, service and speed' (Michael Hammer, 1996).

Business process re-engineering focuses the organization on the whole process of supplying products for customers. This is not a new idea, and BPR offers no new methods, but it is a useful way of summarizing several related ideas. Some of its main principles are:

- organizations should concentrate on the whole process rather than on the separate activities that make up the process;
- the process should be designed across functions and allow work to flow naturally through the process;
- managers should strive for dramatic improvements in performance by radically rethinking and redesigning the process;
- information technology is fundamental to re-engineering as it allows radical new solutions to problems;
- work should be done where it makes most sense;

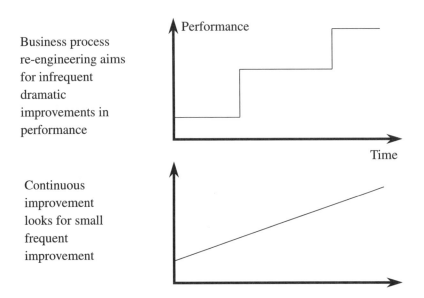

Business process re-engineering aims for infrequent dramatic improvements in performance

Continuous improvement looks for small frequent improvement

Figure 42.1 *Comparisons between BPR and kaizen*

- decisions are made where the work is done, and by those doing the work;
- you do not have to be an expert to help redesign a process, and being an outsider without preconceived ideas often helps.

Business process re-engineering is an approach to change rather than a formal procedure, so we cannot say 'this is how to re-engineer a process'. Perhaps because of this, organizations have mixed experiences with its implementation. Some have reported spectacular successes, but around three-quarters of organizations do not achieve the success they were hoping for. There are many reasons for this lack of success, including:

- adjusting a process rather than fundamentally redesigning it;
- settling for minor improvements;
- stopping before all the work is done;
- pulling back when there is resistance to change;
- not putting enough resources into the BPR;
- not getting senior management support;
- appointing a leader who is not interested;
- setting up a separate and remote working group;
- burying BPR in other initiatives.

The lack of success has been a consistent criticism of BPR, but there are other basic criticisms, including:

- realistically, it is very difficult to get the dramatic improvements promised by BPR;
- sudden changes to the process can be very disruptive and expensive;
- dramatic changes might use new technology with which the organization has no experience;
- a new process can take a long time to settle down before it starts working properly;
- BPR is seen as the latest management fad and is not taken seriously;
- it always uses a radical approach, even when minor adjustments would be best;
- BPR emphasizes staff reductions and becomes an excuse for getting rid of workers;
- it can put short-term goals of costs reduction ahead of longer-term interests;
- radical redesign and downsizing may lose essential experience from the organization;
- re-engineered organizations can be vulnerable to changes in the environment.

INTRODUCING CHANGE

Whatever rate of change seems most appropriate, introducing the changes has to be done carefully. A reasonable approach to this has the following steps:

1. Make everyone aware that changes are needed, describing the reasons, alternatives and likely effects.
2. Examine the current operations, using benchmarking and other comparisons to identify areas that need improvement.
3. Design better operations using the knowledge, skills and experience of everyone concerned.
4. Get people committed to the new methods.
5. Design a detailed plan for introducing the improvements, anticipating likely problems rather than waiting for them to happen.
6. Make any changes necessary to the organization.
7. Do the training and education.
8. Set challenging, but realistic, goals for everyone and make it clear how these can be achieved.
9. Have a specific event to start the new methods.
10. Establish milestones and monitor progress to make sure they are achieved.
11. Give support and encouragement to everyone concerned.
12. Have continuing discussions about progress, problems, adjustments, and so forth.
13. Remain committed to the new methods, updating them as necessary.

Accept that the new methods are only temporary, and continually look for further improvements.

FURTHER READING

Gouillart, F and Kelly, J, *Transforming the Organization,* McGraw-Hill, New York 1995.

Hammer, M, *Beyond Reengineering*, HarperCollins, New York 1996.

Imai, M, *Kaizen, the Key to Japan's Competitive Success*, McGraw-Hill, New York 1986.

Robbins, H and Finley, M, *Why Change Doesn't Work*, Orion Business Books, London 1997.

43

Approach to Planning

DEFINITION

Planning is needed to organize operations and the associated resources. It designs timetables for all aspects of operations, showing exactly what must be done at any time. There is a hierarchy of plans, which starts with a general strategic overview and moves down into detailed operational schedules.

CONTEXT OF PLANNING

The mission, corporate and business plans give the strategic direction of the whole organization. These lead to functional strategies, including an operations strategy. The operations strategy includes all the long-term decisions about products and processes, such as location, capacity, technology used, quality and so on. These strategic plans, in turn, lead to a series of tactical and operational decisions. This gives a hierarchy of decisions, with operations managers making plans at all levels from the broad strategic through to the detailed operational.

Earlier chapters discussed the importance of product planning (Chapters 28 to 30) and forecasting demand (Chapter 34). These give the starting points for the next stages of planning, which make sure that the resources are available to make products to meet the forecast demand. Then a simplified view of planning has organizations:

- analysing customer requirements and designing products to meet them;

- forecasting the demand for the products;
- designing the best process to deliver the products;
- planning the resources needed to support this process.

Planning the resources starts with strategic capacity plans, which make sure there is enough capacity to meet forecast demand. Then the organization designs timetables of production, which show when the product will be made. These production plans are expanded to give timetables for employees, equipment, purchases and other resources. There is some disagreement about the terms used to describe the different levels of planning, but we will use the following standard names:

- *Capacity plans,* which make sure there is enough capacity to meet long-term demand.
- *Aggregate plans,* which show the overall production for families of products, typically by month at each location.
- *Master schedules,* which show a timetable of production for individual products, typically by week.
- *Short-term schedules,* which show detailed timetables of production and resources, typically by day.

PLANNING PROCEDURE

Although all types of planning are different, they share common features, and we can describe a general approach to planning. This compares the resources available with the resources needed, develops plans to overcome any differences between the two, chooses the best plan and implements it. This approach is sometimes called resource requirement planning. It seems quite straightforward, but taking these simple steps does not usually work. In most circumstances there are a huge number of possible plans and an organization cannot look at all of them and find the best. It is also difficult to compare the alternatives as there is a range of competing objectives and non-quantifiable factors. A more realistic view of planning uses an iterative procedure. This designs a plan and sees how close it gets to achieving its objectives; if it performs badly, the plan is modified to find improvements. The general planning procedure then becomes:

- *Step 1* – look at the demand forecasts, higher-level plans and any other relevant information to find the resources needed.
- *Step 2* – look at the process and any other relevant information to find the resources available.
- *Step 3* – compare the resources needed with those available and see if there are any mismatches between supply and demand.

- *Step 4* – suggest a plan for overcoming these mismatches.
- *Step 5* – see how well the plan works, find any problems such as broken constraints or objectives not met, and compare the plan with previous plans.
- *Step 6* – if the plan is not good enough, see how it can be revised and go back to Step 4.
- *Step 7* – if the plan gives reasonable results, is generally acceptable and is the best solution found, implement the results.
- *Step 8* – control the plans, which means continually checking to make sure that they are working properly.
- *Step 9* – move on to the next planning period and go back to Step 1.

This iterative procedure accepts that it is usually impossible to find the 'best' solution. The plans that the marketing department likes may be very inefficient for operations; the best plans for operations may not suit personnel; the best plans for personnel may be too expensive for finance. Planners inevitably look for a compromise that takes into account a large number of factors, including:

- *demand* – forecast sales; sales already made; back orders; variation in demand;
- *operations* – machine capacity and utilization; aim of stable production; plans for new equipment; use of subcontractors; productivity targets;
- *materials* – availability of raw materials; inventory policies; current inventory levels; constraints on storage;
- *finance* – costs; cash flows; financing arrangements; exchange rates; general economic climate;
- *human resources* – workforce levels; levels of skills and productivity; unemployment rates; hiring and training policies;
- *marketing* – reliability of forecasts; competition; plans for new products; product substitution.

Finding a reasonable balance between these factors is difficult, and the iterative planning procedure may be repeated many times before a plan is finally accepted.

Period covered by plans

The iterative procedure described in Steps 1 to 8 above gives plans for a specific period. But planning is continuous and never ends – as plans for one period are finalized and implemented, planning moves on to the next period. In other words, we have to design a series of plans, one for every period, as suggested in Step 9. This actually makes planning a lot easier, as the plans for one period can form the basis of plans further in

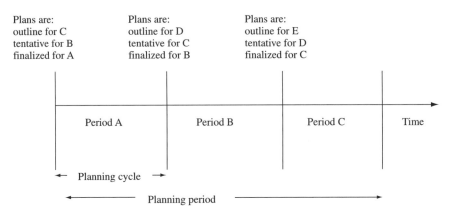

Figure 43.1 *Continual updating of plans in cycles*

the future – next month's production plans can be found by adjusting this month's.

Continuous planning, where organizations keep updating plans for future periods, allows them to work in planning cycles. In one cycle they might finalize plans for the next period and make outline plans for the following period and tentative plans for the period after that. Figure 43.1 illustrates this use of planning cycles. It is difficult to generalize, but strategic plans might cover the next five years and be updated annually; aggregate plans might cover the next six months and be updated every three months. The second half of these plans is fairly tentative, but the first half is more definite and forms the basis of the master schedules.

FURTHER READING

Browne, J, Harhen, J and Shivnan, J, *Production Management Systems*, Addison Wesley, Harlow 1996.

Tomkins, J A and White, J A, *Facility Planning*, John Wiley, New York 1988.

44

Capacity Planning

DEFINITION

The capacity of a process sets the maximum amount of a product that can be made in a given time. The aim of capacity planning is to make sure that there is enough usable capacity to meet demand over the long, medium and short term.

BACKGROUND

All operations have some limitation on their capacity. In Chapter 40 we said that the designed capacity is the maximum rate of output under ideal conditions, whereas the effective capacity is the maximum output that can realistically be expected under normal conditions. The difference between designed capacity and effective capacity allows for set-up times, break-downs, rests, maintenance periods, inefficiencies, scheduling difficulties and so on. Most organizations also do not like to work flat out, as equipment becomes less reliable, people feel overstretched and there is no cushion to deal with sudden changes or unexpected events. The actual output is normally lower than the effective capacity.

MATCHING CAPACITY AND DEMAND

The aim of capacity planning is to make the usable capacity match the demand for products. Any mismatch between capacity and demand will leave either dissatisfied customers or underused resources. If capacity is less than demand, the organization cannot meet all the demand and it loses potential customers. If capacity is greater than demand, the organization meets all the demand but it has spare capacity and underused resources.

To match capacity and demand we can use the general approach to planning described in the last chapter. Unfortunately, there are some specific problems associated with capacity planning, including its discrete nature and the timing of capacity changes.

Discrete capacity

Demand comes in relatively small quantities and can take almost any value, but capacity usually comes in large, discrete amounts. Typically, capacity can be increased by building another factory, buying another machine or employing another person. This gives problems with matching discrete capacity to continuous demand. Suppose that demand for a product rises steadily over time. Capacity is increased at some point, but the increase will come as a discrete step, giving three basic strategies (illustrated in Figure 44.1):

■ capacity can be more or less matched to demand, so that sometimes there is excess capacity and sometime a shortage;
■ capacity can be made at least equal to demand at all times, which needs more investment in facilities and gives lower utilization;
■ capacity can be added only when the additional facilities would be fully used, which needs lower investment and gives high utilization, but restricts output.

There is no way to avoid this problem, but managers need to find the best alternative by balancing the costs and benefits. Factors that encourage organizations to increase capacity early, as shown in Figure 44.1(b), are:

■ uneven or variable demand;
■ high profits, perhaps for a new product;
■ high cost of unmet demand, possibly with lost sales;
■ continuously changing product mix;
■ uncertainty in capacity;
■ variable efficiency;
■ capacity increases that are relatively small;
■ low cost of spare capacity, which might be used for other work.

The main factor that makes organizations delay an increase in capacity until the last possible moment, as shown in Figure 44.1(c), is the capital cost.

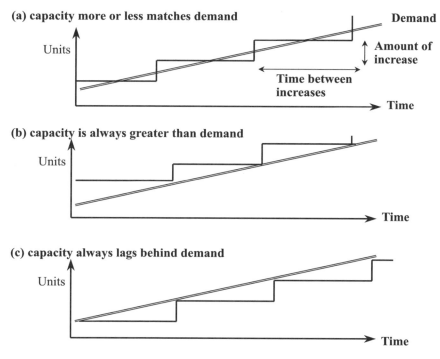

(a) capacity more or less matches demand

Units

Demand

Amount of increase

Time between increases

Time

(b) capacity is always greater than demand

Units

Time

(c) capacity always lags behind demand

Units

Time

Figure 44.1 *Options for timing of capacity increases*

Size of expansion

If an organization is expanding to meet growing demand, it might be better to have one big expansion rather than several smaller ones, as shown in Figure 44.2.

The benefits of large increases include:

- capacity stays ahead of demand for a long time;
- sales are unlikely to be lost;
- there might be economies of scale;
- advantages might be gained over competitors;
- there are less frequent disruptions.

On the other hand, the disadvantages of large increases include:

- capacity does not match demand so closely;
- disruptions may be serious;
- there are high capital costs;
- utilization will be low;
- there is high risk if demand changes;
- the policy is less flexible.

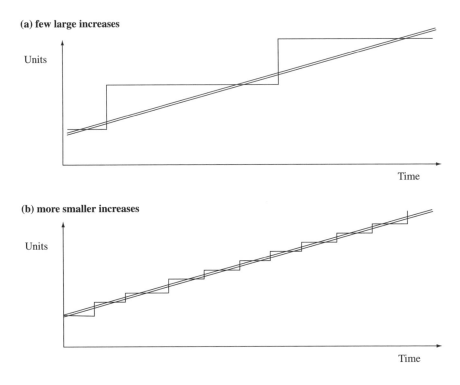

Figure 44.2 *Options for size of capacity increases*

DIFFERENT LEVELS OF CAPACITY PLANS

Changes in capacity might need another facility to be built, replacing an old process, or moving to a new location. Such decisions have long-term consequences and mean that capacity planning is largely a strategic function.

There are, however, other aspects of capacity planning that are shorter term. Leasing extra space or working overtime might increase capacity and these are tactical and operational decisions. The strategic capacity plans give the overall picture, but this is adjusted by shorter-term decisions.

Short-term adjustments to capacity

Short-term mismatches between supply and demand can be corrected in two ways: adjust demand to match available capacity, or adjust capacity to match demand.

Taking the first of these, organizations can adjust demand in a number of ways, including:

- varying the price, with increases for products with too little capacity and decreases for products with spare capacity;
- changing the marketing effort;
- offering incentives, such as free samples of products with spare capacity, or discounts, such as off-peak telephone calls or travel;
- changing related products, so that substitution is possible for products in short supply, such as holiday destinations;
- keeping spare units in stock to be used later;
- varying the lead time, making customers wait for products in short supply;
- using a reservation or appointment system.

One result of this demand management is that business can be actively discouraged at times of high demand. At first this seems strange, but it is really quite common. Professional institutions, for example, put up barriers for entry; expensive cars have long delivery times; artists produce limited editions of prints, perfumes charge very high prices.

The alternative to demand management is capacity management, which looks for short-term adjustments to available capacity. Ways of adjusting capacity include:

- changing the total hours worked in any period, by changing the number of shifts, amount of overtime, or holidays;
- employing part-time staff to cover peak demand;
- scheduling work patterns so the total workforce available at any time varies in line with varying demand;
- using outside contractors, or renting extra space;
- adjusting the process, perhaps making larger batches to reducing set-up times;
- adjusting equipment and processes to work faster or slower;
- rescheduling maintenance periods;
- making the customer do some work, like using automatic cash-dispensing machines in banks or packing their own bags in super-markets.

The first four of these options adjust designed capacity, the next three adjust effective capacity, and the last one reduces the amount of work in operations.

CHANGING CAPACITY OVER TIME

Another problem with capacity planning is that the capacity of a process changes over time. Even if no changes are made to the process, there are

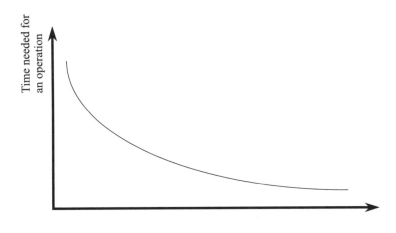

Figure 44.3 *A typical learning curve*

short-term variations due to operator illness, interruptions, breakdowns, efficiency of equipment, and a wide range of other factors. In practice, the amount made by a process and its effective capacity can vary quite widely. So the capacity is not a fixed figure, but it depends on how well the available resources are being used.

Longer-term trends in capacity are brought about by, for example, learning curves and reducing performance of equipment. We will look at the reducing performance of equipment in Chapter 53, but mention the effects of the learning curve here.

The more often you repeat something, the easier it becomes, which is why musicians and sportsmen spend a long time practising. This effect can be seen in almost all operations, where efficiency increases with the number of units produced, and the effective capacity rises. This effect, where the time needed to do an operation reduces with experience, is shown in a learning curve, illustrated in Figure 44.3. Typically, the time needed to do an operation falls by some proportion every time the number of repetitions is doubled. For example, the time taken for an operation might reduce by 10 per cent every time the number of units doubles.

FURTHER READING

Menasse, D, *Capacity Planning: A practical approach*, Prentice-Hall, Englewood Cliffs, NJ 1993.
Tomkins, J A and White, J A, *Facility Planning*, John Wiley, New York 1988.

45

Aggregate Planning

DEFINITION

Aggregate planning uses the long-term forecast demand, capacity and production plans to design medium-term production schedules for families of products. It expands the strategic plans to give tactical production plans.

TACTICAL PLANS

Aggregate plans show the production of each family of products for, typically, each of the next few months. They only look at production of families of products and are not concerned with individual products. So the aggregate plans of a knitwear manufacturer, for example, show the total production of jumpers, but they do not look in more detail at the production of a particular style, colour or size.

The main inputs to aggregate plans are the forecast demand, capacity and strategic production plans. There are a number of other important inputs, including known orders, resources available, people who will be working, stock levels, safety stocks, desired service levels, internal demands, materials available, planned changes to operations, and any other relevant production constraints. The aggregate plans have to look at all of these, and answer questions such as:

- Do we have enough resources to meet the forecast demand?
- Should we keep production at a constant level, or change it to meet varying demand?

- Should we use stocks to meet changing demand?
- Should we use subcontractors to cover for peak demands?
- Should we change the size of the workforce with demand?
- How can we change work patterns to meet changing demand?
- Are shortages allowed, perhaps with late delivery?
- Should we change prices to adjust the demand?
- Can we smooth demand by any other means?

STABLE PRODUCTION

An important question for aggregate planning is how much variation there should be in production levels – should production change with demand or should it be more stable? There are obvious advantages in having stable production, including:

- planning and scheduling resources is easier;
- the flow of products is smoother;
- there are fewer problems with product changes;
- there is no need to 'hire and fire' employees;
- employees have regular work patterns;
- larger lot sizes reduce costs;
- stocks can be reduced as there is less variation;
- throughput can be faster;
- experience with a product reduces problems.

Stable production has many advantages but it is not always the best option. In practice there are three ways in which an organization can meet uneven demand:

- *Chase demand,* where production exactly matches demand. This gives no stocks, but the organization has to change production every period, hiring or firing workers, changing production levels, and so on.
- *Produce at a constant production rate,* where production is constant at the average demand for the planning period. Since demand is variable, the differences between supply and demand are met by building or using stocks.
- *Have a mixed policy,* which is a combination of the first two policies. Here there are some changes in production rate, but not in every period. The policy tries to compromise by having fairly stable production, but reduces the inventory costs by allowing some changes. In practice, this is the most commonly used plan.

DESIGNING AGGREGATE PLANS

The aim of aggregate planning is to:

- design medium-term schedules for families of products;
- meet forecast customer demand;
- keep production relatively stable;
- keep within the constraints of the capacity plan;
- use available resources efficiently;
- meet any other specific objectives and constraints.

There are several ways of designing aggregate plans. We now discuss the most widely used.

Intuitive approaches

Aggregate plans are not usually designed from scratch, but are variations on previous plans. The easiest approach to planning is to ask an experienced planner to review the current plans and, in the light of that planner's knowledge and experience, design an updated version.

This is a very common method of planning and has the benefits of convenience, ease of use and using a well-understood procedure, and experts can give results that are trusted by the organization. Unfortunately, the results can also be of variable and uncertain quality, they may take a long time to design, they rely solely on the skills and knowledge of a planner, they can include bias, and so on.

Expert systems

As we saw in Chapter 38, expert systems use a series of rules to try to duplicate the thinking of a skilled scheduler. Some expert systems for scheduling give very good results. It must be said, however, that expert systems often give disappointing results, are difficult to design and need a lot of expertise before they work properly.

Graphical methods

Planners often find it easier to visualize a plan from a graph. The most popular format draws a graph of cumulative demand over some period. Then an aggregate plan is drawn as a line of cumulative supply. The aim of planners is to get the cumulative supply line nearly straight, giving constant production, and as close as possible to the cumulative demand line.

Graphical approaches have the advantages that they are easy to use and understand, but they are really only one step better than an intuitive method. They do not guarantee optimal solutions, sometimes give very poor results, may take a long time, and still rely on the skills of a planner.

Spreadsheet calculations

Many planners prefer to look at numbers or tables, and an alternative format for planning uses spreadsheets. A common format lists the resources down the left-hand side of the spreadsheet, and the time periods across the top, available capacity for resources down the right-hand side, and demand across the bottom. Then the body of the matrix shows the allocation of resources. These give very fast comparisons of alternative plans and 'what-if' analyses, and can be used with graphical methods.

Simulation

Simulation is a very flexible way of solving a wide range of problems. It gives a dynamic view of problems by imitating real operations over a typical period.

Organizations using simulation for aggregate planning have to start by building a simulation model of the process. Then alternative plans are run on the model and the best identified. This can take some time, but the results often give useful insights into the working of a process.

Mathematical models

The approaches to aggregate planning that we have described so far rely, at least to some extent, on the skills of a planner. A more formal mathematical approach could give better results.

Several approaches are used for aggregate planning, usually based on linear programming. Unfortunately, these methods are too complicated for large problems, or the effort involved is not worthwhile. They are, therefore, limited to fairly small and simple operations.

FURTHER READING

Browne, J, Harhen, J and Shivnan, J, *Production Management Systems* (2nd edition), Addison Wesley, Reading, MA 1996.

Freeland, J and Landel, R, *Aggregate Production Planning: Text and cases*, Reston Publishing, Reston 1984.

Hess, R, *Managerial Spreadsheet Modelling and Analysis*, Irwin, Chicago 1997.

46

Designing a Master Schedule

DEFINITION

The master schedule gives a detailed timetable for making individual products. It shows how the aggregate plan will be achieved as efficiently as possible.

CONTENTS OF MASTER SCHEDULES

Aggregate plans show the timetable for making families of products. Once these plans are accepted, they can be expanded to give more details. Organizations 'disaggregate' the aggregate plans and design detailed schedules for making individual products. These master schedules show the number of individual products to be made in, typically, each week. This is the first time that due dates or completion times are put against individual products.

The master schedule is clearly derived from the aggregate plan, so the overall production levels are largely fixed. However, the schedules are designed relatively close to the start of production, and some orders may have already been received. Then the production level comes from:

- production specified by the aggregate plan;
- adjustments because of more recent forecasts;
- actual customer orders for the period.

Master schedulers have to meet this demand while keeping within the constraints of the process. Their main aims are to:

- identify all known demands for individual products – forecasts, actual sales, internal transfers and so forth;
- design production plans to meet these demands;
- ensure that existing customer orders are met;
- meet the production targets specified in the aggregate plan;
- keep within all other constraints on the process;
- balance the needs of production, marketing, finance and other functions;
- communicate freely with all concerned functions;
- use stocks and other means to keep production relatively stable;
- use available resources efficiently;
- identify any problems and resolve them.

DESIGNING MASTER SCHEDULES

In principle, designing master schedules is similar to designing an aggregate plan. There is a range of possible approaches, from intuitive methods through to mathematical programming. The main difference with master schedules is that they look at lower levels of planning and include a lot more detail, often down to individual customer orders. This inevitably makes the planning more complicated. Because of these complications and the subjective decisions, most master schedules are designed by skilled schedulers using an intuitive approach. They expand the aggregate plan – probably with spreadsheets – and use their experience to modify previous plans.

As usual with plans, it is most common to use an iterative approach. This iterative procedure can be continued up to some period, say three weeks, before the master schedule is finalized and implemented. After this the schedule must be fixed so that it can be used for lower levels of planning. Later changes are only made in emergencies as they affect all the other schedules.

At this stage of planning we have a detailed production plan for each product. This is not the end of planning, however. Now we have to take this plan and see what resources it needs, how these resources should be scheduled, what people are needed, when to buy materials, and so on. This next stage of planning takes the tactical master schedule and uses it to design short-term schedules. Some aspects of short-term scheduling are discussed in the next chapter.

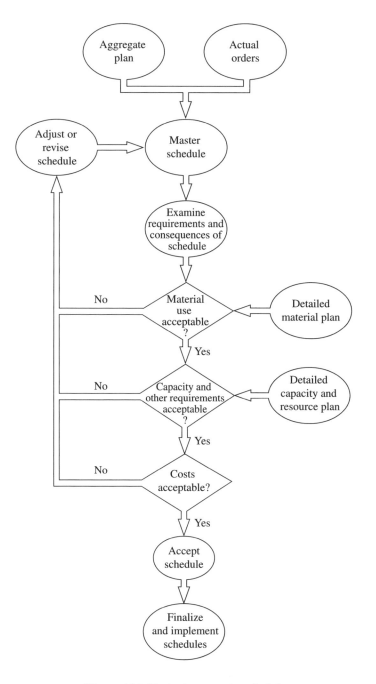

Figure 46.1 *Designing a master schedule*

FURTHER READING

Fogarty, D W, Blackstone, J H and Hoffman, T R, *Production and Inventory Management* (2nd edition), South-Western, Cincinnati, OH 1991.
Proud, J F, *Master Scheduling*, John Wiley, New York 1995.

47

Short-term Scheduling

DEFINITION

Short-term schedules give detailed timetables for jobs, people, materials, equipment and any other resources used in the process. They show what any part of the process is doing at any time.

PURPOSE OF SCHEDULING

The master schedules give a timetable for making individual products, but this is not the end of planning. The organization now knows when each product will be made, but it still has to organize the resources needed for making them. In other words, it has to design timetables for associated equipment, people, materials, facilities and any other resources that are used. These timetables are the result of short-term scheduling.

Designing these operational schedules is one of the most common problems in any organization. They are needed for all resources, and without them operations would be disorganized and chaotic. The basic information given by short-term schedules is:

- the order in which operations use each facility;
- the times when the operations are done;
- timetables for associated resources needed to support the operations.

It is easiest to imagine this in terms of jobs waiting to use equipment. The short-term schedules show the order in which the jobs are done, the time when each is done, and the resources that are needed for each job.

Aims of short-term schedules

The aim of short-term scheduling is to achieve the master production schedule, while giving low costs and high utilization of equipment. Although this may seem fairly straightforward, short-term scheduling is notoriously difficult. Schedules have to balance many different factors, and typically have to:

■ allocate jobs to equipment;
■ allocate staff, materials and other resources to the jobs;
■ set the sequence and timing of jobs on the equipment;
■ control the work, including checking progress and expediting late jobs;
■ revise schedules for late changes;
■ balance the needs of different operations and products.

Although these descriptions talk about scheduling 'jobs' on 'machines', this is just for convenience. Scheduling is one of the most common problems in any organization, and occurs in many different forms.

SCHEDULING JOBS ON MACHINES

A standard scheduling problem has a set of 'jobs' waiting to use a set of 'machines'. The aim is to arrange the jobs so that the work is done as efficiently as possible – perhaps minimizing the waiting time, minimizing the total processing time, keeping stocks low, reducing the maximum lateness, achieving high utilization of equipment, or some other objective. The problem is effectively one of finding the best sequences of jobs. Two basic approaches to this are forward scheduling and backward scheduling.

With *forward scheduling* schedulers know the start date for the first operation. Then they can work through all operations needed for a job and find the date when it will be finished. This has the benefit of doing work early, and any problems are noticed in time to solve them. There may also be advantages in giving customers their products before deadlines and getting earlier payment.

Backward scheduling means that customers are given a due date, which is the time the last operation finishes. Schedulers have to work backwards through the operations to find the date when the job must be started. This has the benefits of reducing the effects of last-minute changes to specifications, and lowering some costs (such as materials that are bought nearer the delivery date).

SCHEDULING RULES

It is very difficult to get optimal solutions to short-term scheduling problems, largely because of the number of variables, including:

- patterns of job arrivals;
- amount and type of equipment used;
- number and skills of operators;
- patterns of workflow through equipment;
- priority rules for jobs;
- disruptions caused by customer changes, breakdowns and so forth;
- different criteria for evaluating schedules;
- objectives of the schedulers.

The most effective way of designing short-term schedules is to use simple rules that give reasonable results. If an organization has a number of jobs waiting to use a single machine, it might look at the following rules:

- *First come, first served.* This is the most obvious scheduling rule and simply takes jobs in the order they arrive. The drawback here is that urgent or important jobs may be delayed while less urgent or important ones are being processed. The benefits are simplicity, ease of use and clear equity.
- *Most urgent job first.* This assigns an importance, or urgency, to each job and the jobs are processed in order of decreasing urgency. Emergency departments in hospitals use this rule to treat their most urgent patients first. The benefit of this rule is that jobs that are more important are given higher priority; the drawback is that those jobs that have low priority may get stuck at the end of a queue for a very long time.
- *Shortest job first.* Taking the jobs in order of increasing duration minimizes the average time spent in the system, where time in the system = processing time + waiting time. This allows jobs that can be done quickly to move on through the system, while longer jobs are left until nearer the end. The disadvantage is that long jobs can spend a long time waiting.
- *Earliest due date first.* Here the queue of jobs is sorted in order of delivery date. Those that are expected first are then processed first. This has the benefit of minimizing the maximum lateness of jobs, but again some jobs may have to wait a long time.
- *Decreasing critical ratio.* The critical ratio is the time remaining until the job is due divided by the time needed to complete it.

$$\text{Critical ratio} = \frac{\text{due date} - \text{today's date}}{\text{time needed for the job}}$$

If this ratio is low, the time to complete the job is short compared with the time available, and the job becomes urgent. If the ratio is high, there is plenty of time left and the job is less urgent.

Other scheduling rules

These examples illustrate the type of scheduling rules that can be used. There are many alternatives, and an organization might schedule jobs in the order of least work remaining, fewest operations remaining, longest first, least slack first (where slack is the time remaining until the job is due minus the time needed for processing it) and so on. There is a huge variety of simple scheduling rules, and more complicated ones to deal with different circumstances.

OPTIMIZED PRODUCTION TECHNOLOGY (OPT)

Simple scheduling rules can give good results, but better solutions might need more complicated rules. Typically these combine a hierarchy of rules, together with more formal analyses and simulations. One method of scheduling that has received a lot of attention was developed by Goldratt, who described the theory of constraints. This concentrates on the capacity of a process – particularly the bottlenecks that limit production. The only way of increasing production is to remove the bottlenecks, but when one bottleneck is removed another is created. The theory of constraints looks for ways of improving efficiency by systematically removing the current bottleneck.

Optimized production technology (OPT) is a software package that is based on the theory of constraints. Like many similar packages, OPT is a proprietary product and the details of its operations are not published – but it is based on a series of well-known principles:

- Balance the flow through the process rather than the capacity. The production schedule should give the best flow of products through the process and need not keep all resources busy.
- The utilization of an operation that is not a bottleneck is not set by its own capacity, but by some other operation in the process.
- Activating a resource (which means doing work that is really needed) is not the same as using the resource (which might include work that is not really needed at the particular time).
- An hour lost at a bottleneck cannot be recovered, and gives an hour lost for the entire process.

- Saving an hour at an operation that is not a bottleneck gives no benefits.
- Bottlenecks control both the throughput of the process and the stocks of work in progress.
- The size of a transfer batch (the number of units moved together between operations) should not equal the size of the process batch (the total number of units made in a production run).
- The size of the process batch should be variable and not fixed.
- Schedules should be designed by looking at constraints simultaneously and not sequentially.
- Lead times are set by the process and cannot be predetermined.
- The sum of local optima is not equal to the optimum of the whole.

Scheduling services

There is no fundamental difference between scheduling services and scheduling in manufacturing. However, services have some features that give added problems for scheduling:

- Customers are more directly involved in services. They often form queues, which makes the time spent waiting for a service particularly important.
- Services cannot be held in stock, so they must be scheduled to arrive exactly when customers want them.
- As services cannot be held in stock, available capacity has to meet peak demands.
- Wide variations in demand give low utilization of resources – and difficult scheduling problems.

FURTHER READING

Baker, K R, *Elements of Sequencing and Scheduling*, Baker Press, Hanover, NH 1995.

Goldratt, E and Cox, J, *The Goal*, North River Press, New York 1984.

Vollman, T E, Berry, W L and Whybark, D C, *Manufacturing Planning and Control Systems* (3rd edition), Richard Irwin, Homewood, IL 1992.

48

Control of Schedules

DEFINITION

Control of the schedules monitors what actually happens in the operations, reports discrepancies with plans, and makes any necessary adjustments.

CONTROL OF SCHEDULES

Short-term schedules give detailed timetables that show what each job, piece of equipment, person and every other resource should be doing at any time. However, there is a difference between designing plans and having them actually happen. The schedules show what an organization intends to do, but during the implementation there may be unforeseen circumstances that prevent the plans actually happening:

- equipment may develop a fault or break down;
- people may be ill and unavailable for work;
- suppliers may not send necessary materials;
- customers may send in new orders;
- customers may change the specifications or cancel existing orders;
- there may be other problems within the organization that disrupt the process;
- the process may be disrupted by external factors that the organization cannot control.

The aim of a planning control system is to monitor actual performance, and allow adjustments when things do not go as planned. There are two main parts to a system.

The first part records the progress of jobs and gives information back to managers. It checks details of jobs' progress, and reports on times, efficiency, productivity, utilization and other measures.

The second part occurs when circumstances change or there is some disruption. Then the control system adjusts the schedules, or takes whatever action is necessary to allow revised plans.

Essentially the control system feeds back all information that managers need to see how operations are going, and whether they need to make any adjustments or more severe changes. To be more specific, the control system:

- ensures that jobs are scheduled according to plans;
- warns of problems with resources, delivery dates and so forth;
- makes sure that materials, equipment and operators are available for each job;
- assigns jobs to specific orders and set delivery times;
- checks progress as jobs move through the process;
- makes small adjustments as necessary to plans;
- allows rescheduling if there is a major disruption to plans;
- gives information on current activities;
- gives feedback on performance.

Associated documents

Many control systems are based around a dispatch list. This shows the schedules as an ordered list of the jobs to be done each day, their importance and how long each will take. In essence, the control system keeps a check of this list, and makes sure that each job is done at the planned time.

Other inputs to the control system might include stock levels, bills of materials (which list all the materials needed for a product), routes that products move through equipment, and delivery dates for specific jobs. The main outputs from a control system are status and exception reports – they show what should be happening and what is actually happening.

Some organizations link the control system to an input/output report, which keeps a check on the units entering an operation and those leaving. Obviously these should match or work is accumulating somewhere.

Control and planning

In principle, planning is done before operations, and then control takes over while the operations are actually being performed. But suppose, as often happens, there are discrepancies between plans and actual performance. Then the control system reports these, or it might take a more active part in overcoming the problems. It might, for example, suggest revisions to the schedules, or actually do the rescheduling. In such cases, there is not really a clear separation between planning and control, and the two functions tend to merge.

FURTHER READING

Browne, J, Harhen, J and Shivnan, J, *Production Management Systems* (2nd edition), Addison Wesley, Reading, MA 1996.

Sink, D S, *Productivity Management: Planning, evaluation, control and improvement*, John Wiley, New York 1985.

49

Material Requirements Planning

DEFINITION

Material requirements planning uses the master schedule to plan the supply of materials for a process. It uses the bill of materials to show what materials are needed for a master schedule, and then designs a timetable for their arrival.

DEPENDENT AND INDEPENDENT DEMAND

Short-term schedules use the master schedules to design timetables for other resources. In the same way, material requirements planning (MRP) uses the master schedules to give a detailed timetable for the delivery of materials. It finds:

- what materials have to be bought in;
- when these materials should be ordered;
- what materials have to be made internally;
- when these materials should be started.

Conventional planning is based on forecasts of demand. It assumes that overall demand for a product is made up of individual demands from many separate customers. Then the demands are independent of each other and the demand for one product is not related to the demand for another. In reality, there are many operations where demands are not independent, and the demand for one product is clearly related to the demand for another product. For example, when a manufacturer uses a number of components to make a product, the demands for each component are related, since they clearly depend on the demand for the final product. This gives a dependent demand system.

Material requirements planning is based on dependent demand. It recognizes that the master schedule gives a timetable for making a product, but the bill of materials shows the materials needed for the product, so these can be combined to find exactly what materials are needed, and when they are needed.

THE MRP APPROACH

Material requirements planning needs a lot of information about products and schedules, and it uses this in a large number of related calculations. These calculations mean that MRP systems are always computerized and their main inputs come from three files:

■ master schedules;
■ bill of materials;
■ inventory records.

Master schedules give the number of every product to be made in every period. Material requirements planning 'explodes' the master schedule using a bill of materials to give details of the materials needed. The inventory records show which of these materials are already available and which have to be bought or made.

A bill of materials is an ordered list of all the parts that are needed to make a particular product. It shows not only the materials, parts and components needed, but also the order in which they are used. If a company makes a table from a top and four legs, a simple bill of materials is shown in Figure 49.1. Every item also has a 'level' that shows where it fits into the process, with level 0 being the finished product. Level 1 items are used directly to make the level 0 item, level 2 items are used to make the level 1 items, and so on.

The full bill of materials keeps going down until it lists all the materials that the organization buys from suppliers. Every product has a bill of materials that is prepared at the design stage.

Calculations for MRP

We can use the example of the table above to illustrate the overall approach of MRP. Suppose the master schedule shows 10 tables to be made in

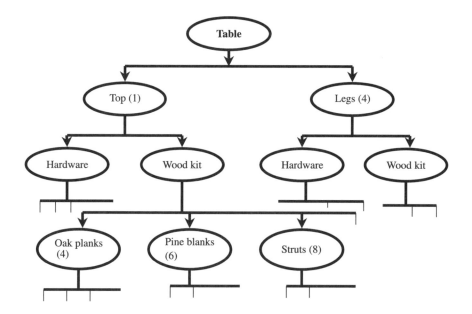

Figure 49.1 *Part of a bill of materials for a table*

February. Then the company will need 10 tops and 40 legs ready for assembly at the beginning of February. This gives the gross requirements for parts. Not all of these have to be ordered, as there may be some already in stock or due to arrive shortly. Subtracting current stocks and expected arrivals from the gross requirements gives the net requirements for new orders.

Now the company has the quantities to order, and knows when these orders should arrive. The next step is to find the time to place the orders. For this it needs to know the lead times, and then orders can be placed in these lead times before the materials are actually needed. Finally, the company may have to consider other information about orders, such as minimum quantities, discounts, safety stocks, supplier reliability, and so on. When all such factors are taken into account, the company can design a detailed timetable for orders. This procedure is summarized in Figure 49.2.

Outputs from MRP

Material requirements planning uses a lot of information, and when this has been collected it can be used in many different kinds of reports. These typically include:

- *timetable of operations* for the supply of materials to achieve the master schedule;
- *list of internal orders* for materials made within the organization;

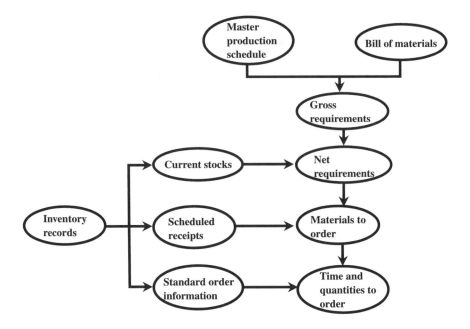

Figure 49.2 *The MRP procedure*

- *list of external orders* for materials from suppliers;
- *changes to previous orders* – whenever there are changes to, particularly, the master schedule or bill of materials, the MRP schedules have to be updated;
- *exceptions* – the system may note exceptions that need management action, problems with schedules, late orders, excessive scrap, requests for non-existent parts, shortage, and so on;
- *performance reports* – which show how well the system is working and might include measures for investment in stocks, inventory turnover, and number of shortages;
- *planning reports* – which can be used in longer-term planning decisions;
- *records of inventory transactions* – allowing the system to maintain accurate records of current stock and to check progress.

BENEFITS AND PROBLEMS OF MRP

Material requirements planning reduces stock levels by relating the supply of materials directly to demand. Then the benefits include:

- materials supply is linked directly to known demand;
- lower stock levels, with savings in capital, space, warehousing and so forth;

- higher stock turnover;
- better customer service, with no delays caused by shortages of materials;
- more reliable and faster delivery times;
- higher utilization of facilities as materials are always available when needed;
- less time spent on expediting and emergency orders;
- it encourages better planning, and sticking to plans;
- material requirements planning schedules can be used for short-term planning;
- it assigns priorities for jobs supplying materials;
- it gives early warning of potential problems.

Problems with MRP

There are also some disadvantages with MRP, the most obvious being the amounts of information and calculation that it needs. The information includes detailed master schedules, bills of materials, current stocks, orders outstanding, lead times, other information about suppliers, and a range of related information. Many organizations simply do not have this information, or they do not have it in enough detail, the right format, or with enough accuracy.

The whole procedure is based on a detailed master schedule that must be designed some time in advance, so MRP cannot be used if:

- there is no master schedule;
- the master schedule is inaccurate;
- plans are changed frequently;
- plans are not made far enough in advance.

Another frequent problem is that MRP reduces flexibility in responding to changes. The only materials available are those needed for a specific master schedule – this plan cannot be changed at short notice as the materials needed for any other plan are simply not available.

Some disadvantages of MRP include:

- it needs a lot of detailed and reliable information;
- it involves a lot of data manipulation;
- systems can be very complex;
- reduced flexibility;
- it assumes that lead times are constant and independent of the quantities ordered;
- in practice, materials are sometimes made in a different order to that specified in the bill of materials;
- if MRP is used to schedule the production of parts, this may give poor schedules;

- material requirements planning may not recognize capacity and other constraints;
- it can be expensive and time consuming to implement.

FURTHER READING

Orlicky, J, *Material Requirements Planning*, McGraw-Hill, New York 1975.

Smolik, D P, *Material Requirements of Manufacturing*, Van Nostrand Reinhold, New York 1983.

Waters, C D J, *Inventory Control and Management*, John Wiley, Chichester 1992.

50

Extensions to MRP

DEFINITION

There are many ways of extending the MRP approach. It was originally developed for manufacturing industry, but it is now used in a range of other operations. Once the dependent-demand MRP mechanism is established, it can be extended to include other resources – such as 'closed-loop MRP', which gives feedback for capacity planning, 'manufacturing resource planning', which extends the ideas to more resources, and 'enterprise resource planning', which eventually looks at controlling operations throughout the whole organization.

MRP AND SERVICES

Material requirements planning was originally developed as a way of organizing the materials supply for manufacturers, who have been developing large MRP systems since the 1970s, when computer power and reliable software became available.

Services also need schedules for materials, and early work adopted MRP to work in service organizations. This can be more difficult, largely because service providers often do not have detailed master schedules or the associated data for bills of materials and inventories. Nonetheless, there are many examples of services that have successfully used MRP. In universities, for example, the finished product is graduating students; the master schedule shows the number of students who will graduate from each programme in each term; the bill of materials shows the courses each student needs to take in each term. Then MRP can find the timetable for materials needed, which are the teachers, classrooms, laboratories and so forth.

Other extensions to MRP improved the procedures for dealing with variable supply, supplier reliability, wastage, defective quality, variable demand, variable lead times, batching rules and so on.

CLOSED-LOOP MRP

In its basic form, MRP designs a schedule for delivering materials for a single period's production. It moves through the master schedule one period at a time, and when it completes the schedules for one period, it moves on to the next. Each MRP run is self-contained and more or less isolated from the runs for other periods. This basic form of MRP does not check that the schedules it designs are efficient or even feasible, and it does not check whether schedules for different periods interfere with each other.

It makes obvious sense to extend MRP so that it checks the resulting schedules to make sure that there are no problems. An important move in this direction came with closed-loop MRP, which makes sure that there is enough capacity in all operations to supply the planned materials. In other words, there are links between the MRP system and other planning systems. The links have two main purposes. First, proposed plans that would break capacity constraints are detected by closed-loop MRP and early rescheduling is done to avoid the problem. Here, MRP takes an active part in capacity planning. Second, if operations are interrupted, the master schedule can be revised quickly with inputs from the MRP system.

A closed-loop MRP system starts with the proposed master schedules. It explodes these and designs schedules for the supply of materials. Then it compares these demands with the available capacity for supplying materials, and if there are any problems it adjusts the master schedules or the available capacities until it finds a reasonable solution. This usually involves some iteration, with repeated adjustments to plans and capacities until a workable and acceptable solution is found. This approach, which is sometimes called capacity requirements planning, is summarized in Figure 50.1.

MANUFACTURING RESOURCE PLANNING (MRP II)

Closed-loop MRP shows how the approach can be extended to other aspects of resource planning. The most significant extension is manufacturing resource planning, or MRP II, which extends the range of resources planned using MRP.

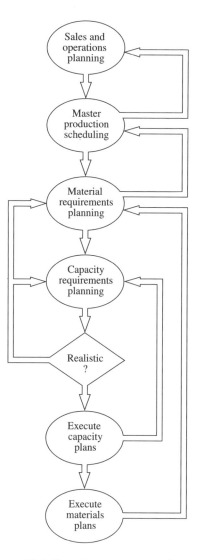

Figure 50.1 *Capacity requirements planning*

Basic MRP gives a timetable for ordering, purchasing and operations needed to supply materials. Closed-loop MRP gives feedback that extends the analyses to planning capacity. But why not extend the MRP approach to a range of other functions? Manufacturing resource planning shows when parts have to be produced, so it can design schedules for the machines that make the parts – and for the people who operate the machines. It shows when deliveries of materials have to be made, so it can design schedules for the delivery vehicles, the drivers and other aspects of logistics.

Continuing this line of reasoning, the approach could design schedules for equipment, people working on the process, cash flows, and many other resources. Eventually the master schedule could form the basis for planning most of the resources used in a process. This is the aim of MRP II. Its purpose is to synchronize all of a manufacturer's operations to achieve the production described in the master schedule.

Manufacturing resource planning II is an integrated system, with all parts linked back to a production plan. In practice it is very difficult to get this level of complete integration. Most organizations do not attempt to develop full MRP II but use parts of the system – perhaps controlling physical distribution through distribution resources planning.

ENTERPRISE RESOURCE PLANNING

Manufacturing resource planning II can produce schedules for a wide range of resources, and in its complete form schedules most of the resources within an organization. But it concentrates on the internal operations. Many organizations recognize that they can get more efficient operations by extending their systems to other activities – and organizations – within the supply chain. In other words, organizations along the supply chain cooperate, exchange information and integrate their systems. A single organization can get benefits by using MRP II to plan its operations, but it can get even more benefits by extending this approach to suppliers. This is the basis of enterprise resource planning (ERP).

Enterprise resource planning extends MRP II to include more functions, particularly those that involve interactions with other organizations. It extends the MRP systems to include a series of suppliers and customers along the suppy chain. Then the production plans of a supplier are co-ordinated to the precise requirements of its customers.

Enterprise resource planning relies on trust and a free flow of information between organizations. Even then, the resulting systems can be extremely complicated. It is fair to say that ERP is currently still being developed and is not widely used.

FURTHER READING

Luscombe, M, *MRP II: Integrating the business*, Butterworth-Heinemann, London 1993.

Wallace, T, *MRP II Making it Happen*, Oliver Wight, Essex Junction, VT 1990.

Wight, O W, *Manufacturing Resource Planning: MRP II*, Oliver Wight Publications, Essex Junction, VT 1984.

51

Just-in-Time Operations

DEFINITION

Just-in-time (JIT) operations try to eliminate all waste within an organization. Their aim is to meet production targets using the minimum amount of materials, with the minimum amount of equipment, the smallest number of operators, and so on. They do this by scheduling all operations to be done at just the time they are needed.

JIT APPROACH

Just-in-time is often seen as a way of minimizing stocks of work in progress. It assumes that the main purpose of stock is to give a buffer between operations, and allow for short-term mismatches between supply and demand. The traditional way of allowing for these is to keep stocks that are high enough to cover any likely problems. Just-in-time gives a more radical solution with the following argument.

Stocks are held in an organization to cover short-term variation and uncertainty in supply and demand. These stocks serve no useful purpose – they only exist because poor coordination does not match the supply of materials to the demand. As long as stocks are held, there are no obvious problems and no incentive for managers to improve the flow of materials. This means that operations will continue to be poorly managed, with problems hidden by the stocks.

Organizations should really try to improve their operations, find the reasons for differences between supply and demand, and then take whatever action is needed to overcome the differences. This will allow them to eliminate stocks and have operations done just as they are needed.

You can imagine JIT on a car assembly line. Just as the chassis moves down the line to a work station, an engine arrives at the same point and is fitted. This is repeated for all parts. As the car body arrives at another work station, four doors also arrive and are added. All the way down the line materials arrive just at the time they are needed, so the car is assembled in one smooth process.

EFFECTS OF JIT

JIT has much wider effects than simple stock control, and really involves a change in the way an organization looks at its operations. Its supporters described it as 'a way of eliminating waste' or 'a way of enforced problem solving'. It starts with the aim of organizing operations to occur at exactly the right time, and becomes a way of eliminating all waste from an organization. We can illustrate its effects on some aspects of operations:

- *Stocks*. Just-in-time assumes that stocks serve no useful purpose but rather hide problems. It is better to solve these problems, remove the differences between supply and demand, and eliminate stocks.
- *Quality*. When operations are done just-in-time, any defects would cause disruptions. This reinforces the need for perfect quality, which was discussed in Chapter 32.
- *Suppliers*. Just-in-time systems rely totally on their suppliers, and they recognize that customers and suppliers are partners with a common objective. They should work closely together and form long-term partnerships and alliances.
- *Employees*. Just-in-time recognizes that the distinction between 'managers' and 'workers' is meaningless, and the welfare of all employees depends on the success of the organization. All employees are treated fairly and equitably, with a stake in the success of the company.
- *Production*. Every time there are changes to a process, there are delays, disruptions and costs. Just-in-time says that these changes waste resources and should be eliminated, so it needs a stable environment, which makes large numbers of a standard product.

If we continue arguing in this way we can list the key elements in JIT operations, which include:

- a stable environment, making standard products with few variations;
- continuous production at fixed levels, probably with automated, high-volume operations;

- a balanced process that uses resources fully;
- reliable production equipment;
- minimum stocks;
- small batches of materials delivered with short lead times;
- low set-up and delivery costs;
- efficient materials handling;
- long-term relationships with reliable suppliers;
- consistently perfect quality of materials;
- flexible workforce, which is treated and rewarded fairly;
- ability to solve any problems;
- an efficient method of control.

Although it is a simple idea, JIT has widespread effects in an organization. Everything is changed, from the way that goods are ordered to the role of people working on the shop floor. This is not done in one step but needs continuous improvement over many years.

PUSH AND PULL SYSTEMS

Just-in-time might seem a good idea in principle but it needs some way of controlling the operations. This is done using a distinctive 'pull' of materials through the process. In a traditional process each operation has a timetable of work that must be finished in a given time. Finished items are then 'pushed' through to form a stock of work in progress in front of the next operation. This ignores what the next operations are actually doing – they might be working on something completely different, or be waiting for a different item to arrive. The result is delays and high stocks of work in progress.

Just-in-time 'pulls' work through the process. When one operation finishes work on a unit, it passes a message back to the preceding operation to say that it is ready to start work on the next unit. The preceding operation only passes materials forward when it gets this request. 'Pulling' materials through only when they are needed eliminates the stocks of work in progress and gives a smooth flow through the process.

In practice, there must be some lead time between an operation requesting material and having it arrive, so requests for materials are passed backwards into this lead time before they are actually needed. Materials are also delivered in small batches, so JIT has some stocks of work in progress, but these are as small as possible.

KANBANS

With JIT, messages are passed between operations using *kanbans*, which is the Japanese for a card, or some form of visible record. There are several ways of using *kanbans*, with the simplest method as follows.

All materials are stored and moved in standard containers. A container can only be moved when it has a *kanban* attached to it. When an operation needs more materials a *kanban* is attached to an empty container and this is taken to the preceding operation. The *kanban* is then attached to a full container, which is returned to the operation. The empty container is a signal for the preceding operation to start work on this material and it produces just enough to refill the container.

There are more complicated uses of *kanbans*, often based on a 'movement *kanban*' and a 'production *kanban*', but you can see the main features as:

■ A message is passed backwards to the preceding work station to start production, and it only makes enough to fill a container.
■ Standard containers are used which hold a specific amount. This amount is usually quite small, and is typically 10 per cent of a day's needs.
■ The size of each container is the smallest reasonable batch that can be made and there are usually only one or two full containers at any point.
■ A specific number of containers and/or *kanbans* is used. This effectively fixes the amount of work in progress.
■ The stock of work in progress can be controlled by limiting the size of containers and the number of *kanbans*.
■ Materials can only be moved in containers, and containers can only be moved when they have a *kanban* attached. This gives a rigid means of controlling the amount of materials produced and time they are moved.

Although it is simple to administer, this system makes sure that stocks of work in progress cannot accumulate.

BENEFITS OF JIT

Some of the benefits of JIT include:

■ always having the right quantities of materials arriving in time for use;
■ lower stocks of raw materials and work in progress;
■ reduced lead times;
■ shorter time needed to make a product;
■ higher productivity and equipment utilization;

- simplified planning and scheduling with less paperwork and decisions made nearer the operations;
- improved quality of materials and products;
- less scrap and waste;
- better relations with suppliers and long-term alliances and partnerships;
- better relations with customers and improved delivery of products;
- better morale and participation of the workforce;
- emphasis on solving problems in the process.

Unfortunately, some of these benefits can only be bought at a high price. Reducing set-up times, for example, can need more sophisticated equipment and give higher costs. A fast response to a demand may mean that spare capacity is needed. It is notoriously difficult to introduce JIT, and it might take many years before the process is working efficiently. Some specific problems listed by JIT users include:

- high initial investment and cost of implementation;
- long time needed to get improvements;
- reliance on perfect quality of materials from suppliers;
- problems with maintaining internal product quality;
- inability of suppliers to adapt to JIT methods;
- need for stable production;
- difficulty making a range of different products;
- reduces flexibility to deal with product changes;
- difficulty of reducing set-up times;
- lack of commitment within the organization;
- lack of cooperation and trust between employees;
- problems linking to existing information systems;
- need to change layout of facilities;
- increased stress in workforce;
- inability of some people to accept devolved responsibilities.

FURTHER READING

Cheng, T C E and Podolsky, S, *Just in Time Manufacturing* (2nd edition), Chapman & Hall, London 1996.

Hutchins, D, *Just in Time*, Gower Press, London 1989.

Schniederjans, M J, *Topics in Just in Time Management*, Allyn & Bacon, Boston 1993.

52

Project Management

DEFINITIONS

A project is a unique job that makes a one-off product. It has a distinct start and finish, and all operations must be coordinated within this time frame. Project management deals with all aspects of planning, organizing, staffing and controlling a project.

FEATURES OF A PROJECT

Chapter 36 looked at different types of processes, which we described as project, job shop, batch, mass and continuous flow. Projects come at one end of this spectrum, making individual units. This gives several distinct features, which include:

- a well-defined objective for the project, usually making a unique product;
- a series of related activities needed to make this product;
- a fixed start and finish date within which all the activities must be completed;
- a budget for the completion of the project;
- a project manager and team who work on the project.

Most organizations work with projects of some kind. Manufacturers have projects of developing new products, consultants work on client projects, agencies work on a series of advertising campaigns, and so on. In recent years many managers have realized that their work is not necessarily a continuous process, but is more like a series of projects. This has the benefit of allowing them to use some of the special methods developed for project management.

Each project is essentially unique, so there is little relevant experience. Plans are made with considerable uncertainty, and projects often go over budget and schedule. They are often large, employing many people and using many resources. Their size and impact means that there can be large numbers of stakeholders.

PHASES OF A PROJECT

Because of the risks, and the size of many projects, a lot of effort is put into project management. This occurs in two main phases: the *planning phase*, during which the project is defined, its feasibility tested, goals are set, detailed design work is done, resources are allocated, times agreed, management and work organized, and so forth; and the *execution phase* – during which materials are purchased and delivered, the work is done, finished products are handed over to customers, initial operations are tested, and so on.

Major projects are usually divided into more parts, and a common approach has the following six phases:

1. *Concept*. This describes in general terms the aims of the project and how these will be achieved. This phase does not show any details, but presents an outline of the likely costs, results, resources and time.
2. *Definition*. If the concept seems reasonable, some details are added in the definition. This gives the objectives that the project is going to achieve, describing the end results in tangible terms. The definition includes a scope that describes all the work to be done in a project.
3. *Planning*. This plans the resources to achieve the definition. These plans are based on a work-breakdown structure, which divides the whole project into smaller manageable bits. There is usually a hierarchy here, with the whole project divided into major elements, each of these elements divided into packages, each of the packages divided into smaller parts, and so on down to individual activities. Some aspects of planning are discussed below.
4. *Execution*. This is the stage where the work is actually done. It implements the plans and does all the work described.
5. *Control*. Throughout the execution stage, the project has to be monitored and controlled to make sure that the work is done according to plans. Projects have a lot of uncertainty, so plans might change quite frequently during execution.

6. *Handover*. At some point the project is finished, when all the work has been done and the end results have been achieved. The results are handed over to the customers.

STAKEHOLDERS IN PROJECTS

Many people may have an interest in a project. Together, these form the stakeholders, who include:

- *owners* – the customers for whom the project is done;
- *sponsors or champions* – who support the project and overcome problems within the owners' organization;
- *project team* – the people who do the actual work and execute the project;
- *project manager* – who controls the project team and is responsible for the work;
- *contractors/subcontractors* – outside organizations that are brought in to do parts of the work;
- *external parties* – other people who may be affected by the project.

From an operations point of view, the key figure in a project is the project manager. Their job is to bring together all the resources and make sure the project is a success. Ideally they bring a range of general management skills, have wide experience of different operations, and act as facilitators, ensuring that conditions are right for other people to do their jobs properly.

Projects usually have a matrix organization, where staff from different functions are brought together into a team for a specific project. Each person is still based within his or her original functional area, but they all have another responsibility to the project manager.

PROJECT PLANNING

The aim of project management is to complete the project successfully – giving customers the product they want, keeping within the specified time and within the budget. This needs effective project planning to:

- identify all the activities in the project, together with the order in which these activities have to be done;
- estimate the time of each activity, the total length of the project, and the time when each activity must be finished;
- find how much flexibility there is in the timing of activities, and which activities are critical to the completion time;

- estimate costs and schedule activities so that overall cost is minimized;
- allocate resources and schedule these so the project can be completed as efficiently as possible;
- identify milestones that can be used to monitor progress on the project, reacting quickly to any deviations from plans and making necessary adjustments;
- anticipate problems and take the actions needed to avoid them;
- give regular reports on progress.

The first five of these are concerned with scheduling the project and are done in the planning phase. The last three are concerned with control of the project in the execution phase.

PROJECT NETWORKS

A work-breakdown structure describes all the activities that are needed for a project. These activities are used for all the detailed planning, including project network analysis.

Project network analysis is based on critical path methods (CPM), which represent the activities of a project as a network. A project network consists of a series of arrows, representing the activities, between nodes, which represent the start and finish of activities. The nodes are called events and a network consists of alternating activities and events, as illustrated in Figure 52.1.

This kind of network is an 'activity on arrow network', but there is an alternative format with 'activity on node'. The choice between the two is largely a matter of personal preference.

There is a wide range of software for drawing networks. This usually starts with a dependence table, which shows the relationships between

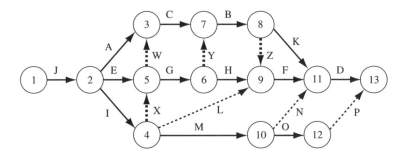

Figure 52.1 *A project network*

activities. In particular, it lists for each activity, the other activities that must be finished before this activity can start. Software will then analyse this table and draw a network in any desired format.

Once the network is drawn, the software can do a series of analyses for the timing of activities and use of resources. These are typically shown as a series of Gantt charts and bar charts. An important part of this analysis finds the critical activities that form a path through the network and fix the project duration. If any of these critical activities is delayed or extended, the whole project is delayed. Delays in the other, non-critical activities are less important and may not affect the duration of the project.

RESOURCE PLANNING

The initial timing of a project is found by CPM, which then finds the resources needed to support the timetable. Often the initial results are unacceptable, and the timing of the project and resource use are adjusted. There are three main reasons for this:

- the initial schedule gives unacceptable use of resources, and the timings are adjusted to increase utilization;
- the timing of the project is unacceptable – perhaps taking more time than the organization has available;
- during execution an activity might take a different time from that originally planned.

Whatever the reason, project schedules need adjusting and this means changing the resource schedules. Another consideration is that the duration of a project is set by the critical activities. A reduction in the project duration can only come by reducing the length of the critical activities, and this inevitably needs more resources and therefore means higher costs.

The total cost of a project is made up of direct costs such as labour and materials, indirect costs such as management and financing, and penalty costs if the project is not finished by a specified date.

Total cost = direct costs + indirect costs + penalty costs

All of these are affected by the duration of the project, so a balance is always needed between cost and duration.

FURTHER READING

Lockyer, K G and Gordon, J, *Project Management and Project Network Techniques* (6th edition), Pitman, London 1996.

Meredith, J R and Mantel, S J, *Project Management* (3rd edition), John Wiley, New York 1995.

53

Maintenance and Replacement

DEFINITION

The performance of most things deteriorates over time. Routine or planned maintenance designs schedules of work that return the performance of equipment to an acceptable level and reduce the chance of breakdowns. Eventually, the cost of this maintenance rises to the point where it is better to replace the equipment rather than continuing maintaining it.

PLANNED MAINTENANCE

The performance of equipment often follows a 'bathtub curve', which plots the probability that equipment fails against its age, as shown in Figure 53.1. There are three main areas in this graph:

- During an initial running-in period, any faults in the equipment are found, people learn how to use it, and there are general teething problems.
- As the teething problems decline, the equipment has a period of stability, which lasts through its normal working life.
- At some point, the equipment begins to wear out, and problems become more frequent as it reaches the end of its life.

Some aspects of this traditional view are becoming less acceptable, and most organizations would not be happy with new equipment that did not

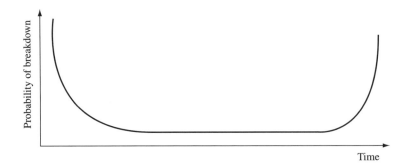

Figure 53.1 *'Bathtub curve' showing the probability of breakdown with age*

work perfectly from the start. At the other end of equipment life, however, there is less that can be done to alleviate the effects of ageing. As equipment gets older it breaks down more often, develops more faults, gives lower quality, slows down and generally wears out.

Sometimes this change is slow – like the fuel consumption of a car, which rises over a period of years. Sometimes the change is very fast, like a bolt that suddenly breaks. The only way of reducing the effects of ageing is to use planned or preventive maintenance.

PREVENTIVE MAINTENANCE

With preventive maintenance, equipment is inspected and vulnerable parts are replaced after a certain period of use. A car, for example, has a regular service to replace filters, oil, plugs and other vulnerable parts. By replacing parts that are worn, or are most likely to wear, the equipment is restored to give continuing, satisfactory performance. There are four approaches to the replacement of these vulnerable parts:

- keep a check on parts, look for specific signs of wear, and replace them when these signs first appear;
- replace parts after a specified period of working;
- replace parts when some measure of performance falls below an acceptable level;
- replace parts when they actually fail.

The first three of these, and particularly the second, have elements of planned maintenance, which have advantages over the alternative of waiting for equipment to fail and then doing the necessary repairs. These advantages include:

- improved overall performance of equipment;
- increased reliability and fewer disruptions;
- maintenance is done at convenient times such as evenings, weekends or holidays;
- equipment has a longer working life;
- lower operating costs;
- higher resale value of equipment;
- safer operations.

FREQUENCY OF MAINTENANCE

An obvious question about routine maintenance asks how often it should be done.

If the maintenance is done too frequently, the equipment will run efficiently but the maintenance costs will be too high.

If it is not done often enough, the maintenance costs will be low but the equipment will still break down.

The best answer comes from an analysis of maintenance and expected failure costs. Plotting these against the frequency of maintenance gives a U-shaped curve that has a minimum (as shown in Figure 53.2). By keeping histories of maintenance – and guidelines from suppliers – it is possible to identify this best time between maintenance periods.

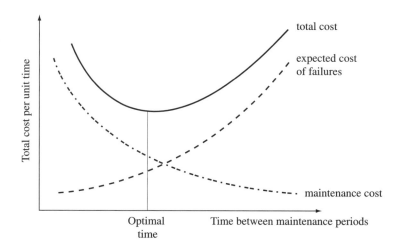

Figure 53.2 *Finding the best time between maintenance periods*

RELIABILITY OF EQUIPMENT

Preventive maintenance can ensure that the performance of equipment remains at a satisfactory level, and extend its useful life. The basic performance of equipment is largely set by its initial design, however. If equipment is poorly designed, no amount of maintenance will make it work better.

The reliability of a piece of equipment is the probability that it continues to work normally throughout a specified period. If a stage light has a reliability of 95 per cent, there is a probability of 0.95 that it will continue to work normally during a performance. The overall reliability of equipment depends on both the reliability of each component and the way these components are arranged. If a single component has a known reliability, putting two identical components in parallel increases the overall reliability. The assumption is that the second component will only start to work when the first one fails. Adding more components in parallel increases reliability, as the equipment will only fail when all components fail. This is the basis of redundancy, where back-up systems are kept to start working whenever there is a breakdown in the main system. (See Figure 53.3.)

On the other hand, if components are added in series, the reliability of the equipment is reduced. This is because equipment with components in series only works if all separate components are working. (See Figure 53.4.)

REPLACEMENT OF EQUIPMENT

Routine maintenance extends the working life of equipment, but there comes a point when maintenance and repairs become too expensive and it

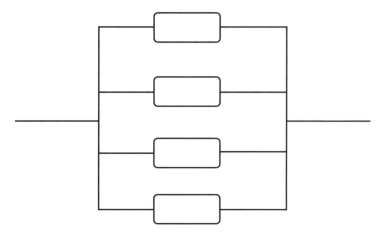

Figure 53.3 *Components in parallel increase reliability*

Figure 53.4 *Components in series reduce reliability*

is cheaper to buy replacements. There are two approaches for the timing of replacements. In the first, equipment is replaced when its performance falls so low that it is no longer acceptable – the output may be too low, quality too poor, breakdowns too frequent, and so on. The drawback with this approach is that its response is too late: it comes when the equipment is already unsatisfactory. The second approach shows a better alternative, which analyses costs and keeps the equipment working for the time that minimizes total costs. This leads to a policy of timed replacement, perhaps replacing delivery vans every five years.

One drawback with this planned replacement is that all equipment is routinely replaced when it appears to be working well. It is sometimes difficult to persuade people that this really is better than waiting until the equipment has obviously declined.

The usual way of finding the best age for planned replacement is based on minimal annual costs. Organizations keep records of all costs, and can forecast the expected costs of keeping equipment working for a given lifetime.

Total operating costs = running + maintenance cost + cost of breakdown + capital costs.

Dividing this cost by the life gives an expected annual cost. Then repeating the calculation for different lengths of life gives a curve with a minimum, which identifies the best age of replacement. In practice, these calculations can be done very quickly using spreadsheets.

FURTHER READING

Moubray, J, *Reliability-centred Maintenance*, Butterworth-Heinemann, London 1991.
Nakajima, S, *Total Productive Maintenance*, Productivity Press, New York 1988.

54

Supply-chain Management

DEFINITION

The supply chain consists of all the organizations and operations along which products move from the original suppliers of materials through to the final customers. Supply-chain management (SCM) is responsible for all the physical movement through this chain.

THE SUPPLY CHAIN

The final product of one organization is the raw material of another, so materials are moved through a series of organizations and operations between original suppliers and final customers. These operations form the supply chain, as illustrated in Figure 54.1 for the supply of paper.

Logistics or supply-chain management is responsible for making sure materials are delivered to the place they are needed at the right time. It looks at three types of movement:

- *Movement of raw materials from supplies into the organization* – including purchasing, inward transport, receiving, storage and retrieval of goods.
- *Movement of work-in-progress within the organization* – including handling, movement and storage of goods during operations.
- *Movement of finished goods from the organization out to customers* – including packaging, storage and retrieval from warehouses, shipping and distribution to customers.

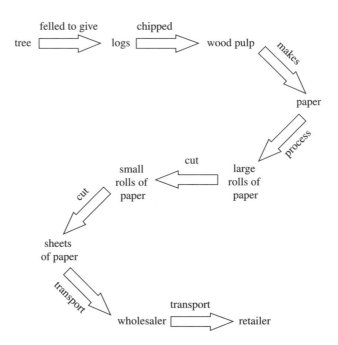

Figure 54.1 *Example of a supply chain*

Sometimes it is convenient to consider the broad range of logistics or SCM in two parts. Then materials management is responsible for the movement of materials into and within the organization. Physical distribution management is responsible for the movement of finished goods out to customers. Whatever we call the activities, SCM includes a range of related functions that include:

- *procurement or purchasing,* which is responsible for buying materials from suppliers (see Chapter 55);
- *traffic and transport,* which moves materials from suppliers to the organization's receiving area;
- *receiving,* which unloads vehicles bringing in materials, inspects the goods for any damage, and checks that the goods delivered match the orders;
- *warehousing or stores,* which stores materials until they are needed;
- *inventory control,* which deals with the replenishment of stocks and controls inventory levels (see Chapter 56);
- *materials handling,* which moves materials as they are needed by operations;
- *shipping,* which takes finished products, checks them and loads them onto vehicles for delivery to customers;
- *distribution,* which delivers finished products to customers;
- *location,* which decides how many warehouses and related facilities should be built, and where they should be (see Chapter 57);
- *communication,* which keeps records for all the logistics system.

AIMS OF SUPPLY-CHAIN MANAGEMENT

Coordinating all movement along the supply chain can be very complicated for even a simple product. The aim of SCM is to provide an integrated function for moving all materials into, through, and out of an organization, while making the best use of available resources, and guaranteeing customer service. This aim is summarized as supplying 'the right materials, to the right place, at the right time, from the right source, with the right quality, at the right price'. The general aim can be expanded to give more detailed objectives, which include:

- designing the best system structure for moving goods through the organization;
- finding the best sizes, locations and type of facilities for the supply chain;
- giving uninterrupted flows of materials into the organization;
- finding and developing reliable suppliers;
- making purchases at lowest long-term cost;
- having efficient movement of work in progress;
- giving efficient and reliable movements of finished goods out to customers;
- giving low costs for holding stocks and high stock turnover;
- maintaining high quality;
- keeping good relations with suppliers and customers;
- designing the most appropriate transport operations;
- having low administration costs and accurate records.

IMPORTANCE OF SUPPLY-CHAIN MANAGEMENT

All organizations rely on the movement of materials. Supply-chain management is important to an organization because such movement:

- is essential;
- is expensive;
- directly affects profitability;
- provides a link between suppliers and customers;
- influences lead time, service levels and so forth;
- gives public exposure with trucks and so forth;
- can be risky, with safety considerations;
- determines the size and location of facilities;
- may prohibit some operations such as moving excessive loads;
- can encourage development of other organizations.

PLANNING FOR SCM

Generally, planning for the supply chain takes place after planning production. Many people say that this is not the best way of organizing logistics, but it is still the most common. Supply-chain management plans can then be based on planned production. In particular, production schedules are analysed to find:

- details of purchases from outside suppliers;
- total volumes, weights and timing of orders brought from suppliers;
- amount of receiving and checking of materials on arrival;
- types and amounts of materials to be moved into storage;
- total amounts of raw materials stored, locations, costs and so forth;
- the mix of materials stored, including space, special conditions, ease of access and so forth;
- arrangements for moving materials to operations and storing until used;
- quantities and weights delivered and stored in finished goods warehouses;
- arrangements for receiving, picking and assembling finished goods for customer orders;
- location of customers and their special conditions for packaging, delivery and so forth;
- timing, size and contents of deliveries from warehouses to customers.

When details of these analyses are complete for every process, the organization can look at the implications in terms of:

- the amount of space needed to store the materials at points on its journey into, through and out of the organization;
- best location and size of warehouses and depots;
- type and amount of equipment needed to handle and transport the materials;
- systems and policies for controlling the stocks within warehouses;
- systems and policies for routing and transporting materials between operations;
- numbers and skills of people needed to run the supply chain.

These decisions will usually lead to a logistics system with the structure shown in Figure 54.2. This system includes separate production, wholesalers and retailers, because many operations are done best in locations that are far away from either customers or suppliers. Intermediaries give a break between production and customers and have benefits that include:

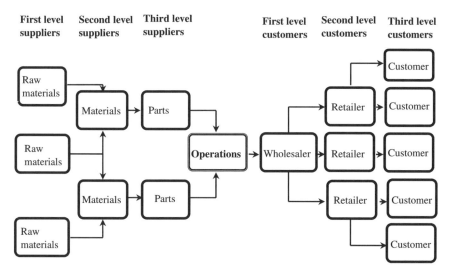

Figure 54.2 *Structure in supply-chain management*

- production can achieve economies of scale by concentrating operations in central locations;
- wholesalers keep stocks from many suppliers, allowing retailers a range of goods;
- wholesalers are near to retailers and have short lead times;
- production facilities do not need to keep large stocks of finished goods;
- retailers can carry less stock as wholesalers offer reliable delivery times;
- wholesalers can place large orders and reduce unit prices;
- distribution costs are reduced by moving large quantities from producers to wholesalers, rather than moving small quantities directly to retailers or customers.

FURTHER READING

Coyle, J J, Bardi, E J and Langley, C J, *The Management of Business Logistics* (7th edition), West Publishing, Minneapolis 1996.
Waters, D (editor), *Global Logistics and Distribution Planning*, Kogan Page, London 1999.

55

Procurement

DEFINITION

Procurement buys the materials needed by an organization. It is responsible for all the activities involved in acquiring materials and moving them from suppliers into the organization.

AIMS OF PROCUREMENT

Many organizations use the terms 'purchasing' and 'procurement' to mean the same thing. Generally, though, purchasing refers to the actual buying of materials, whereas procurement has a broader meaning and can include purchasing, contracting, expediting, materials handling, transport, warehousing and receiving goods from suppliers. The purpose of procurement is to make sure that materials needed to support operations arrive from suppliers at the time they are needed. In more detail, procurement aims to:

- find reliable suppliers, work closely with them and develop good relations;
- buy all the materials that are needed for operations;
- make sure these materials have reliably high quality;
- negotiate good prices from suppliers;
- keep inventory levels low, by buying standard materials, and so forth;
- expedite deliveries when necessary;

- work closely with user department, understand their needs, and get the materials they need at the right times;
- keep informed about price increases, scarcities and so forth.

PURCHASE CYCLE

We can look in more detail at the work done in procurement by considering a typical purchase cycle. This has many variations, but usually includes the following steps:

In the user department:

- the person needing the materials makes an initial request;
- this request is checked against budgets;
- a purchase request is prepared and sent to procurement.

Then procurement:

- receives and analyses the purchase request;
- verifies and checks its details;
- checks current stocks, alternative products and so forth;
- makes a shortlist of possible suppliers, from regular suppliers and/or those who are known to be reliable;
- sends a request for quotations to this shortlist.

Then the supplier:

- examines the request for quotations;
- sees how it could best satisfy the order;
- sends an offer back to the organization, with prices, conditions and so on.

Then procurement:

- clears up any points with potential suppliers;
- chooses the best supplier, based on their product, delivery, price and so forth;
- discusses and finalizes details with the supplier;
- issues a purchase order.

Then the supplier:

- receives and processes the purchase order;
- makes or assembles the order;
- ships the order and sends an invoice.

Then procurement:

- does any follow-up to make sure the materials are delivered;
- expedites late deliveries;
- receives, inspects and accepts the items;
- updates inventory records, notifies the purchasing department;
- approves the supplier's invoice for payment.

Doing all the steps in this cycle can take a lot of effort, so short cuts are usually taken when:

- the item is of low value;
- there is only one possible supplier;
- there is already a successful arrangement with a supplier;
- there is not enough time for extended negotiations;
- the organization has a policy of internal supply.

The whole supply-chain management is important for a successful organization, and this is particularly true of procurement. Many people may not see it as a particularly glamorous job, but it is certainly essential for the smooth running of operations. All materials are purchased somewhere and mistakes in procurement can lead to poor quality, interrupted operations, late deliveries, wrong quantities, high costs and poor customer service. A typical organization spends 60 per cent of its income on purchases, so this is also an area where good management can bring substantial savings. With a profit margin of 10 per cent, a 1 per cent reduction in the cost of purchased goods can increase profits by 6 per cent.

TRENDS IN PROCUREMENT

The role of procurement has changed significantly in recent years. It used to be little more than a clerical job, buying materials as they were requested. Now it is a profession, and managers expect purchasers to take an active part in planning. There are several reasons for this change. One is a consequence of developments like TQM, which have emphasized the importance of procurement, and recognized that there is more to purchasing than getting the lowest price. In fact, TQM specifically advises against giving business on the basis of cost alone.

Traditionally, purchasing departments used competitive bidding to choose their suppliers, and then awarded contracts for the relatively short term. Organizations thought that this gave them good prices because suppliers would compete fiercely to get business. More recently, procurement has moved towards single-sourcing, where organizations give long-term contracts for each item to a single supplier. This creates a relationship with suppliers, who are prepared to pay attention to orders, guarantee performance and become involved in improvements to product design. This can be useful for developments such as value analysis, which is a way of maintaining product quality and performance, while reducing material cost. In effect, value analysis finds substitute materials that are lower in price but equally as good as the original.

Another reason for the changing view of procurement is the recognition that there is an increasing number of ways of purchasing. Many organizations now organize their sales around the internet, or with linked systems in the supply chain giving 'lean operations'. These opportunities rely on skilled people to make the best procurement decisions.

FURTHER READING

Bailey, P, Farmer, D, Jessop, D and Jones, D, *Purchasing Principles* (7th edition), Pitman, London 1994.

Chadwick, T and Rajagopal, S, *Strategic Supply Management*, Butterworth-Heinemann, London 1995.

56

Inventory Control

DEFINITION

Stocks are supplies of goods and materials that are held by an organization. They are formed whenever the organization's inputs or outputs are not used at the time they become available. An inventory is actually a list of items held in stock, but this is often used in the same general sense as 'stock'.

REASONS FOR HOLDING STOCKS

All organizations hold stocks of some kind. The main reason for doing this is to give a buffer between variable and uncertain supply and demand. They allow operations to continue smoothly and avoid disruptions. Other reasons for holding stocks include:

- to act as a buffer between different operations;
- to allow for demands that are larger than expected, or at unexpected times;
- to allow for deliveries that are delayed or too small;
- to take advantage of price discounts on large orders;
- to buy items when the price is low and expected to rise;
- to buy items that are going out of production or are difficult to find;
- to make full loads and reduce transport costs;
- to give cover for emergencies.

These stocks can be classified as:

- Raw materials – the materials, parts and components that have been delivered to an organization but are not yet being used.
- Work-in-progress – materials that have started but not yet finished their journey through the process.
- Finished goods – goods that have finished the process and are waiting to be shipped out to customers.
- Spare parts – for machinery, equipment and so forth.
- Consumables – such as oil, fuel, paper and so forth.

COSTS OF CARRYING STOCK

The traditional approach to stock control uses an independent demand system (see Chapter 49) with forecasts giving the expected demand for an item. Then inventory control is used to design policies which minimize the costs of inventories. These costs come from four main sources:

- Unit cost – the cost of acquiring one unit of the item. It may be fairly easy to find by looking at quotations or recent invoices from suppliers, but it is more difficult when there are several suppliers offering slightly different products or different purchase conditions. If a company makes the item itself, it may be difficult to give a reliable production cost or set a transfer price.
- Reorder cost – the cost of placing a repeat order for an item. It might include the cost of drawing up an order, correspondence and telephone costs, receiving, checking, supervision, use of equipment and follow-up. Sometimes costs such as quality control, transport, sorting and movement of received goods are included in the reorder cost.
- Holding cost – the cost of holding one unit of an item in stock for a unit period of time. This money is either borrowed – in which case interest is paid – or it is cash that the organization could put to other use – in which case there are opportunity costs. Other holding costs are due to storage space, loss, handling, administration and insurance. Typical annual holding costs are around 25 per cent of the value held a year.
- Shortage cost – the cost that occurs when an item is needed but it cannot be supplied from stock. In the simplest case a retailer may lose direct profit from a sale, but the effects of shortages are usually much more widespread and include lost goodwill, loss of reputation and loss of potential future sales. Shortages of raw materials for a production process can cause disruption and force rescheduling of production, retiming of maintenance periods and laying-off of employees. These costs are inevitably difficult to find but they can be very high.

APPROACHES TO INVENTORY CONTROL

An important point about inventory costs is that some rise with the amount of stock held, and others fall. The holding cost is higher when there is more stock, but the shortage cost will be lower. Inventory control must balance these competing costs and suggest policies that give the lowest overall costs. To do this it must answer three basic questions:

- What items should be stocked? No item, however cheap, should be stocked without considering the costs and benefits.
- When should an order be placed? This depends on the inventory control system used, type of demand (high or low, steady or erratic, known exactly or estimated), value of the item, lead time between placing an order and receiving it into stock, supplier reliability, and a number of other factors.
- How much should be ordered? If large, infrequent orders are placed, the average stock level is high but the costs of placing and administering orders is low. If small, frequent orders are placed, the average stock level is low but the costs of placing and administering orders is high.

The first of these questions is largely a matter of management policy, but we can calculate the best answers to the last two questions. One approach finds an economic order quantity (EOQ), which is the order size that minimizes the overall costs for a simple inventory system. In particular:

$$EOQ = \sqrt{\frac{2 \times \text{reorder cost} \times \text{demand}}{\text{holding cost}}}$$

This describes the best order size in many circumstances, but it does not say when an order should be placed. The answer to this comes from the reorder level. (See Figure 56.1.) Suppose there is a constant lead time between placing an order and getting the goods delivered. To get a delivery just as stock is running out, we have to place an order this lead time earlier. The easiest way of finding this point is to monitor current stock and place an order when there is just enough left to last the lead time. With constant demand, an order is placed when the stock level falls to:

$$\text{Reorder level} = \frac{\text{lead time}}{\text{demand}}$$

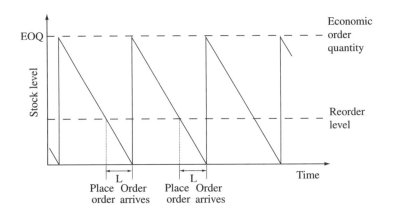

Figure 56.1 *Order quantity and time*

Uncertain demand and safety stock

The EOQ works well provided there is not a lot of variation in demand. In practice, demand can vary widely and have a lot of uncertainty. There are several ways of dealing with this, and the most common uses a safety stock. Although shortage costs are difficult to find, they are usually a lot higher than holding costs, so organizations are willing to hold additional stocks, above their expected needs, to add a margin of safety. These safety stocks are available if the normal working stock runs out. The safety stock has no effect on the reorder quantity, but the reorder level now becomes:

Reorder level = lead time demand + safety stock

The larger the safety stock, the greater the cushion against unexpectedly high demand, and the greater the customer service. The amount of safety stock is largely a matter for management opinion, and they choose an appropriate service level based on their experience, objectives and knowledge of customer expectations. This service level will typically be around 95 per cent, which means that 95 per cent of orders are met from stock – and 5 per cent of orders cannot be met from stock. If demand varies widely, higher service levels need a much larger investment in safety stock.

PERIODIC REVIEW SYSTEM

The EOQ uses a fixed-order quantity, but there is an alternative periodic review system that orders varying amounts at regular intervals. This works by raising the stock level to a specified value, in the way that super-market shelves are refilled to a specified level every evening to replace sales during the day. The operating cost of this system is generally lower and it is better suited to high, regular demand of low-value items. (See Figure 56.2.)

With this approach, the order interval can be any convenient period, but it needs a target stock level. The system works by looking at the amount of stock on hand at the end of a period and ordering the amount that brings this up to the target stock level.

Order quantity = target stock level – stock on hand

ABC ANALYSIS OF INVENTORIES

There is always some effort involved with inventory control, and for some items, especially very cheap ones, this effort is not worthwhile. At the other end of the scale are very expensive items that need special care above the routine calculations. An ABC analysis puts items into categories that show the amount of effort worth spending on inventory control. This is based on a Pareto analysis or the 'rule of 80/20', which suggests that 20 per cent of inventory items need 80 per cent of the attention, while the remaining 80 per cent of items need only 20 per cent of the attention. ABC analyses define:

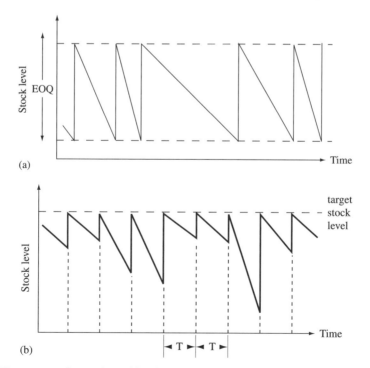

Figure 56.2 *Comparison of fixed-order quantity and fixed-order time systems*

- A items as expensive and needing special care;
- B items as ordinary ones needing standard care;
- C items as cheap and needing little care.

Typically an organization might use an automated system to deal with all B items. The computer system might make some suggestions for A items, but managers make final decisions after reviewing all the circumstances. Some C items might be included in the automatic system, but the very cheap ones may be left out and dealt with using ad hoc procedures.

FURTHER READING

Tersine, R J, *Principles of Inventory and Materials Management* (3rd edition), Elsevier, New York 1987.
Waters, D, *Inventory Control and Management*, John Wiley, Chichester 1992.

57

Facility Location

DEFINITION

Facility location finds the best possible geographical location for an organization's operations.

WHEN ARE LOCATION DECISIONS NEEDED?

There are many reasons for an organization to find a new location for its facilities. These include:

- the end of a lease on their existing premises;
- desire to expand into new geographical areas;
- changes in the location of customers or suppliers;
- significant changes in operations – such as an electricity company changing from coal generators to gas;
- upgrading of facilities – perhaps introducing new technology;
- changes to the logistics system – such as changing from rail transport to road;
- changes in the transport network – such as a new bridge or the Channel Tunnel.

Location decisions have a long-term impact on the performance of an organization, and there are many examples of organizations that have located in the wrong place and suffered heavily as a result. Location decisions are also very complicated, and need to take into account a lot of factors, including operating costs, wage rates, taxes, international exchange rates, competition, current locations, exchange regulations, availability of grants, reliability of supplies, and a whole range of other factors. Many of these can be measured in some way, but the organization must also consider less tangible factors, including the attitude of employees, political situation, international relations, hidden costs, the legal system, future developments of the economy and so on.

Alternatives to locating new facilities

New facilities are inevitably expensive and many organizations prefer to look for alternatives. For example, a company selling its goods in a new market can do this in five different ways, listed below in order of increasing investment:

- *Licensing/franchising* – local operators make and supply the company's products in return for a share of the profits.
- *Exporting* – the company makes the product in its existing facilities and sells it to a distributor operating in the new market.
- *Local warehousing and sales* – the company makes the product in its existing facilities, but sets up its own warehouses and sales force to handle distribution in the new market.
- *Local assembly/finishing* – the company makes most of the product in its existing facilities, but opens limited facilities in the new market to finish or assemble the final product.
- *Full local production* – the company opens complete facilities in the new market.

The choice between these depends on many factors, such as the capital available, the risk that the organization will accept, its target return on investment, existing operations, the timescale, local knowledge, transport costs, tariffs, trade restrictions and available workers. The advantages of local facilities include greater control over products, higher profits, avoidance of import tariffs and quotas, easier transportation, reduced costs and closer links with local customers. These must be balanced against the more complex and uncertain operations.

SELECTING THE GEOGRAPHICAL REGION

When an organization decides that it must look for a new location it has a hierarchy of decisions. These start with a wide view, looking at the attractions of different countries or geographical regions. Then more local views consider alternative areas within this region; then alternative towns and cities within this area are compared; finally alternative sites within the preferred town are considered.

At the top of this hierarchy, an organization may take a decision about the country of operation. Many organizations open facilities in countries not to be near their customers but to take advantage of lower costs. Low wage rates in developing countries have encouraged manufacturers to open factories in the Far East, South America and Eastern Europe. Such arrangements can have high transport costs, but reduced operating costs can more than compensate for this.

Low wage rates do not automatically mean low costs. In many parts of the world low wage rates are accompanied by very low productivity. Perhaps more importantly, manufacturing processes have changed so that labour costs often form a very small part of overall costs.

The location of sites in international markets depends on a number of factors. Some of these are commercial, but experience suggests three other factors are important:

- Culture. It is easier to expand into an area that has a similar language, culture, laws and costs, than to expand into a completely foreign area.
- Organization. There are basically two ways to organize international operations: an international organization maintains its headquarters in the 'home' country and runs its worldwide activities from there; or a multinational organization opens subsidiary headquarters around the world, with each being largely independent.
- Operations. And whether it is better to use the same operations around the world or to adapt to the local environment.

COSTING ALTERNATIVE LOCATIONS

Once a decision has been made about the country or geographical region, more detailed decisions are needed about areas, towns, cities and individual sites. There are two distinct approaches to finding the best site. The *feasible set approach* looks at a small number of feasible sites and finds which of these is the best. The *infinite set approach* uses geometric arguments to show where the best site would be if there were no restrictions on site availability.

The feasible set approach is generally easier, and more realistic. An obvious way of comparing locations is to look at the total costs of each. In principle it is possible to do a full costing, but there are only a certain number of costs that will vary between locations – such as the transport costs and certain operating costs.

Sites near to suppliers will have low costs for inward transport from suppliers, but high costs of outward transport to customers. On the other hand, sites near to customers will have low costs for outward transport, but high costs for inward transport. Some operating costs depend on factors such as wage rates, local taxes, reliability of local suppliers and weather conditions.

We can combine these costs – together with any other relevant ones – and get a direct comparison of sites.

$$\text{Cost of location} = \text{relevant operating cost} + \text{inward transport cost} + \text{outward transport cost}$$

An obvious problem with this approach is that the costs are forecast and not known with certainty in advance. Even reliable costs are likely to change and the analysis will become outdated. This means that the calculated costs are useful for comparisons, but they are not necessarily accurate projections. The weaknesses of costing models include:

- it is difficult to get accurate forecasts of costs;
- data depends on accounting conventions;
- costs vary over time and the analyses become dated;
- customer locations and exact demands may not be known in advance;
- suppliers may move to new locations;
- there are many factors that cannot be costed.

Because of these weaknesses, scoring models are often used to get another viewpoint.

SCORING MODELS

Many important factors in location decisions are intangible. The following factors may be difficult to measure, but they are very important for location decisions.

For the country and region

- availability and quality of workforce;
- climate;
- local and national government policies;
- availability of development grants;
- attractiveness of locations;
- quality of life – including health, education, welfare and culture;
- reliability of local suppliers;
- infrastructure – particularly transport and communications;
- economic stability.

For the city or location

- nearness to customers and suppliers;
- location of competitors;
- potential for expansion;
- local restrictions on operations;
- community feelings.

With location decisions there are some distinct differences between manufacturers and services. Manufacturers generally try to get economies of scale by building large facilities near their raw materials. They will typically look for a site where costs are low, there is a skilled workforce and suppliers are nearby. On the other hand, services must be near to their customers. They cannot keep stocks of their services, so they need small local facilities that meet demand as soon as it arises. Services are more likely to consider factors such as:

- population density;
- socio-economic characteristics of the nearby population;
- location of competitors and other services;
- location of retail shops and other attractions;
- convenience for passing traffic and public transport;
- ease of access and convenient parking;
- visibility of site.

When an organization has listed the most important factors for its location decision, it must find some way of comparing the alternative sites. The most common approach here uses scoring models to:

- decide the relevant factors in a decision;
- give each factor a maximum possible score that shows its importance;
- consider each location in turn and give an actual score for each factor;
- add the total score for each location and find the highest;
- discuss the result and make a final decision.

GEOMETRIC MODELS

Geometric models use an infinite set approach to see where the best location would be in principle. These models are based on the geographic layout of customers and suppliers, and assume that facilities should be somewhere near the centre of potential demands and supplies. A common approach finds the centre of gravity of demand.

These approaches have the problem that the calculated location may not be near any facilities, or near any point where it is feasible to operate. But they can be used as a starting point to look for actual sites. An organization might, for example, find the centre of gravity of demand to identify an area where it would be useful to work, and then look for, and compare, actual sites nearby.

FURTHER READING

Johnson, J C and Wood, D F, *Contemporary Logistics*, Macmillan, New York 1990.

Love, R E, Morris, J G and Weslovsky, G O, *Location: Models and methods*, North-Holland, New York 1988.

Part 3

Financial Management

58

Financial Management: An Overview

DEFINITION

Financial management is concerned with all aspects of how a business deals with its financial resources in order to maximize profit over the long term.

COMPONENTS OF FINANCIAL MANAGEMENT

Financial management involves the following activities:

- *Financial planning*, which predicts the performance of the business in financial terms to give an overall measure of how it is performing and to provide a basis for financial decision making and for raising finance.
- *Financial accounting*, which clarifies, records and interprets in monetary terms transactions and events of a financial nature. Financial accounting will involve maintaining records of transactions (book-keeping), preparing balance sheets and profit-and-loss accounts. The accounts prepared by the firm will be audited to ensure that they present a 'true and fair view' of its financial performance and position. But there is scope within the law and accounting rules for company accountants to indulge in 'creative accounting' to improve the picture the accounts present to the outside world (the City and investors).

- *Financial analysis*, which analyses the performance of the business in terms of variance analysis, cost–volume–profit analysis, sales mix analysis, risk analysis, cost–benefit analysis and cost-effectiveness analysis.
- *Management accounting*, which accounts for and analyses costs, provides the basis for allocation of costs to products or processes, prepares and controls financial budgets and deals specifically with overhead and responsibility accounting. Management accounting provides the data for financial analysis and for capital appraisal and budgeting.
- *Capital appraisal and budgeting*, which selects and plans capital investments based on the returns likely to be obtained from those investments. The capital appraisal techniques comprise accounting rate of return, payback and discounted cash flow.

FURTHER READING

Mott, G, *Accounting for Non-Accountants* (5th edition), Kogan Page, London 1999.

59

Financial Planning

DEFINITION

Financial planning is the process of predicting the performance of a business to give an overall measure of how well it is doing, and to provide the basis for decision making about future requirements for finance and the rates of growth and profitability required to meet the expectations of shareholders and the City.

FINANCIAL PLANNING ACTIVITIES

The main financial planning activities are as follows:

- *Profit forecasting* – predicting future levels of turnover, cost of sales and overheads.
- *Cash-flow forecasting* – predicting the flows of cash into and out of the business and net cash balances in the bank.
- *Tax planning* – forecasting the incidence of corporation tax, capital gains tax, VAT (the extent to which the business is a net payer or a net receiver) and National Insurance payments.
- *Long-range budgeting* – preparing long-range capital and financial budgets indicating what funds will be required in the future.
- *Raising finance* – deciding, on the basis of financial projections and budgets, the amount of capital and liquid funds required in the future and taking whatever steps are required to raise finance and secure cash flow.

- *Profit and dividend planning* – planning to achieve a rate of profit and dividend payment to achieve earnings per share figures and price/earning ratios which will satisfy the City and existing investors.
- *Strategic planning* – generally providing the basis and rationale for the strategic plans for the business in terms of profit, growth, acquisitions, diversifications, overseas investments and portfolio planning.

60

Financial Accounting

DEFINITION

Financial accounting records the revenue received and the expenditure incurred by a company so that its overall performance over a period of time and its financial position at a point in time can be ascertained.

The financial accounting system classifies, records and interprets in monetary terms transactions and events of a financial character.

PURPOSE

The purposes of financial accounting are to meet:

1. the external requirements of shareholders, potential investors, financial analysts, creditors, trade unions, the Registrar of Companies (in the UK) and HM Revenue & Customs; and
2. the internal requirements of the management of the company who require information, not only for control purposes but also as a guide to decision making.

FORMAT OF FINANCIAL ACCOUNTS

Financial accounting systems produce the following financial statements:

1. *The balance sheet*, which is a statement on the last day of the accounting period of the company's assets and liabilities and the share capital and reserves or shareholders' investment in the company.

2. *The manufacturing and trading accounts*, which, for a period of accounts, show the cost of goods manufactured, the cost of goods sold, sales revenue and gross profit (the difference between the sales revenue and the cost of goods sold).

3. *The profit-and-loss account*, which takes the *gross profit* from the trading account and deducts marketing, distribution and administrative costs and expenditure on research and development to determine the company's *trading or operating profit*, for the period. To this, investment income is added and interest payable deducted to give *profit before taxation*, from which corporation tax is deducted to give the *net profit or loss* for the period. (See Chapter 62.)

4. *The profit-and-loss appropriation account*, which indicates the profit available for appropriation to shareholders in the form of dividends, for transfer to reserves and for carrying forward to the next account. The profit available for appropriation is represented by the balance brought forward from the previous account, plus or minus the net profit or loss for the period.

5. *Cash-flow statements*, which identify the movements in assets, liabilities and capital which have taken place during the period and the resultant effect on cash or net liquid funds. It describes the sources from which additional cash (funds) were derived and the application to which this cash was put.

6. *The statement of total recognized gains and losses*, which is produced if there are any gains or losses other than the profit or loss for the year shown in the *profit-and-loss account*. Such gains or losses were previously 'hidden' because they were just accounted for as movements on reserves, for example a revaluation surplus on an asset. The statement's long name has resulted in accountants abbreviating it (albeit normally in an unwritten fashion) to 'strgl', which is pronounced 'struggle'.

Published accounts do not necessarily include all the above statements. Manufacturing and trading accounts are frequently produced only for the management of the company. Published accounts may also include other information of a financial nature, such as a five-year summary, narrative commentary on operating and financial matters and disclosures about the corporate governance of the company. Some companies produce financial statements specifically for their employees; these often include summarized information in pictorial form and may include a *value-added statement* to show how much wealth the company has created. Chapter 63 gives further information on *value-added statements*.

RELATIONSHIP BETWEEN THE BALANCE SHEET AND THE PROFIT-AND-LOSS ACCOUNT

The balance sheet and the profit-and-loss account are the two key financial statements. Their relationship is illustrated in Figure 60.1.

FINANCIAL PRINCIPLES

The following accounting principles are used in financial reporting.

1. Measuring in money

Financial reports express in monetary terms certain facts relating to the assets of the enterprise, the claims against those assets and the profits or losses resulting from the use of those assets. Money is used as the common denominator and accounting therefore only deals with those facts that can be represented in monetary terms.

2. The business as a separate unit

Each business is a separate entity for accounting purposes and accounts are kept for each entity. The directors of a company carry out the important function of *stewardship*, ie they are entrusted with the finance supplied by shareholders, debenture holders, banks and creditors. Financial reports are meant to show how effectively this stewardship has been undertaken.

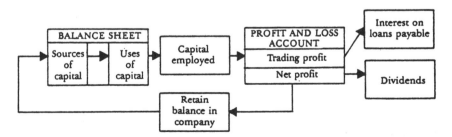

Figure 60.1 *Relationship between balance sheet and profit-and-loss account*

3. Claims equal assets

The company's assets are financed from two sources: its owners and its creditors. The claims of the owners are represented by issued share capital and retained profits. The claims of creditors are called liabilities.

All the assets of the business are claimed by someone, either owners or creditors. At the same time, the total claims against the enterprise cannot exceed what there is to be claimed. An increase in the owners' claims must always be accompanied by an equivalent increase in assets or a reduction in liabilities. This relationship is expressed in the equation:

$$\text{Owners' claims} + \text{Liabilities} = \text{Assets}$$

The claims of the owners can also be treated as a residue, equal to the difference between the sum of the assets and the total liabilities:

$$\text{Owners' claims} = \text{Assets} - \text{Liabilities}$$

4. The going concern

In accounting, the business is viewed as a going concern, one that is not going to be sold or liquidated in the near future. This implies that the existing resources of the business, such as plant and equipment, will be used in order to produce goods, and not simply sold in tomorrow's market. Therefore regular accounting reports do not usually attempt to measure what the business is currently worth to its owners at market rates, ie it is not normally the practice to value capital assets at their net realizable value (the price that could be obtained if the goods were sold on the open market less the cost of selling them).

However, because capital is invested with the expectation of the return *of* that capital as well as a return *on* that capital, investors expect their capital to be maintained, which happens when revenues are at least equal to all costs and expenses. There are two capital maintenance concepts: *financial capital maintenance* (maintain original cash investment) and *physical capital maintenance* (maintain physical operating capability) – see Chapter 66. These raise questions about the use of historical costs as the normal basis of financial reports, which are mentioned briefly below.

5. Measuring actual cost

In the standard balance sheet, the resources of the company are shown at their historical cost (the actual cost at the time of acquisition) less, where appropriate, depreciation, rather than their current or replacement value. The balance sheet does not therefore show the current value of the business. No regular allowance is made for any changes in the values of assets as a result of inflation, although from time to time companies will revalue their assets and incorporate the adjustments in the balance sheet. Systems of current cost accounting have been developed to adjust accounts for the effects of inflation and these are described in Chapter 66.

If a company pays nothing for an item it acquires, this item will usually not appear in the accounting records as an asset. This applies, for example, to the knowledge, skills and expertise of its staff. Attempts have been made to develop a system of human asset accounting to allow for this key asset, but they have so far failed to take root.

6. The treatment of depreciation

The cost of fixed assets, such as plant or machinery, that have a long but limited life are systematically reduced over the life of the asset by the process of *depreciation*. This process gradually removes the cost of the asset from the balance sheet by showing it as a cost of the operation in the profitit-and-loss account. The depreciation charge in this account represents that part of the cost of the asset used during the accounting period. Note that the depreciation process as such does not provide a separate fund to replace the asset at the end of its useful life. It simply reduces the profit available for distribution to shareholders and increases the amount retained in the business. How these retained funds are used – for expansion, acquisitions, replacements or research and development – is a matter for the financial and capital budgeting processes of the company and its system of cash or funds flow management. There are different methods available for depreciation and these are discussed in Chapter 65.

7. Accruals

In accounting, revenues and costs are accrued. The impact of events on assets and equities is recognized in the time periods when services are rendered or utilized instead of when cash is paid or received. That is, revenue is recognized as it is *earned* and expenses are recognized as they are *incurred*, not when cash changes hands. These revenues and costs are entered into profit-and-loss account in the period to which they relate.

This principle means that before producing final accounts *adjustments* have to be made to ensure that the accrual concept of assigning the financial effects of transactions to the accounting period in which they were earned or incurred is implemented.

Adjustments are made in the form of:

■ *accruals* – expenses arising from services that have been provided in the current accounting period, the benefit from which has been used in earning the current period's revenue, but which will not be paid for until the following period; and

■ *prepayments* – recorded expenses which refer to a period beyond that for which the final accounts are being presented.

In addition, *provision* may be made in the accounts this year for prudent reasons for costs, although not yet paid, and even though no benefit may yet have been derived from them.

8. Consistency

Auditors require consistency in the accounting treatments of like items within each accounting period and from one period to the next.

9. Prudence

Accountants have to be conservative in preparing financial statements. Revenues and profits are *never* anticipated and are only included in financial statements when they are realized, but provision is made for *all* known liabilities.

ACCOUNTING BASES AND POLICIES

These accounting principles often require a considerable amount of commercial judgement when they are being applied. Decisions have to be made at the end of each period on the basis of an assessment of future events. For example, it is often necessary to consider the extent to which expenditure incurred in one year can reasonably be expected to produce benefits in the form of revenue in other years and should be carried forward in whole or in part. This means deciding on the extent to which the expenditure should appear in the profit-and-loss account of the current year as distinct from appearing in the balance sheet as a resource at the end of the year. Commercial judgement is also required on matters such as the depreciation of assets, the valuation of stocks and work-in-progress and the treatment of research and development expenditure and long-term contracts. To assist in making consistent and acceptable (from an accounting point of view) judgements, accounting bases and policies are developed.

Accounting bases

Accounting bases are the methods used to express or apply fundamental accounting concepts to financial transactions. These bases are produced in the form of accounting standards issued by accounting professional bodies. In the UK they are issued by the Accounting Standards Board (ASB) and are known as Financial Reporting Standards (FRSs). Statements issued by the predecessor body to the ASB were known as Statements of Standard Accounting Practice (SSAPs). These have been adopted by the ASB. Accounting standards have covered areas such as cash-flow statements (FRS 1), related party disclosures (FRS 8) and goodwill and intangible assets (FRS 10). The International Accounting Standards Committee (IASC) issues International Accounting Standards (IASs) on similar topics. In the United States, the Financial Accounting Standards Board (FASB – pronounced 'fasbee') is the issuing body. There are significant international differences between accounting standards, though progress is being made towards harmonization.

Accounting policies

Accounting policies are the specific accounting bases judged by the business to be the most appropriate to its circumstances and therefore adopted in the preparation of its accounts. For example, of the various methods of accounting for depreciation, the policy adopted may be straight-line depreciation of plant over a period of five years.

FURTHER READING

Davies, M, Paterson, R and Wilson, A (eds), *UK GAAP* (6th edition), Butterworths, London 1999.

Pendlebury, M and Groves, R, *Company Accounts* (3rd edition), Unwin Hyman, London 1994.

61

Balance Sheet Analysis

DEFINITION

Balance sheet analysis assesses the financial strengths and weaknesses of the company primarily from the point of view of the shareholders and potential investors, but also as part of management's task to exercise proper stewardship over the funds invested in the company and the assets in its care.

THE BALANCE SHEET

Components

The three main components of a balance sheet are:

1. *assets* = what the business owns;
2. *liabilities* = what the business owes; and
3. *capital* = the owners' interest in the business.

The balance sheet equation

The balance sheet equation is:

$$Capital + Liabilities = Assets$$

Capital plus liabilities comprise where the money comes from, and assets are where the money is now.

MAKE-UP OF THE BALANCE SHEET

The balance sheet contains four major sections:

1. *Assets or capital in use,* which is divided into the following:

   - Long-term or *fixed assets* which the company owns and needs to carry on its business: land and buildings; plant and machinery; fixtures and fittings; and motor vehicle fleet.
   - Short-term or *current assets* which change rapidly as the company carries on its business: stocks of raw materials; work-in-progress; stocks of finished goods; debtors; bank balances and cash. The heading 'current assets' covers an important operating cycle within the company which is vital for both profitability and liquidity. In this cycle, cash flows out of the business up to the point where the customer, or debtor, takes delivery of the finished goods. When the customer pays, cash flows back, and if the goods yield a profit, current assets increase.

2. *Current liabilities,* the amounts owed which will have to be paid within 12 months of the balance sheet date. These will be shown under the heading of creditors in the balance sheet and will include tax, bank overdraft and dividend payments due to shareholders.

3. *Net current assets* or *working capital,* which is current assets less current liabilities. Careful control of working capital lies at the heart of efficient business performance.

4. *Sources of capital,* which comprise:

   - share capital;
   - reserves, including retained profits, which are distributable, and any funds in the share premium account (money paid in by shareholders over and above the nominal value of the shares they hold), which are non-distributable; and
   - long-term loans.

ANALYSIS

Balance sheet analysis concentrates on two areas: liquidity and capital structure. Information derived from both the balance sheet and the profit-and-loss account also provides a number of key analytical areas and these are dealt with in Chapter 139.

Liquidity analysis

Liquidity analysis aims to establish that the company has sufficient cash resources to meet its short-term obligations. The key balance sheet ratios used in liquidity analysis are as follows:

1. *The working capital ratio (current ratio).* This relates the current assets of the company to its current liabilities and is calculated as:

$$\frac{\text{Current assets}}{\text{Current liabilities}}$$

There is no categorical rule of what this ratio should be, but, clearly, if it is less than 1, there may be danger because the liquid resources are insufficient to cover short-term payments. However, too high a ratio (say more than 2) might be due to cash or stock levels being greater than is strictly necessary and might therefore be indicative of the bad management of working capital requirements.

The working capital ratio is susceptible to 'window dressing', which is the manipulation of the working capital position by accelerating or delaying transactions close to the year end.

2. *The quick ratio (acid-test ratio).* The working capital ratio includes stock as a major item and this may not be convertible very readily into cash if the need arises to pay creditors at short notice. The quick ratio, as its name implies, concentrates on the more readily realizable of the current assets and provides a much stricter test of liquidity than the working capital ratio.

The quick ratio is calculated as:

$$\frac{\text{Current assets minus stocks}}{\text{Current liabilities}}$$

Again, there are no rigid rules on what this ratio should be. But it should not fall below 1 because this would mean that if all the creditors of a company requested early payment there would be insufficient liquid, or nearly liquid, resources available to meet the demands. The company would fail the 'acid test' of being able to pay its short-term obligations and would therefore be in danger of becoming insolvent. The seriousness of the situation would depend on the availability of loan or overdraft facilities.

Capital structure analysis

Capital structure analysis examines the overall means by which a company finances its operations. Companies are usually financed partly by the funds of their ordinary shareholders and partly by loans from banks and other lenders. These two sources of finance are referred to as equity and debt respectively, and the relationship between the two indicates the gearing or leverage of the company.

The higher the proportion of debt to equity, the higher the gearing ratio, ie a company is said to be highly geared when it has a high level of loan capital as distinct from equity capital. The problem which can arise from high gearing is that providers of loan capital have priority for payment over shareholders, and in hard times the latter might suffer. On the other hand, gearing provides the benefit of a predictably fixed amount of interest every year, and the priority given to providers of loan capital over shareholders on liquidation should make the cost of debt capital less than that of equity. The gearing position of a company can be assessed by the use of the following balance sheet ratios:

1. *Long-term debt to equity ratio.* This is the classic gearing ratio and is calculated as:

$$\frac{\text{Long-term loans plus preference shares}}{\text{Ordinary shareholders' funds}} \times 100$$

2. *Long-term debt to long-term finance ratio.* This ratio calculates the amount of debt finance as a proportion of total long-term finance as follows:

$$\frac{\text{Long-term loans plus preference shares}}{\text{Long-term loans plus preference shares plus ordinary shareholders' funds}} \times 100$$

The implications of this ratio are similar to those of the long-term debt to equity ratio. The higher the ratio, the higher the proportion of debt in the capital structure of a company and therefore the higher the amount of the interest charges that might be expected.

There is no such thing as an optimum ratio. It depends on circumstances. But a company with a low level of business risk with stable operating profits may be able to withstand higher gearing than a company whose operating profits fluctuate widely.

3. *Total debt to total assets ratio.* This ratio shows the proportion of the total assets of the company that is financed by borrowed funds, both short term and long term. It is calculated as:

$$\frac{\text{Long-term loans plus short-term loans}}{\text{Total assets}} \times 100$$

The total debt to total assets ratio recognizes the fact that short-term bank loans and overdrafts are often almost automatically renewable and are therefore effectively a source of long-term finance. Again, this ratio gives an indication of the extent to which interest payments will have to be made.

FURTHER READING

Pendlebury, M and Groves, R, *Company Accounts* (3rd edition), Unwin Hyman, London 1994.

62

Profitability Analysis

DEFINITION

Profitability analysis classifies, measures and assesses the performance of the company in terms of the profits it earns either in relation to the shareholders' investment or capital employed in the business, or in relation to sales. Profit (or loss) can be defined as revenue or income minus expenses. Alternatively, profit can be regarded as the increase in the owners' claims or an increase in net assets.

PURPOSE

Profit serves three purposes, as defined by Peter Drucker:[1]

1. It measures the net effectiveness and soundness of a business's effort.
2. It is the premium that covers the cost of staying in business.
3. It ensures the supply of future capital for innovation and expansion.

Profitability is the primary aim and best measure of efficiency in competitive business, and profitability analysis aims to provide the data on which action can be taken to improve the company's business performance.

CLASSIFICATION OF PROFITS

There are four headings under which profits are classified:

1. *Gross profit* – the difference between sales revenue and the cost of goods sold. This is also referred to as *gross margin*, especially in the retailing industry.
2. *Operating or trading profit* – the gross profit less marketing and distribution costs, administrative costs and research and development expenditure.
3. *Profit before taxation* – operating profit plus invested income minus interest payable.
4. *Net profit* – profit before taxation minus corporation tax.

PRESENTATION OF PROFITS

Profit information is derived from the trading account and the profit-and-loss account.

Trading account

The trading account shows the cost of goods manufactured, the cost of sales, sales and the gross profit, which is transferred to the profit-and-loss account. This is shown in Table 62.1.

Table 62.1 *Trading account*

	£000
Finished goods to warehouse	
Opening stock	500
Factory production	6,500
	7,000
Less closing stock	400
Cost of sales	6,600
Sales	8,000
Gross profit to profit-and-loss account	1,400

Profit-and-loss account

The profit and loss account is set out along the lines shown in Table 62.2. (This lists the typical main headings, but the presentation will vary between companies.)

MEASUREMENT OF PROFITABILITY

Profitability is a measure of the return in the shape of profits that shareholders obtain for their investment in the company. It is expressed in the form of the following ratios.

Table 62.2 *Profit-and-loss account*

	£000	£000	£000
Gross profit from trading account			1,400
Selling and distribution costs			
Sales reps' salaries and expenses	150		
Sales office salaries	30		
Distribution costs	100	280	
Advertising		50	
Administration expenses			
Office salaries		150	
Directors' salaries		100	
Depreciation		20	
Audit fees		10	
Provision for bad debts		30	
Bank interest		20	
			660
Operating profit			740
Investment income			40
Profit before interest and taxation			780
Less loan interest			50
Profit before taxation			730
Taxation			200
Net profit to appropriation account			530

1. Return on equity

This ratio shows the profitability of the company in terms of the capital provided by the owners of the company, ie the shareholders. The formula for this ratio is:

$$\frac{\text{Profit after interest and preference dividends but before tax}}{\text{Average ordinary share capital, reserves and retained profit for the period}} \times 100$$

This ratio therefore focuses attention on the efficiency of the company in earning profits on behalf of its ordinary shareholders. This is regarded by many analysts as the basic profitability ratio.

2. Return on capital employed

The return on capital employed ratio aims to provide information on the performance of a company by concentrating on the efficiency with which the capital is employed. The basic formula is:

$$\frac{\text{Trading or operating profit}}{\text{Capital employed}} \times 100$$

The profit figure taken is the one which reflects the ordinary activities of the company, including the interest paid on current liabilities, or received on current assets. Interest charges to loan creditors are not deducted because, assuming the capital employed represents the total assets of the company, it will be partially financed by creditors, and the profit figure should therefore be the amount before any interest payments to those creditors are made. Taxation charges are not deducted because the amount of taxation paid by a company depends on a variety of circumstances, which may not all be under the control of the company.

Capital employed is usually taken as either the total assets of the company, ie fixed assets plus current assets, or the net total assets, ie fixed assets plus current assets minus current liabilities. Use of the total assets figure focuses attention on the efficiency with which all the resources available to the managers of the company have been utilized, and this is the basis which is referred to most frequently. The argument for using net total assets is that these are the resources which are most under the control of the company and any distortions caused by variations in working capital policy will be minimized.

The alternative formulae are therefore:

1. *Return on total assets*

$$\frac{\text{Trading profit before interest and taxation}}{\text{Average total assets for the period}} \times 100$$

2. *Return on net total assets*

$$\frac{\text{Trading profit before interest and taxation}}{\text{Net total assets for the period}} \times 100$$

3. Earnings per share

Earnings per share are calculated as:

$$\frac{\text{Profit after interest, taxation and preference dividends}}{\text{The number of ordinary shares issued by the company}}$$

This is widely used as a variation on the return on equity indicator of profitability. Its disadvantage for intercompany comparison purposes is that the earnings per share clearly depend on the number of shares issued, which has nothing to do with profitability. Similarly, comparisons over a period of time within a company will be affected if any bonus share issues have taken place.

4. Price–earnings (P/E) ratio

This ratio is calculated as follows:

$$\frac{\text{Market price of ordinary shares}}{\text{Earnings per share}}$$

It reflects the expectations of the market concerning the future earnings of the company (market price), and the earnings available for each ordinary share, based on the results of the most recent accounting period.

If the market price is £5 per share and earnings per share are 50p, the price/earnings ratio is 5.00 ÷ 0.50 = 10. This means that, if £5 is paid for a share, then the shares are selling at 10 times earnings, ie 10 years of current earnings at 50p have been bought. For comparison purposes, companies with higher P/E ratios are regarded as having better prospects.

5. Return on sales or profit margin

The return on sales or profit margin is a key ratio. It shows how well the company is doing in maximizing sales and minimizing costs. It is calculated as a percentage:

$$\frac{\text{Profit}}{\text{Total sales}} \times 100$$

The ratio therefore expresses the profit in pounds generated by each pound of sales. The profit figure used is generally, but not always, the trading profit before interest and taxation, as is the case in the formulae for return on capital employed.

6. Asset turnover ratio

Although a much-used ratio, the return on sales may be misleading because it fails to take account of the assets available to achieve the profit margin. It can be used in association with the return on capital employed, but the problem can also be overcome by adopting the asset turnover ratio, which is calculated as:

$$\frac{\text{Total sales}}{\text{Assets}}$$

This ratio expresses the number of times assets have been 'turned over' during a period to achieve the sales revenue. It measures the performance of the company in generating sales from the assets at its disposal.

REFERENCE

1. Drucker, P, *The Practice of Management*, Heinemann, London 1955.

FURTHER READING

Westwick, C A, *How to Use Management Ratios* (2nd edition), Gower, Aldershot 1987.

63

Value-added Statement

DEFINITION

A value-added statement sets out the details of the value added to the cost of raw materials and bought-out parts by the process of production and distribution. It seldom appears in the annual company accounts but is sometimes used in employee reports.

FORMAT

The format recommended in the discussion paper, *The Corporate Report* (1975), issued by the predecessor body of the Accounting Standards Board, is as follows:

Value added

1. Turnover.
2. Bought-in items (materials and services).
3. Value added (ie turnover minus the cost of bought-in items).

Distribution as follows

4. To employees (wages, salaries and other employment costs).
5. To government (taxation).
6. To providers of capital (interest on loans, dividends).
7. To provide for maintenance and expansion of assets: depreciation, retained profits.

CONTENT

The content of the value-added statement comprises the following.

Calculation of the value-added figure

1. The turnover figure that appears in the profit and loss account.
2. The cost of bought-in items, which will include raw materials, bought-in parts, heating and lighting, printing, and professional and specialist services. This is deducted from the turnover figure to give a figure of the value added by the efforts of the company's employees to make the best use of the capital and other resources available to them.
3. Turnover minus cost of bought-in items.

Distribution of value added

4. The share allocated to employees, comprising gross pay, employers' National Insurance and pension contributions, and the costs of fringe benefits and employee facilities.
5. The payments to government, normally corporation tax, but some reports include National Insurance contributions, value added tax, customs and excise duty, etc.
6. The share allocated to the providers of long-term capital – interest paid and payable on loans, dividends paid and payable to shareholders.
7. The extent to which a proportion of value added is being retained for the future development of the business and the maintenance of the fixed asset base. Some people argue that depreciation should not be included in this category, but should be treated as a deduction from gross value added at the head of the statement.

USE

The value-added statement does not add anything to the information already given in the profit-and-loss account and other financial statements issued by companies. But it does rearrange this information in order to highlight the fact that a company is operated for the benefit of a number of different interests – employees, shareholders, lenders and government – who each have certain rights which have to be satisfied to the best of the company management's abilities.

For employees in particular, value-added statements focus attention on their contribution and are often expressed in the form of value added per employee. But the statements also draw the attention of employees and others to the fact that the results obtained additionally depend on the contribution of shareholders and lenders, who provide capital and have to be rewarded for the risk they take. Finally, the statement indicates quite clearly the size of the obligations companies have to the government as well as to the other interested parties.

64

Cash Management

DEFINITION

Cash management forecasts cash flows (inflows or outflows of cash) as part of the working capital cycle, prepares cash and financial budgets and fund-flow statements, and manages the cash or funds flowing through the company.

PURPOSE

Basic aim

The basic aim of cash management is to ensure that cash in exceeds cash out. In other words, the purpose of cash or funds management is to ensure that the company has the cash and working capital for its expanding or fluctuating needs without either tying up funds which could be more profitably invested or used elsewhere, or relying too heavily on bank overdrafts or other short-term loans.

Overtrading

Cash management aims to minimize the danger of overtrading. This takes place when a rapidly expanding company achieves increased profits but has a deteriorating cash position because the profits generated by sales are not translated into cash flows.

Extra sales require more stock, labour and capital expenditure. Sales result in the first place in the creation of debts with a time lag before they are paid. These factors could more than absorb the cash flow being generated.

The extent to which a company can and should rely on overdrafts to finance a deficit is limited. There is always the danger that in hard times banks will reduce or even withdraw overdraft facilities, resulting in a cash crisis.

THE WORKING CAPITAL CYCLE

The working capital cycles for a manufacturing and a retailing company are illustrated in Figures 64.1 and 64.2 respectively. They show the significant role of cash in the operation of a business.

COMPONENTS OF CASH MANAGEMENT

Cash management starts with the construction of *operating* and *capital expenditure cash budgets*. These are combined with information on investment receipts and outflows as a result of taxation, dividend or

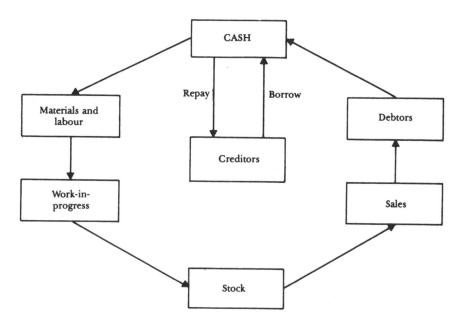

Figure 64.1 *Working capital cycle – manufacturing company*

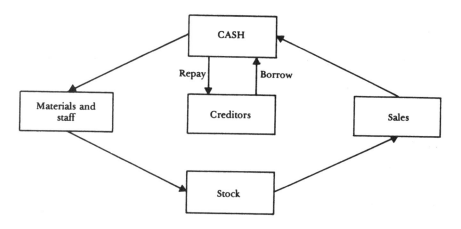

Figure 64.2 *Working capital cycle – retailing company*

interest payments to form the *finance budget*. As an ancillary to this budget a *funds-flow statement* shows the source and application of all the funds used by the company. Finally, the process of *funds-flow management* ensures that all cash or fund flows are handled effectively.

THE OPERATING CASH BUDGET

The operating cash budget deals with budgeted receipts (forecast cash inflows) and budgeted payments (forecast cash outflows). It includes all of what is sometimes referred to as the revenue expenditure incurred in financing current operations, ie the costs of running the business in order to generate sales – buying materials, parts and non-capitalized tools and equipment, labour and staff costs, and selling, administration and research and development costs.

The operating cash budget is based on forecasts of cash inflows and outflows for each accounting cycle of the year and is set out as shown in Table 64.1. If the first budget run reveals any cash-flow problems, steps can be taken to see if any adjustments can be made to outflows (delays in paying creditors) or inflows (calling in debts more vigorously). Contingency plans can also be made to raise short-term finance if necessary.

Table 64.1 *Operating cash budget*

			Period		
	1	2	....	13	Total
Budgeted receipts					
Cash sales					
Receipts from debtors	⎯⎯	⎯⎯		⎯⎯	⎯⎯
	⎯⎯	⎯⎯		⎯⎯	⎯⎯
Budgeted payments					
Materials					
Cash purchases					
Payments to creditors					
Factory payroll					
Other production outlays (excluding depreciation)					
Selling outlays					
Administrative outlays					
Total payments	⎯⎯	⎯⎯		⎯⎯	⎯⎯
Operating cash surplus or (deficit)	⎯⎯	⎯⎯		⎯⎯	⎯⎯

CAPITAL EXPENDITURE CASH BUDGET

The capital expenditure cash budget plans cash outlays on capital expenditure projects. The projected outflows have to be considered carefully in relation to the operating cash budget to ensure that cash-flow problems are avoided. Capital expenditures can often be rephased to avoid embarrassment.

Neither the operating nor the capital expenditure budget makes any reference to the charge for depreciation shown in the profit-and-loss account. The intention of this depreciation charge is to spread the cost of the fixed assets to the particular periods or products that benefit from their use, so that the capital of the company remains intact. No cash outflow is included in the depreciation charge, which is why it is excluded from the operating cash budget.

FINANCE BUDGET

The finance budget is prepared from the information supplied by the operating cash and capital expenditure budgets together with further information on inflows or receipts (investment income) and outflows or payments (taxation, dividends and interest payments).

This analysis may indicate the need to rearrange the flows in the finance budget to overcome any forecast cash-deficit problems. If cash deficits cannot be smoothed out, the analysis will show when there will be a need to raise finance. A forecast surplus will assist in the planning of investments.

A finance budget is set out along the lines shown in Table 64.2.

Table 64.2 *Finance budget*

	£			£	
Inflows					
Opening cash balance					
Operating cash surplus					
Investment income	───	───		───	───
Total receipts	───	───		───	───
Outflows					
Taxation					
Preference dividends (net)					
Ordinary dividends (net)					
Interest payments (net)					
Bank interest					
Capital expenditure					
Operating cash deficit	───	───		───	───
Total payments	───	───		───	───
Surplus finance or deficit to be financed					
Sales or purchase of investments	───	───		───	───
Closing cash balance	───	───		───	───

THE CASH-FLOW STATEMENT

Purpose

The cash-flow statement reports the significant elements of cash generation and cash absorption for a period. It provides information that can help in assessing liquidity, solvency and financial adaptability.

Preparation

In published accounts, where applicable, FRS 1 'Cash-flow statements' prescribes the format of the statement (see Table 64.3). The amounts disclosed in the statement are derived from the differences between the balance sheets at the beginning and end of the period. The statement shows the increase or decrease in cash arising analysed into the following categories: net cash inflow from operating activities, returns on investments and servicing of finance, taxation, capital expenditure, equity dividends paid, management of liquid resources, and financing. Other statements and notes provide further information and reconcile these movements back to the balance sheets and profit-and-loss account. For example, Table 64.4 shows how the net cash inflow from operating activities is reconciled back to the operating profit in the profit-and-loss account. Adjustments are made for non-cash aspects of that profit for depreciation and increases in amounts still tied up in balance sheet assets, such as debtors.

A further note shows the gross cash movements that relate to the items in the cash-flow statement. For example, the financing cash movement may result from the issue of ordinary share capital (with associated expenses paid) less the repayment of a debenture loan.

Table 64.3 *Example of a cash-flow statement*

	£000
Net cash inflow from operating activities	3,463
Returns on investments and servicing of finance	1,501
Taxation	(1,433)
Capital expenditure	(725)
	2,806
Equity dividends paid	(1,200)
Management of liquid resources	1,606
Financing	72
Increase in cash	1,454

Table 64.4 *Reconciliation of operating profit to net cash inflow from operating activities*

	£000
Operating profit	3,017
Depreciation charges	445
Increase in stocks	(87)
Increase in debtors	(36)
Increase in creditors	124
Net cash inflow from operating activities	3,463

FUNDS FLOW MANAGEMENT

Cash management is more than simply ensuring that cash in exceeds cash out, however important that form of liquidity may be. It is about managing money in the broader sense of the systems concept of funds. Funds flow through all the assets of a business, and funds flow management is the critical task of deciding on and controlling the volume of funds and the speed with which they travel through the system.

Funds flow management therefore ensures that:

1. forecasts are made of all the funds circulating through the system;
2. steps are taken to ensure that, as far as possible, inflows and outflows are balanced to enable an appropriate degree of liquidity to be maintained, thus avoiding excessive deficits that cannot be financed by normal means;
3. credit and bad debts are controlled properly in order to speed up and maximize cash inflows;
4. the cost of financing short-term deficits is minimized by such means as negotiating beneficial overdraft facilities or, within reason, delaying payments to creditors;
5. the total capital resources of the company are sufficient to meet current and forecast levels of trading;
6. surplus cash resources are invested profitably, both in the shorter and in the longer term; and
7. cash inflows and outflows are continuously monitored in order to action the various measures listed above.

BENEFITS

Cash management is a systematic process of ensuring that problems of liquidity are minimized and that funds are managed effectively. It enables the company to recognize the potential dangers of overtrading. Steps can then be taken to modify trading plans to keep them in line with cash resources or, preferably, in an expanding business, to raise the additional capital required before a crisis hits the company.

65

Depreciation

DEFINITION

Depreciation is the measure of the cost (or revalued amount) of the economic benefits of the tangible fixed assets of the company that have been consumed during the period. This consumption arises from wearing out, using up or otherwise reducing the useful economic life of an asset. It can arise from use, passage of time or obsolescence. An asset may become obsolete through either changes in technology or demand for the goods or services it produces.

REASON FOR DEPRECIATING ASSETS

Assets are depreciated because if, during the year's operations, some of their life has been used, then this should be taken as a 'cost' in the profit-and-loss account before declaring a profit. The purpose of depreciation is to remove gradually the cost of the asset from the accounting records by showing it as an operational cost. A false profitability figure would result from a failure to charge depreciation for the accounts.

Note that the depreciation process does *not* provide a separate fund to replace the asset at the end of its useful life. The sum allowed for depreciation has been retained in the business, and it is impossible to separate depreciation money from retained profit money. If liquid funds are required for replacements, a separate provision must be made for them by means of a corresponding investment in a cashable security.

METHODS

The depreciation charge for each period in the profit-and-loss account should arise from a systematic allocation of the depreciable amount of a tangible fixed asset over its useful economic life. In practice, in many industries, simple 'rules of thumb' are applied when deciding useful economic lives. This saves effort and, where there are many similar assets (such as motor vehicles), does not distort results significantly from year to year. Where an asset has been revalued, the current period's depreciation charge is based on the revalued amount.

The two main ways of calculating depreciation are as follows:

1. *Straight-line method*. This is the simplest to operate and is done by taking the cost of the asset, dividing it by the anticipated life of the asset in years and charging the result each year to the accounts. Thus a £10,000 asset with a life of five years will be depreciated at the rate of £2,000 a year.
2. *Reducing-balance method*. This method recognizes that assets such as motor vehicles may depreciate at a greater rate in their early life, and therefore deducts a constant percentage of the asset balance. If 25 per cent were used as the rate for an asset worth £10,000, the depreciation figures would be: year 1 – £2,500; year 2 – £1,875; year 3 – £1,406, etc.

DEPRECIATION AND INFLATION

If depreciation is based on the historical cost of acquiring the asset, then in times of inflation the application of the normal straight-line or reducing-balance method will not take account of the fact that the current or replacement cost of the asset is higher. As a result, profits may be over-stated. The technique of current cost inflation accounting, as defined in Chapter 66, is designed to overcome this difficulty.

66

Inflation Accounting

DEFINITION

Inflation accounting is the technique used to adjust financial accounts to allow for the effect of inflation. Inflation can be defined as a decline in the purchasing power of money due to an increase in the general level of prices.

REASONS FOR INFLATION ACCOUNTING

Financial accounts are the basis on which the success of a business is measured and on which investors can find out whether or not their investment is safe and will produce a reasonable return for them. Financial accounts therefore have a significant effect on the business, and shareholders are particularly interested in them from the point of view not only of obtaining a good return on their investment but also of maintaining the value of that investment. But if this value is expressed in terms of historical costs, without allowing for the impact of inflation, it could be illusory. Hence the need for inflation accounting. These issues are considered in more detail below.

Influence of financial accounts

Financial accounts have a major influence on:

1. the level of dividends declared by the directors;
2. the willingness of investors to risk their capital in the company, ie, to buy or sell shares;
3. the willingness of a potential creditor to lend to the company;
4. the interest displayed by other companies in taking over the company;
5. the agreement of shareholders to the re-election of directors;
6. the basis for company taxation;
7. the attitude of employees and trade unions to the company; and
8. government policies relating to monopolistic practices and price control.

The concept of income and the maintenance of capital

Income is increase in wealth, ie capital, and invested capital is traditionally regarded as a financial rather than a physical concept. The focus is on the potential profitability of money invested, no matter what inventory or other capital resources have been acquired.

Financial resources (capital) are invested with the expectation of the return *of* that capital as well as an additional amount representing the return *on* that capital. The expectation is that capital will be maintained, and this happens when revenues are at least equal to all costs and expenses. There are two concepts of capital maintenance:

1. *Financial capital maintenance*, in which costs and expenses are measured by the financial resources (usually, historical, ie original, costs) used up in earning the revenue;
2. *Physical capital maintenance*, in which costs and expenses are measured as the amount required to preserve the capacity of the company to maintain previous levels of output of goods or services.

The historic cost illusion

The problem with the financial capital maintenance concept is that it is based on historical costs and, because of inflation, these are illusory. In times of inflation, they can produce misleadingly high levels of profit when current revenues are matched against costs incurred in previous years, and these costs are expressed in historic pounds.

Purpose of inflation-adjusted accounting

The purpose of inflation-adjusted accounting is to restore the principle of matching current revenues with current costs or current purchasing power to the profit-and-loss account, thus removing the inflationary element from historic cost profit and/or allowing the concept of physical capital maintenance to be adopted.

TECHNIQUES

The two techniques used in inflation accounting are:

1. current purchasing power accounting (CPP); and
2. current cost accounting (CCA).

Current purchasing power accounting

The CPP system adjusts all accounting figures for changes in the index of retail prices between the date of the original transaction and the accounting date, thereby providing an overall adjustment to the accounts for the effects of inflation. This approach is linked to financial capital maintenance in that it meets the needs of proprietors or businessmen and women who seek to preserve the value of their investment and look at accounts to assess its growth. CPP accounting expresses incomes, expenditure and costs in 'real' terms, thus avoiding the illusion of growth, which is simply a function of the falling value of money.

The problem with the CPP system is the use of an overall index to deflate the accounts when, in practice, the replacement costs of some assets may have changed at a rate which is quite different from the movement in the index of retail prices.

Current cost accounting

The CCA system matches current revenues with the current cost of the resources which are consumed in earning them. Historic cost figures are adjusted individually for the changes in prices which are specific to the physical resources (stock, plant or equipment). This avoids the blanket approach of the CPP system and satisfies the concept of physical capital maintenance, ie that the capital to be maintained is not the proprietary investment (the financial capital maintenance concept) but the physical resources of the business itself.

Current costs in CCA are usually replacement costs and are therefore based on the assumption that the business will continue in its present form as a 'going concern'. CCA does not, however, show the value of these assets. This can be done if the net realizable value (NRV) concept is used, ie the amount of money for which an asset can be exchanged in the marketplace (selling price less selling cost). But NRV is not so relevant to a continuing business as the replacement cost concept, and the latter approach is usually adopted in a current value system.

The current cost method separates income from continuing operations from income arising from holding gains. The income from continuing operations is defined as the excess of revenue over the current costs of the assets consumed in obtaining that revenue. Holding gains are defined as increases in the replacement costs of the assets held during the current period. The advocates of a physical concept of capital maintenance claim that all holding gains should be excluded from income and become a part of revalued capital called revaluation equity. The point being made is that for a going concern, no income can result unless the physical capital devoted to operations during the current period can be replaced.

USE OF INFLATION ACCOUNTING

Inflation accounting is now only used for internal reporting purposes. CCA may be used both to establish pricing policies and because it provides a more reliable measure of the return on capital employed, which can be used to assess the comparative performance of different divisions within a company. Current cost profit-and-loss accounts and balance sheets can be prepared in addition to the historic cost accounts to provide more insight into the performance of a business in current terms. It might be revealed, for example, that after a period of high inflation a company may have much less to distribute to its shareholders on a current cost basis than if historical costs had been used.

BENEFITS

The main benefit of inflation accounting is that the emphasis on current values provides a more realistic picture on which managerial decisions and the views of investors can be based. It directs attention to real increases or decreases in income by removing the effect of inflation and concentrates the minds of businessmen and women on the need for physical capital maintenance so that the capacity of the business to continue is preserved.

FURTHER READING

Lewis, R and Pendrill, D, *Advanced Financial Accounting* (3rd edition), Pitman, London 1991.

67

Raising Finance

DEFINITION

Raising finance requires initial decisions on the capital structure of the company. Financing demands a knowledge of the sources of funds and the advantages and disadvantages of each source. Further decisions are then made on the most appropriate method of satisfying either short-term requirements to finance current trading, or medium- and longer-term needs to provide funds for growth, capital investments and acquisitions.

CAPITAL STRUCTURE AND GEARING

When considering capital structure the major consideration is the proportion of debt finance the company should undertake to maintain. This proportion of fixed interest capital to equity or ordinary shares is known as gearing or leverage.

The pursuit of an optimum level of debt as compared with equity finance, while an important consideration, is not necessarily the only one that exercises the mind of financial managers. Some analysts assert that the value of the company cannot depend on the manipulation or distortion of financial policy with regard to the proportion of debt finance, but rather depends upon the investment performance and risk characteristics of the particular enterprise.

Despite these views, however, managements have to make decisions on the level of gearing or leverage they want, and may have to justify these decisions to the shareholders. If preference for debt finance results in a high proportion of fixed-interest capital, the company is said to be highly geared. A low-geared company has a high proportion of equity capital.

Advantages of high gearing or leverage

A preference for debt finance and therefore high gearing may be justified for one or more of the following reasons:

1. The cost of debt capital may normally be expected to be lower than that of equity.
2. Income-producing assets can be financed without immediate reference to shareholders and therefore without having to justify an increase in equity capital.
3. The creation of new equities may increase the risk of potential loss of control.
4. Earnings per share should be increased if the fixed-interest capital is used to earn a return in excess of the interest charge, and this benefit accrues to the ordinary shareholders of the company.
5. Gearing or leverage increases the value of the company through the tax advantages of debt finance. Interest payment is a tax-deductible expense.

Disadvantages of high gearing

High gearing can be risky, even to the point of bankruptcy, if earnings are not sufficient to cover additional interest costs. This may result in an increase in the equity capitalization rate needed to compensate shareholders for the additional financial risks they must now carry. It is normally desirable to cover interest payments at least three or four times by profit before interest (ie profit before interest should be three or four times as high as the interest payments).

Many companies take a cautious view of gearing and, while they recognize its advantages, prudently require five times cover and use this as a guide to the maximum amount of fixed-interest debt they can incur.

SOURCES OF FINANCE

The main sources of finance available to a company are:

1. short-term borrowing;
2. medium-term finance;
3. longer-term debt capital;

4. convertibles;
5. equity capital; and
6. venture capital.

Short-term borrowing

Short-term (less than one year) funds to finance current trading can be obtained by means of the following:

1. *Trade credit* – delaying payment for goods received.
2. *Short-term bank lending* – through self-liquidating loans or overdrafts. An overdraft or, in the United States, a line of credit facility, is relatively cheap and can be used flexibly. It is particularly useful for companies where the demand for and supply of cash fluctuate widely throughout the year.
3. *Bill finance and acceptance credits* – where the borrower signs a promissory note or trade bill, issued by his or her creditor, for a stated term for repayment and an appropriate rate of interest. An acceptance credit allows the borrower to draw his or her bill directly on the bank and this bill can be rediscounted or sold in the market, thereby generating immediate cash. Trade or bank bills usually carry a modest interest rate.
4. *Intercompany loans and the interbank market.* Limited facilities exist in the UK for intercompany loans, when companies bypass the banking system by placing deposits directly with one another or through a broker. Alternatively, bank money-market lines exist for bank loans for a stated period negotiated at a percentage against the interbank 'wholesale' money-market rate, usually referred to as the London Inter-Bank Offer Rate, or LIBOR.
5. *Commercial paper* – a facility is available in the United States that allows companies to issue fully negotiable paper or promissory notes direct to the public.
6. *Factoring.* A factor purchases his or her client's book debts and, on an agreed maturity date, pays to the client the full value of the approved debt purchased less the agreed service fee of between 1 and 3 per cent of turnover. The factor collects the debts and thus relieves his or her client of sales ledger handling costs. Thus factoring provides a credit facility and can reduce debts.

Medium-term finance

Medium-term finance is provided over a period of one to five or even as many as 15 years by banks, specialist brokers and finance houses. The main sources are as follows:

1. *Term loans* – a business loan with an original maturity of one to five years which is not repayable on demand unless the borrower breaches

stipulated conditions. Term loans are usually made to purchase a fixed asset and banks prefer them to be self-amortizing. Such loans can be matched to the expected payback period of an investment.

2. *Hire purchase* – where the borrower is regarded as a hirer but can purchase the equipment when all instalments have been paid. Interest rates are high.

3. *Leasing* – a method of financing the use of equipment as distinct from financing ultimate ownership. Operating leases are for a period of up to three years and carry a full maintenance service. Contract hire applies to the provision of motor vehicles. A third form of leasing, financial leasing, allows the borrower to acquire the use of an asset on terms which correspond to those obtainable on a medium-term loan, for which it can be regarded as a straight substitute. Leasing at one time offered significant tax advantages in the UK but this is no longer the case, except for companies which may be unable to make full use of their capital allowances to reduce their tax liabilities.

Longer-term debt capital

Longer-term debt capital can be obtained in the following forms:

1. *Loan capital* – long-term bank loans, mortgages, loan stocks and debentures which constitute a fixed-term debt and usually carry a fixed rate of interest. Loan stocks and debentures are normally secured on the assets of the borrower. Both adequate asset and earnings cover will be expected if a Stock Exchange listing for the debt is sought, and constraints may be placed on the borrower on the use of assets arising under the terms of the security.

   For example, if a debenture is secured by a floating charge on the general assets of the company, it may be specified that stock and work-in-progress (termed 'inventory' in the United States) should not fall below a certain level.

2. *Preference shares* – shares of the company whose holders rank as non-voting owners with prior rights over ordinary shareholders for the distribution of income or capital. They provide a greater rate of return for shareholders than fixed-interest stocks, although with less security. Cumulative preference shares provide the right to receive dividends missed in previous years.

   The disadvantage of this form of finance is that the borrower is committing him- or herself to a long-term fixed-rate debt, probably at historically high rates of interest.

   Many companies prefer floating rate, medium-term finance or have simply rolled over short-term bank borrowings.

Convertibles

Convertible loans are issues of debt stock, carrying a rate of interest and specified maturity date and giving the holder the right to convert into issues of equity at stated prices. Their value from the point of view of the company is that such issues provide it with relatively cheap, fixed (tax-deductible), interest debt capital. Although convertible into equity at a later date, convertible stock affords for the present a given volume of cheaper, fixed-rate loans. If it is converted in the future, it can be replaced by issues of new convertibles to preserve the gearing rate.

Equity capital

Equity capital normally represents the largest proportion of capital employed by a company. It can be obtained in the following ways:

1. *By internal finance* supplied from retained earnings. This does not require any formal issue of securities to shareholders, but adds to the value of shareholders' securities by the creation of reserves attributable to ordinary shareholders.
2. *By raising finance on the open market* through the issue of new securities in exchange for capital supplied by new shareholders.
3. *By a rights issue* restricted to existing shareholders.

Venture capital

Venture capital can be raised from or through merchant banks or agencies. Common to all venture capital is the identification by the banker of what he or she considers strong growth potential so that the high risks he or she takes are balanced by the hope of a correspondingly high return. Venture capital investment almost always includes an equity shareholding of between 5 and 40 per cent, and very often the holding company requires a seat on the board of the client company. This implies a much closer relationship between the two sides than is common between lender and borrower.

The advantage of using venture capital is that smaller companies can gain access to long-term finance without recourse to a public share issue or without saddling themselves with heavy, fixed-interest payments. A potential drawback to some companies is the loss of a degree of independence because of the direct interest taken by the suppliers of the finance.

CHOICE OF METHODS

The following factors have to be taken into account in choosing a method of raising finance:

1. the term over which it is required;
2. the level of gearing or leverage existing in the company and the policy on the limits to which gearing can be increased;
3. the cost of the finance in terms of interest rates;
4. the degree to which the company wishes to tie itself down with fixed commitments or, put another way, the extent to which it needs to vary its requirements for finance in the short or medium term;
5. the relative tax advantages of different forms of borrowing;
6. the size and reputation of the company (when raising equity finance);
7. the costs of raising finance, eg the cost of a new issue of securities;
8. the readiness of the company to accept a degree of involvement in its affairs by providers of venture capital or, in some cases, institutional shareholders.

68

Creative Accounting

DEFINITION

Creative accounting is defined by Michael Jameson (see Further Reading section at the end of this chapter) as the process of 'structuring transactions so as to produce the required financial outcome, rather than allowing accounting to report transactions in a neutral and consistent way'.

Creative accounting operates within the letter both of the law and of accounting standards but is clearly against the spirit of both. It is essentially a process of using the rules, the flexibility provided by the rules and the omissions from those rules to make financial statements look somewhat different from what was intended by the rules.

Some of the main areas in which creative accounting can take place are described below.

FIXED ASSETS

Fixed assets are those assets such as property and plant which have a useful life beyond the current accounting period – they are depreciated over their useful economic life. The amount at which they are shown in the balance sheets will not necessarily represent their value.

Useful economic life

Creative accountants can exercise choice over the length of the useful economic life. If the company wants to maintain its fixed assets in the balance sheet at the highest level it can, then the useful economic life will be as long as possible. If, on the other hand, the company wishes its fixed asset values to reduce quickly, it will choose much shorter lives. As Jameson suggests, 'the useful life decision is taken by determining first, what answer is required and second, by assessing what useful life will give that answer'.

Depreciation method

Different methods of depreciating assets (eg straight-line, reducing-balance – see Chapter 65) can influence the balance sheet value of an asset. Changing from one method to another can make a significant impact on profits. Terry Smith (see, also, Further Reading section) quotes a major company as having inflated the average growth in profits over the years 1985–90 from 14.3 to 16.7 per cent by changing the depreciation method.

CURRENT ASSETS

Legal manipulation when accounting for current assets can take place in the areas of stocks and work-in-progress, debtors and cash.

Stocks

The higher the value of stock at the end of the year, the higher the profit. However, this year's closing stock is next year's opening stock, so a high figure at the end of one year will reduce next year's profits. Massaging stock values from one year to the next will not create profit in the long run but will enable a creative accountant to smooth profits by either boosting one year's profit or hiding an unexpected and embarrassingly high profit in a particular year.

Massaging stock figures can be achieved by varying methods of accounting for stock. For example, stock can be valued at the direct, out-of-pocket cost of its acquisition, or on the basis of the additional costs of getting the stock into place. Indirect labour costs and certain overheads can be included or excluded from the stock valuation.

Stock holdings can be increased deliberately at the end of the year, which allows companies to carry forward production overheads and boost the current year's profits. Alternatively, stocks could be run down to reduce current profit levels. Thus the accounting system will have the effect of advancing or retarding the recognition of profit, and this has the appearance of creating or hiding profit in the short run.

Debtors

The debtors figure in the current assets can be manipulated by adjusting the provision for bad debts. In the short term, a higher provision will hide profits and a lower provision will boost profits. If there has been over-provision for bad debts, profits can be increased in later years by reducing the provision.

In the short run, profit or balance sheet changes between one year and the next can be smoothed by advancing the issue of invoices to boost profits or by delaying their issue to reduce profits.

Cash

Cash holding can be manipulated by varying the timing of payments and receipts. If a company wants to show high levels of cash in the bank at the end of the financial year it will ensure that as many payments as possible are banked before the year end. Profits can also be boosted in one year by delaying payment until after the year end. These are, of course, only short-run devices.

LIABILITIES

Judgement can be exercised on the recognition of liabilities in the balance sheet and there is scope for creativity in moving liabilities off the balance sheet.

Current liabilities

The actual amount due to creditors can be varied according to whether any discounts available have been included or excluded. There is also scope for adjusting the level and timing of accruals (expenses arising from services provided in the current accounting period, the benefit from which has been used in earning the current period's revenue, but which will not be paid for until the following period).

Long-term liabilities

It is often in the interests of a company to show that as many of its debts as possible will become due for settlement as far into the future as can be arranged. Where loans are of an indeterminate duration it may be possible to 'roll them over' into the future, especially where the debts exist between companies in the same group.

Off-balance sheet liabilities

The amount of debt carried by a company can be seemingly reduced by placing debts 'off-balance sheet'. Financial reporting standards issued by the UK Accounting Standards Board during the 1990s have had the effect of reducing the scope for off-balance sheet schemes. In particular FRS 5 'Reporting the substance of transactions' insisted on disclosure of such things as 'quasi-subsidiaries'. The quasi-subsidiary is a company effectively owned by another but with ownership structured so that it falls outside the company law requirement for its balance sheet to be consolidated with that of its owner (parent company). The quasi-subsidiary would often be heavily financed by third party debt, which its parent company wanted to conceal from its own shareholders.

INCOME

The basis of company accounting is not cash but the accrual system. This means that the income a company receives in a year is not the same as the net increase in its bank account over the year. Its revenue is the value of the goods and services that it has delivered to customers during the year. Cash expected next year is treated as an accrual and included in the current year's profit-and-loss account.

Accountants have, however, to make assumptions about accruals. Judgement is required. This is especially the case when long-term contracts are involved, and the creative accountant may be able to provide for the sales revenue to increase at a desirable rate (neither too fast nor too slow). It is also possible to manipulate bad debt write-offs by charging them against revenue and thus maintaining gross margin.

This propensity of creative accountants to smooth out profit figures has been encouraged by the City's enthusiasm for steady increases in turnover and profitability without any sudden fluctuations.

EXPENSES

Expenses are deducted from revenue in arriving at profit. To maximize profits and produce favourable price–earnings (P/E) ratios, creative accountants may wish to massage expenses by deferring costs into the future. This can be done by including expenditure in the valuation of stock or work-in-progress and carrying it forward.

Another popular method of deferring costs into the future is to capitalize them, ie to include them on the balance sheet as fixed assets. This can include intangible assets such as research and development expenditure, goodwill, patents and trademarks.

In some cases accountants might want to accelerate the charging of expenses to smooth profits. They do so by making provisions against future expenses. If the provision is too large it can be released in future periods to boost profits. Auditors have had difficulty in challenging over-provisions as they are at least prudent in effect in the year they are set up. The practice of making large provisions when taking over another company (known as 'big bath' provisions) became so prevalent that in 1998 the UK Accounting Standards Board issued FRS 12 'Provisions, contingent liabilities and contingent assets' to restrict the making of provisions to very specific circumstances. Accordingly, the scope for creative accounting in this area is much diminished.

CONCLUSION

The existence of creative accounting in the above fields and others such as pre-acquisition write-downs, disposals, brand accounting, pension fund accounting and currency mismatching has been demonstrated clearly by Terry Smith. It flourishes because of pressure from the City for sustained profitability, and because total precision in the application of the law and accounting standards is virtually impossible in these and other areas. There is often room for judgement, and although auditors are there to ensure that a 'true and fair view' is expressed by the accounts, they are not always in a position to challenge the judgements and assumptions made by company accountants.

The UK Accounting Standards Board responded to the challenge of creative accounting and many of its pronouncements during the 1990s were directly aimed at curtailing the worst practices. FRS 5 'Reporting the substance of transactions' did much to curb the use of artificial structures and transactions. Its theme was 'substance over form'. In addition, the enforcement of accounting standards became a reality in the 1990s with the formation of the Financial Reporting Council and its enforcement body the Financial Reporting Review Panel. The Panel has the power to investigate and force the correction of accounts that it believes do not show a true and fair view.

FURTHER READING

The original version of this chapter drew heavily on Michael Jameson's *A Practical Guide to Creative Accounting* (Kogan Page, London 1988). Illustrations of creative accounting techniques used by companies may be found in *Accounting for Growth* by company financial analyst Terry Smith (Century, London 1992 and 1996). This book became famous for its 'blob guide', which scored companies by the number of creative accounting practices used.

Creative Accounting and the Cross-eyed Javelin Thrower (McBarnet, D and Whelan, C, Wiley, Chichester 1999) is an academic review of the challenge of creative accounting and the battle against it during the 1990s. It does not set out to be a creative accounting guide, although it does offer some strategies for taking on the Financial Reporting Review Panel. It has several informative appendices dealing with the enforcement process.

69

Management Accounting

DEFINITION

Management accounting provides information to management on present and projected costs and on the profitability of individual projects, products, activities or departments as a guide to decision making and financial planning.

TECHNIQUES

Management accounting uses the following techniques:

- *Cost accounting* – the recording and allocation of cost data.
- *Cost analysis* – the classification and analysis of costs to aid business planning and control.
- *Absorption costing* – the assignment of all costs, both fixed and variable, to operations or products.
- *Marginal costing* – the segregation of fixed and variable or marginal costs and the apportionment of those marginal costs to products or processes.
- *Standard costing* – the preparation of predetermined or standard costs and their comparison with actual costs to identify variances.
- *Variance analysis* – the identification and analysis of differences between actual and standard costs, or between actual and budgeted overheads, sales and profits, with a view to providing guidance on any corrective action required.

- *Cost–volume–profit analysis* – the study of the relationship between expenses, revenue and net income in order to establish the implications on profit levels of changes in costs, volumes (production or sales) or prices.
- *Profit–volume charts,* which specifically reveal the impact of changes in volume on net income.
- *Break-even analysis,* which indicates the point where sales revenue equals total cost and there is neither profit nor loss. It also shows the net profit or loss that is likely to arise from different levels of activity.
- *Sales mix analysis,* which calculates the effect on profits of variations in the mixture of output of the different products marketed by the company.
- *Financial budgeting,* which deals with the creation of budgets (statements in quantitative and financial terms of the planned allocation and use of the company's resources). The basic form of budget is a static budget, ie one which assumes a constant level of activity.
- *Flexible budgets,* which take account of a range of possible volumes or activity levels.
- *Zero-based budgeting,* which requires managers to justify *all* budgeted expenditure and not to prepare budgets as no more than an extension of what was spent last year.
- *Budgetary control,* which compares actual costs, revenues and performance with the fixed or 'flexed' budget so that, if necessary, corrective action can be taken or revisions made to the budget.
- *Overhead accounting* – direct attention to the identification, measurement and control of overheads.
- *Responsibility accounting,* which defines responsibility centres and holds the managers of those areas responsible for the costs and revenues assigned to them.
- *Capital budgeting* – the process of selecting and planning capital investments based on an appraisal of the returns that will be obtained from the investments. The main capital appraisal techniques comprise *accounting rate of return, payback* and *discounted cash flow.*
- *Risk analysis,* which assesses the danger of failing to achieve forecasts of the outcome or yield of an investment.

USES

Objective

The main objective of management accounting is to provide management information which will help managers to optimize their decisions with a view to improving present performance and providing for longer-term profitable growth. Management accounting could therefore be described as the development and maintenance of a management information system.

Principles

In carrying out this task, management accountants are governed by two key principles:

1. *Comparison.* Either of:
   - what has been achieved with what should have been achieved – this is a feedback process designed to point the way to corrective action and improved performance, not simply a stick with which to beat managers; or
   - alternative courses of action with a view to deciding which, on balance, is the best in terms of cost/benefit, cost-effectiveness or return on investment – this is an evaluative process.

2. *Relevance.* Management accounting as a decision making tool must only be concerned with relevant data, ie information that will lead the manager to the best decision. When managers make decisions they are choosing between alternatives in order to predict which one has the best future. Historical costs only help to shape predictions, and the relevant data or costs are the expected future data that will *differ* among alternatives. Any item is irrelevant if it will remain the same regardless of the alternative selected.

Decisions and problem solving

Management accounting is used to assist in making decisions or in solving problems in the following areas:

1. Long-range planning.
2. Budgetary and financial control.
3. Profitability measurement and analysis and profit improvement planning.
4. Cost reduction.
5. Investment appraisal and portfolio management.
6. Pricing.
7. Make or buy.
8. Product development and product mix.
9. Capacity planning.
10. Distribution planning.

BENEFITS

Management accounting brings together a wide range of quantitative and analytical techniques. By understanding what is available in the way of these techniques and how they can be used, management is placed in the best position to make good decisions and to prepare realistic plans for the future.

FURTHER READING

Drury, C, *Management and Cost Accounting* (3rd edition), Van Nostrand Reinhold, London 1992.

Mott, G, *Management Accounting for Decision Makers* (2nd edition), Pitman, London 1991.

70

Cost Accounting

DEFINITION

Cost accounting is concerned with the classification, recording, allocation and analysis of cost data to provide information for product costing, operational control, inventory valuations and decision making.

OBJECTIVES

1. *Pricing.* To provide guidance on pricing decisions and to ensure that prices at least cover the costs of developing, manufacturing and selling the products of the company and the costs of administering and financing the firm.
2. *Control.* To provide a basis for controlling expenditure by ensuring that managers are involved in budgeting costs in their departments and have the information which will enable them to control their costs within their budget. Operational control systems provide feedback to production and department managers on the resources consumed (labour, materials, energy, overheads) during an operating period.
3. *Profit management.* To provide information on fixed and variable costs which enables profits and contributions to be forecast and will ensure that profits achieved are measured accurately.
4. *Inventory valuation.* To ensure that inventory is valued correctly and thus provide a basis for the realistic measurement of profit. This involves allocating periodic production costs between goods sold and goods in stock.

5. *Appraisal of alternative courses of action.* To provide information which will help in decision making concerned with strategic planning, product planning and the appraisal of capital investment projects.

COST ACCOUNTING TECHNIQUES

Cost accounting techniques are concerned with:

1. Cost classification.
2. Costing.
3. Cost analysis.

Costs need to be classified according to the type of expense (direct or indirect) or behaviour (fixed or variable) and by reference to the product, job or order and the location of the activity incurring the expense. Costing determines product costs by allocating prime costs and overheads to products and provides the basis for analysis, decision making and control.

COST CLASSIFICATION

Classification of costs by type of expense

This classification distinguishes *direct manufacturing costs*, which are clearly identified with the product, and others. Direct costs are divided into:

- *direct materials*, which form part of the finished product and can be directly associated with it;
- *direct labour*, the labour which contributes to the conversion of the direct material or components into the finished product;
- *direct expenses*, those costs other than material or labour which can be charged direct to the product (eg the cost of processing the product by a subcontractor).

The total of direct material and labour costs plus direct expenses is also known as the *prime cost* of production.

Indirect manufacturing costs cannot readily be identified with the product or ultimate cost unit. Indirect costs consist of:

- *indirect materials*, such as the tools and consumables used in a production department;
- *indirect labour*, such as quality control and inventory control staff, shop cleaners;

■ *indirect expenses*, such as rent and rates, depreciation of plant and insurance.

The total of indirect material and labour costs plus indirect expenses is known as the *factory overhead*. *The total product cost* or total manufacturing expense is the sum of prime costs and factory overheads. *Other indirect expenses or overheads* which are incurred on activities or to pay for facilities or services other than those connected with production include:

■ marketing and selling costs;
■ distribution costs – warehousing, depots or transportation;
■ research and development costs; and
■ administration expenses – the costs of administrative departments such as finance, personnel and the corporate office, plus any corporate costs such as rent, rates and insurance that cannot be charged directly to manufacturing.

The relationship between these costs is illustrated in Figure 70.1.

Classification of costs by behaviour

Costs may be classified into three patterns of behaviour:

1. *Variable*, where the cost varies directly or proportionately to the level of activity. Direct material is an example of a variable cost. In this case the variable cost per unit is constant, irrespective of changes in the level of activity.
2. *Non-variable or fixed*, where the total cost remains unchanged over a period of time regardless of changes in the levels of activity. The most regular fixed-cost items are rent and rates, management salaries and

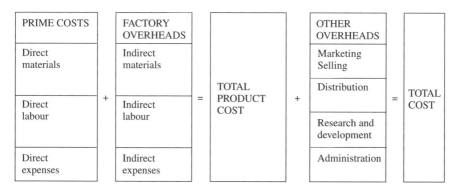

Figure 70.1 *The make-up of total costs*

depreciation of fixed assets. In these cases the fixed cost per unit will fall as output increases and will rise as output decreases.

3. *Semi-variable*, where the total costs tend to vary with significant changes in activity levels but are fixed at certain levels of activity.

4. *Stepped*, where there is a significant change in costs at specific activity levels (a type of semi-variable cost). Graphical representations of fixed and variable costs are shown in Figures 70.2 and 70.3 respectively.

Classification of costs by product, order or job

A product, order or job cost is determined by calculating the direct labour and direct material costs. In addition, departmental overheads are allocated in accordance with one of the following measures of activity:

1. Direct labour costs.
2. Direct labour hours.
3. Machine hours.
4. Units of product.

Figure 70.4 shows how fixed and variable costs combine to produce total costs.

Classification of costs by location

Costs may be classified according to function, department, location or designated cost centre. Directly attributable costs will be allocated to the cost centre and are controllable by the manager of that cost centre. In a fully absorbed costing system, other costs which cannot be attributed directly will be apportioned to departments on some arbitrary basis, eg building occupation costs might be apportioned on the basis of floor area. Apportioned costs are largely uncontrollable by the departmental manager.

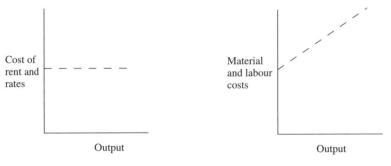

Figure 70.2 *Fixed costs*   **Figure 70.3** *Variable costs*

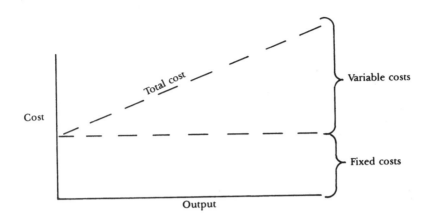

Figure 70.4 *Total costs*

The semi-variable and stepped cost categories exist because costs do behave that way. But when carrying out *cost–volume–profit* (CVP) analysis (see Chapter 76), or preparing break-even charts, it may be necessary to make assumptions as to whether costs are truly variable or whether they should be regarded as fixed for the purpose of the calculation.

It is also necessary to bear in mind the concept of *relevant range* when examining fixed costs. A fixed cost is fixed only in relation to a given period of time – the budget period – and a given, though wide, range of activity called the relevant range. For example, output above a particular range may require more space or extra managerial or supervising staff. This is illustrated in Figure 70.5.

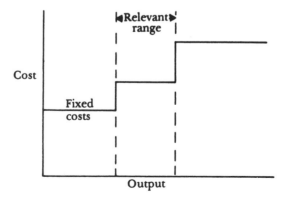

Figure 70.5 *The relevant range for fixed costs*

Classification of costs by product, order or job

A product, order or job cost is determined by calculating the direct labour and direct material costs. In addition, overheads are allocated in one of the ways described below.

COSTING

Costing techniques are used to establish the total cost of a product for stock valuation, pricing and estimating purposes and to enable the company to establish that the proposed selling price will enable a profit to be made. Costing techniques also, and importantly, provide information for control and decision making. The approaches to costing are all based on some form of measurement and take account of the need for overhead recovery.

Cost measurement

Cost measurement involves measuring the direct costs of materials and labour plus the indirect costs (overheads) originating in the factory (factory overheads) and elsewhere in the company (distribution, marketing, advertising, servicing, research and development, purchasing, information systems and administration).

Overhead recovery

Overheads are charged to cost units to provide information on total costs – this process is called overhead recovery. It involves some method of allocating overheads to products on the grounds that all company resources support production and sales – even corporate expenses should be allocated to product costs. There are a number of methods of doing this, as summarized below.

Absorption costing

The most widely used method of overhead recovery is called absorption costing and involves allocating all fixed and variable costs to cost units. The global recovery method charges out all overheads to cost units on the basis of the direct labour hours, although this can be arbitrary and is certainly flawed in situations where direct labour costs are not a particularly high proportion of total costs. This can result in a situation where a very small change in the number of direct labour hours worked can have an unrealistic and dramatic effect on the costs allocated to products. The more refined departmental recovery method allocates overheads to departmental cost centres but these overheads are only charged out to those cost units passing through that cost centre, which means that overheads can be more accurately apportioned according to the use the cost centre makes of the facility which generated the overhead cost. Absorption costing is described more fully in Chapter 71.

Activity-based costing

The problem of allocating costs referred to above has led to the development of the activity-based costing (ABC) method. This is founded on the assumption that activities cause costs and a link is made between activities and products by assigning costs of activities to products on the basis of an individual product's demand for each activity. Activity-based costing is treated more fully in Chapter 72.

Marginal costing

Marginal or direct costing (see Chapter 73) segregates fixed costs and apportions the marginal or variable costs to products. It is used, often in association with an absorption costing system, for cost–volume–profit analysis (see Chapter 76) and planning.

Standard costing

Standard costing (see Chapter 74) is the preparation of predetermined or standard costs and their comparison with actual costs to identify variances. Standard costs are used to measure performance and express what a product or activity should cost, not what it actually costs. It is used mainly in mass or large-batch production factories.

COST ANALYSIS

When analysing costs the following concepts need to be considered:

1. The distinction between product costs and period costs.
2. The distinction between total costs and marginal costs.
3. The need for relevance.
4. The use of differential costing.
5. Opportunity costs.

Product and period costs

Product costs are related to goods produced or purchased for resale and are initially identifiable as part of inventory. These product or inventory costs become expenses in the form of cost of goods sold only when the inventory is sold.

Period costs are costs that are being deducted as expenses during the current period without having been previously classified as product costs. The distinction between product and period costs when analysing gross margin and operating profit is illustrated in Figure 70.6.

Total and marginal costs

If some costs are variable while others are fixed, the total cost per unit of output is representative of only one level of activity. A change in the volume of output will affect the total unit cost, because the fixed costs will spread over a larger or smaller number of units.

Marginal costing recognizes the variability of cost items and differentiates throughout the costing system between the variable or marginal costs and the fixed or period costs.

When calculating the marginal cost of a product, the total of prime cost and variable overheads is computed. The difference between the marginal cost of the product and the selling price is the marginal income or contribution.

Relevance

Cost analysis has to be relevant. It has to provide information that will lead to the best decisions concerning future courses of action when alternatives are available.

Cost analysis is therefore concerned with the expected future data which will influence choices of action. In cost analysis terms, relevance is therefore about the expected future costs of alternatives and is not simply about historical or past data which may have no bearing on the decision.

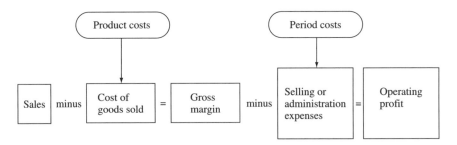

Figure 70.6 *Product and period costs*

Differential costing

Differential costing is used in decision making, which is essentially a process of choosing between competing alternatives, each with its own combination of income and costs. Problems of choice include capital expenditure decisions, make or buy decisions, the length of production runs, sales mix decisions and product planning.

Differential costing is concerned with the effects on costs and revenue of a certain course of action. Differential costs are increases or decreases in total costs, or the change in specific elements of costs that result from any variations in operations. Economists use the term *incremental costs* for the same concept and define them as the additional costs of a change in the level or nature of an activity.

Differential costing only uses *relevant* costs as defined above. In other words, it eliminates residual costs (usually historical or sunk costs) and concentrates on the costs that will be incurred as a result of company decisions, ie future costs.

Differential costing is more difficult if an absorption costing system is used because average unit costs produced by such a system include past costs, which are irrelevant to decisions about the future.

Opportunity costs

Opportunity costs represent income forgone by rejecting alternatives. They are therefore not incorporated into formal accounting systems because they do not incorporate cash receipts or outflows. Opportunity costs are, however, very relevant when examining alternative proposals or projects. When deciding whether or not to allocate capital to a project it is highly desirable to consider if the money could produce a better or worse return if invested elsewhere.

BENEFITS

The provision of comprehensive but relevant cost data is an essential component in successful management. The classification of costs as direct or indirect and fixed or variable, and the allocation or apportionment of those costs to products and cost centres is vital to the process of cost–volume–profit analysis. This analysis then provides the basis for output and pricing decisions. The analysis of costs and the provision of cost data are the basis for *responsibility* accounting, in which managers take part in constructing their budgets and are held responsible for any variances that occur which are within their control.

71

Absorption Costing

DEFINITION

Absorption or full costing is the practice of assigning all costs, both fixed and variable, to operations or products. Some absorption costing systems set expenses such as general administration, financial costs and selling expenses against revenue in the profit-and-loss account so that the outcome is simply the cost of production. In a full historical cost system, however, all administration and sales expenses are also absorbed into production costs.

COST OF PRODUCTION

In an absorption cost system the cost of production consists of:

1. *Prime costs* – direct material and direct labour.
2. *Production overheads* – indirect materials and wage costs arising in such areas as stores, packing, maintenance, the salaries of factory managers and supervisors, and the costs of power, heating and lighting, and depreciation.

The process of relating these costs to production is called assignment.

The selling value of the goods produced minus the full cost of production is the factory profit.

OVERHEAD ABSORPTION OR RECOVERY

The overhead which is charged to cost units is called absorbed or recovered overhead. Overhead absorption or recovery is achieved by one or a combination of overhead rates, for example, labour hour rate, machine hour rate, direct material costs percentage. The difference between the amount of overhead recovered during a period and the actual overhead incurred is called under- or over-recovered overhead.

The methods used to allocate or assign overheads to production are as follows:

1. *Direct allocation*, where there is a demonstrable relationship between the cost and the product to which it is being applied. Such costs may be direct to the cost centre but indirect to the production process. Depreciation and fixed process costs may be treated this way.
2. *By proration and apportionment* – establishing some basis for apportioning overheads which are not directly related to products. Some aspect of size in the department or production volumes is usually the base, although there is no one generally accepted approach to apportioning overhead costs. Examples of methods used are:

   ■ dividing the total overhead figure by the number of units produced, but this is too crude as each unit may not be identical and, if so, they should not share indirect costs equally;
   ■ direct labour hours or costs for the various products or units produced – this is best in a labour-intensive operation, but is the most frequently used method;
   ■ machine hours where machines dominate, as in a machine shop; and
   ■ floor space, for power, heat, lighting, rent and rates.

FULL ABSORPTION

For pricing and inventory valuation purposes it is necessary to know the full cost of producing a cost unit. This is not only the prime cost plus factory overheads, which make up the cost of production, but also all the other overheads, which include selling and administration expenses. These overheads are distributed to the cost unit by apportionment and absorption, using one or more of the bases mentioned earlier, eg direct labour hour rate or machine hour rate. Thus the cost unit is based on the total unit cost inclusive of full overhead recovery. This process is sometimes referred to as the global recovery method.

ADVANTAGES AND DISADVANTAGES

Advantages

The apparent advantage of absorption or full costing is that all the costs are covered. Nothing seems to be hidden away. Absorption costing based on the full recovery of overheads highlights the danger of cutting prices to achieve volume sales without paying enough attention to the need to allow for fixed costs in the longer term. Absorption costing is also recognized by the International Accounting Standards Body as the appropriate method of valuing stocks and work-in-progress.

Disadvantages

The main disadvantages of absorption costing are as follows:

1. The fixed costs are apportioned on the basis of assumptions about the level of output and are, in fact, representative of only one level of activity. A change in the volume of output will affect the total unit cost, since the fixed costs will be spread over a larger or smaller number of units. Overheads are then either under- or over-absorbed and the total cost per unit will have been under- or over-stated. The danger is that once a budget has been prepared on an absorption cost basis with built-in assumptions about the level of activity, the figures which it reveals are likely to continue to be used for pricing and profit planning decisions even though changes in output levels make them invalid. For example, if fixed costs remain unchanged, reduction in output levels will mean they have to be apportioned over a smaller number of units. The factory profit per unit of output will therefore be less. But management may still expect the higher budgeted profit fixed for a larger output figure to apply at the lower level. Their expectations of profit will therefore be too high.

   The concept of operating leverage is relevant to this problem. Operating leverage is the ratio of fixed costs to total costs. The higher this is, the more sensitive overhead recovery is to volume forecasting errors.
2. There is no satisfactory method of allocating indirect fixed expenses to the final product. Arbitrary methods are adopted, usually related to the volume of production (eg direct labour hours), even though the results obtained from one method in a given circumstance may differ significantly. However, the technique of activity-based costing aims to overcome this problem (see Chapter 72).
3. Absorption costing does not provide adequate guidance on the relationships between cost, volume and profit or on the pricing decisions

which are dependent on these relationships. In other words, absorption costing does not permit the proper analysis of the impact of volume changes on profitability.

4. The full historical method of costing, which absorption costing becomes if all overheads are charged or allocated to each unit of cost, is based on the cost when it is incurred. There is no reference to possible changes in price if the product is to be produced in the future. The adoption of a historical basis for assessing expenses can have a misleading effect if the costs are required to tell management whether or not it is worthwhile continuing production of a particular product. The difficulty of changing prices is particularly relevant in the case of materials whose prices vary considerably over short periods of time.

OTHER APPROACHES

The disadvantages listed above refer mainly to the global recovery method which aggregates all overheads and then charges them out to cost units according to the direct labour hours going into each product. The more refined departmental overhead recovery method is used by many larger firms with diversified products and production systems. This involves charging out all overheads to operational cost centres when they arise. These operational cost centres then charge out their overheads but only to those cost units passing through that cost centre.

Activity-based costing is described in Chapter 72. This aims to provide better management accounting information for product costing, decision support and cost control purposes. It may be used in conjunction with a global overhead recovery system which provides financial accounting information for valuing inventory.

In addition, some companies use marginal costing, as described in Chapter 73, to help them make decisions which allow for volume and price changes. But they will continue to use some form of absorption costing as the main method of recording historical costs (ie costs that have already been incurred) and valuing stocks and work-in-progress.

72

Activity-based Costing

DEFINITION

Activity-based costing (ABC) systems are based on the belief that activities cause costs and that a link should therefore be made between activities and products by assigning costs of activities to products based on an individual product's demand for each activity.

RATIONALE

The concept of activity-based costing was developed by Robert Kaplan and Robin Cooper from the Harvard Business School.[1,2] They argued that managers in companies selling multiple products are making important decisions about pricing, product mix and process technology based on distorted cost information.

The reason for this distortion is that the traditional method of allocating factory and corporate overheads by burden rates on direct labour (absorption costing or global overhead recovery) was designed several decades ago when overhead costs were relatively small and distortions arising from arbitrary overhead allocations were not significant. This was especially the case in the typical situation where a company was making a limited range of products and the costs of direct labour and materials, the most important production factors, could be traced easily to individual products. Today, however, product lines and marketing channels have proliferated. Direct labour now represents a relatively small proportion of corporate costs, while expenses covering factory support operations, marketing, distribution and engineering have exploded.

In any case, the resources consumed by products are unrelated to direct labour costs. Costs are therefore allocated to products in ways which are not connected to actions taken within a cost centre.

Some companies have recognized the declining role of direct labour and use two additional allocation bases – materials-related expenses and machine hours or processing time. According to Kaplan and Cooper, however, this still does not guarantee that the allocation of overheads will not distort product costs, and cost centre managers may not get the control information they need.

As a result, decisions on pricing and product mix are being made on the basis of inaccurate data. Profits are frequently understated on high-volume products and overstated on speciality items. A further problem is that cost centre managers do not get the right information for controlling their costs. Operating costs are reported too late and are too aggregated to benefit production cost centre managers.

One reason for this reluctance to trace overheads to products and allocate costs more accurately according to the use of resources was that the expense of collecting data made it hard to justify more sophisticated allocation procedures. However, information costs are no longer a barrier. And for operations under computer control, digital data is easily captured to record what, when and how much was produced. Automatic bar-code reading of parts combined with local area networks permit continual tracking of parts and operatives. Cost control systems can record these data and provide frequent, accurate reports on output and resource consumption.

A further reason for the reliance on traditional methods is that they were originally designed for inventory valuation, which, in accordance with financial accounting principles, requires manufacturers to allocate periodic production costs to all items produced. For this purpose, an aggregated, simplistic method of assigning overhead costs to products is quite acceptable – accountancy principles do not require that allocated overhead costs be casually related to the demands of individual products.

But as Kaplan argues, cost system designers have failed to recognize that their systems need to address three different functions:

■ inventory valuation for financial and tax statements, allocating period production costs between goods sold and goods in stock;
■ operational control, providing feedback to production and department managers on the resources consumed (labour, materials, energy and other services) during an operating period;
■ individual product cost measurement.

Kaplan and Cooper argue that no single system, especially one based on the aggregate allocation of overheads, can adequately cover all three functions. The traditional method of allocation is appropriate for inventory valuation but is inadequate as a means of providing data for operational control and product pricing. They therefore suggest that an additional system – activity-based costing – should be used for these purposes.

THE PHILOSOPHY OF ACTIVITY-BASED COSTING

The assumption underpinning activity-based costing (ABC) is that virtually all of a company's activities exist to support the production and delivery of goods and services. They should therefore all be considered as product costs. And because nearly all factory and corporate support costs are separable, they can be split apart and traced to individual products or product families.

On the basis of this assumption, the philosophy of activity-based costing is that costs can be controlled more effectively by focusing directly on managing the forces that cause the activities – the 'cost drivers' – rather than cost.

The reporting of the costs consumed by the significant activities of a business, and their cost drivers, provides the basis for understanding what causes overhead costs and directs attention to where steps can be taken to improve profitability. Knowing the high costs of material movements, or the cost of producing many different components or maintaining many different machines, highlights the need to carry out these activities more effectively.

Thus activity-based costing provides better, more accurate, information for decision making on prices and product mix, and for the control of manufacturing operations.

DEVELOPING AN ACTIVITY-BASED COSTING SYSTEM

The steps required to develop an activity-based costing system are as follows:

1. Identify the main activities performed in the organization, such as manufacturing and assembly, as well as support activities, including purchasing, packing and dispatching.
2. Identify the factors which influence the cost of each activity – the cost drivers.
3. Collect accurate data on direct labour and material costs and on the costs of each of these factors.

4. Establish the demands made by particular products on activities, using the cost drivers as a measure of demand.
5. Trace the cost of activities to products according to a product's demand for each activity.

The rules developed by Kaplan and Cooper for this process are:

- focus on expensive resources, thus directing attention to resource categories where the new costing process has the potential to make big differences on product costs;
- emphasize resources whose consumption varies significantly by product and product type – look for diversity; and
- focus on resources whose demand patterns are uncorrelated with traditional allocation measures, such as direct labour, materials and processing time, thus identifying resources with the greatest potential for distortion under traditional systems.

This process cannot be done with surgical precision, but, as Kaplan and Cooper say:

> It is better to be basically correct with activity-based costs, say within 5 or 10 per cent of the actual demands a product makes on organizational resources, than to be precisely wrong (perhaps by as much as 200 per cent) using outdated allocation techniques.

ABC may not be appropriate for all companies, particularly those where overheads are relatively small and which do not produce a wide range of products. But many of the benefits of ABC can still be obtained by implementing a partial system which focuses only on the most important activities.

Nor should the method be used to produce monthly profit statements. Traditional methods can be used for that, leaving ABC to support strategic decision making, profitability analysis and the control of manufacturing costs.

BENEFITS

Activity-based costing ensures that management accounting information is not merely a by-product of external financial accounting systems. While it provides a more accurate basis for calculating product costs, perhaps its greatest benefit is that it is a mechanism for managing costs. It is in this area of cost management and resource planning, rather than product costing, that ABC has the greatest potential.

In particular, the benefits of ABC are that:

- the cost-driver rates established by the system can be used to measure activity performance and efficiency and provide a more suitable basis for budgeting;
- accurate feedback can be provided to cost centre managers on their performance based on their consumption of resources during a period rather than the allocations of costs over which they have no control; and
- the provision of accurate information on product costs enables better decisions to be made on pricing, marketing, product design and product mix.

REFERENCES

1. Kaplan, R, 'One cost system isn't enough', *Harvard Business Review*, January–February 1988, pp. 61–66.
2. Cooper, R and Kaplan, R, 'Measure costs right: make the right decisions', *Harvard Business Review*, September–October 1988, pp. 96–103.

FURTHER READING

Drury, C *et al*, *A Survey of Management Accounting Practices in UK Manufacturing Companies*, Chartered Association of Certified Accountants, Glasgow 1993.

73

Marginal Costing

DEFINITION

Marginal or direct costing divides costs into fixed and variable costs. The latter tend to vary in total, in relation to output, and are regarded as marginal costs. Marginal costing first segregates fixed costs and then apportions the marginal costs to products or processes.

Marginal costing may be incorporated into the system of recording and collecting costs or it may be used as an analytical tool for studying and reporting on the effects of changes in volume and type of output. Where it is incorporated into the system of recording and collecting costs, stocks are valued at variable costs, while fixed costs are not charged to production but are instead written off to the profit-and-loss account in the year in which they are incurred.

Marginal costing is also sometimes called variable costing.

BACKGROUND TO MARGINAL COSTING

The background to the marginal costing concept is the marginal theory in economics which refers to the ambition of the entrepreneur to expand his or her business at the point where the additional cost of producing one more unit equals the additional revenue from selling it. The reason for this is that, as output increases, the pressures of demand and supply will cause prices and wages, and therefore costs, to increase. As more units are produced which need to be sold, prices will have to be reduced to ensure their disposal. This increase in cost and reduction in revenue will mean that, eventually, the additional cost of producing one more unit will be exactly the same as the additional revenue from selling it. No further profits will therefore be made and it will no longer be in the interests of the company to continue to expand production.

Marginal costing is known as direct costing in the United States, where it was developed in the 1930s to overcome the distortion caused by fluctuations in the level of stocks, and to eliminate the problem of the volume variance where there are large seasonal variations in the level of sales.

MAKE-UP

Marginal cost

Marginal cost comprises material, labour and expenses, plus variable works, administration and selling expenses.

Contribution

Sales revenue minus marginal cost equals the contribution or margin. This indicates the amount which sales of the product contribute to the fixed expenses of the enterprise and to profit, thus highlighting the fact that until those fixed expenses have been covered, no profit has been made.

Comparison of full, or absorption, and marginal costing

The distinction between full and marginal costing for a product is illustrated in Table 73.1.

USES

Marginal costing has the following uses:

1. *Cost–volume–profit analysis.* Marginal costing is an essential tool in *cost–volume–profit analysis*. It demonstrates the relationships between cost and volume and, therefore, the effect on profit of a change in volume. Thus it assists in making decisions on selecting products, outlets and markets.
2. *Relationship between fixed costs and profits.* Marginal costing highlights the significance of fixed costs on profits. It indicates whether or not, in a

Table 73.1 *Comparison of full and marginal costing*

		Full cost		Marginal cost	
	p	*p*	*p*	*p*	*p*
Sales price			50		50
Direct material costs		5		5	
Direct labour costs		3		3	
Direct expenses		2		2	
Prime cost		10		10	
Works expenses					
Fixed	8	12		4	
Variable	4	22			
Administration expenses					
Fixed	6				
Variable		6			
Cost of production		28			
Selling expenses					
Fixed	10				
Variable	6	16		6	
Total of above costs and expenses			44		20
Net profit			6		
Margin or total contribution					30
Contribution to fixed costs				24	
Contribution to profit				6	

highly competitive situation, it may well be wise to take an order which covers marginal costs and makes some contribution towards fixed costs, rather than lose the order and the contribution by insisting upon a price above full cost.

3. *Contribution analysis.* The analysis of the contribution per unit each product makes towards fixed or current period costs and profit leads to the preparation of statements showing the total contribution each product class has made towards the recovery of period costs. These statements may be further refined by deducting any discretionary or separable period costs (ie costs such as annual tooling and product advertising) which should be avoided if the product line were dropped.

4. *Sales mix decisions.* These can be made by analysing the respective contributions of each product line after charging separable period costs.

5. *Overcoming the volume variance problem.* The problems of volume variance in a standard absorption costing system are overcome. In absorption costing, the under- or over-absorbed fixed production

overhead is represented by the volume variance. In businesses with large variations in stock levels and a high ratio of fixed costs this approach can lead to serious distortions in the profit figures. It is perfectly possible in these circumstances for profits to decline when sales increase and vice versa, and it is hard to explain with absorption costing what is happening or why. Profit planning and control are therefore made more difficult. With the marginal costing approach, stocks are valued at variable cost and there is no volume variance. Consequently, the relationship between sales volume and contribution is much easier to explain and understand.

6. *Make-or-buy decisions.* These are best taken with full knowledge of the marginal or variable cost of making rather than buying a product. But it is also helpful to know through marginal costing what contribution to fixed costs will result from a 'make' decision.

7. *Limiting factor decisions.* Decisions on which orders to accept have often to be made when plant is being operated at capacity. The order to be accepted is the one that marginal costing shows will make the highest contribution per unit of the limiting factor. For example, if labour were the limiting factor, the product to be chosen for production would be the product which yields the largest contribution per unit of labour employed.

8. *Pricing decisions.* The marginal cost approach to pricing decisions recognizes that decision making is about choosing between competing alternatives, each with its own combination of income and costs. The relevant concepts to employ are therefore future incremental costs and revenues and opportunity costs, not full costs, which include historical or sunk costs. The marginal approach answers the question 'What will happen to profits if the selling prices of particular products are raised or lowered?' With marginal pricing, the company seeks to fix its prices so as to maximize its total contribution to fixed costs and profit. This is achieved by considering each product separately and fixing its price at a level which is calculated to maximize its total contribution.

ADVANTAGES AND DISADVANTAGES

Advantages

Marginal costing systems are simple to operate and do not involve the problems of overhead apportionments. Fluctuations in profits are easier to explain because they result from cost–volume interactions and not from changes in inventory. Marginal costing emphasizes the contribution made by sales to fixed cost recovery and profit and clarifies decision making in many key areas of management accounting where volume and product mix and pricing considerations are important.

Disadvantages

Marginal costing diverts attention from full costs, especially in the longer term. But in the long run it is important to have an understanding of the full cost of a product to the company, since the company must make sufficient contribution from all products to cover fixed costs and provide an adequate return on capital employed. In the short term, it may be desirable to price products below full cost as long as the price covers the variable cost and makes some contribution. But it is important to know what the implications of such decisions are on fixed-cost recovery at the time they are made. Marginal pricing can lead to danger if it is indulged in too readily and without proper foresight.

CONCLUSION

Marginal costing is an essential tool for cost–volume–profit analysis and planning. It is often operated as such in association with an absorption costing system which provides information on full costs for longer-term control and for the valuation of stocks in financial accounts.

74

Standard Costing

DEFINITION

Standard costing is the preparation of predetermined or standard costs, their comparison with actual costs to identify variances, and the analysis of variances to determine causes and to decide on any corrective actions required.

A standard is the required value of an item, given current capacity and working methods. Standards are developed by analysis for each of the cost components in a product. The total of these components is the total standard cost of the product.

USE

Standard costs are used to measure performance. They express not what a product or activity actually cost, but what it should have cost.

In theory, standard costs are the real costs of the product and can properly be used as a means of charging production and, therefore, for valuing work-in-progress and finished stocks. Any deviation from standard is said to be the result of inefficiency, excessive waste or some other abnormal condition and is chargeable only to the period in which it is incurred.

METHOD

Basic approach

Standards are set after a careful analysis of the job, the methods which are used and the efficiency of performance. Detailed standards are often only established for the two major elements of cost: direct labour and direct materials, and all other costs are controlled with the help of departmental overhead budgets. Before setting direct labour or direct material standards, however, it is necessary to decide on the type of standards to be used.

Types of standards

The two main types of standards are:

1. *ideal or perfection standards*, which are expressions of the absolute minimum costs possible under the best conceivable conditions, using existing specifications and equipment; and
2. *currently attainable standards*, which are those that can be attained by very efficient operations.

Currently attainable standards are most commonly used because:

■ they do not demotivate employees by setting almost unachievable goals, as ideal standards do; and
■ they provide a more realistic basis for cash budgeting, inventory valuation and departmental budgets.

Direct labour standards

Direct labour standards consist of two elements – standard time and standard pay:

1. *Standard time*. The standard time to produce a limit of output is based on standard hours. Work study is used to determine the standard work output for an average worker working at an average pace. This average output per working hour is the standard hour, which gives the labour content of a cost unit expressed as standard time (hours or minutes) per unit. In departments with a number of products all units of hours are expressed in terms of the standard input of hours allowed for their production. Standard hours thus become the common denominator for measuring total volume.
2. *Standard pay*, which is stated as the hourly wage rate.

The unit labour cost is calculated by multiplying the standard time per unit by the standard hourly pay rate.

Direct material standards

Direct material standards are built up by:

1. establishing the price per unit of each material or ingredient used in manufacturing the product;
2. working out the standard usage of each of those materials or ingredients in manufacturing one unit of the product; and
3. multiplying price per unit by standard usage to obtain the standard material cost per unit.

Make-up of standard unit costs

The standard unit cost is the standard labour cost per unit plus the standard material cost per unit. To this are added the variable expenses or overheads which are recovered on a basis such as so much per labour hour. The standard costs plus standard variable expenses give the total variable costs. If fixed costs are added, the total cost per unit is obtained as set out in the example of a standard cost profile in Table 74.1. This profile includes variable and fixed overheads for which standards are also required.

Table 74.1 *Standard cost profile*

	Per unit £
Direct materials	6.00
Direct labour	2.00
Variable expenses	.70
Variable costs	8.70
Fixed costs	.30
Total costs	9.00
Profit	1.00
Sales price	10.00

OVERHEADS

Overhead standards are set on the basis of an estimate of the activity levels in the coming period. They are split into the part that varies in relation to changes in output, and the part which remains fixed – a variable overhead and a fixed overhead component. Overheads are applied as a standard rate per unit of output on the basis of direct labour or machine hours or direct material.

VARIANCE ANALYSIS

Variance analysis is the technique of analysing the difference between planned and actual costs.

Variances for labour or material are either price (wages or ingredients) or quantity (standard hours or material usage). Differences between standard and actual overhead rates are expressed as volume, cost or efficiency variances.

Variance analysis is treated in more detail in Chapter 75.

BENEFITS

Standard cost systems are used to overcome some of the weaknesses of historical cost accounting, which only provides information on what costs have been, gives no indication of what costs ought to be, and only allows managers to compare present performance with past results. The information provided by a standard cost system is used to promote cost control and improve managerial efficiency.

75

Variance Analysis

DEFINITION

Variance analysis identifies differences between actual and standard costs or between actual and budgeted overheads, sales and, ultimately, profits. The reasons for variances are then established to provide guidance for any corrective action required.

CLASSIFICATION OF VARIANCES

The classification of variance headings and the reasons why variances occur are shown in Figure 75.1.

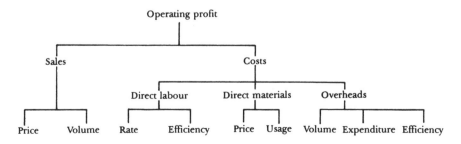

Figure 75.1 *Classification of variances*

OPERATING PROFIT VARIANCE

Operating profit is revenue less current expenses. Variances in operating profit are caused either by sales revenue being above or below budget or because of positive or negative variances under the headings of direct labour, direct materials and overheads.

SALES VARIANCE

Sales variance is the difference between the budgeted value of sales and the actual value of sales achieved in a given period. Sales variances may be caused by a sales price variance or a sales volume variance. The latter is subdivided into sales quantity variance and sales mix variance.

Sales price variance

Sales price variance is that portion of the sales variance which is due to the difference between the actual value of sales (actual quantity × actual price) and the actual quantities sold, valued at standard price. In other words, it is the difference between the actual price at which the product was sold and the standard or budgeted price.

Sales volume variance

Sales volume variance is that portion of the sales variance which is due to the difference between the actual quantities sold and the standard quantity specified. It can be subdivided into two types of variance:

1. *Sales quantity variance* – that portion of the sales volume variance which is due to the difference between actual and budgeted units sold. Under absorption costing, these variances are valued at the standard unit profit, and under marginal costing they are valued at the standard unit contribution.
2. *Sales mix variance* – that portion of the sales volume variance which is due to differences between the actual and the standard or forecast composition of the sales mix, ie the proportions of each type of product sold.

DIRECT LABOUR AND MATERIAL VARIANCES

Direct labour

Direct labour variances are classified as follows:

1. *Labour rate variance* – the difference between the actual and budget/standard hourly rate of pay applied to the actual hours paid. This is the price variance for labour costs.
2. *Labour efficiency variance* – the difference between the actual working and standard hours to produce the actual output. This variance can be subdivided into:

   ■ labour productivity variance – the variance caused by the standard mix of labour producing more or less than expected;
   ■ labour mix variance – the variance caused by differences between the proportions of the different grades of labour actually used and the budgeted or standard proportions; and
   ■ labour idle time variance – the difference between budgeted hours paid and actual hours worked; this difference is idle time, which will have been budgeted at zero, so that any idle time causes an adverse variance.

Direct materials

Direct materials variances are classified as follows:

1. *Materials price variance* – the difference in unit prices between standard/budget and actual applied to the actual quantity of materials used.
2. *Materials usage variance* – the materials quantity variance; the variance arising from using more or fewer units of material input than budgeted/standard to produce the actual quantity of units. This variance can be subdivided into:

   ■ materials yield variance – that part of the materials usage variance arising from the materials process loss being different from budget/standard; and
   ■ materials mix variance – that part of the materials usage variance arising from the proportion in which materials are used being different from the budgeted standard proportions.

Interrelationships

The interrelationships between price (or rate) and quantity (efficiency or usage) variance is illustrated in Figure 75.2. In this example, the rectangle represents standard costs and its sides represent standard price and standard quantity. Both variances are adverse. The upper right-hand area is treated as a price variance so that the analysis of the quantity variance can concentrate on the factors other than price which produced it.

OVERHEAD VARIANCES

Overhead variances are classified thus:

1. *Volume* – the overhead quantity variances arising from the volume against which overheads are recovered being different from standard/budget.
2. *Expenditure* – the overhead price variances arising because of a difference between standard/budget overhead expenditure in the month and actual expenditure applied to the actual recovery volume.
3. *Efficiency* – that part of the volume variance arising from labour productivity variances when overheads are recovered against labour hours.

BENEFITS

Variance analysis is a key part of control, especially when it is based on properly measured standards. It uses the management by exception principle which means that problems are brought into prominence so that action can be taken where it is most needed, and efforts are made directly where they can produce the best results.

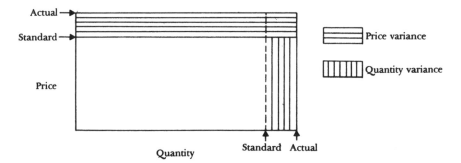

Figure 75.2 *Interrelationship between variances*

76

Cost–Volume–Profit Analysis

DEFINITION

Cost–volume–profit (CVP) analysis studies the relationships between expenses (costs), revenue (sales) and net income (net profit). The aim is to establish what will happen to financial results if a specified level of activity or volume fluctuates, ie the implications on profit levels of changes in costs, volume of sales or prices.

USES

CVP analysis is used to study the effects of changes in volume on variable costs, and the relationship between profit and volume (the profit–volume or P/V ratio). It answers the key question: 'What effect would increases or decreases in one or more of labour cost, material cost, fixed costs, volume of sales have on profits?' CVP analysis is used in profit planning and as a guide to making tactical decisions on sales effort and prices.

CONCEPTS AND TECHNIQUES

CVP analysis combines the following management accounting concepts and techniques:

1. the variable and fixed elements of cost;
2. profit–volume (P/V) ratio analysis;
3. differential costing;
4. break-even analysis;
5. margin of safety ratio; and
6. sales mix analysis.

Variable and fixed costs

1. *Variable costs* vary directly with the level of business activity and are constant per unit of production.
2. *Fixed costs* remain constant over a particular period of time, whatever the level of business activity, within a given, though wide, range known as the relevant range.

Profit–volume ratio

The profit–volume or contribution ratio is sales revenue minus variable costs (contribution) divided by sales revenue. It shows the rate at which profit increases or decreases with an increase or decrease in volume.

Differential costing

Differential or incremental costing measures the effects on total costs that result from any changes in operations. In CVP analysis it is used to assess the impact of alternative decisions about activity volumes on fixed or variable costs and on contribution or profit. Differential costing can be linked with *sensitivity analysis*, which takes an overall look at the effect of different assumptions, including activity levels and costs, on profit levels.

Break-even analysis

Break-even analysis shows the point at which sales revenue is just sufficient to cover total costs, ie the number of units which must be sold before the company begins to earn a profit.

Margin of safety ratio

The difference between actual or budgeted sales and break-even sales is known as the margin of safety. The margin of safety ratio, therefore, indicates the extent to which sales volume could decrease before profits would disappear, other things being equal. In other words, the margin of safety represents that proportion of sales which determines the profits of the company.

Sales mix analysis

Sales mix analysis establishes the effects of changes in the sales mix on cost–volume–profit relationships. When a sales mix is chosen it can be shown on a P/V or break-even chart by assuming average revenues and costs for a given mix.

METHOD

CVP analysis combines the concepts and techniques listed above by initially:

1. establishing the fixed and variable costs related to products;
2. calculating the relationship between sales volume and revenue by reference to actual or assumed unit prices;
3. working out the profit–volume (P/V) ratio by calculating contribution (sales revenue minus variable costs) as a proportion of sales revenue;
4. using differential costing and sensitivity analysis to assess the impact of alternative decisions on activity levels on costs and profits;
5. drawing up break-even charts which establish the point at which sales begin to produce profits;
6. deducing from the break-even analysis the margin of safety ratio to indicate the levels of profit as different volumes of sales above the break-even point; and
7. determining the cumulative or combined effect of each product on profitability to assess the effects of changes in the product mix.

The outcomes of each of the above analyses are then linked to answer such questions as follows:

- What sales revenue must be achieved to recover fixed costs?
- By what percentage can current sales drop before the margin of safety is exhausted and the break-even point is reached?
- How will profits be affected by different levels of sales?
- What level of sales revenue must be achieved to reach profit targets?
- What are the implications of increases or decreases in costs per unit or fixed costs on profits?
- What is the optimum mix of products from the point of view of profitability?
- What effect will price changes have on profits (on the basis of assumptions about the impact of such changes on demand and therefore revenue)?

BENEFIT

The benefit of CVP analysis is that it highlights the key factors that affect profits and enables the company to understand the implications of changes in sales volume, costs or prices. This knowledge of cost behaviour patterns and profit–volume relationships provides insights which are valuable in planning and controlling short- and long-run operations.

77

Profit–Volume Charts

DEFINITION

Profit–volume (P/V) charts show the impact of changes in volume on net income.

DESCRIPTION

A P/V chart is illustrated in Figure 77.1. It is constructed as follows:

1. The vertical axis represents total profit (net income) or loss.
2. The horizontal axis represents volume in units.
3. Unrecovered fixed costs are shown as losses below the horizontal axis, and at zero volume the net loss equals total fixed costs, of £25,000 in this example.
4. The profit line slopes upwards from the intercept with the vertical axis at a loss of £25,000.
5. The profit line intercepts the horizontal volume axis at the break-even point of 50,000 units. This is where sales minus variable costs (ie total contribution) equals fixed costs.
6. Each unit sold beyond the break-even point will contribute to profits (total costs being completely recovered). In this example, every 10,000 units sold above the break-even point adds £5,000 to profits.
7. The P/V ratio represents the slope of the profit line on the profit–volume chart. It is the ratio at which profit increases/decreases with an increase/decrease in volume and is given by the formula:

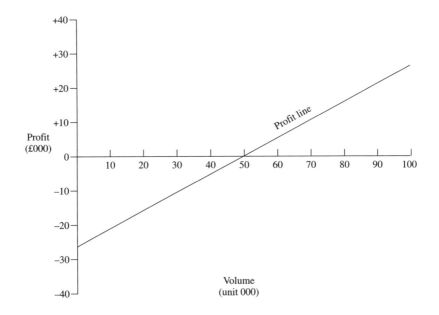

Figure 77.1 *Profit–volume chart*

$$P/V = \frac{\text{sales} - \text{variable costs (total contribution)}}{\text{sales}}$$

The P/V chart differs from the *break-even chart* in the following respects:

1. It contains a single line whose slope is equal to the average unit contribution rather than separate curves for cost and revenue.
2. The vertical axis represents total profit or loss rather than total revenues and costs.

USES

The P/V chart provides indicative answers to the following questions:

1. If unit selling prices, unit variable costs and total fixed costs remain constant, how many units need to be sold to achieve targets for profit, percentage return on sales or percentage return on investment? The sales to give a required profit can be calculated by the formula:

$$\frac{\text{Fixed cost} + \text{required profit}}{\text{P/V ratio}}$$

2. If the unit variable costs can be reduced, what additional profits can be expected at any given volume of sales?
3. What will be the effect on profits of a reduction in selling price according to the number of units sold?

Impact of price reductions

The third question referred to above is vital. To improve profits the best approach is to increase sales rather than simply cut costs. Although cost reduction exercises are part of a profit improvement plan, they should not be the only resource – if profits cannot be increased by more sales, then the future of the product or even the company is in doubt.

One way of increasing sales is to reduce prices. But there are three limitations on the effectiveness of this action:

1. If the demand for the product is inelastic, volume will not respond to changes in price and the only result will be lower profits.
2. Even if greater quantities can be sold at a lower price, any advantage gained will be lost if competitors retaliate by lowering their prices as well.
3. While sales volume may increase with reductions in price, it may not increase sufficiently to overcome the handicap of selling at a lower price.

Demand analysis and assessments by the marketing department can establish the degree to which the first two limitations apply. The third limitation can be dealt with by use of the P/V chart. A reduction in the selling price of a product has the same general effect on the marginal contribution as an increase in the variable cost. The profit line, in either case, will rise at a slower rate on the P/V chart. A percentage change in the selling price of a product will have a greater impact than the same percentage change in variable costs because the selling price must be assumed to be greater than the variable cost.

BENEFITS

The great advantage of the P/V chart is that profits or losses at any level of activity can be read directly off the vertical scale. It is therefore a valuable aid to profit planning and to making decisions on pricing and sales targets. It does not, however, reveal how costs may vary following a change in activity as does the break-even chart.

78

Break-even Analysis

DEFINITION

Break-even analysis is a method for identifying the relationships between costs, volume of output and profit. It indicates the break-even point, the point where sales revenue equals total cost (the sum of fixed and variable costs) and there is neither profit nor loss. Profits are made if revenue exceeds this point, while a loss is incurred if revenue falls below it.

THE BREAK-EVEN CHART

Break-even analysis is carried out by means of a break-even chart, which is illustrated in Figure 78.1 and shows:

1. variable costs in relation to sales units or output added to fixed costs to produce total costs;
2. sales revenue in relation to number of units sold;
3. the break-even point, where the sales revenue line crosses the total cost line;
4. the profit-and-loss wedges above and below the break-even point respectively;
5. the margin of safety in sales units or cash, ie, the extent to which sales volume or revenue exceeds the break-even point; and
6. the angle of incidence – the angle at which the sales revenue line crosses the total cost line. The aim of management will be to achieve as large an angle of incidence as possible, since this gives a correspondingly high rate of profit once the break-even point has been passed.

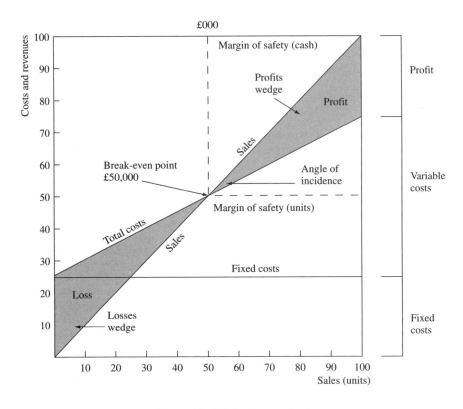

Figure 78.1 *A break-even chart*

An alternative method of drawing a break-even chart is shown in Figure 78.2. This clearly indicates the contribution to fixed costs and profits achieved above the break-even point. There are a number of assumptions built into break-even charts, which are often unrealistic. These can limit their usefulness. The main assumptions are:

1. the variable costs associated with producing the various levels of output are constant and can be represented by a straight line. This is linked to the assumption that volume is the only factor affecting variable costs and all other factors (eg wage levels and the cost of materials) remain unchanged;
2. the fixed costs remain constant over the range of output;
3. the selling price per unit is constant (ie no discounts), making sales revenue a straight line;
4. production and sales are equal and there are no significant changes in inventory levels; and
5. there is only one product or, if there is more than one product, a constant sales mix exists over the whole range.

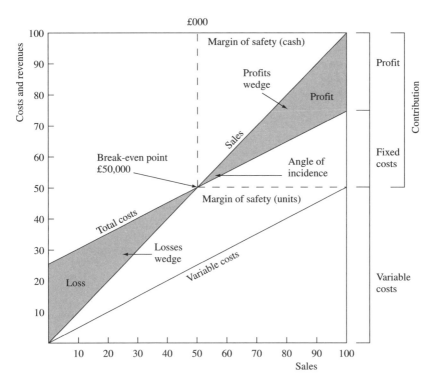

£000

Figure 78.2 *Break-even chart showing contribution*

It has also to be remembered that the picture presented in a break-even chart is correct only for a defined period of time and if the production capacity is used within certain maximum and minimum levels.

BENEFITS

In spite of the limitations mentioned above, break-even analysis still provides the following benefits:

1. It gives a useful indication of the net profit or loss that is likely to arise from different levels of activity.
2. It forces attention on the incidence of fixed and variable costs.
3. It ensures that pricing decisions are considered from the point of view of the revenues produced at different levels of output in relation to costs.
4. It conveys clearly the role of contribution in the relationship of volume to profit and highlights the amount of fixed cost not yet recovered by contribution.

79

Sales Mix Analysis

DEFINITION

The sales mix is the combination of quantities of a variety of company products that comprise total sales. Sales mix analysis calculates the effect on profits of variations in the mixture of output of the different products.

METHOD

When comparing the relative profitability of different products the contribution concept is used (contribution is sales revenue minus variable costs). This is a CVP (*cost–volume–profit*) analysis technique. It is carried out by multiplying the units to be produced of the product by the contribution per unit. For example, if the limiting factor on increasing the output or sales of three related products A, B and C was an additional 5,000 units, the following calculation would indicate which was the most profitable product to expand:

	Units	Contribution per unit	Total contribution
A	5,000	1.5	7,500
B	5,000	2.0	10,000
C	5,000	2.5	12,500

Contribution or *marginal costing* is used because it would be misleading to make comparisons on the basis of profits calculated after all costs, fixed and variable, have been fully absorbed. This is because, using *absorption costing* methods, the profitability figure for a product is only correct at the given level of output and is false if that level changes. The true impact of any changes in output can only be compared between products if this comparison is made by reference to the marginal impact of additional sales on revenues and costs.

Sales mix or multiple-product analysis can be conducted with the help of a P/V (*price–volume) chart* as in the following example of a two-product company:

1. The unit contribution margin for product A is £1 and for product B £2.
2. Fixed costs are £100,000.
3. The break-even point, Fixed costs/Contribution margin, is therefore 100,000 units if only B is sold.
4. If the planned mix is three units of A for each unit of B, the contribution margin for this package of products will be $(3 \times £1) + (1 \times £2) = £5$.
5. The average contribution margin per unit of product would be £5 divided by four units in each package = £1.25.
6. The break-even point, assuming that the mix is maintained, is: £100,000 $\div$ £1.25 = 80,000 units (consisting of 60,000 units of A and 20,000 of B).

These relationships are illustrated in Figure 79.1. The slopes of the solid lines show the unit contribution margins of each product.

The slope of the broken line shows the average contribution. If a target of 160,000 units is achieved consisting of 120,000 units of A and 40,000 of B, the profit (net income) would be £100,000. However, if the mix changes and the sales of B are higher than expected, net income increases. Selling a higher proportion of A would have the opposite effect. When the sales mix changes, the break-even point and the expected profits at various levels of sales are altered.

THE LIMITING FACTOR CONCEPT

Sales mix analysis can be used when a limiting factor or constraint applies. A limiting factor is a factor in the activities of an undertaking which at a point in time over a period of time will limit the volume of output. It is frequently sales potential, but it may be a limitation in plant, skilled labour or floor space.

The limiting factor concept deals with a single constraint. For example, if the constraint is plant capacity and a choice has to be made in a batch production factory of the priority between jobs, the contribution each job will make can be divided by the machine hours and the jobs ranked according to contribution per machine hour.

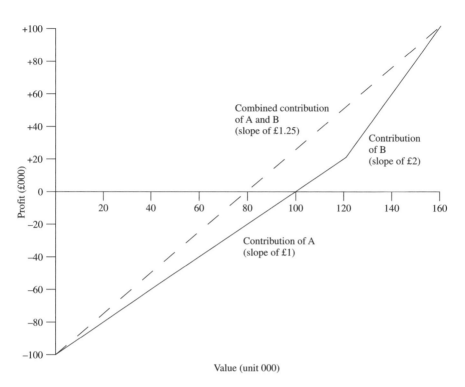

Figure 79.1 *Sales mix shown on a P/V chart*

If there are more constraints, *linear programming* techniques may have to be used.

BENEFITS

Sales mix analysis helps management to make decisions on changes in sales and production policies. These decisions are made on the basis of comparisons between the contribution to profit and fixed cost made by different combinations of products, especially when limited factors apply.

80

Financial Budgeting

DEFINITION

Budgeting deals with the creation of budgets: statements in quantitative and usually financial terms of the planned allocation and use of the company's resources. Budgets are usually prepared annually, but may be updated during the year.

Instead of budgeting for one financial year and then the next, some companies have adopted the discipline of the 'rolling budget' that is continuously updated, typically every three months. For this, the basic budgeting techniques are no different, but a less detailed approach may be adopted to keep the amount of budgeting work at realistic levels.

PURPOSE

Budgets are needed for three reasons:

1. to show the financial implications of plans;
2. to define the resources required to achieve the plans;
3. to provide a means of measuring, monitoring and controlling results against the plans.

THE PROCESS OF BUDGETING

The process of budgeting is shown in Figure 80.1. The components of this process are as follows:

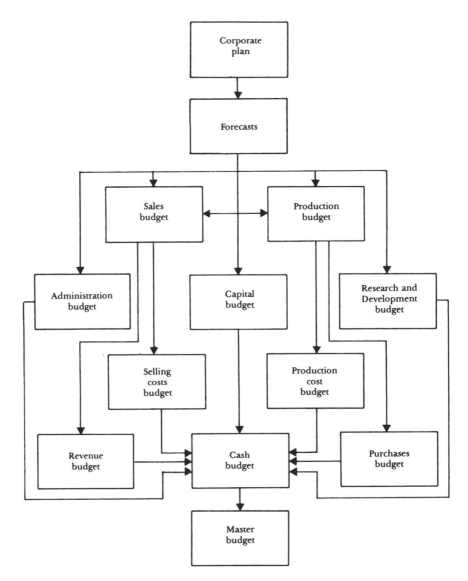

Figure 80.1 *The budgeting process*

1. *The corporate plan*, which has defined the longer-range objectives of the company in terms of return on shareholders' investments, return on capital employed and growth in revenue and profits. The annual budget can be regarded as the first year of the long-range financial plan. The corporate plan will include capital investment plans and the research and development programme.

2. *Forecasts* of the sales revenue that can be obtained in the coming financial year, accompanied by forecasts of the capital and research and development expenditure that will be needed to achieve the forecasts. The sales forecast will have been made with the help of market research and will take into account both likely demand and any limiting factors or constraints in such areas as production capacity. It will be the mainspring for the rest of the budget.

3. *The sales budget*, which will define what is going to be sold, in what volume and at what price. The budget will set out sales targets in total and for each product line. It will include contribution targets. Sales will be analysed by area or unit.

4. *The production budget*, which defines what needs to be produced and at what cost. The first requirement is an examination of the plant capacity and the availability of the other resources needed to satisfy the sales budget. Bottlenecks and other limiting factors are isolated and decisions taken about their treatment. Management decisions are also needed about the stock levels of finished goods and new material and bought-in parts. The budgeted costs of buying materials, finished parts and tooling are also set out. The production budget is built up for each department, showing the numbers of different products to be made in the individual control periods which together form the total budget period.

5. *Departmental budgets*, which set out what needs to be spent in each department to achieve the sales and production budgets and the research and development programme, and to provide the administrative and service facilities required to operate the business. They will be based on forecast and budgeted activity levels. Each departmental budget will set out staff or labour costs and the costs of any activities controlled by the department. In addition:

   ■ the *selling costs budget* will include the costs of running the marketing function and the field sales force, plus the costs of distribution, advertising, promotions, market research and customer servicing;

   ■ the *production cost budget* will cover the expenses incurred in operating the production departments and in maintaining plant and machinery, and the depreciation to be charged for that plant and machinery;

   ■ the *administration budget* will cover the costs of all central services provided by finance, personnel, management services, legal, property, public relations, pensions and the corporate office. Any other expenses such as insurance, depreciations and outside professional services which cannot be charged directly to other departments will be included in this budget, which will be divided into sections for each service department or area; and

■ the *research and development budget* will cover all the research and development expenses of the company, including the operation of research establishments, the costs of buying external research and the costs of any materials used.

The departmental budgets will be analysed into the direct costs incurred in buying in materials and finished parts, the departmental expenses or overheads and the central or corporate overheads and expenses. From these will be devised overhead budgets for each department against which they will control expenditure, and these will be added to form the corporate overhead or master budget.

6. *The revenue or debtors' budget,* which is derived from the sales budget and sets out the sales revenue budgeted for each period. This will be analysed into gross revenue, bad debts and the net revenue (gross revenue less bad debts) that will flow into the cash budget.

7. *The purchases or creditors' budget,* which is derived from the production budget and sets out the expenditures on raw materials, finished parts and tooling for each period.

8. *The capital expenditure budget,* which will be derived from the corporate plan and forecasts and will cover all capital investments or equipment needed in the budget year. Each department will be required to submit its own capital expenditure proposals which will be incorporated into the capital budget as long as they are accepted as forming a valid part of the longer-term capital investment programme.

9. *The cash or finance budget,* which translates the operating budgets for each function and department which have been prepared as revenues and expenses into cash inflows and outflows. The object of the cash budget is to ensure that the right amount of cash is on hand to operate the business, yet at the same time to ensure that no cash is lying idle. It is necessary to plan and budget for the inflow and outflow of cash from all other sources so that a funds-flow budget can be prepared and cash flows controlled against that budget.

10. *The master budget,* which will collate all the information prepared during the budgeting process. Besides setting out the sales, production, capital and cash budgets, the master budget will include a balance sheet, a profit-and-loss account and a cash-flow statement. Departmental budgets will be prepared which will be the basis for controlling expenses.

FINANCIAL BUDGETING PROCEDURE

The procedure for preparing financial budgets consists of the following steps:

1. *Budget guidelines* are prepared which have been derived from the corporate plan and forecasts. These will include sales and output targets and the activity levels for which budgets have to cater.

   Policies will be set out on the profit margins or contribution to be achieved and the ratios to be met, eg return on capital employed, overheads to sales revenue, bad debts to sales revenue, stock to sales, stock to current assets, current liabilities to current assets.

   Finally, the assumptions to be used in budgeting are given. These include rates of inflation and increases in costs and prices.
2. *Initial budgets* are prepared by departmental managers with the assistance of budget accountants where possible and necessary. Changes to previous budgets which are not in line with changes in activity levels or assumptions on inflation and cost or price increases have to be justified. These departmental budgets are checked by higher management to ensure they meet the guidelines.
3. *Functional and departmental budgets* are collated and analysed to produce the master budget. This is reviewed by top management, who may require changes at departmental level to bring it into line with corporate objectives for profitability and growth.
4. *The master budget* is finally approved by top management and budget packs are issued to each departmental or budget centre manager for planning and control purposes.

BENEFITS

Budgets translate policy into financial terms, which in business is the only way in which, ultimately, policies can be expressed. It is certainly the only basis upon which control can be exercised, as described in Chapter 83.

81

Flexible Budgets

DEFINITION

A flexible budget is one that takes account of a range of possible volumes. It is sometimes referred to as a multi-volume budget. The range of possible outputs may be known as the relevant range. 'Flexing' a budget takes place when the original budget is deliberately amended to take account of changed activity levels.

REASON FOR FLEXIBLE BUDGETS

A static budget, as described in Chapter 80, is prepared for only one level of activity, eg volume of sales. This means that both fixed and variable costs are assumed to remain constant at any level of activity. Fixed costs may do so, but variable costs, by definition, will not, as is shown in Figure 81.1. Because the actual output will almost certainly be different from the budgeted output, the original budget will be inaccurate. It is therefore necessary to 'flex' budgets to reflect different levels of output – assumed or actual.

PREPARATION OF FLEXIBLE BUDGETS

Flexible budgets are prepared by assuming different levels of output or activity and preparing cost and overhead budgets for each level. For example, in an assembly shop, activity levels, if a standard costing system

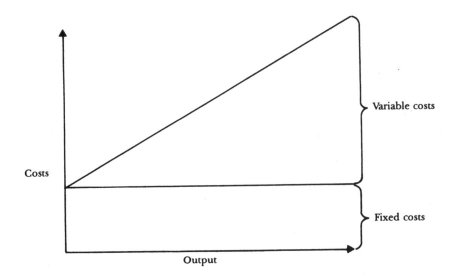

Figure 81.1 *Relationship of total costs to output*

is used, would be expressed in standard hours and the activity level would be expressed as a percentage of the standard hours achieved. Thus, the targeted standard hours would be shown as the 100 per cent activity level. A weekly budget for such an assembly shop is shown in Table 81.1.

Table 81.1 *Weekly flexible budget for assembly shop*

Performance		Budget		
Standard hours produced		2,850	3,000	3,150
Activity (%)		95	100	105
Costs		£	£	£
Directly allocable				
Direct materials	V	3,700	4,000	4,300
Direct labour	V	11,400	12,000	12,600
Indirect labour	F	2,750	2,750	2,750
Tools and consumables	V	50	55	60
Power	V	20	30	30
Repair materials and labour	V	150	160	170
Depreciation of plant	F	60	60	60
Apportioned				
Associated labour costs	SF	290	300	310
Rent and rates	F	200	200	200
Factory administration and services	F	4,500	4,500	4,500
Total costs		23,120	24,055	24,980

(V = Variable, F = Fixed, SF = Semi-fixed)

Budgets based on fixed output levels can be 'flexed' during the year on the basis of revised activity forecasts. In companies where activity levels do not vary dramatically month by month, the reforecast may be made no more than twice a year. The result of the reforecast is a completely recast master budget, incorporating a revised balance sheet and profit-and-loss account.

CONTROL OF FLEXIBLE BUDGETS

The control of flexible budgets is carried out on the same basis as any other control process, ie actuals are compared with budget to show any variances. The budget with which the actuals are compared, however, is the adjusted budget based on achieved activity levels. In a standard costing system these would be shown as standard hours produced. Table 81.2. is an example of a departmental operating statement which shows the original budget for a performance of 3,000 standard hours compared with the adjusted budget for a performance of 3,150 standard hours, an activity ratio of 105 per cent. The actual costs recorded are compared with the adjusted budget to indicate favourable or unfavourable (in brackets) variances.

Table 81.2 *Departmental operating statement*

	Original budget £	Adjusted budget £	Actual cost £	Variances £
Direct materials	4,000	4,300	4,400	(100)
Direct labour	12,000	12,600	13,000	(400)
Variable overheads	245	260	240	20
Fixed overheads	2,750	2,750	2,750	–
Depreciation of plant	60	60	60	–
Apportioned costs	5,000	5,010	5,010	
	24,055	24,980	25,460	(480)

BENEFITS

Flexible budgetary control overcomes the major disadvantage of fixed budgeting, which is that it does not allow for almost inevitable variations in activity levels which will affect costs. If such allowances are not made, a completely unrealistic picture of variances is built up and control cannot be overcome.

82

Zero-base Budgeting

DEFINITION

Zero-base budgeting is a technique that requires budget managers to re-evaluate all their activities completely in order to decide whether they should be eliminated, or funded at a reduced, similar or increased level. Appropriate funding levels, from zero to a significant increase, will be determined by the priorities established by top management and the overall availability of funds.

BASIS

The traditional approach to budgeting tends to perpetuate commitments that had their origin in the past. This practice begins with the past level of expenditures as a base and concentrates on projected increases or decreases from that base. Only a small portion of the budget is analysed, rather than close scrutiny being made of every part of it. The minds of managers concentrate only on justifying increases rather than on challenging the need for any function or activity in its present form.

The term 'zero-base' does not mean that everybody's position is automatically 'zeroed', or that operations and structure must again be built from the ground up. This would be unrealistic. But it does demand a systematic evaluation and review of all activities and programmes, current as well as new, on a basis of output as well as cost, emphasizing managerial decision making. The approach recognizes that, ultimately, the production of a budget is a matter of assessing priorities against margin and profit targets, in the light of an analysis of the costs and benefits of alternative approaches.

METHOD

Zero-base budgeting covers all activities, although it would not be necessary to include direct labour if standard costs are used. For each activity the basic elements or decision units are defined and each unit is analysed to establish:

1. its objectives;
2. the activities carried out;
3. the present costs of these activities;
4. the benefits resulting from each activity;
5. the standards and other performance measures that exist;
6. alternative ways of achieving objectives, and the priorities between them; and
7. the advantages and disadvantages of incurring different levels of expenditure.

BENEFITS

Zero-base budgeting is no panacea and it has often failed because companies have introduced over-elaborate procedures which have sunk almost without trace in a sea of paperwork. But the approach is right: cost control is about challenging and justifying proposed expenditures as well as monitoring what has actually been spent. The most elaborate control system in the world is useless if it relates to an unsound base. Zero-base budgeting techniques can and should be used to develop an attitude of mind on the part of managers to the examination and control of all their activities. They should not be used in a threatening way. The emphasis should be on their value in getting priorities right and ensuring that costs and benefits are thoroughly reviewed to the advantage of all concerned.

83

Budgetary Control

DEFINITION

Budgetary control compares actual costs, revenues and performances with the budget so that, if necessary, corrective action can be taken or revisions made.

PRINCIPLES OF CONTROL

The five principles of control are:

1. *plan* what needs to be achieved;
2. *measure* regularly what has been achieved;
3. *compare* actual achievements with the plan;
4. *take action* to correct deviations from the plan; and
5. *feed back* results to amend the plan as required.

APPLICATION TO BUDGETARY CONTROL

The application of these principles to budgetary control requires the following:

1. *A budget* for each cost centre which sets out under each cost heading (to which a cost code will have been attached) the budgeted expenditure against whatever activity levels have been built into the budget.

2. A system of *measurement* or recording which allocates all expenditures to the current cost code and cost centre and records the activity levels achieved.

3. A system for *comparison* or reporting which sets out actuals against budgets and indicates the positive and negative variances that have occurred. This system of comparison must ensure that performance reports are available quickly to the right person and are presented in such a way that variances are immediately identifiable.

4. A procedure for *acting* on the control information received. This requires reports to higher management on what is being done to deal with variances.

5. A procedure for *feeding back* changes in activity or performance levels or revised forecasts so that the budget guidelines can be amended and budgets updated.

The process is illustrated in Figure 83.1.

BENEFITS

Budgetary control is the only basis on which performance can be monitored and, consequently, improved. It will not work effectively, however, unless:

1. the budget is based on adequate assumptions and forecasts;
2. the budget is realistic – the targets are not so high as to be unattainable or so low as to be meaningless;
3. control information clearly specifies deviations or variances;

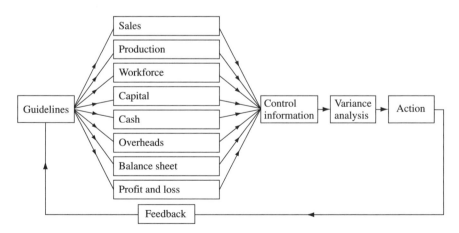

Figure 83.1 *The process of budgetary control*

4. control information goes to the right people, who are responsible for the results and will analyse variances and can take action; and
5. steps are taken by higher management to ensure that variances are analysed and reported on and that corrective action is planned, implemented and successful.

Note, however, that what has been described in this chapter and in Chapter 80 on financial budgeting is a static budgeting system which is based on predetermined activity or volume levels. But these volumes change, and many assumptions about the incidence of variable costs and the amount and allocation of overheads or expenses included in the original budget will no longer be valid. A system for 'flexing' budgets, ie adjusting them in the light of actual or forecast changes in activity levels, is required. This was described in Chapter 81.

84

Overhead Accounting

DEFINITION

Overhead accounting is directed specifically to the identification, measurement and control of overheads. Overheads, for the purpose of overhead accounting, are costs that are not specific to a particular activity. They are, in fact, costs that arise from the execution of a set of activities within which each individual activity is seen as an integral part of the whole set.

PRINCIPLES OF OVERHEAD ACCOUNTING

The following principles apply to overhead accounting:

1. Overhead cost accounting is done for two reasons:

   - analysis of existing operations for cost control purposes and to ensure that costs are minimized for any given level of output;
   - analysis for making economic decisions which will govern alterations to the existing operational system;

2. Overheads should only be analysed for specified accounting units and over a defined period of time.
3. No overhead analysis can be relevant by itself for all decisions and control purposes. The analysis will provide information and guidance, but the ultimate decision may have to take into account other factors in the internal and external environment of the company.

4. Overhead accounting should only concern itself with relevant costs, ie those costs that will be affected in the future by current decisions (this approach is also termed incremental costing). Historical costs provide a base for projections into the future but are not relevant in themselves.

OVERHEAD CONTROL

Overhead control is a matter first of identifying overheads and then of defining responsibility for those overheads. An overhead cost is only controllable if the manager concerned can influence the level of cost incurred.

Overhead control is thus achieved by introducing a system of *responsibility accounting* which is related to the decision-making structure that influences the incurrence of particular costs. Overhead costs are therefore classified in a way which is consistent with that structure. Because, by their very nature, it may be difficult to pin down the responsibility for overhead costs, strenuous efforts have to be made to identify who is primarily responsible. A proper system of overhead accounting avoids arbitrary allocation of overheads.

The system of responsibility accounting will start at the top, where the key ratio of overheads to sales revenue will receive continuous attention in budgeting and control. Significant variances in this overall figure should prompt investigations at each level of responsibility so that reasons can be established and corrective action taken.

BENEFITS

Overhead accounting brings into prominence a significant area of costs which it is often difficult to control. This problem typically arises because the overheads are not classified accurately and responsibility for their control is diffuse. Overhead accounting aims to overcome these defects.

FURTHER READING

Drury, C, *Management and Cost Accounting* (3rd edition), Van Nostrand Reinhold, London 1992.

85

Responsibility Accounting

DEFINITION

Responsibility accounting defines responsibility centres throughout the organization. The managers of each of these centres are held responsible for the costs and revenues assigned to them.

The three main areas of responsibility covered are:

1. *Cost centres*, where only costs are reported formally. They are the smallest segment of activity or area of responsibility for which costs are accumulated. Typically, cost centres are departments, but a department may contain several cost centres.
2. *Profit centres*, where costs and revenues are reported formally. They are usually segments of a business responsible for the sales and profits of a product line.
3. *Investment centres*, where there is a formal reporting of revenues, expenses and related investment. Their success is measured not only by their income but also by relating that income to their invested capital. Typically, a whole business or subsidiary can be treated as an investment centre.

BASE

Responsibility accounting is based on four principles.

1. Objectives

The overall objectives of the business are divided and subdivided into the objectives of each of its constituent parts, expressed as profit, contribution or cost. This is illustrated in Figure 85.1.

2. Controllable costs

Responsibility accounting excludes or segregates costs which are not controlled directly by the manager. For example, in a machine shop the level of waste is directly controllable but the rent is not.

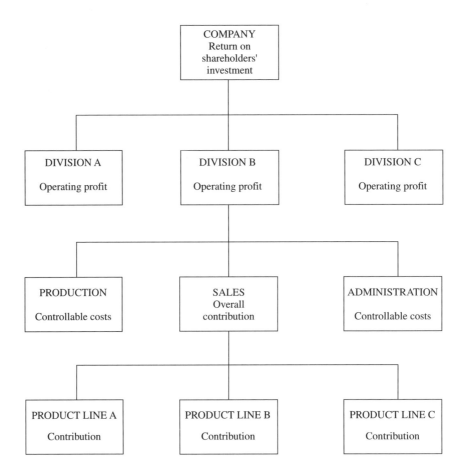

Figure 85.1 *Organizational assignment of responsibilities*

3. Explanation

The results achieved in a profit centre are not all directly controllable by the profit centre manager. External factors will affect both revenues and expenditures. But responsibility accounting requires managers to *explain* why the actual results obtained differ from those in the forecast or budget. Even if the changes are caused by the external environment, managers are still expected to predict and measure the behaviour of relevant parts of that environment and to act appropriately. Only by seeking and offering such explanations will they be able to adopt a proactive rather than a reactive stance to the management of change. It is the job of the manager of a responsibility centre to explain outcomes regardless of his or her personal influence over the results.

4. Management by exception

The feedback of information on actual revenues and costs to the responsibility centre manager concentrates on the important deviations from the budget. This is the principle of management by exception, whereby the attention of managers is focused on exceptions to the norm so that they do not waste time on those parts of the reports that reflect smoothly running phases of operations.

STRUCTURE

The structure of a system of responsibility accounting for controllable costs is illustrated in Table 85.1.

METHOD

The steps taken to develop and implement a responsibility accounting system are as follows:

1. The organization is divided and subdivided into responsibility centres – for return on investment, profit, contribution, revenue or controllable costs.
2. Managers are identified who will be accountable for the results achieved in each responsibility centre.
3. Objectives, standards, targets and budgets are agreed for the organization as a whole and for each responsibility centre.
4. An information system is set up which reports actuals against standards, targets or budgets and highlights variances.

Table 85.1 *Responsibility accounting for controllable costs*

Cost centre	Budget (£000)		Variances (£000) (favourable/ unfavourable)	
	This period	*Year to date*	*This period*	*Year to date*
Level 1. Board				
Production	250	700	(20)	(40)
Sales	150	400	10	25
Administration	200	600	5	10
Total	600	1,700	(5)	(5)
Level 2. Production Director				
Plant A	100	280	(10)	(30)
Plant B	70	200	–	10
Plant C	80	220	(10)	(20)
Total	250	700	(20)	(40)
Level 3. Plant A Manager				
Department A	50	140	(4)	(15)
Department B	30	80	(4)	(10)
Department C	20	60	(2)	(5)
Total	100	280	(10)	(30)
Level 4. Department A Manager				
Line A	10	35	(1)	(3)
Line B	20	60	(2)	(8)
Line C	20	45	(1)	(4)
Total	50	140	(4)	(15)

5. Procedures are instituted for the analysis of control reports, for taking any action required and for providing information on outcomes.

BENEFITS

Responsibility accounting first facilitates the delegation of decision taking. Responsibility centre managers can be given an appropriate and controlled degree of authority over their units in the knowledge of what they are expected to achieve and what they can do.

Second, exception reporting, which is built into any fully developed responsibility accounting system, enables managers to concentrate on the key issues which need their attention.

Finally, responsibility accounting provides individual managers with incentive through performance reports, and top management with a quantitative basis for evaluating each manager's performance.

86

Capital Budgeting

DEFINITION

Capital budgeting is the process of selecting and planning capital investments based on an analysis of the cash flows associated with the investments and appraisals of the benefits that are likely to arise from them. Capital budgeting is based on the belief that the object of any investment is that in return for paying out a given amount of cash today, a larger amount will be received back over a period of time. Capital budgeting and investment appraisal procedures frequently require choices to be made from several options.

FACTORS

The basic factor to be considered in making a capital expenditure decision is that there will be a pattern of cash outflows and inflows, as illustrated in Figure 86.1.

The problem is to determine whether the cash outflow required for the investment is justified by the cash inflows which will be created over its life.

The detailed factors to be evaluated in making investment decisions are:

1. the initial cost of the project;
2. the phasing of expenditure over the project;
3. the estimated life of the investment; and
4. the amount and timing of the resulting income.

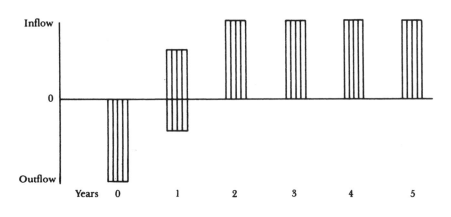

Figure 86.1 *Capital investment cash flows*

The outflow of funds needed to acquire a capital asset is called 'the investment'. The inflows represent funds generated by the investment and can be called 'returns'. The returns on a project are represented by the excess of added revenue over added costs (other than depreciation, since in capital investment decisions depreciation over the life of the investment is represented by the investment).

OPPORTUNITY COST

An overriding principle in investment appraisal is that the company should value projects on the basis of the opportunity cost of capital – the cost in terms of lost income or profit of the forgone alternative investment: in other words, what could be earned if the money available was invested in other projects. Projects which earn a rate of return less than could be earned by other means (less than the opportunity cost of capital) should be rejected, and those that yield a superior rate of return should be accepted.

THE COMPARISON OF RETURNS WITH INVESTMENT

Capital investment decisions require the comparison of two streams of funds. A favourable decision is indicated if returns less investment is positive. But in many projects, returns from the initial outlay are yielded over long periods of time. Some adjustment for this time difference is desirable for two reasons:

1. Investors have to wait for the returns to materialize and such waiting implies uncertainty due to the inherent difficulty of long-term forecasting.
2. The waiting requires the sacrifice of present consumption or other investment opportunities.

Because of the importance of this principle, the most favoured approach to investment appraisal as part of the capital budgeting procedure is discounting. This adjusts for the time differential and takes into account uncertainty and the sacrifice of the alternative uses of funds. The effect of discounting is to express the two streams of investment and returns in present value equivalents.

The incidence of taxation also has a significant effect on the timing of the streams of returns, and if a discounting procedure is used, the decision to go ahead with an investment will only be made if the total present value of returns after tax charges minus the total present value of the investment after tax relief results in a positive figure.

INVESTMENT APPRAISAL TECHNIQUES

The four main techniques for appraising investment proposals are as follows:

1. *Payback* – the length of time which must elapse before the cash inflow from the project equals the total initial cash outflow.
2. *Accounting rate of return* (also known as the unadjusted rate of return), which calculates the average annual profit as a percentage of the original cash outlay.
3. *Discounted cash flow (DCF)*, which is a discounting method expressing future cash inflows in present values.
4. *Net present value (NPV)*, which is related to DCF and consists simply of adding the present values of all the cash inflows.

Although the discounted cash flow and the net present value methods are in many ways the most appropriate techniques because they involve discounting cash flows to present values, this does not mean that the payback or accounting rate of return method cannot or should not be used to provide a quick and simple, although somewhat crude, view on how long it will take the company to get its money back (payback), or how the average rate of return compares with other rates that could be earned.

These methods are dealt with at great length in Chapters 87–89.

CAPITAL BUDGETING PROGRAMME

A capital budgeting programme consists of the following stages:

1. *The search for investment opportunities.* To provide for profitable growth, management generates a constant flow of investment opportunities for appraisal.
2. *The identification of relevant alternatives.* There is rarely only one way of carrying out a project and relevant alternatives need to be evaluated to seek the best approach and to highlight opportunity costs.
3. *The determination of costs.* The emphasis is on relevant cost information, ie future incremented cash flows, not traditional historical cost accumulations. It is cash flows and net book values that are important in the long-term assessment.
4. *The determination of revenues.* Again these are forecast in the form of cash flows over a period of time. This requires estimates of the probabilities of different levels of revenue being attained, taking into account possible variations in the factors such as demand built into the forecast. *Risk analysis* techniques such as the calculation of expected values, utility theory, mean variance analysis, game theory, Monte Carlo simulations and decision trees are all used for this purpose.
5. *The screening and ranking of projects.* Alternative proposals are screened and ranked in accordance with the rates of return, generally at the net present values that it is believed they will generate. The payback period and the accounting rate of return from different projects may also be considered. Potential rates of return are compared with the company's policy on the minimum satisfactory rate of return it requires from an investment. This policy will be influenced by the target rates of return on shareholders' capital or on capital employed, and by the cost of obtaining capital.
6. *Capital expenditure control.* When the decision to incur capital expenditure has been made, a capital budget is set up for the project and procedures are introduced for the authorization of expenditure. Project control information is needed as part of the system of *project management*. This control data will show progress, expenditure to date against budget and total anticipated expenditure compared with the overall capital budget for the project.
7. *Rate of return control.* Information is generated which compares net cash flows with budget and enables corrective action to be taken when required.

BENEFITS

Capital budgeting ensures that:

1. projects are properly evaluated in terms of the cash outflows and inflows involved and the payback, rate of return and net present value of the investment;
2. alternative proposals can be compared so that the opportunity costs of investments are identified and the choice of project takes into account both those costs and the minimum rate of return targeted by the company; and
3. procedures are set up for the controlling expenditure within agreed budgets for the lifetime of the project and for comparing returns with forecasts so that corrective action can be taken when necessary.

FURTHER READING

Mott, G, *Investment Appraisal*, Pitman, London 1993.

87

Payback Method of Capital Appraisal

DEFINITION

The payback period method of capital appraisal forecasts when a project or capital investment will reach its break-even point, ie the length of time which will elapse before the cash inflow from the project equals the total initial cash outflow.

PURPOSE

The purpose of the payback period technique is to discover how long it takes each project to generate enough cash inflows to recoup the initial outlays. The time taken to recoup is called the payback period, and it should be as short as possible. The longer the payback period, the longer money is tied up in the project.

CALCULATING PAYBACK

Payback is calculated by:

1. totalling the initial capital outlays;
2. estimating the cash inflows for year 1 (if any), then year 2, year 3 and so on until the total of inflows equals or slightly exceeds the outlay and

any further deductions would be negative. The number of years' inflow deducted in this way will be the payback period in years; and

3. if, having deducted the inflows, there is a residue left which is less than the next year's inflow, that inflow figure is divided into the residue. The result of this division is the fraction of a year to be added to the payback period to give the exact period. This process is called interpolation.

USES

Payback is a quick and easy way of assessing the speed with which projects can turn round their funds, a factor which is important in times of cash shortage. It is also an easy method of assessing the relative merits of different investments. Guidelines can be used in the payback method to indicate whether or not a project is worth investigating further. For example, it may be decided that no investment should be considered if the payback period is longer than three years.

The main objective to the payback method is that it tells you nothing about the rate of return on investment that is being achieved after the initial outlay has been covered, and rate of return is the key measure of performance. The payback method also ignores the timing of cash flows.

88

Accounting Rate of Return

DEFINITION

The accounting or average rate of return method of capital investment appraisal calculates the forecast average rate of annual profit from an investment as a percentage of the original cash outlay. It is also known as the unadjusted rate of return.

METHOD

The accounting rate of return is calculated by taking the following steps:

1. Tabulate the capital outlays for each year of the project.
2. Divide the total capital outlay by the number of years over which the project runs to obtain the average annual capital outlay.
3. Tabulate the net inflows for each year.
4. Total the net inflows and divide that total by the number of years of project life in order to obtain the average annual return.
5. Divide the average annual return by the annual average capital outlay and multiply the result by 100 to obtain the percentage average annual rate of return.

USES

The accounting rate of return method is the traditional method of appraisal and is based on the familiar financial statements prepared under accrual accounting which recognize revenues and costs as they are earned or incurred, not as money is received or paid. It is thus a simple measure of profitability, producing a figure which is easily compared with the return from alternative projects, the return that can be obtained from alternative investments (eg bank deposits), or the dividend yield expected from an ordinary public company share.

The disadvantage of this technique is that it ignores the time value of money concept, ie that £1 received today is worth more than £1 receivable at some future date, because £1 received today could earn interest in the intervening period. The discounted cash-flow method is designed to overcome this defect.

89

Discounted Cash Flow

DEFINITION

The discounted cash-flow (DCF) technique is used to establish and compare the return on investment in projects by discounting future cash flows to establish their present value. It focuses on cash inflows and outflows rather than on net income as computed in the accrual accounting sense. The DCF return is the true annual rate of return on the capital outstanding in the investment.

BASIS OF THE TECHNIQUE

The DCF technique recognizes that £1,000 receivable in one year's time is worth less than £1,000 receivable now. If, for example, the rate of interest is 15 per cent, the £1,000 receivable in one year's time is worth £870 now. The £870 could be invested at 15 per cent, which would represent a total of £1,000 in one year's time. On these terms, the company would not want to pay more than £870 today for the investment.

This process of expressing future inflows in present values is known as discounting and it is, in effect, compound interest in reverse. A DCF calculation matches cash out against cash in over the life of the investment and relates the cash flow back to the initial outlay. The return from a project is calculated before any depreciation charges are deducted.

Taxation is an important factor in investment appraisal and must be deducted in the year in which it is paid, not the year in which it is incurred. This will incorporate all taxation allowances on the capital equipment, as this is a tax saving which increases the actual cash inflow of the project.

A DCF calculation works out the present value of an investment over a period of years at an assumed rate of interest. The present value is compared with the initial cost and the actual rate of return is the discount rate required to equalize the present value with the original cost. This rate of return is compared with target rates of return to see if the investment is viable. Alternative investments can be evaluated by comparing their respective rates of return.

THE DCF TECHNIQUE

The DCF technique comprises three elements:

1. Calculation of present value.
2. Calculation and use of net present value.
3. Calculation and use of internal rate of return.

Calculation of present value

The first step in DCF is to calculate the present value. This is the current discounted value of the cash flow expected in a future year. A present value can be calculated by using the basic discounting equation:

$$PV = \frac{CF}{(1 + r)^n}$$

Where PV stands for present value
$\quad\quad\quad$ CF stands for cash flow in the year concerned
$\quad\quad\quad$ r $\quad$ stands for the annual interest rate expressed as a decimal, not a percentage
$\quad\quad\quad$ n $\quad$ stands for the year number concerned.

Alternatively, present value tables can be used which are set out as in Table 89.1.

Table 89.1 *Extract from present value table*

		Discount rate	
Year	8%	9%	10%
1	0.9259	0.9174	0.9091
2	0.8573	0.8417	0.8264
3	0.7938	0.7722	0.7513

Using this table, the present value of £50,000 received in year 2 and discounted at 10 per cent is 50,000 × 0.8264 = 41,320.

Net present value

The net present value (NPV) technique assumes some minimum desired rate of return (discount factor), adds the present values for each year of the project of all the cash inflows, and deducts from this figure the sum of all the present values of the cash outflows for each year of the project. Put another way, having selected a target minimum rate of return, the NPVs for each year (the present value of inflows minus the present value of outflows) are added to produce a total NPV for the whole project. An example of this calculation is given in Table 89.2.

If, having worked out the NPV, the result is positive, the project is desirable, and vice versa. When choosing among several investments the one with the largest NPV is the most desirable.

Table 89.2 *Calculation of net present value (NPV)*

Year	Inflow	Outflow	Net cash flow	Discount factor	Net present value
	£000	*£000*	*£000*	*10%*	*£000*
1	10	70	(60)	0.9091	(54.55)
2	30	80	(50)	0.8264	(41.32)
3	90	60	30	0.7513	22.54
4	100	50	50	0.6830	34.15
5	110	40	70	0.6209	43.46
Total net present value =					4.28

Internal rate of return

The internal rate of return (IRR) is the discount rate that makes the NPV of a project equal to zero. Expressed another way, the internal rate of return can be defined as the discount rate that makes the present value of a project's expected cash inflows equal to the present value of the expected cash outflows, including the investment in the project. The IRR indicates the maximum cost of capital a project may incur without making a loss, ie without its NPV becoming negative. The higher the IRR, the more attractive the project.

The IRR can be found by trial and error. For example, in Table 89.2 a discount factor of 10 per cent gave a positive NPV of 4.28. If the discount factor were 14 per cent, the NPV would be minus 4.89. A discount factor of 12 per cent gives minus 0.50, so the IRR is just under 12 per cent (11.98 per cent).

The IRR is computed on the basis of the investment tied up in the project from period to period instead of solely the initial investment. The IRR in the above example is just under 12 per cent of the capital invested during each year. If money were borrowed at the same effective interest rate, the cash inflow produced by the project would exactly repay the hypothetical loan plus the interest over five years.

The IRR is used to ensure that the project will at least achieve the target rate of return set by the company, which will be related to the cost of capital. If there is more than one project to evaluate, then clearly, the higher the IRR, the more advantageous the project.

BENEFITS

The discounted cash-flow technique, including the use of NPVs and the IRR, is the only capital appraisal method which indicates the value of a project after accounting for the opportunity cost of money. Because it explicitly and automatically weighs the time value of money, it is the best method to use for long-range decisions where the overriding goal is maximum long-term net cash inflows. It has to be remembered, however, that the DCF is based on two fundamental assumptions: first, that the predicted cash flows will occur in the amounts and at the times specified; second, that the original amount of the investment can be looked upon as being either borrowed or loaned at some special rate of return.

Doubts about the uncertainty of forecasts lead many companies to rely more on the traditional payback or accounting return techniques. But these also have assumptions about future inflows built into them. While these methods have their uses, only DCF properly measures the return on cash flows over time. To minimize the problems of uncertainty, *risk analysis* techniques can be used. These are considered further in Chapter 90.

FURTHER READING

Mott, G, *Investment Appraisal*, Pitman, London 1993.

90

Risk Analysis

DEFINITION

Risk analysis assesses the danger of failing to achieve forecasts of the outcome or yield of an investment or investments, the risk attached to a project being largely its loss-making chances. Outcomes are generally expressed as net present values (NPVs), following discounted cash-flow calculations of the probabilities of variations occurring to the basic data built into the forecast, such as demand, costs, inflation and cash flows.

THE NEED

Estimates of cash flows prepared when appraising investments are subject to the possibility of forecasting error, like all such estimates. Errors occur because:

1. demand is never wholly predictable, and forecasts of cash inflows are therefore uncertain;
2. costs and therefore cash outflows are time based, but unforeseen circumstances can change them; and
3. inflation cannot be predicted accurately and reduces the value of money, while increasing interest rates.

TECHNIQUES

The most commonly used techniques in risk analysis are:

1. three-level estimates;
2. expected value.

Three-level estimates

The preparation of three-level estimates is a fairly crude method of comparing risks. It is similar to *sensitivity analysis* in that, unlike other risk analysis techniques, it does not incorporate probability assessments of variations into the basic factors.

Three forecast cash flows are produced: one for the best conditions (optimistic), the second for the worst conditions (pessimistic), and the third for the most likely outcome. These provide an overall feel for what might happen to the project upon which management can base its decisions. More analytical techniques are available, as described below, but to a greater or lesser degree all of these depend on certain subjective assumptions.

Expected value

The expected value is a forecast based on the weighted average of all the reasonably probable levels that sales might achieve. Probability is expressed as the percentage chance of obtaining a given result. In risk analysis, expected values are also called certainty equivalents.

The expected value is obtained by multiplying each of the alternative demand forecasts expressed as cash flows by its probability and adding the results together as shown in Table 90.1.

Table 90.1 *Expected value calculation*

Forecast demand in units	Cash flow £	Probability %	Expected value £
2,000	20,000	20	4,000
3,000	30,000	40	12,000
4,000	40,000	30	12,000
5,000	50,000	10	5,000
		100	33,000

BENEFITS

Risk analysis ensures that the factors influencing the likely outcomes of investments are identified and that the probabilities of their occurrence are fully explored. It provides guidance for decision making, but, because of the assumptions that have to be built into all estimates of probabilities, risk analysis can never completely supplant managerial judgement, that is to say, the gut feeling that an investment will or will not work.

FURTHER READING

Mott, G, *Investment Appraisal*, Pitman, London 1993.

91

Programme Budgeting*

DEFINITION

Programme budgeting, also known as output budgeting, is the integration of a number of planning, budgeting and control techniques for:

1. establishing priorities and strategies for major public sector developments or operational programmes;
2. identifying, allocating and costing the resources required;
3. planning the work to be done to achieve the expected outputs; and
4. monitoring performance and controlling results.

In programme budgeting, a programme is an activity or sequence of activities which needs to be carried out to achieve a desired output over a set period of time and within a predetermined budget.

The process of programme budgeting is also referred to as a *planning, programming, budgeting system (PPBS)*.

CONCEPT OF PROGRAMME BUDGETING

The concept of programme budgeting was developed in the United States in the 1960s. Its use was rapidly extended to the UK and elsewhere. It became fashionable in the UK at the time of the Fulton Report on the Civil Service,

---

* Referred to in the United States as program budgeting.

which advocated the use of more management techniques and emphasized the need for accountable management, ie holding individuals and units responsible for performance measured as objectively as possible. Possibly because it was oversold as a panacea at the time, programme budgeting as such is not heard about much today. But the concept and the approach remain valid and are still used or advocated, even if the name has changed.

The need

The belief that programme budgeting was necessary arose because of the indissoluble connection between budgeting and the formulation and conduct of national policy. Governments are constrained by the scarcity of economic resources at their disposal, but the extent to which a government desires to pursue its objectives will influence the resources available to itself by taxation and other means. Planning, programming and budgeting constitute the processes by which it was thought that objectives and resources, and the interrelationships between them, could be taken into account to achieve a comprehensive and coherent programme of action for a government as a whole.

No government nor, indeed, any commercial enterprise can avoid a degree of compromise when selecting goals and strategies. The task of helping to make the necessary compromises among various objectives is a function of planning, programming and budgeting. To make these compromises, programme budgeting attempts to express the various activities for which plans have to be made in terms of the only common denominator available, which is, of course, money.

A government, like a private business, can determine its policies most effectively if it chooses rationally among alternative courses of action, with as full knowledge as possible of the implications of those alternatives. And because these choices are often fundamentally the same as those made in private enterprise, programme budgeting uses business management techniques such as corporate planning, investment appraisal and, particularly, management accounting.

The importance of management accounting

The significance attached to the role of management accounting in the planning and control processes of the government was emphasized in a UK government White Paper reprinted in 1983 on *Efficiency and Effectiveness in the Civil Service*. This paper stated that management accounting systems enable all those who incur, control or influence costs 'to consider options, formulate plans to meet objectives, and subsequently to compare actual expenditure against those plans'. The emphasis in management accounting is not only to assess cash expenditure on an input basis, as in the British government vote system, but also, and more importantly, to allocate such costs to outputs or objectives so that they can provide a proper basis for monitoring performance against plans.

Cost–benefit analysis

However, many of the outputs resulting from government programmes are difficult to evaluate in purely financial terms, especially those concerned with social issues. Hence the use of cost–benefit techniques to measure inputs and outputs in these more subjective areas.

OVERALL APPROACH TO PROGRAMME BUDGETING

The overall approach to programme budgeting follows these stages:

1. Appraisal and comparison of various government activities in terms of their contribution to national objectives.
2. Determination of how given objectives can be attained with minimum expenditure and resources.
3. Projection of government activities over an adequate time horizon.
4. Comparison of the relative contribution of private and public activities to national objectives.
5. Revision of objectives, programmes and budgets in the light of experience and changing circumstances.

THE PROCESS OF PROGRAMME BUDGETING

The process of programme budgeting is illustrated in Figure 91.1. The techniques used in this process, as described elsewhere in this book, are:

1. strategic planning (Chapter 2);
2. management accounting (Chapter 69);
3. investment appraisal (Chapter 87);
4. cost–benefit analysis (Chapter 92);
5. cost-effectiveness analysis (Chapter 93); and
6. budgetary control (Chapter 83).

In addition, the analytical process of establishing objectives and drawing up alternative programmes can be assisted by building a hierarchical programme structure to illustrate how departmental or functional

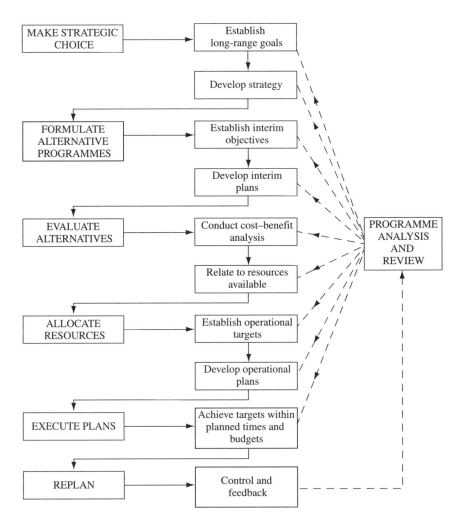

Figure 91.1 *The process of programme budgeting*

programmes with overriding objectives can be split into a hierarchy of dependent and interrelated sub-objectives. This is shown in Figure 91.2.

DEVELOPMENTS IN PROGRAMME BUDGETING

Although little reference is now made, in the UK at least, to the original notion of programme budgeting, the basic concepts are retained in one form or another, although the emphasis may have changed.

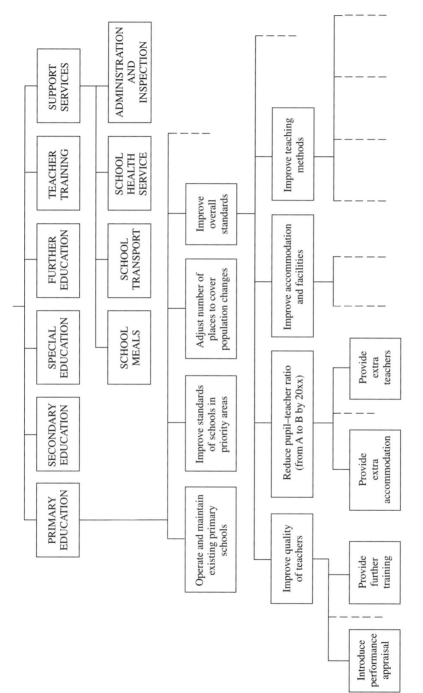

Figure 91.2 *Possible educational objectives for an education authority*

In the United States, rational policy analysis has become a major feature of the administration, using 'hard edge' quantitative techniques in a logic-of-choice approach to decision making, drawn from economics, statistical decision theory and operation research.

BENEFITS

Programme budgeting as originally conceived, or as modified by more recent governments, is designed to help higher-level decision takers who are concerned with broad questions of whether to embark upon, maintain, modify or discontinue particular activities.

In the UK, the emphasis on output budgeting coupled with increasing attention to management accounting techniques has focused attention on the assessment of the cost-effectiveness of present and future activities in order to ensure the efficient use of available resources and, in particular:

1. to reveal uneconomic activities, under-utilized capacity and wastage and to assist corrective action; and
2. to ensure that decisions are taken with full knowledge of all relevant financial information.

The potential benefits of using this approach are obvious. What is interesting to management in the private sector, however, is that although programme budgeting has been developed and adapted for use in public administration, the way it brings together its planning, evaluation and control techniques into a coherent package has much of interest to those involved in corporate planning and financial control in industry or commerce.

FURTHER READING

Jones, R and Pendlebury, M, *Public Sector Accounting* (4th edition), Pitman, London 1996.

92

Cost–Benefit Analysis

DEFINITION

Cost–benefit analysis conducts a monetary assessment of the total costs and revenues or benefits of a project, paying particular attention to the social costs and benefits which do not normally feature in conventional costing exercises.

AIM

The underlying object of cost–benefit analysis is to identify and quantify as many tangible and intangible costs and benefits as possible. The aim is then to see a strategy which achieves the maximum benefit for the minimum cost. Only where benefits exceed costs should a project be undertaken.

BACKGROUND

In business, the usual method for testing the 'soundness' of proposed activities is investment appraisal, which requires a calculation of the value of the resources to be employed in them (the costs) and a comparison with the value of the goods or services to be produced (the benefits). In appraising an investment, it is the normal practice to subtract from the annual value of receipts all variable or running costs, leaving a residual which can be expressed as an annual rate of return on the capital employed. Because money in the hand is worth more than money in prospect, *discounted cash-flow* (DCF) techniques are often used to discount expected future cash flows at arbitrary chosen rates to arrive at a present value. If the anticipated return compares favourably with the prospective rates obtainable from the alternative uses to which the capital might be put, the prospective project may be regarded as sound.

In contrast, in the public sector many services are provided, such as roads and schools, without direct prices being charged for them. The cost can usually be calculated, but it is more difficult to place a financial value on the benefits resulting from the satisfaction of group wants. And there may be social costs involved which are difficult (in some cases, perhaps, impossible) to measure. The concept of welfare economics, as developed by Professor A C Pigou, argues that there are circumstances in which market forces fail to encompass all costs and all benefits. To obtain a full picture of the likely costs and benefits of projects in the public sector, it may be necessary to try to assess these social costs and benefits. This is the particular feature of cost–benefit analysis which distinguishes it from the investment or project appraisal techniques used in business.

METHOD

A cost–benefit analysis is conducted in the following stages:

1. The project and its overall objectives (described as benefits) are defined.
2. A more detailed list is prepared of the anticipated benefits and likely costs. Social benefits and costs will be included in this list.
3. The list of benefits and costs, direct or indirect, is reduced to monetary values in order to arrive at an estimate of the current net benefit of the project (if any). The assessment of social benefits or costs often relies on judgement and may therefore be questionable. The fact that the term sometimes used for these values is 'shadow price' is revealing. In a transportation study, for example, accessibility and speed may be assessed as benefits, and noise as a cost. But how is the effect of noise on local residents to be measured? One way is to ask individuals how much they would pay to have a quieter house. This then becomes an estimate of the value of peace and quiet. This will not, of course, give a precise answer. It is not like using a scientific measuring instrument. But the advocates of attaching values to social benefits and costs will say that at least, if consistent methods are used, a basis is provided for comparing the total costs and benefits of alternative projects, which is the main object of cost–benefits analysis.
4. The stream of net benefits is predicted for each year of the project. The net benefit will be the value of the benefit accruing from the project minus the running costs incurred. This stream will be expressed as a

positive or negative cash flow depending on whether benefits exceed costs or costs exceed benefits.

5. The stream of annual net benefits is compared with the capital cost of the project, and this can be expressed as a percentage rate of return on the investment. Three methods of appraisal are available:

   ■ In the net present value method a discount rate is chosen and used to convert a time stream of net benefits into present value terms. Investment costs are then deducted and the projects appraised in the light of the resulting net present values. The discounted cash-flow approach is the preferred method.
   ■ The implicit rate of return on capital employed yielded by each project may be found by mathematical methods. The resulting internal rates of return can then be used in the appraisal process to identify the project where the rate is highest.
   ■ The present values of the benefit stream can be expressed as 'benefit–cost' ratios with the denominator representing total costs. Choice of project in this case would depend on the size of the resulting ratios.

6. The final appraisal is made. Crudely, if costs exceed benefits, ie the benefit–cost ratio is less than 1, the project should not be considered. The comparison between alternative projects may look at the respective benefit–cost ratios, but it should also consider the different net present values and the discounted rates of return on the investment.

BENEFITS

Cost–benefit analysis can be used simply to ensure that value for money is obtained from a project which requires the investment of funds. It can and does go beyond this by providing a basis for assessing the merits of different projects in terms of the benefits they produce and the costs that will be incurred.

Cost–benefit studies attempt to allow for social costs and benefits. And as these are a feature of most, if not all, public sector projects, the discipline of trying to apply a consistent method of measurement in these areas should help to produce better decisions which take important subjective factors into account. The difficulty is, of course, placing realistic values on such things as good health, quiet houses or protection from a potential enemy. Cost–benefit analysts have sometimes attempted the impossible, and Professor Peter Self described the efforts of the Roskill Commission on London's third airport as 'nonsense on stilts'. But at least cost–benefit analysis concentrates attention on basic issues. And the task of listing relevant costs and benefits is in itself a valuable discipline.

FURTHER READING

Jones, R and Pendlebury, M, *Public Sector Accounting* (4th edition), Pitman, London 1996.

93

Cost-effectiveness Analysis

DEFINITION

Cost-effectiveness analysis compares alternative courses of action in terms of their costs and their effectiveness in attaining some specific objectives.

AIMS

The aims of cost-effectiveness analysis are to:

1. assist decision makers to identify a preferred choice among possible alternatives;
2. ensure that the course of action selected will provide good value for money – better than any other course of action; and
3. generally provide for the better allocation and use of resources.

METHOD

Cost-effectiveness analysis is carried out in the following stages:

1. *Establish objectives* – an analysis of what the decision maker is trying to attain through their policy or programme. At this stage, preliminary information will be obtained about how to measure the extent to which

objectives are achieved. This will mean that the outputs and potential benefits of the programme will need to be specified, at least in outline.

2. *Identify alternatives* – the means by which the objectives will be attained.

3. *Assess costs* – actual costs *and* opportunity costs for each alternative. Because the choice of an alternative implies that certain specific resources can no longer be used for other purposes, the true measure of their cost is the opportunities they preclude.

4. *Construct model* – a simplified representation of the real world which abstracts the features of the situation relevant to the question being studied. The means of representation may vary from a set of mathematical equations to a purely verbal description of the situation, in which judgement alone is used to predict the consequences of various choices. In cost-effectiveness analysis, as in any analysis of choice, the role of the model is to predict the costs that each alternative would incur and the extent to which each alternative would assist in attaining the objectives.

5. *Select criteria* – the rules or standards by which to rank the alternatives, selected in order of desirability; the most promising is chosen. They provide a means for weighing cost against effectiveness.

6. *Conduct analysis* – the consequences of choosing an alternative as indicated by means of the model. These consequences show how effective each alternative is in the attainment of objectives (which means that a measure of effectiveness for each objective is required) and what the costs are. The criteria can then be used to arrange the alternatives in order of preference.

7. *Implement and review* – the selected policy or programme is implemented and its cost and effectiveness are measured against budgets and performance criteria. The review will then determine any changes needed to improve cost-effectiveness.

BENEFITS

Cost-effectiveness analysis can help a decision maker to understand the relevant alternatives and the key interactions by giving him or her an assessment of the costs, risks and possible pay-offs associated with each course of action.

FURTHER READING

Jones, R and Pendlebury, M, *Public Sector Accounting* (4th edition), Pitman, London 1996.

Part 4

Human Resource Management

94

Human Capital Measurement

DEFINITION

Human capital measurement is concerned with finding links, correlations and, ideally, causation, between different sets of human resource data, using statistical techniques. The aim is to provide information on how well the human capital of an organization is managed as a guide to future action. Human capital represents the human factor in the organization: the combined intelligence, skills and expertise that gives the organization its distinctive character.

THE NEED FOR HUMAN CAPITAL MEASUREMENT

There is an overwhelming case for evolving methods of valuing human capital and as an aid to decision making. This may mean identifying the key people management drivers and modelling the effect of varying them. The issue is to develop a framework within which reliable information can be collected and analysed such as added value per employee, productivity and measures of employee behaviour (attrition and absenteeism rates, the frequency/severity rate of accidents, and cost savings resulting from suggestion schemes).

The recognized importance of achieving human capital advantage has led to an interest in the development of methods of measuring the value of that capital for the following reasons:

- Human capital constitutes a key element of the market worth of a company, typically over 36 per cent of total revenue.
- People in organizations add value and there is a case for assessing this value to provide a basis for HR planning and for monitoring the effectiveness and impact of HR policies and practices.
- The process of identifying measures and collecting and analysing information relating to them will focus the attention of the organization on what needs to be done to find, keep, develop and make the best use of its human capital.
- Measurements can be used to monitor progress in achieving strategic HR goals and generally to evaluate the effectiveness of HR practices.
- You cannot manage unless you measure.

APPROACHES TO MEASUREMENT

The main approaches to measurement are described below.

The human capital index – Watson Wyatt

On the basis of a survey of companies that have linked together HR management practices and market value, Watson Wyatt[1] identified four major categories of HR practice which could be linked to a 30 per cent increase in shareholder value creation. These are:

Practice	Impact on market value %
total rewards and accountability	16.5
collegial, flexible workforce	9.0
recruiting and retention excellence	7.9
communication integrity	7.1

The organizational performance model – Mercer HR Consulting

The Organizational Performance Model developed by Mercer HR Consulting as explained by Nalbantian et al[2] is based on the following elements: people, work processes, management structure, information and knowledge, decision making and rewards. Each of these plays out differently within the context of the organization creating a unique DNA. If these elements have been developed piecemeal, as often happens, the potential for misalignment is strong and it is likely that human capital is not being optimized to create opportunities for substantial improvement in returns. Identifying these opportunities requires disciplined measurement of the organization's human capital assets and the management practices that affect their performance. The statistical tool 'Internal Labour Market Analysis' used by Mercer draws on the running record of employee and labour market data to analyse the actual experience of employees rather than stated HR programmes and policies. Thus gaps can be identified between what is required in the workforce to support business goals and what is actually being delivered.

The human capital monitor – Andrew Mayo

Andrew Mayo[3] has developed the 'human capital monitor' to identify the human value of the enterprise or 'human asset worth' which is equal to 'employment cost × individual asset multiplier'. The latter is a weighted average assessment of capability, potential to grow, personal performance (contribution) and alignment to the organization's values set in the context of the workforce environment (ie how leadership, culture, motivation and learning are driving success). The absolute figure is not important. What does matter is that the process of measurement leads you to consider whether human capital is sufficient, increasing, or decreasing, and highlights issues to address. Mayo advises against using too many measures and, instead, concentrate on a few organization-wide measures that are critical in creating shareholder value or achieving current and future organizational goals.

MEASUREMENT ELEMENTS

The main data elements used for measurement are as follows:

- *Basic workforce data* – demographic data (numbers by job category, gender, race, age, disability, working arrangements, absence and sickness, turnover and pay).
- *People development and performance data* – learning and development programmes, performance management/potential assessments, skills and qualifications.
- *Perceptual data* – attitude/opinion surveys, focus groups, exit interviews.
- *Performance data* – financial, operational and customer.
- *Non-financial variables* – the top 10 are:

1. quality of corporate strategy;
2. execution of corporate strategy;
3. management credibility;
4. innovation;
5. research leadership;
6. ability to attract and retain talented people;
7. market share;
8. management expertise;
9. alignment of compensation with shareholders' interests;
10. quality of major business processes.

APPROACHES TO HUMAN CAPITAL MEASUREMENT

The points that should be borne in mind when measuring human capital are:

■ Identify sources of value including the competencies and abilities that drive business performance.
■ Analyse the relationships between people management practices and outcomes and organizational effectiveness.
■ Remember that human capital measurement is concerned with the impact of people management practices on performance so that steps can be taken to do better. It is not just about measuring the efficiency of the HR department in terms of activity levels. It needs to be value focused rather than activity based. For example, it is not enough just to record the number of training days or the expenditure on training; it is necessary to assess the return on investment generated by that training.
■ Keep measurements simple – concentrate on key areas of outcomes and behaviour.
■ Only measure activities if it is clear that such measurements will inform decision making.
■ Analyse and evaluate trends rather than simply record actuals – compare the present position with base line data.
■ Focus on readily available and reliable quantified information; however, although quantification is desirable, it should not be based on huge, loose assumptions.
■ Remember that measurement is a means to an end not an end in itself. Do not get so mesmerized by the process of collecting data as to forget that the data is there to be used to support decision making and generate action.

REFERENCES

1 *Watson Wyatt Human Capital Index*, Watson Wyatt, London 2002.
2 Nalbantian, R, Guzzo, R A, Kieffer, D and Doherty, J, *Play to Your Strengths: Managing your internal labour markets for lasting competitive advantage*, McGraw-Hill, New York 2004.
3 Mayo, A, *The Human Value of the Enterprise: Valuing people as assets*, Nicholas Brealey, London 2001.

95

Human Resource Planning

DEFINITION

Human resource planning uses demand and supply forecasting techniques to determine the future workforce requirements of the company.

THE PROCESS OF HUMAN RESOURCE PLANNING

While human resource planning is primarily concerned with ensuring that the company gets the quantity and quality of people it needs, it is also linked with productivity planning to ensure that the best use is made of the company's human resources.

Human resource planning consists of six interrelated areas of activity:

1. *Demand forecasting* – estimating future needs by reference to corporate and functional plans and forecasts of future activity levels.
2. *Supply forecasting* – estimating the supply of employees by reference to analyses of current resources and future availability, after allowing for wastage.
3. *Determining human resource requirements* – analysing the demand and supply forecasts to identify future deficits or surpluses.
4. *Productivity and cost analysis* – analysing productivity, capacity, utilization and costs in order to identify the need for improvements in productivity or reductions in cost.

5. *Action planning* – preparing plans to deal with forecast deficits or surpluses of personnel; to improve utilization and productivity or to reduce costs.
6. *Human resource budgeting and control* – setting human resource budgets and standards and monitoring the implementation of the plans against them.

These are illustrated in Figure 95.1.

DEMAND FORECASTING

Demand forecasting is the process of estimating the future quantity and quality of human resources required. The basis of the forecast is the annual budget and longer-term corporate plan, translated into activity levels for each function and department. The three techniques used in demand forecasting are:

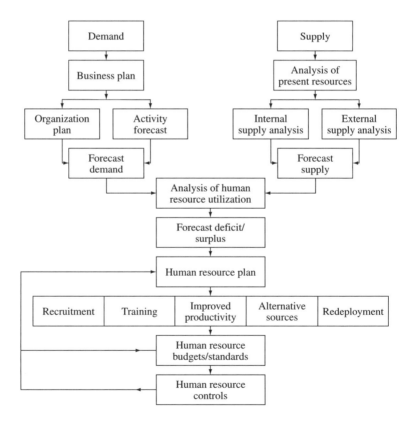

Figure 95.1 *The process of human resource planning*

1. ratio-trend analysis;
2. work study;
3. econometric models.

Ratio-trend analysis

Ratio-trend analysis is carried out by studying past ratios between, say, the number of direct and indirect workers in a manufacturing plant, and forecasting future ratios, having made some allowance for changes in organization or methods. Activity level forecasts are then used to determine direct labour requirements, and the forecast ratio of indirects to directs is used to calculate the number of indirect workers needed.

Work study

Work study techniques can be used when it is possible to apply work measurement to calculate how long operations should take and the amount of labour required. The starting point in a manufacturing company is the production budget prepared in terms of volumes of saleable products for the company as a whole, or volumes of output for individual departments. The budgets of productive hours are then compiled by the use of standard hours for direct labour, if standard labour times have been established by work measurement. The standard hours per unit of output are then multiplied by the planned volume of units to be produced to give the total planned hours for the period. This is divided by the number of operators required. Allowance may have to be made for absenteeism and forecast levels of idle time. The following is a highly simplified example of this procedure:

1. Planned output for year: 20,000 units.
2. Standard hours per unit: 5 hours.
3. Planned hours for year: 100,000 hours.
4. Productive hours per worker/year (allowing normal overtime, absenteeism and downtime): 2,000 hours.
5. Number of direct workers required: $100,000 \div 2,000 = 50$.

Work study techniques for direct workers can be combined with ratio-trend analysis to calculate the number of indirect workers needed. Clerical staff requirements may also be estimated by these methods if clerical work measurement techniques are used.

Econometric models

To build an econometric model for human resource planning purposes it is necessary to analyse past statistical data and to describe the relationship between a number of variables in a mathematical formula. The variables affecting human resource requirements may be identified under headings such as investment, sales or the complexity of the product line. The formula could then be applied to forecasts of movements in these variables to produce a human resource forecast.

SUPPLY FORECASTING

Human resources comprise the total effective effort that can be put to work as shown by the number of people and hours of work available, the capacity of employees to do the work, and their productivity. Supply forecasting measures the quantity of people that is likely to be available from within and outside the organization, having allowed for absenteeism, internal movements and promotions, wastage and changes in hours and other conditions of work. The supply analysis covers:

1. existing human resources;
2. potential losses to existing resources through labour wastage;
3. potential changes to existing resources through internal promotions;
4. effect of changing conditions of work and absenteeism; and
5. sources of supply from within the company.

BENEFITS

Human resource planning techniques ensure that the demand and supply factors in assessing future requirements are fully taken into account. They provide the basis for action plans dealing with recruitment, management, training, retraining, career progression, redundancy (if necessary) and the improvement of productivity.

96

Role Analysis

DEFINITION

Role analysis is the process of finding out what people are expected to achieve when carrying out their work and the competencies and skills they need to meet these expectations. The result of role analysis is a *role profile* that defines the outcomes role holders are expected to deliver in terms of key result areas or accountabilities. It also lists the competencies required to perform effectively in the role – what role holders need to know and be able to do. Role profiles can be individual or generic (covering a number of similar roles).

PURPOSE OF ROLE ANALYSIS

Role analysis aims to produce the following information about a role for use in recruitment, performance management and learning and development evaluation:

- *Overall purpose* – why the role exists and, in essence, what the role holder is expected to contribute.
- *Organization* – to whom the role holder reports and who reports to the role holder.
- *Key result areas or accountabilities* – what the role holder is required to achieve in each of the main elements of the role.

- *Competency requirements* – the specific technical competencies attached to the role; what the role holder is expected to know and to be able to do.

For job evaluation purposes, the role will also be analysed in terms of the factors used in the job evaluation scheme.

METHODOLOGY

The essence of role analysis is the application of systematic methods to the collection of information required to produce a role profile under the headings set out above. The steps required to collect this information are:

1. Obtain documents such as the organization structure, existing job descriptions (treat these with caution, they are likely to be out of date), and procedure or training manuals which give information about the job.
2. Ask managers for fundamental information concerning the overall purpose of the role, the key result areas and the technical competencies required.
3. Ask the role holders similar questions about their roles.

The methods that can be used are interviews, questionnaires or observation.

Interviews

To obtain the full flavour of a role, it is best to interview role holders and check the findings with their managers or team leaders. The aim of the interview is to obtain all the relevant facts about the role to provide the information required for a role profile. It is helpful to use a check list when conducting the interview. Elaborate check lists are not necessary; they only confuse people. The basic questions to be answered are:

1. What is the title of your role?
2. To whom are you responsible?
3. Who is responsible to you? (An organization chart is helpful.)
4. What is the main purpose of your role? ie in overall terms, what are you expected to do?
5. What are the key activities you have to carry out in your role? Try to group them under no more than 10 headings.
6. What are the results you are expected to achieve in each of those key activities?
7. What are you expected to know to be able to carry out your role?
8. What skills should you have to carry out your role?

The answers to these questions may need to be sorted out – they can often result in a mass of jumbled information which has to be analysed so that the various activities can be distinguished and refined to seven or eight key areas.

The advantages of the interviewing method are that it is flexible, can provide in-depth information and is easy to organize and prepare. It is therefore the most common approach. But interviewing can be time-consuming, which is why in large role analysis exercises, questionnaires as described below may be used to provide advance information about the job. This speeds up the interviewing process or even replaces the interview altogether, although this means that much of the 'flavour' of the job – ie what it is really like – may be lost.

Questionnaire

Questionnaires about their roles can be completed by role holders and approved by the role holder's manager or team leader. They are helpful when a large number of roles have to be covered. They can also save inter-viewing time by recording purely factual information and by enabling the analyst to structure questions in advance to cover areas which need to be explored in greater depth. The simpler the questionnaire the better. It need only cover the eight questions listed above.

The advantage of questionnaires is that they can produce information quickly and cheaply for a large number of jobs, but a substantial sample is needed and the construction of a questionnaire is a skilled job which should only be carried out on the basis of some preliminary fieldwork. It is highly advisable to pilot test questionnaires before launching into a full-scale exercise. The accuracy of the results also depends on the willingness and ability of job holders to complete questionnaires. Many people find it difficult to express themselves in writing about their work.

Observation

Observation means studying role holders at work, noting what they do, how they do it and how much time it takes. This method is most appro-priate for routine administrative or manual roles but is seldom used because of the time it takes.

97

Selection Testing

DEFINITION

Selection testing consists of the application of standard procedures to subjects which enables their responses to be quantified. The differences in the results represent differences in abilities or behaviour. The tests used for selection are intelligence tests, aptitude and attainment tests, and personality tests.

CHARACTERISTICS OF TESTS

The main characteristics of a test are that:

1. it is a sensitive measuring instrument which discriminates well between subjects;
2. it will have been standardized on a representative and sizeable sample of the population for which it is intended so that any individual's score can be interpreted in relation to that of others;
3. it is reliable in the sense that it always measures the same thing – a test aimed at measuring a particular characteristic, such as intelligence, should measure the same characteristic when applied to different people at the same or a different time, or to the same person at different times; and
4. it is valid in the sense that it measures the characteristic which the test is intended to measure – thus an intelligence test should measure intelligence (however defined) and not simply verbal facility, and a test

meant to predict success in a job or in passing examinations should produce reasonably convincing (statistically significant) predictions.

INTELLIGENCE TESTS

Intelligence tests are the oldest and most frequently used psychological tests. The first test was produced by Binet and Simon in 1905, and shortly afterwards Stern suggested that the test scores should be expressed in the form of intelligence quotients, or IQs. An IQ is the ratio of the mental age as measured by a Binet-type test to the actual (chronological) age. When the mental and chronological ages correspond, the IQ is expressed as 100. It is assumed that intelligence is distributed normally throughout the population, ie, the frequency distribution of intelligence corresponds to the normal curve shown in Figure 97.1. The most important characteristic of the normal curve is that it is symmetrical – there are an equal number of cases on either side of the mean, the central axis. Thus the distribution of intelligence in the population as a whole consists of an equal number of people with IQs above and below 100.

APTITUDE AND ATTAINMENT TESTS

Aptitude tests are designed to predict the potential an individual has to perform a job or specific tasks within a job. They can cover such areas as clerical, numerical and mechanical aptitude, and dexterity. They may come in the form of well-validated single tests, or as a battery of tests such as those developed some years ago by the British National Institute of Industrial Psychology for selecting apprentices.

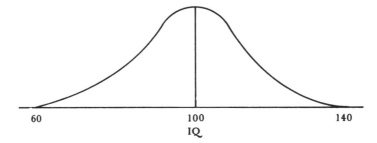

Figure 97.1 *An IQ normal curve*

All aptitude tests should be properly validated. The usual procedure is to determine the qualities required for the job by means of a job analysis. A standard test or a test battery is then obtained from a test agency. Alternatively, a special test is devised by or for the company. The test is then given to employees already working on the job and the results compared with a criterion, usually supervisors' ratings. If the correlation between test and criterion is sufficiently high, the test is then given to applicants. To validate the test further, a follow-up study of the job performance of the applicants selected by the test is usually carried out.

Attainment tests measure abilities or skills that have already been acquired by training or experience. A typing test is the most typical example. It is easy to find out how many words a minute a typist can type and compare that with the standard required for the job.

PERSONALITY TESTS

Personality tests attempt to assess the type of personality possessed by the applicant in terms of personality traits (styles of behaviour such as aggressiveness or persistence) or personality types (salient features which characterize the individual such as extroversion or introversion).

They need to be treated with great caution. For selection purposes they are almost meaningless if they have not been validated by a thorough correlation of test results with subsequent behaviour. And such validations present great difficulties.

BENEFITS

Selection testing provides an objective means of measuring abilities or characteristics. Tests are most likely to be helpful when they are used as part of a selection procedure for occupations where a large number of recruits are required, and where it is not possible to rely entirely on examination results or information about previous experience as the basis for predicting future performance. In these circumstances it is economic to develop and administer the tests and a sufficient number of cases can be built up for the essential validation exercise. Intelligence tests are particularly helpful in situations where intelligence is a key factor but there is no other reliable method of measuring it.

FURTHER READING

Toplis, J, Dulewicz, V and Fletcher, C, *Psychological Testing: A Practical Guide*, Institute of Personnel Management, London 1987.

98

Job Evaluation

DEFINITION

Job evaluation schemes:

1. establish the rank order of jobs within an organization, measure the difference in value between them and group them into an appropriate grade in a job grade structure;
2. ensure that, so far as possible, judgements about job values are made on objective rather than subjective grounds; and
3. provide a continuing basis for assessing the value of jobs which is easy to understand, administer and control and is accepted by the staff as fair.

TECHNIQUES

The basic techniques used in job evaluation are as follows:

1. *Job analysis*. Information is obtained about the content of the job and the levels of responsibility involved.
2. *Whole-job comparison*. Following job analysis, whole jobs are compared with one another to determine their relative importance and their place in a hierarchy. (Job evaluation is essentially a comparative process.)
3. *Factor comparison*. Separately defined characteristics or factors which are assumed to be common to all jobs are analysed and compared. It is assumed that differences in the extent to which the characteristics are found in the jobs will measure differences between the jobs.

TYPES OF JOB EVALUATION

Job evaluation schemes are usually grouped into two basic types:

1. *Non-analytical*, based on whole-job comparisons. The main non-analytical schemes are job ranking and job classification.
2. *Analytical*, based on factor comparisons. The basic scheme is points rating, although there are a number of proprietary brands, of which the best known is the Hay/MSL scheme.

Job ranking

The simplest form of job evaluation is job ranking. This is a non-analytical approach which aims to judge each job as a whole and to determine its relative value in a hierarchy by ranking one job against another. The rank order is established by considering the worth of each job to the organization. A grading structure has then to be developed and the jobs are slotted into the grades.

Job classification

Job classification is based on an initial definition of the number and characteristics of the grades into which the jobs will be placed. The grade definitions attempt to take into account discernible differences in skill and responsibility and may refer to specific criteria, such as level of decision, knowledge, equipment used and education or training required to do the work. Jobs are allotted to grades by comparing the whole-job description with the grade definition.

Points rating

Points rating schemes use factor comparison techniques. The factors selected are those considered to be most relevant in assessing the comparative value of jobs. Typical factors include resources controlled, decisions, complexity, and knowledge and skills.

Each factor is given a range of points so that a maximum number of points is available. The relative importance or 'weighting' of a factor is determined by the maximum number of points allotted to it. In each factor, the total range of points is divided into degrees according to the level at which the factor is present in the jobs. The characteristics of each degree in terms of, say, level of complexity, are defined as yardsticks for comparison purposes.

Jobs are evaluated by studying job descriptions containing analyses of the degree to which the factor is present in the job and comparing them with the factor level definition. The jobs are graded for each factor and the points for each grading are added to produce a total score. This score can then be related to the scores of other jobs to indicate the rank order. For example, an evaluation of two jobs using a four factor scheme could produce the results shown in Table 98.1.

Table 98.1 *An example of points rating*

Factor	Job A		Job B	
	Level	*Points*	*Level*	*Points*
Resources	4	20	5	25
Decisions	4	60	4	60
Complexity	5	25	3	15
Knowledge and skills	3	15	3	15
		120		115

JOB EVALUATION PROGRAMME

A job evaluation programme consists of the eight stages shown in Figure 98.1:

Stage 1 is the preliminary stage in which information is obtained about present arrangements; decisions are made on the need for a new scheme or to revise an existing scheme; and a choice is made of the type of scheme to be used.

Stage 2 is the planning stage when the programme is drawn up; the staff affected are informed; arrangements are made as required for setting up working parties; and the representative sample of benchmark jobs to be analysed is selected.

Stage 3 is the analysis stage when information is collected about the sample of benchmark jobs as a basis for the internal and external evaluation.

Stage 4 is the internal evaluation stage when the jobs are ranked by means of the chosen evaluation scheme and graded, usually on a provisional basis pending the collection of market rate data, except where a job classification scheme is used to slot jobs into an existing job grade structure.

Stage 5 is the external evaluation stage when information is obtained on market rates.

Stage 6 is the stage in which the salary structure is designed.

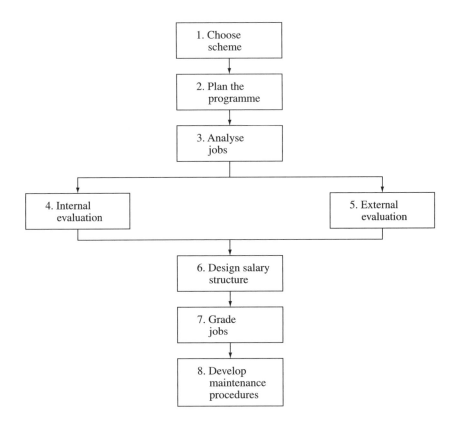

Figure 98.1 *Job evaluation programme*

Stage 7 is the grading stage in which the jobs are slotted into the salary structure.

Stage 8 is the final stage, in which the procedures for maintaining the salary structure are developed so that salary levels can be adjusted in response to inflationary pressures by means of general cost-of-living increases; new jobs can be graded into the structure; and existing jobs can be regarded as their responsibilities or market rates change.

BENEFITS

If job evaluation is based on proper job analysis and a systematic approach is used to make comparisons, it will provide a consistent and agreed framework within which defensible differentials can be maintained. It will not be completely objective. However elaborate the analysis or complicated the scheme, judgement is still required to rank or grade jobs or to allocate points to them. But, even if an element of subjectivity inevitably creeps in, at least the judgements are based on fact and are made on an organized basis. Job evaluation can be described as, in effect, a process of systematic subjectivity.

FURTHER READING

Armstrong, M and Baron, A, *The Job Evaluation Handbook,* Institute of Personnel and Development, London 1995.

99

Salary Surveys

DEFINITION

Salary surveys obtain information on the rates of pay in comparable companies for similar jobs. The purpose is to obtain data on market rates so that a competitive salary structure can be maintained.

METHOD

Salary surveys obtain and analyse information from the sources described below:

1. *General published surveys*, which give information on the average or median (ie middle of the range) salaries for typical jobs. An indication of dispersion is usually given in the form of the upper-quartile salary (the point above which 25 per cent of jobs are paid) and the lower quartile (the point below which 25 per cent of the jobs are paid).

   All published surveys depend on attracting the right range and type of participants and their success in doing this can vary from year to year. It is not possible to ensure a representative sample in all regions, industrial sectors or job types and it is essential that the survey user is aware of the areas where data are thin and can accordingly treat them with caution. This, together with the problems associated with correct matching of the job type and level, often means that while published survey data are usually relatively cheap to obtain, they can, at best, give only a very broad indication of market rates.

2. *Specialized surveys*, which consist of three types:

- analyses of members' salaries conducted by professional institutions;
- local or national surveys of particular industrial groups produced by employers or trade associations;
- local or national market studies carried out on a 'one off' basis by consultants either for a single employee or for a group of organizations.

3. *Company surveys*, which cover selected benchmark jobs which are special to the industry or are not dealt with adequately by other surveys. Surveys are either conducted by a single company approaching others on a reciprocal basis, or they are carried out by a group of independent companies acting as a 'salary survey club'. The data from a company survey can be presented in the form illustrated in Figure 99.1.

The translation of salary market data into an acceptable company salary structure is a process based on judgement and compromise. The aim is to extract a derived market rate based on effective estimates of the reliability of the data, and to strike a reasonable balance between the competing merits of the different sources used. However 'scientific' the approach, this is essentially an intuitive process. Once all the available data have been collected and presented in the most accessible manner possible (ie job by job for all the areas the structure is to cover), a proposed scale midpoint has to be established for each level based on the place in the market the company wishes to occupy, ie its 'market posture'. The establishment of this midpoint will be based not only on assessment of current and updated

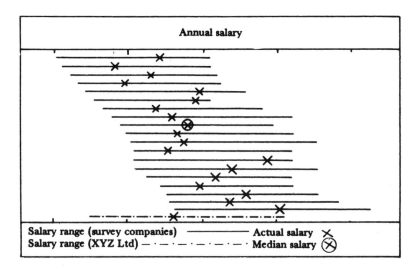

Figure 99.1 *Salary survey data presented graphically*

salary data but on indications of movements in earnings and the cost of living, which are likely to affect the whole structure. For organizations needing to stay ahead of the market this point will often be around the upper quartile; for others, closer alignment with the median is adequate.

100

Grade and Pay Structures

DEFINITIONS

Grade structures

A grade structure consists of a sequence or hierarchy of grades, bands or levels into which groups of jobs which are broadly comparable in size are placed. There may be a single structure which contains grades or bands and which is defined by their number and width (width is the scope the grade or band provides for pay progression). Alternatively the structure may be divided into a number of career or job families consisting of groups of jobs where the essential nature and purpose of the work are similar but the work is carried out at different levels. A grade structure becomes a pay structure when pay ranges, brackets or scales are attached to each grade, band or level.

Pay structure

A pay structure defines the different levels of pay for jobs or groups of jobs by reference to their relative internal value as determined by job evaluation, to external relativities as established by market rate surveys and, sometimes, to negotiated rates for jobs. They provide scope for pay progression in accordance with performance, competence, contribution or service.

TYPES OF GRADE AND PAY STRUCTURE

Narrow-graded structure

Narrow-graded structures consist of a sequence of job grades into which jobs of broadly equivalent value are placed. There may be 10 or more grades. Grades may be defined by a bracket of job evaluation points so that any job for which the job evaluation score falls within the points bracket for a grade would be allocated to that grade. Alternatively, grades may be defined by grade definitions or profiles.

Broad-graded structures

Broad-graded structures have six to nine grades rather than the 10 or more grades contained in narrow-graded structures. The grades and pay ranges are defined and managed in the same way as narrow-graded structures except that the increased width of the grades means that organizations sometimes introduce mechanisms to control progression in the grade so that staff do not inevitably reach its upper pay limit.

Broad-banded structures

Broad-banded structures compress multi-graded structures into four or five 'bands' each with, typically, a range of pay from 70 per cent to 100 per cent of the minimum. Bands may have a structure of reference points or zones or, less frequently, they may be unstructured. Pay can be managed more flexibly than in a conventional graded structure and more attention is paid to market rate relativities. Bands may be described verbally, not by reference to the results of analytical job evaluation.

Career family structures

Career families consist of jobs in a function or occupation such as marketing, operations, finance, IT, HR, administration or support services which are related through the activities carried out and the basic knowledge and skills required, but in which the levels of responsibility, knowledge, skill or competence needed differ. In a career family structure the different career families are identified and the successive levels in each family are defined by reference to the key activities carried out and the knowledge and skills or competencies required to perform them effectively. They therefore define career paths – what people have to know and be able to do to advance their career within a family and to develop career opportunities in other families. Typically, career families have between six

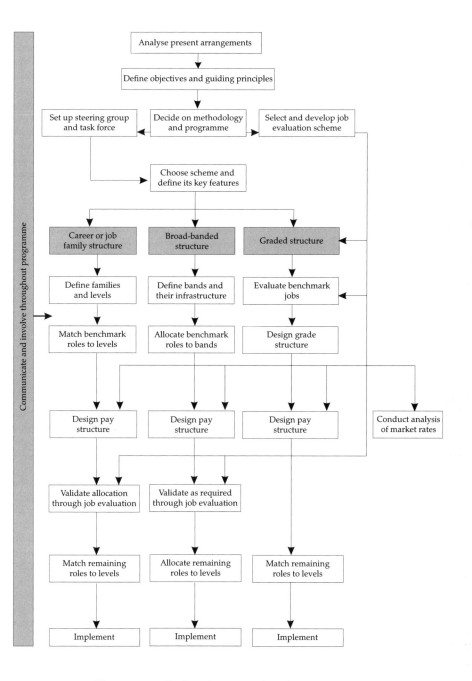

Figure 100.1 *Design of a new grade and pay structure*

Table 100.1 *Advantages and disadvantages of different grade and pay structures*

Type of structure	Advantages	Disadvantages
Narrow-graded	• Clearly indicate pay relativities • Facilitate control • Easy to understand	• Create hierarchical rigidity • Prone to grade drift • Inappropriate in a delayered organization
Broad-graded	As for narrow-graded structures but in addition: • the broader grades can be defined more clearly • better control can be exercised over grade drift	• Too much scope for pay progression • Control mechanisms can be provided but they can be difficult to manage • May be costly
Broad-banded	• More flexible • Reward lateral development and growth in competence • Fit new style organizations	• Create unrealistic expectations of scope for pay rises • Seem to restrict scope for promotion • Difficult to understand • Equal pay problems
Career family	• Clarify career paths within and between families • Facilitate the achievement of equity between families and therefore equal pay • Facilitate level definitions	• Could be difficult to manage • May *appear* to be divisive if 'silos' emerge
Job family	• Can appear to be divisive • May inhibit lateral career development • May be difficult to maintain internal equity between job families unless underpinned by job evaluation	• Facilitate pay differentiation between market groups • Define career paths against clear criteria

and eight levels as in broad-graded structures. Some families may have more levels than others.

Job family structures

Job family structures resemble career structures in that separate families are identified and levels of knowledge, skills and competency requirements defined for each level, thus indicating career paths and providing the basis for grading jobs by matching role profiles to level definitions. The main difference between job family and career family structures is that each job family has in effect its own pay structure which takes account of different levels of market rates between families (this is sometimes called 'market grouping'). In contrast, career family structures have common ranges of pay or job evaluation points for similar levels in different families.

FURTHER READING

e-research, Survey of grade and pay structures, e-reward, Stockport 2004.
Armstrong, M and Stephens, T, *Handbook of Employee Reward*, Kogan Page, London 2005.

101

Salary Control Systems

DEFINITION

Salary control systems ensure that the salary policies of the company are implemented and that salary costs are kept within budget.

BASIS OF THE SALARY CONTROL SYSTEM

The salary control system is based on:

- a clearly defined and understood salary structure;
- defined methods of salary progression;
- budgets of salary costs;
- a method of monitoring salary costs and the implementation of salary policies;
- clearly defined salary review guidelines;
- well-defined procedures for grading jobs and fixing salaries; and
- clear statements of the degree of authority managers have at each level to decide salaries and increments.

TECHNIQUES

There are four techniques for monitoring salary costs and checking on the stability and effectiveness of the salary system:

1. salary budget;
2. attrition measurement;
3. compa-ratio;
4. salary audit.

SALARY BUDGET

The annual salary budget is a product of the numbers of staff to be employed and the rates at which they will be paid during the budget year. It is therefore based on human resource plans, present salary levels and forecasts of additional costs arising from general or individual salary reviews. Actual costs should be monitored against budget using a return such as that illustrated in Table 101.1.

Table 101.1 *Salary cost return*

Category of staff	Budget for year		Budget for period		Period actual		Year to date	
	No	*Cost*	*No*	*Cost*	*No*	*Cost*	*No*	*Cost*
Grades 3–2								
Grades 7–4								
Grades 12–8								
Total								

SALARY ATTRITION

Salary attrition takes place when entrants join on lower salaries than those leaving so that salary costs over a period are likely to go down, given a normal flow of starters and leavers and subject to the effect of general and individual salary increases. In theory at least, attrition helps to finance merit increases. It has been claimed that fixed incremental systems can be entirely self-financing. But the conditions under which this can be attained are so exceptional that a completely self-financing system rarely, if ever, occurs. But some amount of attrition of merit-increased costs is normal and should be measured in order to assess actual costs and to forecast future expenditure.

Attrition can be measured over a period by the following formula: *total percentage increase to payroll arising from general promotional and merit increases* minus *total percentage increase in average salaries.*

COMPA-RATIO

A compa-ratio (short for comparative ratio) provides a measurement of how far average salaries in a range differ from the target salary, defined as the salary which should be earned by a fully competent individual in a job. A line drawn through the target salaries for each range in a salary structure is the salary policy line for an organization and it is this line which is related to market rates. If, typically, the target is the midpoint of the salary range for a grade, the compa-ratio can be calculated as follows:

$$\frac{\text{Average of all salaries in grade} \times 100}{\text{Midpoint of range}}$$

If the distribution of salaries is on target (ie the average salary is equal to the midpoint), the compa-ratio will be 100. If the ratio is above 100, this would suggest either that staff are overpaid or that there are a large number of long-serving employees paid at the top of the range. Conversely, if the ratio is below 100, the causes would probably be that salaries are too low or that a large number of entrants on lower salaries have affected the relationships. The identification of the reasons for a high or low compa-ratio can suggest policy adjustments to correct the imbalance, although there can be many situations where a ratio of over or under 100 is perfectly justified.

SALARY AUDIT

The salary system needs to be audited to check that:

1. salary levels are keeping pace with changes in market rates so that salary policies on external relativities are being maintained;
2. the salary structure is not being eroded by grade drift (unjustifiable upgradings) or because salaries for new starters or promoted staff are fixed at too high a level;
3. appropriate differentials are being maintained internally; and
4. salary progression policies are being implemented properly.

The audit is conducted by monitoring external and internal relativities and procedures.

Monitoring external relativities

Market rate surveys are conducted or analysed regularly and comparisons made with salaries paid within the company to assess whether salaries are generally keeping pace with the market or whether any particular groups of staff are out of line. The best way to summarize and compare the data is to chart (as shown in Figure 101.1):

1. the salary practice line (the average of actual salaries paid in each grade);
2. the salary policy line (the line joining together the target salaries for each grade – usually the midpoint salary); and
3. the median and/or upper-quartile market rate trend lines.

Monitoring internal relativities

Internal relativities are monitored by carrying out periodical studies of the differentials that exist vertically within departments or between categories of staff. For example, if there is an established hierarchy in departments of, say, departmental manager, section heads, senior and junior clerks, the average salaries at each level are analysed periodically to reveal any changes in differentials between levels. There is nothing sacrosanct about the pattern of differentials. Structural adjustments within the company and alterations in market rates can justify changes. But it is desirable to know what is happening so that action can be taken, if required and if feasible, to restore the proper relationships.

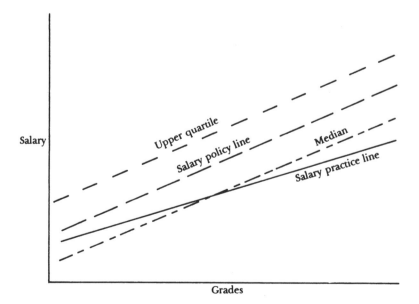

Figure 101.1 *Analysis of salary structure policy and practice in relation to market rates*

It may also be interesting to analyse key ratios, for instance between the salary of the chief executive and the average earnings without overtime of semi-skilled employees. If, for example, this ratio has changed from 7:1 to 5:1 the implications will need to be studied, not only for the chief executive but also for intermediate jobs in the hierarchy.

Monitoring procedures

The following procedures are monitored to ensure that they are operating in accordance with the company's salary policies:

1. *General salary reviews*. The audit should ensure that general increases are not above the rate of inflation or the general level of market rate increases, and that the amount they cost is what the company can afford to pay.
2. *Individual salary reviews*. If variable merit increases are given, the audit checks that guidelines on the amounts that can be paid in relation to performance are available and that the total cost of the review falls within the guideline budget, and that increases are properly authorized.
3. *Regradings*. The audit checks that regradings are justified by job evaluation and that the new salaries resulting from regradings or promotions are in line with responsibility levels as indicated by the salary structure. The aim is to avoid 'grade drift', ie regradings made simply to obtain a higher salary and not related to an increase in responsibility.
4. *Appointment salaries*. The audit checks that salaries for new staff are in line with policies on where jobs fit into the salary structure and how much can be paid above the minimum to attract candidates.

BENEFITS

Salary control systems are needed to avoid excessive salary costs, staff being overpaid or underpaid for what they do, difficulties in recruiting or retaining staff, and lack of motivation because the salary system is inequitable.

102

Contingent Pay

DEFINITION

Contingent pay is the term used to describe schemes for providing financial rewards that are related to individual performance, competence, contribution or skill.

TYPES OF SCHEME

Performance-related pay

Individuals receive financial rewards in the form of increases to basic pay or cash bonuses which are linked to an assessment of performance, usually in relation to agreed objectives. Scope is provided for consolidated pay progression within pay brackets attached to grades in a grade and pay structure (see Chapter 99). Such increases are permanent – they are seldom if ever withdrawn. (See also Chapter 103.)

Competence-related pay

People receive financial rewards in the shape of increases to their base pay by reference to the level of competence they demonstrate in carrying out their roles. It is a method of paying people for the ability to perform now and in the future.

Contribution-related pay

Contribution-related pay is a process for making pay decisions which are based on assessments of both the outcomes of the work carried out by individuals and the inputs in terms of levels of competence and competency which have influenced these outcomes. It focuses on what people in organizations are there to do, that is, to contribute by their skill and efforts to the achievement of the purpose of their organization or team.

Skill-based pay

Skill-based pay provides employees with a direct link between their pay progression and the skills they have acquired and can use effectively. Rewards are related to the employee's ability to apply a wider range or a higher level of skills to different jobs or tasks.

DEVELOPING AND IMPLEMENTING CONTINGENT PAY

The 10 steps required to develop and implement contingent pay are:

1. Analyse culture, strategy and existing processes including the grade and pay structure, performance management and methods of progressing pay or awarding cash bonuses.
2. Set out aims which demonstrate how contingent pay will help to achieve the organization's strategic goals.
3. Communicate aims to line managers staff and involve them in the development of the scheme.
4. Determine how the scheme will operate covering:
    -   the use of performance and competence measures;
    -   the performance management processes required;
    -   the scope for awarding cash bonuses as well as base pay increases;
    -   the approach to making decisions on awards;
    -   the amount of money that will be available for contribution pay, and how that money should be distributed;
    -   the guidelines and procedures needed to govern contribution pay reviews and ensure that they are carried out fairly and consistently and within available budgets;
    -   the basis upon which the effectiveness of contingent pay will be evaluated.
5. Develop competence framework and role profiles.
6. Develop or improve performance management processes covering the

Table 102.1 *Comparison of contingent pay schemes*

Type of scheme	Advantages	Disadvantages	When appropriate
Performance-related pay	• May motivate (but this is uncertain) • Links rewards to objectives • Meets the need to be rewarded for achievement • Delivers message that good performance is important and will be rewarded	• May *not* motivate Relies on judgements of performance which may be subjective • Prejudicial to teamwork • Focuses on outputs, not quality • Relies on good performance management processes • Difficult to manage well	• For people who are likely to be motivated by money • In organizations with a performance-orientated culture • When performance can be measured objectively
Competence-related pay	• Focus attention on need to achieve higher levels of competence • Encourages competence development • Can be integrated with other applications of competency-based HR management	• Assessment of competence levels may be difficult • Ignores outputs – danger of paying for competencies that will not be used • Relies on well-trained and committed line managers	• As part of an integrated approach to HRM where competencies are used across a number of activities • Where competence is a key factor where it may be inappropriate or hard to measure outputs • Where well-established competency frameworks exist
Contribution-related pay	• Rewards people not only for what they do but how they do it	• As for both PRP and competence-related pay – it may be hard to measure contribution and it is difficult to manage well	• When it is believed that a well-rounded approach covering both inputs and outputs is appropriate
Skill-based pay	• Encourages and rewards the acquisition of skills	• Can be expensive when people are paid for skills they don't use	• On the shop floor or in retail organizations

selection of performance measures, decisions on competence requirements, methods of agreeing objectives and the procedure for
conducting joint reviews.

7. Communicate intentions to line managers and staff.
8. Pilot test the scheme and amend as necessary.
9. Provide training to all concerned.
10. Launch the scheme and evaluate its effectiveness after the first review.

FURTHER READING

Armstrong, M and Murlis, H, *Reward Management* (5th edition), Kogan Page,
London 2004 .
e-research, *Survey of Contingent Pay*, e-reward, Stockport 2004.

103

Performance-related Pay

DEFINITION

Performance-related pay (PRP) links reward or salary progression to some form of performance rating. This could be part of a performance management or appraisal system, or it could be based on an entirely separate appraisal of performance exclusively for pay purposes.

TYPES OF PERFORMANCE-RELATED PAY SCHEMES

The main types of individual PRP schemes are variable salary progression, variable increments and achievement bonuses.

Variable salary progression

In a variable salary progression system, movement through a salary range is governed by performance ratings, as shown in Figure 103.1.

In this typical example there are four performance levels:

A = exceptional
B = above average
C = average
D = below average

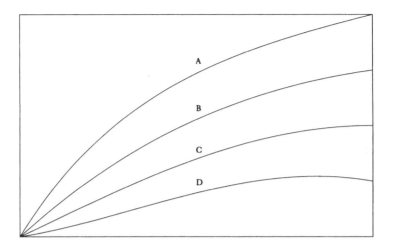

Figure 103.1 *Variable salary progression*

Some organizations simplify the system by having only three ratings which indicate whether an individual should have an above-average, average or below-average increase. Guidelines are provided on the increases that can be awarded in each category. There is much to be said for this approach in that it does not label people and avoids asking managers to make fine discriminations in what is essentially a subjective process.

Variable increments

In an incremental or pay spine structure, pay can be varied according to performance by giving extra increments for good performance or by withholding increments for poor performance. The achievement of high ratings can also provide for job-holders to be awarded extra increments on top of their scale.

Achievement bonuses

Achievement or success bonuses are lump-sum payments related to performance. They are sometimes the only variable element in pay, but they can be used to recognize exceptional performance or as a means of rewarding people who have reached the top of their salary scale when they perform particularly well. People in that position will be required to re-earn their bonus every year – it should not be regarded as an automatic handout.

CRITERIA FOR EFFECTIVENESS

Performance-related pay is more likely to work as a motivator if:

- it is appropriate to the type of work carried out and the people employed on it and fits the culture of the organization;
- the reward is clearly and closely linked to the effort of the individual or team;
- the reward follows as closely as possible the accomplishment which generated it;
- employees are in a position to influence their performance by changing their behaviour;
- they are clear about the targets and standards of performance required;
- they can track their performance against these targets and standards;
- fair and consistent means are available for measuring performance;
- the reward is clearly and closely linked and proportionate to the effort of the individual or team;
- employees expect that effective performance (or specified behaviour) will certainly lead to worthwhile rewards;
- the performance-related pay scheme operates by means of a defined and easily understood formula;
- provisions are made in the scheme for amending the formula in specified circumstances;
- constraints are built into the scheme which ensure that employees cannot receive inflated rewards which are not related to their own performance;
- the scheme is properly designed, installed and maintained; and
- employees covered by the scheme are involved in its development and operation.

BENEFITS

The main benefits of performance-related pay (PRP) are:

- rewarding people according to their performance will motivate them to achieve higher levels of performance;
- it is right and equitable to reward people according to their contribution, and PRP provides a tangible means of recognizing achievement; and
- PRP is a means of ensuring that everyone understands the performance imperatives of the organization – the existence of a well-conceived and properly managed PRP scheme delivers a message to employees about the expectations of the organization for high-level performance.

These benefits are, however, dependent on the scheme meeting the exacting criteria set out above.

FURTHER READING

Brown, D and Armstrong, M, *Paying for Contributions*, Kogan Page, London 1999.

104

Payment by Results

DEFINITION

Payment by results systems relate the pay or part of the pay received by individual workers or groups of workers to the number of items produced or the time taken to do a certain amount of work.

The main schemes are:

1. straight piecework;
2. differential piecework systems;
3. measured day work;
4. group incentive schemes;
5. factory-wide incentive schemes.

STRAIGHT PIECEWORK

The most common of the schemes of payment by results which are purely individual in character is what is called straight piecework. This means payment of a uniform price per unit of production and it is most appropriate where production is repetitive in character and can easily be divided into similar units.

Straight piecework rates can be expressed in one or two main forms: 'money piecework' or 'time piecework'. In the case of money piecework, the employee is paid a flat money price for each piece or operation completed. In the case of time piecework, instead of a price being paid for an operation, a time is allowed (this is often called a time-allowed system).

Workers are paid at their basic piecework rate for the time allowed, but if they complete the job in less time, they gain the advantage of the time saved, as they are still paid for the original time allowed. Thus, an operator who completes a job timed at 60 hours in 40 hours would receive a bonus of 50 per cent of his or her piecework rate, namely: $(60 - 40/40) \times 100$.

Piece rates may be determined by work study using the technique known as effort rating to determine standard times for jobs. In situations where work is not repetitive, especially in the engineering industry, times may be determined on a much less analytical basis by rate-fixers using their judgement. This often involves prolonged haggles with operators.

DIFFERENTIAL PIECEWORK SYSTEMS

Straight piecework systems result in a constant wage cost per unit of output, and management objections to this feature led to the development of differential systems where the wage cost per unit is adjusted in relation to output. The most familiar applications of this approach have been the premium bonus systems such as the Halsey/Weir or Rowan schemes. Both these systems are based on a standard time allowance and not a money piece rate, and the bonus depends on the time saved. Unlike straight piecework, the wages cost per unit of production falls as output increases, but the hourly rate of workers' earnings still increases, although not in proportion to the increased output. For obvious reasons, these systems are viewed with suspicion by unions and workers, and many variations to the basic approach have been developed, some of which involve sharing the increments of higher productivity between employers and workers.

MEASURED DAY WORK

In measured day work the pay of the employee is fixed on the under-standing that he or she will maintain a specific level of performance, but the pay does not fluctuate in the short term with his or her performance. The arrangement relies on work measurement to define the required level of performance and to monitor the actual level. Fundamental to measured day work is the concept of an incentive level of performance, and this distinguishes it clearly from time rate systems. Measured day work guarantees the incentive payment in advance, thereby putting employees under an obligation to perform at the effort level required. Payments by results, on the other hand, allows employees discretion as to their effort level but relates their pay directly to the output they have achieved. Between these two systems are a variety of alternatives that seek to marry the different characteristics of payment by results and measured day work, including banded incentives, stepped schemes and special forms of high day rate.

GROUP INCENTIVE SCHEMES

Group or area incentive schemes provide for the payment of a bonus either equally or proportionately to individuals within a group or area. The bonus is related to the output achieved over an agreed standard or to the time saved on a job – the difference between allowed time and actual time.

FACTORY-WIDE INCENTIVE SCHEMES

Factory-wide incentive or gainsharing schemes provide a bonus for all factory workers which is related to an overall measure of performance. They are sometimes referred to as share-of-production plans. The basic type of scheme links the bonus to output or added value (the value added to the cost of raw materials and bought-in parts by the process of production). Other schemes such as the Scanlon and Rucker plans have more elaborate formulae for calculating the bonus and built-in arrangements for joint consultation.

In their simplest form these schemes provide for a direct link between the bonus and output or added value. Alternatively, a target for output or added value may be set and the bonus paid on a scale related to achievements above the target level.

BENEFITS

The benefits claimed for payment-by-results schemes are that people who work primarily for money will work harder if they are paid more.

Some commentators question the significance of money as an incentive. But even if it is accepted, as it is by most people, that money is a prime motivator, incentive schemes can only work if the following conditions are fulfilled:

1. There is a direct and easily recognizable link between effort and reward.
2. Incentive payments do not fluctuate too widely for reasons beyond the worker's control (especially when the bonus is a significant sum).
3. There is no undue delay in paying bonuses.
4. The scheme is manifestly fair and easy to understand.

From management's point of view, the increases in effort arising from a well-run scheme based on proper work measurement can be considerable in the right circumstances (ie when the conditions listed above can be met). But incentive schemes can too easily lead to wage drift (rewards creeping up at a higher rate than effort) and endless wrangles between managers and ratefixers, and the workers and their representatives.

105

Systematic Training

DEFINITION

Systematic training is specifically designed to meet defined needs which will be satisfied by improving and developing the knowledge, skills and attitudes required by individuals to perform adequately a given task or job.

COMPONENTS

The components of systematic training are as follows:

1. *The identification and analysis of training needs.* All training must be directed towards the satisfaction of defined needs: for the company as a whole, for specific functions or groups of employees, or for individuals.
2. *The definition of training objectives.* Training must aim to achieve measurable goals expressed in terms of the improvements or changes expected in corporate, functional, departmental or individual performance.
3. *The preparation of training plans.* These must describe the overall scheme of training and its costs and benefits. The overall scheme should further provide for the development of training programmes and facilities, the selection and use of appropriate training methods, the selection and training of trainers, and the implementation of training plans, including the maintenance of training records.
4. *The measurement and analysis of results.* These require the validation of the achievements of each training programme against its objectives and

the evaluation of the effect of the whole training scheme on company or departmental performance.

5. *The feedback of the results of validations and evaluations.* So that training plans, programmes and techniques can be improved.

The relationships between these components are shown in Figure 105.1.

BENEFITS

Training can be defined variously as: the modification of behaviour through experience; the transfer of skills and knowledge from those who have them to those who do not; or the bringing about of a significant improvement in performance as a result of instruction, practice and experience.

These definitions indicate what training is but not how it can be effective. And the only way of getting good results from training is to tackle it systematically. The benefits that result from this approach are:

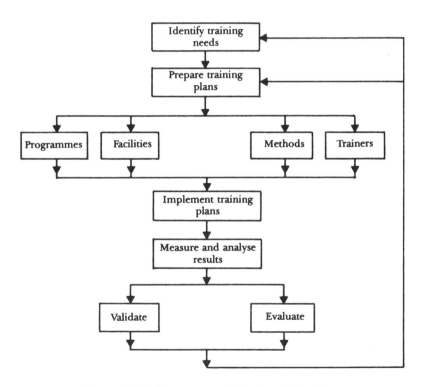

Figure 105.1 *The components of systematic training*

1. learning time is shortened and the costs of training and the losses resulting from too lengthy a learning curve are reduced (the learning curve is the time taken to reach an acceptable level of performance);
2. the performance of existing employees is improved;
3. commitment to the job and identification with the company are increased; and
4. people's capacities are developed so that they can be better prepared for positions of greater responsibility in the future.

FURTHER READING

Kenney, J and Reid, M, *Training Interventions*, Institute of Personnel Management, London 1988.

106

Identifying Training Needs

DEFINITION

Identifying training needs is the process of analysing training requirements as a basis for preparing relevant training programmes.

AIMS

The analysis of training needs aims to define the gap between what is happening and what should happen. This is what has to be filled by training (see Figure 106.1). The gap may consist of the difference between:

■ how the company or a function within the company is performing and how it should perform;

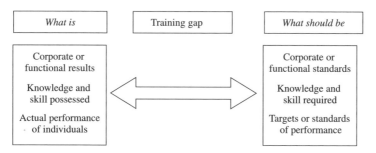

Figure 106.1 *The training gap*

- what people know and can do and what they should know and do; and
- what people actually do and what they should do.

TRAINING NEEDS ANALYSIS

Training needs analysis covers corporate, group and individual needs as shown in Figure 106.2.

Corporate training needs should come from the analysis of company strengths and weaknesses as part of the corporate planning process. The company human resource plan will also indicate the numbers and types of people required in the future.

Group needs are identified by analysing functional or departmental human resource plans or by conducting special surveys using question-naires and interviews. Job analysis can be used to determine the knowledge and skills required in specific jobs and this information can be supplemented by analysing the results obtained from the assessment of individual needs.

Individual training needs are identified by using the techniques of job analysis (Chapter 104), skills analysis (Chapter 107) and performance management systems (Chapter 101).

BENEFITS

Training programmes are too often shots in the dark. If they are not relevant to what is required by the organization, then they are pointless. The only way to ensure relevance is to carry out a systematic training needs analysis exercise as an essential starting point in developing a training programme.

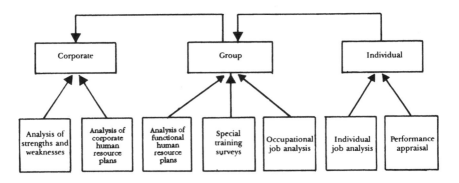

Figure 106.2 *Training needs – areas and methods*

107

Skills Analysis

DEFINITION

Skills analysis identifies what the worker needs to know and be able to do to perform a job satisfactorily at experienced worker standard. Skills analysis leads to the production of a training specification or breakdown. This is used as the basis for the instruction given to trainees and for the design of the overall training programme.

THE TRAINING SPECIFICATION

The training specification breaks down the broad duties contained in the job description into the detailed tasks that must be carried out. It then sets out the characteristics that the worker should have in order to perform these tasks successfully. These characteristics are as follows:

1. *Knowledge* – what the worker needs to know. It may be professional, technical or commercial knowledge; or it may be about the commercial, economic or market environment – the machines to be operated, the materials or equipment to be used or the procedures to be followed, the customers, clients, colleagues and subordinates he or she is in contact with and the factors that affect their behaviour; or it may refer to the problems that will occur and how they should be dealt with.
2. *Skills* – what the worker needs to be able to do if results are to be achieved and knowledge is to be used effectively. Skills are built

gradually by repeated training or other experience. They may be manual, intellectual or mental, perceptual or social.

3. *Attitudes* – the disposition to behave or to perform in a way which is in accordance with the requirements of the work.

TECHNIQUES

Skills analysis starts with *job analysis,* as described in Chapter 104. Skills analysis goes into further detail, however, about what workers have to be able to do and the particular attributes they need to do it.

The specific techniques used in skills analysis are:

1. job breakdown;
2. manual skills analysis;
3. task analysis;
4. faults analysis.

JOB BREAKDOWN

Definition

The job breakdown technique analyses a job into separate operations, processes or tasks which can be broken down into manageable parts for instructional purposes.

Method

A job breakdown analysis is recorded in a standard format of three columns:

1. *The stage column.* The different steps in the job are described – most semi-skilled jobs can easily be broken down into their constituent parts.
2. *The instruction column.* Against each step a note is made of how the task should be done. This, in effect, describes what has to be learned by the trainee.
3. *The key points column.* Against each step any special points such as quality standards or safety instructions are noted so that they can be emphasized to a trainee learning the job.

MANUAL SKILLS ANALYSIS

Definition

Manual skills analysis is a technique developed by W D Seymour from work study. It isolates for instructional purposes the skills and knowledge employed by experienced workers performing tasks which require a high degree of manual dexterity. It is used to analyse short-cycle, repetitive operations such as assembly tasks and other similar factory work.

Method

The hand, finger and other body movements of an experienced operative are observed and recorded in great detail as he or she carries out his or her work. The analysis concentrates on the tricky parts of the job which, while presenting no difficulty to the experienced operative, have to be analysed in depth before they can be taught to trainees. Not only are the hand movements recorded in great detail but particulars are also noted of the cues (vision and other senses) which the operative absorbs when performing the tasks. Explanatory comments are added when necessary.

TASK ANALYSIS

Definition

Task analysis is a systematic analysis of the behaviour required to carry out a task with a view to identifying areas of difficulty and the appropriate training techniques and learning aids necessary for successful instruction. It can be used for all types of jobs but is specifically relevant for clerical tasks.

Method

The analytical approach used in task analysis is similar to those adopted in the job breakdown and manual skills analysis techniques. The results of the analysis are usually recorded in a standard format of four columns as follows:

1. *Task* – a brief description of each element.
2. *Level of importance* – the relative significance of each task to the successful performance of the whole job.

3. *Degree of difficulty* – the level of skill or knowledge required to perform each task.
4. *Training method* – the instructional techniques, practice and experience required.

FAULTS ANALYSIS

Definition

Faults analysis is the process of analysing the typical faults which occur when performing a task, especially the more costly faults. It is carried out when the incidence of faults is high.

Method

A study is made of the job and, by questioning workers and supervisors, the most commonly occurring faults are identified. A faults specification is then produced which provides trainees with information on what faults can occur, how they can recognize them, what causes them, what effect they have, who is responsible for them, what action the trainees should take when a particular fault occurs, and how a fault can be prevented from recurring.

BENEFITS

Skills analysis is an essential element in systematic training. It is only by breaking down the job into its constituent parts and identifying what the worker needs to know to be able to do to complete each task satisfactorily that relevant training programmes can be prepared.

Skills analysis enables instruction to be based on the progressive part method in which the trainee is taught and practises each part until it can be done at target speed and at an acceptable level of quality. When two successive parts can be done separately in the target time they are practised jointly until the required speed is attained. Then a third part is added and so on, until the complete job has been learned. This is by far the best method of extending training in any job where there is more than one task to do, to the point at which trainees attain the training objective by achieving the experienced worker's level of output and quality.

108

Training Techniques

DEFINITION

A training technique is a specific and systematic approach to imparting knowledge or developing skills. The more important techniques are described below.

ACTION LEARNING

Action learning, as developed by Professor Revans, is a method of helping managers to develop their talents by exposing them to real problems. They are required to analyse them, formulate recommendations and then, instead of being satisfied with a report, actually take action. It accords with the belief that managers learn best by doing rather than being taught.

This approach conforms to the principle on which all good training should be based, ie it is problem-based and action-orientated. It recognizes that the most perplexing task managers face is how to achieve change – how to persuade their colleagues and others to commit themselves to a different way of operating. An action-learning programme therefore concentrates on developing the skills which managers need to take action effectively, without ignoring the need for knowledge of relevant techniques.

The concept of action learning is based on five assumptions:

1. Experienced managers have a huge curiosity to know how other managers work.

2. Learning about oneself is threatening and is resisted if it tends to change one's self-image. However, it is possible to reduce the external threat so that it no longer acts as a total barrier to learning about oneself.
3. People only learn when they do something, and they learn more the more responsible they feel the task to be.
4. Learning is deepest when it involves the whole person – mind, values, body, emotions.
5. The learner knows better than anyone else what he or she has learned. Nobody else has much chance of knowing.

COMPUTER-BASED TRAINING

Computers can be used for training in the following ways:

1. To simulate actual situations so that trainees can 'learn by doing'. For example, technicians can be trained in troubleshooting and repairing electronic circuitry by looking at circuit diagrams displayed on the screen and using a light pen to measure voltages at different points in the circuit. When faults are diagnosed, 'repairs' are effected by means of the light pen, this time employed as a soldering iron.
2. To extend programmed learning texts (see below) to provide diagrammatic and pictorial displays in colour and to allow more interaction between the trainee and the information presented on the screen.
3. To provide a database for information which trainees can access through a computer terminal.
4. To measure the performance of trainees against predefined criteria.
5. To provide tests or exercises for trainees. The technique of adaptive testing uses a program containing a large number of items designed to test a trainee's comprehension of certain principles. But it is not necessary for him or her to work through all of them or even to satisfy them sequentially in order to demonstrate understanding. His or her responses to a limited number of questions will show whether or not he or she has grasped the appropriate concepts to satisfy given training objectives. The process of testing can thus be speeded up considerably and can prove less frustrating for the trainee.

JOB INSTRUCTION

Job instruction techniques are based on *skills analysis*. The sequence of instruction follows four stages:

1. *Preparation*. The instructor has a plan for presenting the subject matter and using appropriate teaching methods and aids.

2. *Presentation*. This consists of a combination of telling and showing (demonstration).
3. *Practice*. The learner imitates the instructor and constantly repeats the operation under guidance. The aims are to reach the target level of performance for each element of the total task and to achieve the smooth combination of these elements into a whole job pattern.
4. *Follow-up*. The trainer follows up and helps the trainee as required.

109

Total Loss Control

DEFINITION

Total loss control is a comprehensive programme of activities designed to prevent personal injury and accidents and to minimize losses to a business arising from damage or pollution.

Total loss control goes beyond simply preventing accidents by attacking all potential causes of loss whether caused by injury or damage. However, although the technique as a whole is referred to as total loss control, it is divided into two main areas: accident control and loss control. These are linked together in the total loss control programme.

ACCIDENT CONTROL

An accident is an unintentional or unplanned happening that may or may not result in property damage, personal injury, a work stoppage or interference, or a combination of those circumstances. The essence of total accident control is that *all* accidents as defined above are reported and investigated, whether or not they produce injury or loss. Only in this way can preventive measures be taken to avoid a recurrence. Moreover, safety audits and spot checks will consider every potential source of an accident, even if the risk of injury or damage is negligible.

An accident control programme consists of the following steps:

1. *Audit*. Regular surveys of all work areas are made using checklists to identify potential causes of injury or loss.

2. *Spot checks.* Periodical spot checks, especially in higher-risk areas, are made to investigate possible problems or to follow up preliminary information which indicates the likelihood of an accident.
3. *Control centres.* These are set up to report on and analyse injuries (first-aid posts) or damage (maintenance units). They ensure that information is collected for further analysis and investigation by designated health and safety advisers or loss control officers.
4. *Reporting rules.* Strict rules are published and enforced on reporting incidents. They may be phrased like this: 'Whenever you or the equipment you operate is involved in any accident that results in personal injury or damage to property, regardless of how minor, you must report it immediately to your foreman or supervisor.'
5. *Investigation.* This is carried out initially by the foreman or supervisor following a standardized procedure. The officer responsible for accident control will investigate more serious cases but will also carry out spot checks on relatively minor cases to ensure that local investigations are being conducted properly and to further the training of foremen and supervisors in accident investigation and control.
6. *Remedial action.* The designated accident control officer recommends remedial action to prevent potential accidents or to eliminate a hazard.
7. *Proactive advice.* Accident control involves not only improving existing safety arrangements but also providing proactive advice at the time when equipment, plant or buildings are being designed, installed or constructed.
8. *Training.* Foremen, supervisors and workpeople need specific induction and continuous training in safety practices and methods of preventing accidents.
9. *Education.* A continuous programme of educational propaganda or good safety practice is essential.
10. *Follow-up.* The designated accident control officer continually follows up to ensure that remedial action has been taken and that training and education are effective.

LOSS CONTROL

Functions

The functions of loss control are to:

1. locate and define errors involving incomplete decision making, faulty judgement, bad management or individual behaviour leading to incidents which result in loss of any kind to the business; and
2. provide sound advice to management as to how such mistakes can be avoided.

Methods

Loss control follows broadly the same procedures as accident control except that it covers a wider variety of potential problem areas, ie not only potential damage but any losses, direct or indirect, arising from accidental damage *or* the standard processing methods used in the company. For example, loss control will monitor potential losses arising from pollution, vibration, lack of hygiene, fire, security lapses and even product liability. It will also consider the losses that might arise from interruptions to production in order to assess priorities in high potential-loss areas for remedial work.

The major elements of loss control management are:

1. *identification* of possible loss-producing situations (risk determination);
2. *analysis* of the causes of actual or potential losses;
3. *measurement* of any actual losses sustained by the company;
4. *selection* of methods to minimize losses, including remedial engineering, revised procedures, training and education; and
5. *implementation* of these methods within the organization.

BENEFITS

The benefits of a systematic approach to the control of accidents and losses are quite clear. The overriding benefit of a system of total loss control is that it can produce significant reductions in losses and accidents if it is introduced and maintained as a comprehensive programme with full backing from the top and properly trained and qualified accident or loss prevention officers.

FURTHER READING

Fletcher, A and Douglas, H M, *Total Loss Control*, Associated Business Programmes, London 1971.

Part 5

Management Science

110

Operational Research

DEFINITION

Operational research (OR) has been defined by the Operational Research Society of the United Kingdom as follows:

> Operational research is the application of the methods of science to complex problems arising in the direction and management of large systems of men, machines, materials, and money in industry, business, government, and defence. The distinctive approach is to develop a scientific model of the system, incorporating measurements of factors such as chance and risk, with which to predict and compare the outcomes of alternative decisions, strategies, or controls. The purpose is to help management determine its policy and actions scientifically.

OPERATIONAL RESEARCH TECHNIQUES

The main operational techniques are described below.

Decision theory

In one sense, all operational research is about decisions. It is about decision rules, evaluating alternative decisions, optimizing decisions, predicting the outcome of decisions, helping to cope with uncertainty and risk, and sorting out the complexity of the situations in which decisions are frequently made so that management can swiftly exercise judgement on what is the best course of action in the circumstances (see Chapter 111).

The techniques available are:

1. the clarification of decision rules: optimistic, pessimistic, opportunity cost or expected value;
2. means-end analysis to clarify a chain of objectives and identify a series of decision points;
3. decision matrix analysis to model relatively simple decisions under uncertainty so as to make explicit the options open to the decision taker;
4. decision trees to assist in making decisions in uncertainty when there is a series of either/or choices;
5. algorithms which set out the logical sequence of deductions required for problem solving;
6. subjective probability techniques which aim to systemize the process of making intuitive decisions or decisions based largely on personal experience; and
7. Bayesian analysis, which aims to translate subjective probabilities into mathematical probability curves, thus providing a clearer analytical framework for the decision.

Modelling

Modelling is a representation of a real situation. It is a fundamental technique of operational research because, by representing a situation in mathematical terms, it increases management's understanding of the circumstances in which decisions have to be made and the possible outcomes of those decisions (see Chapter 112).

Simulation

Simulation is the construction of mathematical models to represent real-life processes or situations as they develop over a period of time. Simulation enables the model to be manipulated so that the dynamics of the system can be reproduced or simulated. One of the most commonly used simulation techniques is the Monte Carlo method, which builds into the system the chance elements that will affect outcomes. Simulation enables the likely effects of many decisions on complex situations to be estimated in conditions of uncertainty when chance elements may play an important part (see Chapter 113).

Linear programming

Linear programming uses a mathematical approach to solving problems where there are many intersecting variables and only limited resources are available. Its aim is the combination of variables that satisfies the constraints in the system and achieves the objectives sought (see Chapter 114).

Queuing theory

Queuing theory uses mathematical techniques to describe the features of queues of people, materials, work-in-progress, etc in order to find the best way to plan the sequence of events so that bottlenecks can be avoided (see Chapter 115).

ABC analysis

ABC analysis classifies items such as stock levels or sales outlets into three groups: A (very important), B (fairly important) and C (unimportant) depending upon their impact on events. Decisions can then be made on how to concentrate on the A items where the best results will be obtained in relation to the effort expanded. ABC analysis is based on Pareto's law, or the 80/20 rule, which describes the tendency for only a small number of items (20 per cent) to be really significant in that they produce 80 per cent of the results.

Sensitivity analysis

Sensitivity analysis is a technique, also used frequently in management accounting, to predict the impact on results (eg profits or contribution) of varying the levels of the parameters which affect those results (see Chapter 116).

Network analysis

Network analysis is a critical-path technique for planning and controlling complex projects by recording their component parts and representing them diagrammatically as a network of interrelated activities (see Chapter 118).

Statistical techniques

Operational research, in its use of mathematics to assist in describing the circumstances in which decisions are made, deploys statistical techniques extensively. Because chance and uncertainty play a major part in the sort of decisions OR deals with, probability estimates are important. So are the analysis of distributions of data and the study of the interrelationships or correlations between interacting variables.

APPLICATIONS

The following are examples of the main applications of operational research:

- Decision making, providing general help in making decisions, especially in complex situations with many interacting variables and in conditions of uncertainty or risk.
- Distribution planning, using statistical analysis, linear programming, simulations or algorithms to solve, with the aid of computers, standard transportation problems of how to achieve the best and cheapest distribution pattern.
- Facility and operation control systems planning, using simulation to enable alternative design concepts to be evaluated and to understand the sensitivity of output to changes in shop configurations and process track speeds.
- Forecasting, where models are developed to predict likely changes in demand or the impact of alternative marketing approaches, including new product development and changes in the marketing mix.
- Inventory control, where models and simulations are used to deal with problems of minimum safety or minimum reorder level, and ABC analysis is used to concentrate thinking on the key decision areas.
- Long-range financial planning, where models are used to predict profit, contribution and sales turnover figures.
- Product mix decisions, where linear programming is used to determine the combination of products which will maximize contribution to profits and fixed costs;
- Production planning, where linear programming is used to decide on what manufacturing facilities are needed and the best way to load these facilities, bearing in mind fluctuations in requirements and uncertainty in demand.
- Profit planning, where sensitivity analysis is used to predict the outcome of alternative assumptions about demand, prices and costs.
- Project planning, where network analysis is used for planning and scheduling, and to assist in resource allocation.
- Queuing problems, where queuing theory is used to plan sequences of events in order to optimize service levels to customers and to minimize bottlenecks.
- Resource allocation, where linear programming is used to work out the workforce, materials, machine time and other resources needed to complete construction or development projects or to maintain budgeted production schedules.

OPERATIONAL RESEARCH METHOD

OR is based on a sequence of three key tasks:

1. Gain understanding of the system and the relevant factors affecting it, including uncertainty and risk, so that the problem can be defined in useful terms for analysis by means of a mathematical model that represents the system (see also Chapter 112 on modelling).
2. Collect and analyse relevant data using appropriate statistical and other quantitative techniques and, often with the aid of a computer, formulate and test a practical solution. This frequently requires a degree of optimization, ie obtaining the best answer *in the circumstances* by balancing the parameters and variables.
3. Present proposals for action and assist in implementing decisions.

BENEFITS

1. Its ability to deal in a quantitative manner with conditions of uncertainty, bearing in mind Bertrand Russell's dictum that 'we are not able to predict the future with complete certainty but equally we are not entirely uncertain about the future'.
2. Its use of objective methods to sort out in complex situations what information is relevant and what information from past experience has a causal relationship with the situation being examined.
3. Its capacity to illustrate the likely outcomes of alternative courses of action based upon the information analysed (ie answering 'what if' questions).
4. The assistance it gives to managers in understanding the many inter-related factors affecting their decision.
5. Its provision of various logical approaches to decision making in complex situations.
6. Its ability to handle masses of data with the help of the computer.

FURTHER READING

Duckworth, W E, Gear, A E and Lockett, A G, *A Guide to Operational Research*, Chapman & Hall, London 1977.
Littlechild, S C (ed), *Operational Research for Managers*, Philip Allan, Deddington 1977.

111

Decision Theory

DEFINITION

Decision theory deals with the process of making decisions, especially in conditions of uncertainty, when a number of alternative courses of action may have to be evaluated before the final decision is made. Decision theory analyses types of decisions, sets out ground rules for making decisions and develops decision making methods using various kinds of models or procedures.

TYPES OF DECISION

Decisions can be classified according to their purpose, their structure, their complexity, the degree of dependence and influence on other decisions, the extent to which conditions of uncertainty exist, the circumstances in which the decisions are made and the timescale available. Features contained in any of these categories may be present in a single decision.

Purpose

Decisions may be either:

- strategic – long term, dealing with wide issues affecting the whole or a major part of an organization; or
- tactical – shorter term, dealing with operational issues which, although they may affect the whole organization, are more likely to make an impact upon a particular function or department.

Structure

Decisions may be either:

- structured and unambiguous in that they are well defined, the options are clear and explicit, and evaluation criteria exist; or
- unstructured and ambiguous in that the circumstances in which the decisions are being made are unclear, the reasons for making the decisions are ill-defined, the options available are not apparent, and criteria for judging the outcome of the decisions are not readily available.

Complexity

Decisions may be more or less complex depending on the number of factors that affect them. These may be internal, arising from such factors as complex technology or processes, a multiproduct production line or a complicated distribution network. Alternatively, complexity may arise from the external environment caused by such factors as a highly segmented market, rapid changes in technology and political, social and economic complications.

Degree of dependence and influence

Decisions may be more or less dependent on other decisions – past, current or future. They may also exert a greater or lesser degree of influence over other decisions. The extent to which they are dependent or exert influence has to be taken into account and may increase the complexity of the decision making process.

Uncertainty

Decisions may be made in conditions of certainty where all the relevant facts are known and all the likely consequences can be reliably forecast. Alternatively, they may be made in conditions of uncertainty, either because the facts are not known or because the outcomes may be affected by the unforeseeable results of human behaviour.

When the uncertainties are inherent in the system, what is termed a stochastic modelling process may be used to describe them. ('Stochastic' simply means, as defined by the *Oxford English Dictionary*, 'pertaining to conjecture', in other words, guesswork.)

Circumstances

Decisions may be:

1. opportunity decisions made voluntarily to exploit a chance to develop a new product or enter a new market;
2. problem decisions to deal with an immediate but not too critical problem – the decisions may be proactive in that they aim to anticipate a difficulty, or they may be reactive in that they deal with a problem which has already arisen; or
3. crisis decisions – major problems imposed on management often from outside the company.

Timescale

Decisions have to be made under conditions of greater or lesser urgency, depending upon circumstances.

DECISION RULES

The four basic decision rules are as follows:

1. *Optimistic.* Choose the option which yields the best possible outcome (the maximax rule).
2. *Pessimistic.* Choose the option with the highest value of the lowest possible outcome (called the maximin rule, the revenue rule or the maximax cost rule).
3. *Opportunity cost.* What opportunity is forgone when one course of action is chosen rather than another? This is sometimes called the regret rule and has been formulated as 'If we decide on one particular option, then, with hindsight, how much would we regret not having chosen what turns out to be the best option for a particular set of circumstances?'[1]
4. *Expected value.* Choose the option in accordance with an estimate of the likelihood of a particular situation occurring.

DECISION TECHNIQUES

The decision techniques available which are classified under the broad heading of decision theory are:

■ means–ends analysis;
■ decision matrix;

- decision trees;
- algorithms;
- subjective probability;
- Bayesian analysis.

These are considered below.

Other techniques designed to assist in decision taking, described elsewhere in the handbook, are:

- linear programming (Chapter 114);
- modelling (Chapter 112);
- simulation (Monte Carlo and deterministic) (Chapter 113).

Means–ends analysis

Means–ends analysis as described by Cooke and Slack[1] is a method of clarifying a chain of objectives and thus identifying a series of decision points. The concept is based on the fact that what is an objective to one decision maker will be a means of achieving a higher objective to a higher (hierarchically) decision maker. In other words, one person's means is another person's end.

Means–ends analysis is carried out by charting a means–ends chain as illustrated in Figure 111.1.

Decision matrix

A decision matrix, as described by Cooke and Slack,[1] is a method of modelling relatively straightforward decisions under uncertainty in such a way as to make explicit the options open to the decision taker, the factors or 'states of nature' relevant to the decision, and the probable outcomes from a combination of each option with each factor as shown on the matrix. The form in which a decision matrix is constructed is shown in Figure 111.2.

Decision trees

Decisions are often made in conditions where there are a number of alternative courses of action and when the outcomes of these actions are uncertain. Furthermore, earlier actions may affect subsequent actions and these likely effects need to be considered at the earlier stage.

Decision trees are a means of setting out problems of this kind, which are characterized by the interaction between uncertainty and a series of 'either/or' decisions. They display the anatomy of sequential decision points, the implications of which lead to branches on the tree. Thus the

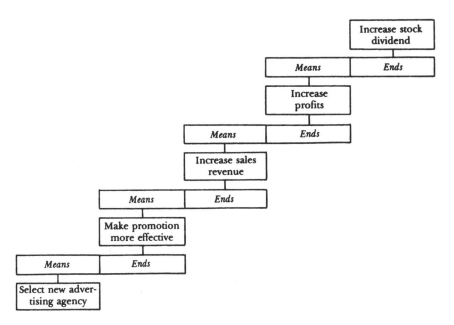

Figure 111.1 *A means–ends chain.* From *Making Management Decisions*, S Cooke and N Slack, Prentice-Hall International, London 1984

consequences of future decisions can be traced back to assess their influence on the present decision.

The stages in the construction of a decision tree are:

1. list decisions and uncertainties in chronological order;
2. construct tree showing decision points or nodes and choice nodes as illustrated in Figure 111.3 (an example is shown in Figure 111.4);
3. assign costs, benefits or probabilities to appropriate branches; and
4. analyse using the 'roll-back' method, ie tracing the costs and benefits back from the final point to the original objective as defined in the first decision point.

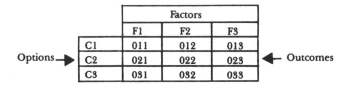

Figure 111.2 *A decision matrix*

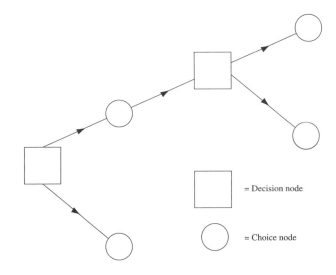

Figure 111.3 *Decision tree structure*

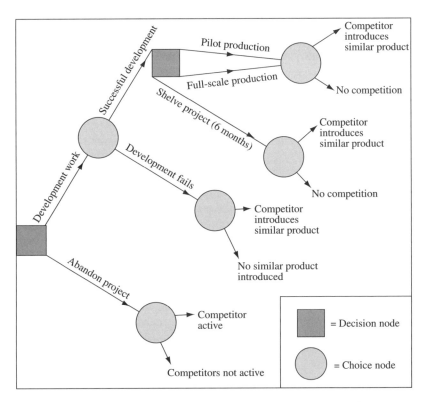

Figure 111.4 *Example of a decision tree.* From *International Dictionary of Management,* fourth edition, H Johannsen and G T Page, Kogan Page, London 1990

Algorithms

Algorithms contain a logical sequence of deductions for problem solving. They are used to reduce problem-solving tasks to a comparatively simple series of operations which at the same time indicate the order in which the operations are carried out. Illustrations of an instructional and an analytical type of algorithm are given in Figures 111.5 and 111.6 respectively.

Subjective probability

Decisions are frequently made which require a judgement of the probability of an outcome without the aid of objective measures. The subjective perception of the likelihood of an event occurring and the allocation to it of a probability figure (eg there is a 70 per cent chance that x will happen) is known as subjective probability, and is an expression of the degree of belief in an event happening.

The following generalizations about subjective probability were made by Lindsay and Norman:[2]

1. People tend to overestimate the occurrence of events with low probability and underestimate the occurrence of events with high probability.
2. People tend to adopt the gambler's fallacy of predicting that an event that has not occurred for a while is more likely to occur in the near future.
3. People tend to overestimate the true probability of events that are favourable to them and underestimate those that are unfavourable.

The technique of making subjective probability judgements is based on:

- being aware of the tendencies listed above and attempting to minimize them;
- understanding that probability assessments are usually based on experience but that memory can be selective – we tend more easily to recall events that were pleasurable to us or that support the line of reasoning we are adopting; and
- an analytical approach to considering any experience and other evidence available which attempts to increase the objectivity of the judgement by assessing the relevance of each piece of data to the situation.

Bayesian analysis

Bayesian statistical analysis aims to translate subjective forecasts into mathematical probability curves in situations where there are no normal

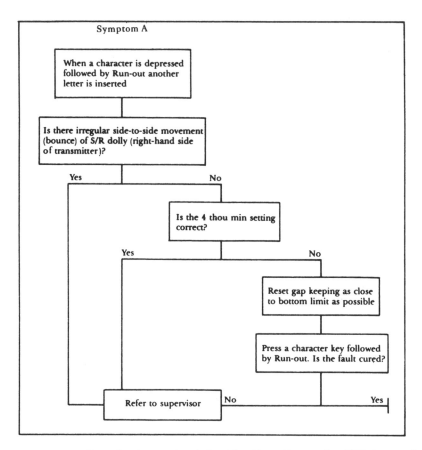

Figure 111.5 *Part of an instructional algorithm.* From *International Dictionary of Management,* H Johannsen and G T Page, Kogan Page, London 1986

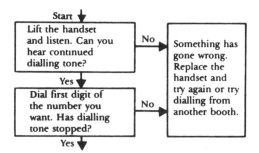

Figure 111.6 *An algorithm used for fault analysis.* From *International Dictionary of Management,* fourth edition, H Johannsen and G T Page, Kogan Page, London 1990

statistical probabilities because alternatives are unknown or have not been tried before. Bayesian statistics use the best estimate of a given circumstance as if it were a firm probability. They enable revisions to be made to probabilities after further information becomes available. The end result of Bayesian analysis depends on the stated prior probabilities. However, although Bayesian statistics can lead to spurious accuracy, like any manipulation of subjective probabilities, they do provide a useful logical structure in making probability revisions as more is learned about the assumptions built into the decision.

BENEFITS

Decision theory provides a method for dealing with complex situations in conditions of uncertainty. The analytical approach ensures that the danger of superficial judgements is minimized and that the alternatives available are properly evaluated.

REFERENCES

1. Cooke, S and Slack, N, *Making Management Decisions*, Prentice-Hall, London 1984.
2. Lindsay, P, and Norman, D, *Human Information Processing*, Academic Press, London 1977.

112

Modelling

DEFINITION

A model is a representation of a real situation. It depicts interrelationships between the relevant factors in that situation and, by structuring and formalizing any information about those factors, presents reality in a simplified form.

USES OF MODELLING

Models can help to:

1. increase the decision maker's understanding of the situation in which a decision has to be made and the possible outcomes of that decision;
2. stimulate new thinking about problems by, among other things, providing answers to 'what if' questions (*sensitivity analysis*); and
3. evaluate alternative courses of action.

CHARACTERISTICS OF MODELS

Models have been classified by Cooke and Slack[1] according to the extent to which they are:

1. *concrete or abstract* – scales exist which define the degree of correspondence with reality that a model possesses, ranging from a replication of

the original process to a completely synthetic extraction of essential elements of the original situation;

2. *static or dynamic* – the situation can be described by a static model at a particular point in time, while a dynamic model will use time as a major element and will examine phenomena in relation to preceding and succeeding events;

3. *deterministic or stochastic* – deterministic models use single estimates to represent the value of each variable, while stochastic models show ranges of values for variables in the form of probability distributions; and

4. *normative or descriptive* – normative models are prescriptive in that they evaluate alternative solutions and indicate what *ought* to be done, while descriptive models simply describe the solutions and make no attempt to evaluate them.

THE PROCESS OF MODELLING

The steps followed in developing a model are as follows:

1. Decide on the objectives of the model by answering the basic questions:

   ■ What problems is this model meant to solve?
   ■ What decisions will this model help to make?

2. Consider whether the purpose of the model is to:

   ■ provide optimal solutions to the problem (linear programming and decision trees come into this category); or
   ■ provide satisfactory or workable solutions to the problem (corporate models, queuing theory, stock control simulations and heuristic models do this – a heuristic model adopts short cuts in the reasoning and uses rules of thumb or a form of trial and error in its search for a satisfactory solution).

3. Describe in general terms the situation that the model is meant to represent and the factors or variables that impinge on that situation. The extent to which the model will be deterministic (using single estimates for the value of variables) or stochastic (using probability distributions) is considered at this stage. A typical situation will be a long-range profit forecast, and the factors will be the production, marketing and financial resources of the company and the broad strategies developed for their future.

4. Classify the variables, which may be exogenous or endogenous. Exogenous variables are the independent inputs to the model which act on decisions. They can be either controllable or uncontrollable.

Endogenous variables are the outputs of the system which are generated from the interaction of the system's inputs or exogenous factors and the structure of the decision itself.

5. Identify the parameters or constants which will be fed into the model and will not vary over the period of time studied or the range of options considered. The rate of interest, for example, may be taken as a constant.

6. Analyse the interactions to determine the influence of one factor on another and therefore the cause-and-effect relationship. From this analysis may be derived a cause–effect model of the situation which can be used as the basis for a mathematical model. An example of a cause–effect model is shown in Figure 112.1.

7. Build a mathematical model containing a set of symbols which describe decision variables and the relationships between them. Computers are used when the model becomes too complex to be used manually. Special modelling systems exist which compile the models directly into computer-readable statements.

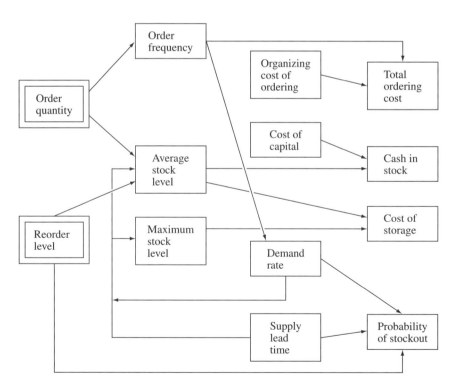

Figure 112.1 *A cause–effect model of a stock control process.* From *Making Management Decisions*, S Cooke and N Slack, Prentice-Hall International, London 1984

SELECTING A MODELLING SYSTEM

When selecting a modelling system the following factors are considered:

1. Is the system interactive?
2. Is the language and command structure easily understood by a non-specialized user?
3. How soon could a novice write and run a simple model for, perhaps, a project approval?
4. What are the processing costs?
5. Has the modelling system the facilities to handle large and complex problems? For example:

   ■ flexibility of data file handling;
   ■ advanced language facilities;
   ■ consolidation facilities to interpret company structures or hierarchies; or
   ■ flexibility of report formats.

APPLICATIONS

Typical modelling applications include:

■ budgetary planning models which forecast out-turns, help to allocate resources, determine the optimal product mix and indicate the sensitivity of the budget to changes in key variables during the planning period, eg the impact of varying rates of inflation, or changes in working capital and cash flow;
■ transport and distribution models aimed at increasing the profitability of fleet operations and the scope for economics by better routeing and scheduling techniques;
■ production planning models to allocate production to departments and production lines in a way which will maximize throughput, reduce delays and minimize manufacturing, distribution and inventory holding costs; and
■ resource allocation models to plan future machine loading and work-force requirements;
■ inventory models to optimize stock holding and define minimum safety stock and reorder stock levels.

BENEFITS

1. Clarification of all the issues, factors and variables surrounding a decision.
2. The improvement of decision making by providing information on alternatives and outcomes.
3. The scope to ask 'what if' questions and therefore to evaluate different opportunities.
4. Bringing data and decision rules into the open so that assumptions can be questioned.
5. Shortening planning cycles by removing much of the manual calculation.
6. Improving the accuracy of forecasts by using the power of the computer.

REFERENCE

1. Cooke, S and Slack, N, *Making Management Decisions*, Prentice-Hall, London 1984.

FURTHER READING

Hammond, J S, III, 'Dos and don'ts of computer models for planning', *Harvard Business Review*, March–April 1974.

113

Simulation

DEFINITION

Simulation is the construction of mathematical models to represent the operation of real-life processes or situations. The object is to explore the effect of different policies on the model to deduce what might happen in practice without going to the risk of trial and error in the real environment. Ackott and Sasieni[1] have defined the distinction between modelling and simulation as follows: 'Models represent reality, simulation imitates it. Simulation always involves the manipulation of a model so that it yields a motion picture of reality.'

The distinction between simulation and queuing theory is defined at the end of Chapter 115.

THE PROCESS OF SIMULATION

Simulation makes use of logical models as the basis of its attempts to copy the dynamics of a real situation and, thereafter, to predict actual behaviour. It usually relies on a statement of procedure which underlies the logical relationship between variables. A simulation model takes the form of a logical flow chart which describes this interrelationship. The model is then used to execute the procedure described in the flow chart, and thus the behaviour of the system which is being modelled is simulated. The next step is to transfer the logical model on to the computer and put it to work in an attempt to copy the dynamic operation of the real system.

Because in the real situation events are often triggered off by random or chance influences, simulation sometimes uses techniques such as the so-called Monte Carlo method to represent this random process.

SIMULATION TECHNIQUES

The main simulation techniques are:

1. stochastic digital simulation, usually called the Monte Carlo method, because early applications used roulette wheels to simulate the chance events inherent in this approach;
2. systems dynamics, sometimes called industrial dynamics – a method of simulating certain kinds of total complex systems; and
3. deterministic simulation – a method used to test a series of decision rules whose effects cannot be found out easily; single estimates represent the value of each variable in the decision.

Monte Carlo method

The Monte Carlo method starts from a logical flow chart to represent the system by showing the cause–effect logic which links the variables. An example of such a flow chart is shown in Figure 113.1. The Monte Carlo technique is used when the flow of inputs into the system has random characteristics, although the random nature of these inputs may follow some form of pattern. The aim is to simulate the chance element so that all the possible outcomes are understood before the system is tried out in practice. For example:

■ in a stock control system like the one illustrated in Figure 113.1, the inputs will be the daily demand and delivery lead times. Previous records are examined to show the frequency distributions of these inputs. The operation of any stocking policy (the combination of order quantity and reorder level) is simulated by random sampling values of demand and lead time; and
■ when considering the size and scope of port facilities the input will be the interval between the arrival of ships. It will be possible to establish from records the average inter-arrival time and also the distribution of times. But although over a long period the arrival pattern is known, it is not possible to predict precisely the time of the next arrival. These random arrivals within the overall pattern can be simulated by using random numbers.

Random numbers as used in the Monte Carlo method are a series of numbers that have no pattern whatsoever and have no relation to one

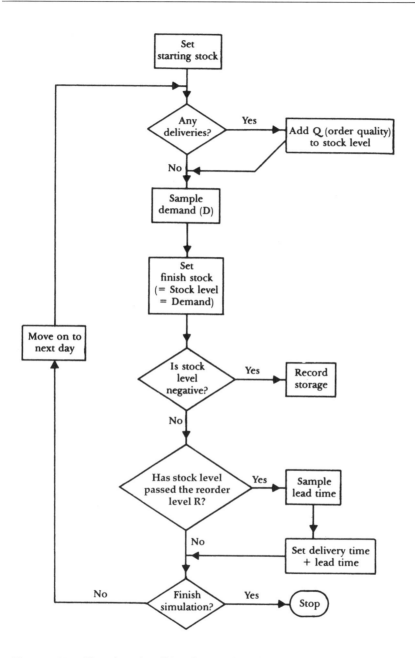

Figure 113.1 *Flow chart describing the procedural logic involved in simulating stock behaviour.* From *Making Management Decisions,* S Cooke and N Slack, Prentice-Hall International, London 1984

another. The characteristics of such a series are that over a large set the digits 0 to 9 should occur with equal frequency. Random numbers can be read off compiled tables or calculated by computer. Random numbers are allocated in proportion to the frequency in the distribution as established by records of past experience.

Using a systematic method of selecting random numbers from those allocated in the table, the corresponding value of the event being simulated is established. In the examples given above these events would be either daily deliveries and lead times or the inter-arrival time of ships.

Systems dynamics

Systems or industrial dynamics as developed by Forrester[2] studies the complex information feedback characteristics of industrial activity to see how structures, policies and the timing of decisions and actions influence outputs. It simulates the interactions between the flows of information, money, orders, personnel and capital equipment in a company, an industry or a national economy.

The underlying assumption, as described by Pidd[3], is that socio-economic systems may be regarded as analogous to servo-mechanisms, and central to this analogy is the concept of feedback of information. A decision is made which leads to action, but there is a time-lag or delay between the decision to act and the act itself. The action leads to results, once again following a delay. The results are then fed back to the decision maker as information on which to base a further decision, and so on. The situation is further complicated by the fact that the information may be distorted and/or delayed. The system will have properties which are quite distinct from the elements which compose it. It is therefore necessary to view it as a whole and not merely as a collection of parts.

In essence, systems dynamics is a method of simulating certain kinds of total complex situations such as a complete production distribution system. A special computer compiler called Dynamo has been written for use when developing simultaneous programmes.

Deterministic simulation

Deterministic simulation is used to clarify the decisions required in situations such as the accurate calculation of the resources needed to achieve a given throughput time and output with a known level of input. Simulation helps to test the effects of different decisions or decision rules. Deterministic simulation excludes the uncertainty present in everyday life for the sake of convenience, clarity or tractability.

A typical application of deterministic simulation given by Duckworth, Gear and Lockett[4] is in a machine shop where the manager wanted to experiment by changing the number of types of machine, the number of workers employed and the input, and then see what happened to work-in-progress, throughput time and labour and machine utilization, so that he could find out where bottlenecks developed and plan how to eliminate them. A flow chart showing the main stages of the programme drawn up is shown in a simplified version in Figure 113.2.

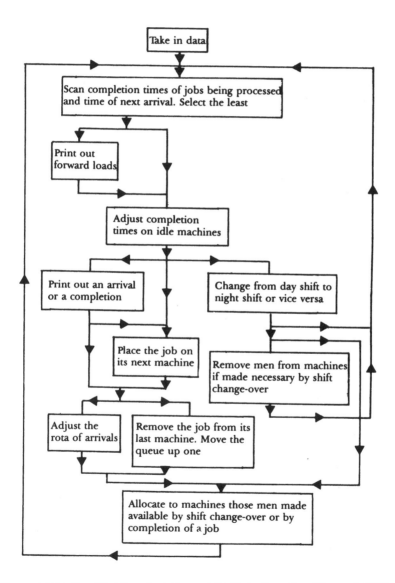

Figure 113.2 *Simplified flow chart.* From *A Guide to Operational Research*, W E Duckworth, A E Gear and A G Lockett, Chapman & Hall, London 1977

A computer working according to predetermined decision rules, such as the priorities for allocating people and jobs to machines, simulated alternative loadings and the effect on queues, and throughput time. The implications of various alternative methods of loading machines and progressing were then identified so that a choice could be made of the optimum method.

BENEFITS

Simulation enables the likely effects of many decisions in complex situations to be estimated so that harmful consequences can be avoided and more beneficial methods introduced.

REFERENCES

1. Ackott, R L and Sasieni, M W, *Fundamentals of Operational Research*, Wiley, New York 1986.
2. Forrester, J, *Industrial Dynamics*, Wiley, New York 1961.
3. Pidd, M, 'Computer simulation models,' in *Operational Research for Managers*, Littlechild, S G (ed), Philip Allan, Deddington 1977.
4. Duckworth, W E, Gear, A E and Lockett, A G, *A Guide to Operational Research*, Chapman & Hall, London 1977.

114

Linear Programming

DEFINITION

Linear programming is a mathematical approach to solving business problems where there are many interacting variables and it is necessary to combine limited resources to obtain an optimized result. It is a decision model under conditions of certainty where constraints affect the allocation of resources among competing uses. The model analyses a list of actions whose outcomes are known with certainty and chooses the combination of actions that will maximize profit or minimize cost.

THE BASIC TECHNIQUE

The aim of linear programming is to find the specific combination of variables that satisfies all constraints and achieves the objectives sought.

The technique is based on simultaneous linear equations. A linear equation is simply $x + 3 = 9$. Simultaneous equations have two or three unknowns and become progressively more difficult to solve. Linear programming:

- constructs a set of simultaneous linear equations, which represent the model of the problem and which include many variables; and
- solves the equations with the help of a digital computer.

The formulation of the equations – the building of the model – is the most difficult part. The computer does the rest.

The term 'linear' is used because when the relationships between two variables are plotted on a graph they are represented by a straight line.

THE LINEAR PROGRAMMING METHOD

The linear programming approach can be divided into four steps:

1. *Formulate the objectives* (called the objective function). This is usually to maximize profit or minimize cost.
2. *Determine the basic relationships* (particularly the constraints). For example, in a manufacturing application the constraints may be the production capacity of various machines.
3. *Determine the feasible alternatives*. If the simplex method is used (the most common approach), a step-by-step process is followed. This begins with one feasible solution and tests it algebraically, by substitution, to see if it can be improved.
4. *Compute the optimum solution*. The simplex method goes on substituting feasible solutions until further improvement is impossible, given the constraints. The optimum solution is therefore achieved.

APPLICATIONS

Linear programming can be used to provide solutions to problems such as the following:

1. Production planning where the requirement is to maximize production with the optimum use of resources yet there are numerous constraints on the use of those resources, eg machine capacity, storage space, labour availability. The solution to a production planning problem may contain decisions on the production levels at each plant, the machine capacity required, stock levels, raw material inputs and transportation resources.
2. Product mix decisions where the objective is to determine the combination of products which maximizes the total contribution towards fixed costs and profit. The variables will be marginal cost, marginal revenue, units sold and price per unit. The constraints will include production capacity and the level of demand expected for each product at different prices. A product mix problem of this kind may involve the substitution of resources. This is not simply a matter of comparing margins per unit of product and assuming that the production of the product with the greatest margin per unit should be maximized. Such substitutions are a matter of trading a given contribution margin of a

limiting factor (ie a critical resource) for some other contribution margin of a limiting factor.

3. The blending of materials to satisfy technical requirements and capacity constraints while maximizing profits.

4. The formulation of animal feed products to ensure that the cheapest combination of raw materials is used which meets the required nutritional specifications.

5. Human resource planning to decide how many people are required in different occupations and with different skills to meet future needs, taking into account growth in the business, availability of staff from within the company, promotions, natural wastage and retirements.

BENEFITS

Linear programming can help to produce optimal decisions where there are a number of predictable variables and constraints. It is particularly useful in sorting out production planning and product-mix problems. Linear programming is a good technique for combining materials, labour and facilities to best advantage when all the relationships are linear, where outcomes are known with certainty and where many combinations are possible.

115

Queuing Theory

DEFINITION

Queuing theory uses mathematical techniques to describe the character-istics of queues of people, material, work-in-progress, etc, in order to find the best way to plan the sequence of events so that bottlenecks can be avoided.

USES

Queuing theory deals with problems such as congestion in telephone systems, airports and harbours, machines out of action waiting for repair or materials (machine interference problems) and the design of production schedules.

QUEUING SYSTEMS

As described by Littlechild,[1] queuing systems have three characteristics:

1. *The arrival of items or customers.* The arrival pattern may be known or deterministic, as in an appointment system, or random, as in a super-market. Such arrival patterns are described by means of probability distributions. Units may arrive singly or in bulk and arrival time may be constant or may vary over time.

2. *Queue discipline*. Items or customers may be dealt with strictly in turn and service may be on a first-in first-out (FIFO) basis, a last-in first-out (LIFO) basis, or on a random basis. There may be several queues and queue-jumping may take place. Constraints in the system may limit queue size.
3. *Service mechanism*. There may be any number of servers or service points and they may differ in respect of the speed at which they work and the type of customer or item they can handle. Speed of operation may vary or be constant.

AIM

The aim of queuing theory is to optimize service levels in relation to the demands placed on the service department or facility.

Optimization means minimizing delays, and therefore queues, while still operating at an acceptable level of costs. It is necessary to bear in mind the physical as well as the cost constraints that might restrict the capacity of the system to speed up the rate at which queues are processed.

SOLVING QUEUING PROBLEMS

The basic information required to solve a queuing problem is traffic intensity. This is demand divided by capacity or, in other words, the mean service time divided by the mean interval between successive arrivals. Traffic intensity is denoted by the Greek symbol ρ.

Traffic intensity is calculated by measuring the time intervals between the arrival of jobs or customers and computing the average of these intervals. Thus a frequency distribution is built up and calculations are made of the mean or average arrival rate and the variance or standard deviation of that rate. The average service time is found in a similar way.

Queuing problems arise when jobs or customers arrive at random so that the probability of an arrival in a particular interval of time depends on the length of the interval and not on the time of day or the number of previous arrivals. In these circumstances it can be shown mathematically that the probable number of arrivals in any time interval is given by the Poisson probability distribution. This describes the occurrence of isolated events in a continuum. If the average number of occurrences of a particular event is known, and is constant, Poisson probability paper can be used to calculate the probabilities of all the various possible frequencies with which the event might occur. (For a full description of this graph paper, refer to M J Moroney, *Facts from Figures*, Penguin, pp. 104–05.[2])

In a Poisson probability distribution, the number of items or users is very large and the chance of any one item occurring or any request originating from a particular individual is small. But because the population of items or users is so large, the average occurrence or usage can still be high. An example of Poisson distribution is that of telephone subscribers using long-distance lines. The chance that any one subscriber will require a long-distance line in a given short period of, say, one minute, is very small. Yet there are a large number of subscribers to any exchange, so the average number of long distance calls over the same short period may be considerable.

If the arrival pattern follows a Poisson distribution, it can be shown mathematically that the probability distribution of time intervals between successive arrivals is described by what is termed the negative exponential function. A property of this function is that the probability of arrivals happening at a particular time is not related to the time already elapsed since the previous arrival.

An application of queuing theory in manning a telephone enquiry bureau was described by Sparrow (in Littlechild[1]) as follows:

> It was assumed that calls arrived at random from an infinite number of sources, so that the inter-arrival times had a negative exponential distribution and the number of calls within a given time interval had a Poisson distribution. This was a reasonable assumption, since there was a large number of customers acting independently of each other, as long as the grade of service achieved was good enough to ensure few repeated calls.
>
> The service time was assumed to be negatively exponentially distributed, ie the probability of a call finishing at any time is independent of the duration of the call up to that time. Figure 115.1 illustrates the nature of this assumption. The histogram was drawn from data on call durations taken at an off-peak time. The exponential fit is a good one. At peak times the exponential fit is not so good, but there is still a long tail to the distribution and the average call duration is not significantly different.

Starting from this point, the average calling and service rates were calculated, to determine the traffic intensity, ie the average service time. Grades of service (ie the proportion of calls which are lost) and waiting time (ie the length of time callers are kept waiting) were then assessed. Finally a model was produced to show how increasing the number of operators improves both the grade of service and the waiting time, thus indicating the staff required at various times of the day to meet different levels of service.

The costs of providing service and of queuing can then be added to produce the total cost, which can be recalculated for various values of the average service time so that a decision can be made on the optimum service arrangements. A typical relationship between total costs and average service times is shown in Figure 115.2.

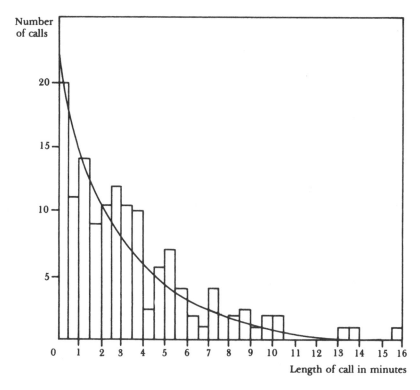

Figure 115.1 *Histogram showing number of calls of a given length at half-minute intervals. The curve shows the expected number of calls of a given length from a negative exponential distribution with mean call length of 3.322 minutes.*
From 'Manning the telephone enquiry building at West Midlands Gas' L B Sparrow in *Operational Research for Managers* ed S G Littlechild, Phillip Allan, Deddington 1977

BENEFITS

By employing the mathematics of queuing theory, the probable efficiency of a system can be assessed in terms of its service levels and productive capacity and plans can be made to eliminate undue and over-costly delays and bottlenecks.

There is a limit, however, to the extent to which queuing theory can deal with highly complex problems in dynamic situations with many variables. In these circumstances simulation techniques may be used as described in Chapter 113.

Littlechild has explained succinctly that:[1]

> The difference between simulation and queuing theory is that the former involves the repeated trial of a particular system, under different patterns of customer arrivals or service performance, until

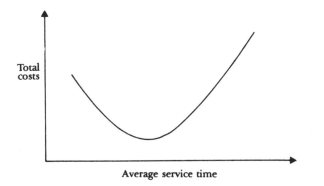

Figure 115.2 *Total servicing costs as a function of average service time*

one has built up an adequate picture of how the system behaves. Queuing theory gives an explicit picture, generally in the form of a mathematical function or graph, relating behaviour to certain system parameters. In this case, one may see immediately how the system would respond to changes in these parameters, whereas with simulation one would have to repeat a whole exercise. Simulation allows one to test out ideas for different system designs but does not, of itself, lead to a 'best' design. Queuing theory thus has a distinct advantage in the limited number of situations where it can be applied, but simulation is a more flexible technique.

REFERENCES

1. Littlechild, S G (ed), *Operational Research for Managers*, Philip Allan, Deddington 1977.
2. Moroney, M J, *Facts from Figures*, Penguin, Harmondsworth 1984.

116

Sensitivity Analysis

DEFINITION

Sensitivity analysis is the study of the key assumptions or calculations on which a management decision is based in order to predict alternative outcomes of that decision if different assumptions are adopted. It is a 'what if ' technique that measures how the expected values in a decision model will be affected by changes in the data.

METHOD

1. List the key factors or parameters. For example, when estimating the likely profitability of a project the factors may be market growth rate, market share, selling price, and the costs of direct labour and direct materials.
2. Attach the most likely values to each of these parameters, and from these predict the most likely level of profits.
3. Calculate the effect of varying the values of all or a selected few of these parameters. This may be done by working out what the impact would be if all the values varied equally by, say, 1, 3 or 5 per cent. Different incidences of variation between the values may be calculated if appropriate.
4. List the outcomes of the alternative assumptions and make a subjective assessment of their likelihood.
5. Draw conclusions on any actions required which would make the achievement of the better outcomes more likely.

An example of part of a sensitivity analysis is shown in Table 116.1. The likely level of profits was forecast at £380,000 and the effect on this figure is calculated for a change of 1 per cent in a number of factors.

Table 116.1 *Example of sensitivity analysis*

A difference of 1%	Will change profits by £
Market growth rate	10,000
Market share	12,600
Selling price	190,000
Direct labour	1,200
Direct materials	4,500

BENEFITS

Sensitivity analysis helps to prevent rash predictions about the outcome of plans by ensuring that the assumptions on which the plans are based are examined and that the effect of changes in these assumptions is gauged. This process may involve challenging the original assumptions and could result in a rethink about the project. Sensitivity analysis can indicate areas where improvements are likely to have the greatest impact on results. In presenting a range of possible outcomes, sensitivity analysis facilitates the development of alternative or contingency plans if the basic assumptions have to be changed.

117

Cybernetics

DEFINITION

Cybernetics is the study of control systems in humans and machines and the relations between them. In the words of Stafford Beer:[1] 'Cybernetic systems are complex, interacting, probabilistic networks... How are such systems organized? They seem to be cohesive, self-regulating, and stable, yet adaptive to change and capable of learning from experience.'

BASIC PRINCIPLES

Cybernetics involves three control principles: the most basic are error-actuated feedback and homeostasis; the third is that of the Black Box.

Error-actuated feedback

In error-actuated feedback the difference or error between what is required and what actually happens is transmitted (fed back) to whoever is involved so that a correction can be made. Feedback systems may only operate effectively if overcorrection is avoided by making the correction somewhat less than the error.

Homeostasis

Homeostasis is the property that all living organisms have of making use of error-actuated feedback to adjust their metabolism to changing environmental conditions so that certain essential parameters remain constant. The homeostatic mechanism is one that itself responds to the error-actuated feedback instead of relying on an outside agent.

The Black Box

In cybernetics, a Black Box is a system too complex to understand fully in the existing state of knowledge. In macro terms, the economic system of a country is a Black Box. In micro terms, in a complex department run by a number of interacting human beings, it may never be possible to find out exactly how inputs to the department are transformed into outputs. But it may not matter too much. The most important task in any manufacturing or processing system is to transform inputs into outputs as economically as possible. If this is achieved satisfactorily, it may be a futile exercise to try to find out precisely what is going on.

The Black Box principle states that the behaviour of a complex system is discovered merely by studying the relationship between the input and output, and not by considering what happens inside the box.

APPLICATIONS

Cybernetics can be applied to the design of manufacturing processes. Comprehensive feedback mechanisms can be built into the system. Some of these can automatically initiate corrections on the principle of homeostasis. Others use a systematic procedure for producing control information for process operators who have clearly defined rules on what action they take in response either to the information or to their observations in order to restore the system to normal.

Cybernetics applied to management ensures that feedback on performance is available so that corrections can be made. It is the basic principle behind budgetary control and management by objectives, but cybernetics aims to introduce much more comprehensive information systems which will enable corrections to be made more swiftly and without having any drastic effect.

The Black Box principle can be used to control systems that are highly complex. An example given by Duckworth, Gear and Lockett[2] is of a production controller with the problem of scheduling a tool room. The operations in the tool room were so complex that three or four clerks would be required to record all the necessary information. But on the basis of an analysis of inputs and outputs it was established that an input of 40 jobs per week would keep the tool room fully occupied and ensure an output of 40 jobs per week. Without worrying too much about what precisely was happening inside the tool room, it was possible to schedule work to it on the basis of an output of 40 jobs and keep production flowing smoothly and economically.

REFERENCES

1. Beer, S, *Cybernetics and Management*, EUP, London 1959.
2. Duckworth, W E, Gear, A E and Lockett, A G, *A Guide to Operational Research*, Chapman & Hall, London 1977.

Part 6

Planning and Resource Allocation

118

Network Analysis

DEFINITION

Network analysis is a technique for planning and controlling complex projects and for scheduling the resources required on such projects. It achieves this aim by analysing the component parts of a project and assessing the sequential relationships between each event. The results of this analysis are represented diagrammatically as a network of interrelated activities.

BASIC TECHNIQUE

Networks are built up from the following basic elements:

1. *Events* – stages reached in a project at which all preceding activities have been completed and from which succeeding activities start.
2. *Nodes* – circles used to represent an event, ie the start or completion of a task, at a point in time.
3. *Activities* – arrows which link up events and indicate the time or resources which will be used in completing the task.

The basic sequence shown in a network is illustrated in Figure 118.1, where the two circles represent project events and the arrow joining them denotes the activity which must take place in order to progress from the first event to the second.

Figure 118.1 *Basic network sequence*

Rules for constructing networks

The rules for constructing networks are as follows:

1. *No dangling activities.* All activities must be connected to the end event. They must not be allowed to appear in isolation, as in Figure 118.2.

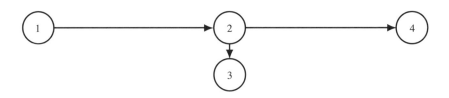

Figure 118.2 *A dangling activity*

Activity 3 is 'dangling'. Either it is not a real part of the project or it must be linked directly to 4 with an activity which does not consume time or resources. This type of activity is known as a 'dummy' and is represented by a broken line, as shown in Figure 118.3.

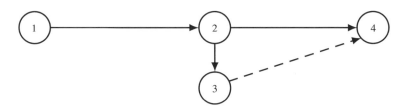

Figure 118.3 *A dummy activity introduced to avoid a dangling activity*

2. *Dummy activities* are constructed not only to prevent dangling but also to link events which are interdependent, even though no time or resources are consumed because of this link. This is illustrated in Figure 118.4, which is a miniature network. There are three routes from 1 to 6. One of these lies directly from event 1 through events 2 and 3. The second also lies directly from 1 through events 4 and 5. But activity 3 to 6 cannot start until activity 1 to 4 is completed. The broken line from 4 to 3 is the third route, a dummy activity for which no time or resources are

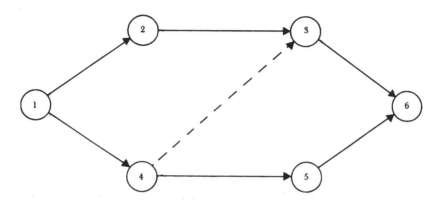

Figure 118.4 *A dummy activity introduced to show the dependence of activities 3 to 6 on the completion of activities 1 to 4*

consumed but which indicates that activity 3 to 6 is dependent on the completion of 1 to 4.
3. *Parallel activities* cannot have the same start and end events, as shown in Figure 118.5, because this leads to confusion. To avoid this happening a dummy activity is inserted, as shown in Figure 118.6.

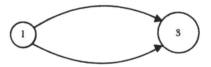

Figure 118.5 *Incorrectly drawn parallel activities*

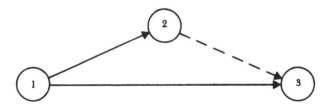

Figure 118.6 *A dummy activity introduced to avoid parallel activities having the same start and end events*

4. *Closed loops* are not allowed. The activities must take the project forwards. A situation like the one shown in Figure 118.7 is a cyclical activity between events 1 and 2 and is fully described by the arrow drawn between those two events.

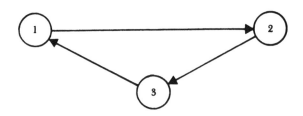

Figure 118.7 *An incorrect closed loop*

5. *Preceding and succeeding activities.* An event can only have two or more preceding activities and two or more succeeding activities if *none* of the succeeding activities can start until all the preceding activities have been completed. This is illustrated in Figure 118.8, where neither activities 3 to 4 nor 3 to 5 can begin until both activities 1 to 3 and 2 to 3 have finished. If the start of 3 to 5 depends on the completion of 2 to 3 and not 1 to 3 as well, then an additional event (6) and a dummy activity (3 to 6) are needed, as shown in Figure 118.9.

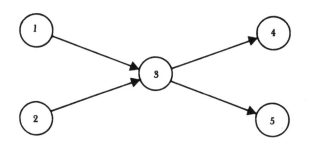

Figure 118.8 *Completion of preceding and succeeding activities*

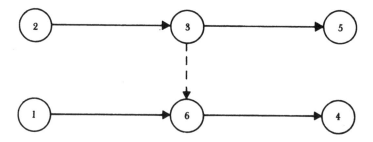

Figure 118.9 *Use of a dummy activity to clarify the sequence of events between preceding and succeeding activities*

THE COMPLETE NETWORK

An example of a complete network is shown in Figure 118.10. This network follows the convention of treating time as increasing from left to right. Events or nodes are numbered and activities are shown by arrows and defined by the events at each end.

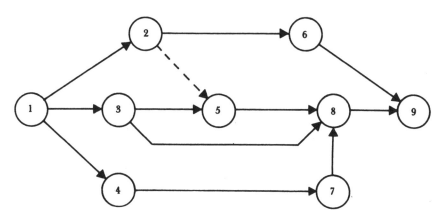

Figure 118.10 *A complete network*

The relationships in this network are as follows:

■ Event 1 is the starting point of the network.
■ Activities 2 to 6, 3 to 5, 4 to 7 cannot start until, respectively, activities 1 to 2, 1 to 3 and 1 to 4 have been completed.
■ Activity 2 to 5 is a dummy activity and activity 5 to 8 therefore cannot start until both activities 3 to 5 and 1 to 2 have been completed.
■ Activities 6 to 9 and 7 to 8 cannot start until, respectively, activities 2 to 6 and 4 to 7 have been completed.
■ Activity 8 to 9 cannot start until activities 3 to 8, 5 to 8 and 7 to 8 have been completed.

TECHNIQUES

When the network has been drawn, it is used as the basis for timing the duration of each activity in order to determine the duration of the whole project. It then provides the information required for project planning and control (these techniques of project management are described in Chapter 52).

The main network analysis techniques are:

1. critical path method;
2. programme, evaluation and review technique (PERT);
3. activity-on-node or precedence networks;
4. resource allocation.

Critical path method

Basic construction

The critical path method aims to determine those activities which are critical for the successful completion of the project within the scheduled timescale. It starts with a time analysis of the duration of each activity. The start time of event 1 is set at zero, and the start times of subsequent events are determined by adding the activity times, working through the network until the end event is reached. This process is illustrated in Figure 118.11.

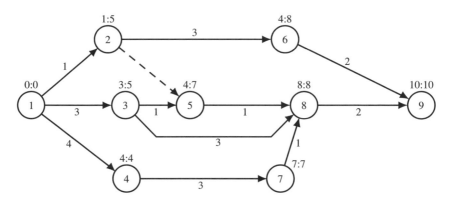

Figure 118.11 *Network showing critical path*

Working out the critical path

The timings on the network are determined by taking the following steps:

1. The estimated time for each activity is entered against the activity arrow. For example, in Figure 118.11 activity 1 to 2 takes one week and activity 3 to 8 takes three weeks.
2. The earliest completion times for each activity are obtained by taking each path and adding the times of all the activities that form that path from left to right along the network. This figure is the first one entered

above the event circle or node. For example, the earliest time to reach event 6 is the time for activity 1 to 2 (one week) plus the time for activity 2 to 6 (three weeks), making four weeks in all.

When there is a choice of paths the longest route is taken to work out the earliest completion time. For example, event 8 can be reached via activities 1 to 3, 3 to 5 and 5 to 8 making a total of five weeks. It can also be reached via activities 1 to 3 and 3 to 8 with a combined time of six weeks. But the longest path is formed by activities 1 to 4, 4 to 7 and 7 to 8, and following this route will delay the earliest possible completion time to eight weeks, which is the figure entered above the node for event 8.

3. The shortest or critical time to complete the project as planned, which is the earliest completion time of the end event, is established by working sequentially through the network, as described in step 2, to find the longest path. In the example, this is 10 weeks, which is the sum of the times for activities 1 to 4, 4 to 7, 7 to 8 and 8 to 9, ie $4 + 3 + 1 + 2 = 10$.

4. The critical path is determined by following the route formed by the activities leading to the shortest or critical time. In the example, the activities listed in step 3 (1 to 4, 4 to 7, 7 to 8 and 8 to 9) are the critical activities and the critical path they form is denoted by a double bar on the network.

5. The latest start times of each event in the network, if the critical time is not to be exceeded, are determined by starting at the end event and working backwards to the start event. The latest time of the end event is equal to the critical time for the project, in this example 10 weeks. Working backwards from event 9, the latest start time for event 6 is the critical time of 10 weeks, less the time for activity 6 to 9 of two weeks, which equals eight weeks. This is entered as the right-hand figure above the node alongside the figure for the earliest completion time.

In the case of event 3 there are two paths from event 8. The first, via event 5 takes two weeks which, if this were the only route, would result in the latest start time for event 3 being six weeks, ie $8 - 2$. But by the direct route from 8 to 3, the latest start time for event 3 becomes five weeks (ie $8 - 3$) and, clearly, this event must be reached within five weeks, not six if the project is not to be delayed.

6. The 'float' time, which is the extra time that can be taken over an activity without delaying the start of another activity, is calculated by deducting at each event the earliest start time from the latest start time. For example, in Figure 118.11, there is four weeks' float available to complete activity 1 to 2 $(5 - 1)$. By definition, there is no float available for the activities forming the critical path.

Uses

The critical path method is used to determine:

- The latest start times for each activity.
- The amount of float or leeway in completing non-critical activities without delaying the completion of the project on time. The *total float* will be the maximum increase in activity duration which can occur without increasing the project duration. The *free float* will be the maximum increase in activity duration which can occur without altering the floats available to subsequent activities.
- The critical activities along the critical path where there is no float and where any delay in carrying them out will delay the project. These are the activities to which most attention must be paid, although this should not lead to the neglect of other activities, especially where the float is limited.

Pert

The programme evaluation and review technique (PERT) considers activity durations in the network as uncertain. Instead of a single estimate of each activity time, three estimates are used as follows:

m = the most likely duration of the activity;
a = the optimistic estimate of the activity duration (the shortest);
b = the pessimistic estimate of the activity duration (the longest).

PERT is frequently used in construction projects where jobs may be delayed by unfavourable weather, etc.

Because of their complexity, PERT systems are run on computers which generate the planning and control data required.

Activity-on-node

Activity-on-node or precedence networks provide an alternative notation to the arrow diagram. In this notation, activities are shown in the nodes and the arrows simply show logical precedence and do not denote activities. Its format is shown in Figure 118.12 where the numbers within the nodes refer to an activity.

When two or more arrows terminate at an activity, all must be followed before the activity can begin. When two or more arrows leave an activity, all may be pursued as soon as the activity is complete.

No dummy activities are required in precedence networks, but it is not so easy to draw them against a timescale. They do, however, allow more general dependencies between the activities to be represented.

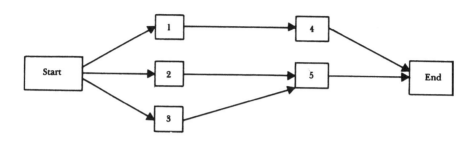

Figure 118.12 *Activity-on-node network*

Resource allocation

The time analysis provided by the network can be used as the basis for defining resource requirements such as labour. The number of people needed for each activity is sometimes entered on the network alongside the time estimate. This can then be transferred to a Gantt or bar chart showing against each activity the resource requirements for the different types of labour required. This visual picture forms the basis for any rescheduling of the programme which is needed, if possible within the critical time, to maintain a steady level of resource usage and to contain resource requirements within presented limits.

BENEFITS

The main benefit of network analysis is that it takes into account the inter-relationship of all the activities comprising a major project. Bar charts can be used successfully to show the starting and finishing times of different activities but they do not reveal dependencies and they cannot highlight the critical activities or the leeways allowed in completing non-critical activities (float) as the critical path or PERT can.

FURTHER READING

Battersby, A, *Network Analysis for Planning and Scheduling Studies in Management*, Macmillan, London 1978.
Lockyer, K G, *Critical Path Analysis*, Pitman, London 1991.

119

Line of Balance

DEFINITION

The line of balance technique is used in production scheduling and control to determine, at a review date, not only how many items should have been completed by that date but also how many items should have passed through the previous operations by this time so as to ensure completion of the required quantity of items in later weeks.

METHOD

The five stages required in the line of balance technique are:

1. prepare operation programme;
2. prepare completion schedule;
3. construct line of balance;
4. prepare programme progress chart; and
5. analyse progress.

These stages are illustrated in the simplified example that follows.

STAGE 1. OPERATION PROGRAMME

The operation programme shows the 'lead time' of each operation, ie the length of time prior to the completion of the final operation by which intermediate operations must be completed. Figure 119.1 illustrates an operation programme chart. The final delivery date is zero and the timescale runs from right to left. The programme shows that purchased part A must be combined with item B in operation 4 three days before completion. Item B, prior to this combination, has undergone a conversion operation which has to be finished five days before completion. The longest lead time is 10 days, which is when the purchased part for item B must be available.

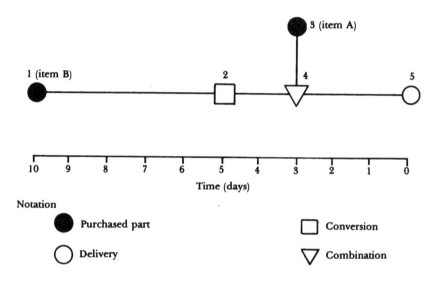

Figure 119.1 *Operation programme*

STAGE 2. COMPLETION SCHEDULE

The completion schedule simply lists how many items have to be completed week by week and cumulatively, as shown in Table 119.1.

Table 119.1 *Completion schedule*

Week no	Completed items	Cumulative items
0	0	0
1	5	5
2	10	15
3	10	25
4	10	35
5	15	50

The completion schedule can be shown graphically, as in Figure 119.2, where the scheduled, cumulative completions week by week can be compared with actual completion.

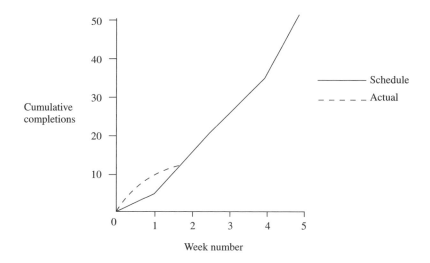

Figure 119.2 *Completion schedule (graphical version)*

STAGE 3. CONSTRUCT LINE OF BALANCE

The line of balance shows the numbers of items of each operation that should have been finished in a particular week to meet the completion schedule. It can be prepared analytically or graphically, as illustrated in Figure 119.3.

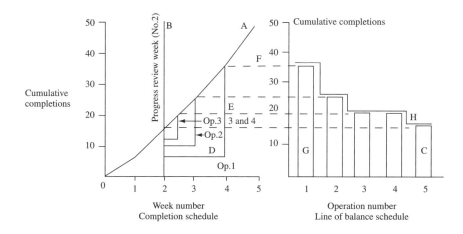

Figure 119.3 *Construction of a line of balance*

The steps required to construct the line of balance graphically are as follows:

1. Graph the completion schedule as the cumulative number of units to be completed each week (A on Figure 119.3).
2. Draw a vertical line on the completion schedule at the week in which the review is to take place (B).
3. Show by means of a vertical bar on the line of balance schedule (the right-hand graph) how many items have been completed for delivery (operation 5) by the review week (week 2). In this example, production is on schedule at 15 items (C).
4. For each of the other operations find out how many items should have been completed by week 2. This will be the total of not only the requirements for the completed item by the two-week review date but also the number to be completed in the lead time for that operation. This is done graphically for each operation by:

   (a) extending a line horizontally from the two-week point to the amount on the horizontal timescale equal to the lead time; for example, on Figure 119.3 this is line D, which adds the lead time of 10 days for operation 1 to the two-week review period;
   (b) extending a vertical line from that point to cut the completion schedule line, thus showing how many items of this operation should be completed (E);
   (c) extending a horizontal line from this point towards the line of balance schedule to the point above the appropriate operation number (F);
   (d) drawing a vertical bar from the operation number on the line of balance schedule to the line drawn at step 4(c) (G); and
   (e) joining the tops of the bars for each operation drawn up at step 4(d) to produce the line of balance (H).

STAGE 4. PROGRAMME PROGRESS CHART

The programme progress chart for a review week (week 2 in this example) is illustrated in Figure 119.4. This graphs the numbers of items produced at each item against the line of balance, thereby indicating clearly any shortfalls or overproduction.

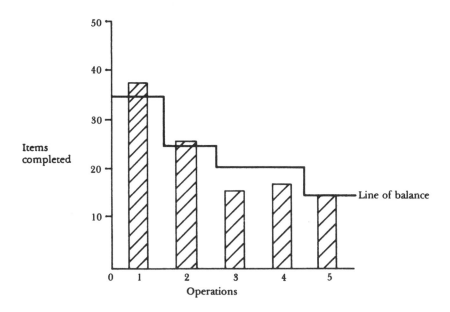

Figure 119.4 *Programme progress chart*

STAGE 5. ANALYSE PROGRESS

Progress can be analysed by reference to the programme progress chart which is prepared at regular intervals, probably week by week. This example reveals that while the delivery of the item is on schedule, there is a shortfall on the conversion operation, number 4. There is also a shortfall for operation 3, which is a purchased part. Steps will have to be taken to increase output at the conversion stage and to expedite delivery of the bought-in part. The other two operations are marginally ahead of schedule and do not present a problem.

In complex operations, the line of balance calculations can be performed by a computer, which will also generate control reports.

BENEFITS

The line of balance is a simple planning and control technique which, like *network analysis*, formalizes and enforces planning discipline and enables control to be exercised at each stage of the production line. It prevents any feeling of false security which might be engendered if the delivery of an item is on schedule but unappreciated shortfalls at early stages are building up trouble. By identifying such shortfalls, or even excessive production or purchasing levels, corrective action can be taken in good time.

FURTHER READING

Wild, R, *Production and Operations Management*, Holt, Rinehart & Winston, Eastbourne 1984, pp. 426–33.

Part 7

Efficiency and Effectiveness

.

120

Balanced Scorecard

DEFINITION

The balanced scorecard was defined by Kaplan and Norton, who introduced the concept as follows:

> The Balanced Scorecard (BSC) translates an organization's mission and strategy into a comprehensive set of performance measures that provides the framework for a strategic measurement and management system. The scorecard measures organizational performance across four linked perspectives: financial, customer, internal business process, and learning and growth.

AIM

As described by Kaplan and Norton, the balanced scorecard enables companies to track short-term financial results while simultaneously monitoring their progress in building the capabilities and acquiring the intangible assets that generate growth for future financial performance. Its aim is to ensure that a broader and more balanced view is taken of the factors affecting business performance. This replaces the focus on financial indicators alone, which could lead to short-term decisions, over-investment in easily valued assets through mergers and acquisitions with readily measurable returns, and underinvestment in intangible assets, such as produce and process innovation, employee skills and motivation or customer satisfaction, whose short-term returns are difficult to measure.

The balanced scorecard is, however, not simply a measuring device. It can and should be used as a fundamental approach to managing a business by ensuring that strategic goals in key performance areas are defined and communicated to all employees. If this is done, individual goals can be aligned to corporate goals within a clearly defined framework, which can also be used as a basis for measuring, rewarding and improving their performance.

METHODOLOGY

The steps required to introduce and operate a balanced scorecard approach are listed below.

Define the elements of the scorecard

First, it is necessary to establish the constituents of the balanced scorecard – the perspectives from which performance requirements will be defined and measured as a basis for improvement. The elements usually include financial, process and customer factors. People factors covering development, motivation, leadership, and so forth, are sometimes substituted for learning and growth.

In the retail network of Halifax plc the four areas are:

- how people are managed;
- how internal processes are managed;
- levels of customer service;
- business performance (sales).

At this stage it is also necessary to define clearly the objectives of the balanced scorecard approach.

Identify performance drivers

The second step is to identify the performance drivers for each of the categories – for example, repeating and expanding sales from existing customers, the internal processes at which the company must excel, the needs and wants of customers and the particular people skills the organization needs now and in the future.

Links will need to be established between each of these areas so that they are mutually reinforcing. For example, high levels of customer service in defined areas will lead to better financial performance; customer service levels can be improved by attention to processes such as on-time delivery, and customer care will be enhanced if the right people are selected and given the training to develop the necessary skills.

Identify performance measures

The third step is to determine how performance in each of the categories will be measured. In some areas such as finance and customer service it may be quite easy to determine quantitative measures such as sales or levels of service as assessed by surveys, questionnaires and mystery shopping. The measures for the process and change in perspectives may, however, have to focus on the achievement of development programmes to meet defined specifications and to deliver expected results.

Communicate

This fourth step is to communicate to all employees what the balanced scorecard is, why it is important, how it will work, the part they will be expected to play and how they and the organization will benefit from it.

Operationalize

The fifth step is to operationalize the system. This means developing policies, procedures and processes that ensure that it is applied at all levels in the organization – strategically at the top, tactically in the middle – and as a matter of continuing importance so far as working practices are concerned to all employees.

Operationalization might include the definition of performance requirements in terms of targets and the introduction of new processes, the communication of these requirements, and the development and application of processes for measuring outcomes and taking corrective action when required. At an individual level, performance management processes may be based on the four elements of the scorecard. Objectives and standards of performance and competencies that are aligned to corporate objectives would be agreed for each element and performance reviews would assess progress and lead to agreed improvement and personal development plans.

Train

The sixth step is to provide training for everyone in the organization on the operation of the balanced scorecard and on what, on their different levels, they are expected to do about managing and implementing the process.

Monitoring, evaluation and review

Finally, the operation of the balanced scorecard should be monitored and its effectiveness evaluated in agreement with its objectives. A review can then take place to decide on where improvements or amendments need to be made and how they will take place.

BENEFITS

The benefits of the balanced scorecard are that it:

- communicates corporate and departmental objectives to the people and teams performing the work;
- enables a comprehensive view to be taken of the various aspects of a company's performance;
- provides a framework within which performance can be managed at corporate, unit, team and individual levels.

REFERENCE

Kaplan, R S and Norton, D P, 'The balanced scorecard – measures that drive performance', *Harvard Business Review,* January–February 1992, pp 71–79.

121

Benchmarking

DEFINITION

Benchmarking involves identifying best practices in other organizations, comparing them with existing practices within the benchmarker's own organization, and taking action to improve those practices in the light of information on best practices elsewhere, comparing and measuring the performance of the benchmarker's own organization in particular respects with the performance in those areas of other organizations.

AIM

The aim of benchmarking is to improve the performance of the organization by incorporating appropriate best practice into existing procedures and practices, and by identifying areas where performance is inadequate compared with other organizations so that corrective action can be taken.

METHODOLOGY

The process of benchmarking involves:

- identifying the aspects of policy, procedure and practice for which information from other organizations is required;
- identifying the critical performance areas or factors within the organization for which comparative data are required;

- identifying other organizations or sources of information about these aspects or factors (some information will be published and some industrial or professional associations have such information);
- approaching organizations to reach agreement on obtaining information – this is usually given on a reciprocal basis;
- gathering the data from other organizations – it is important to find out as much as possible about *how* any policy, procedure or practice works *and* how *well* it works, the extent to which the approach is transferable from that organization to the benchmarker's organization (it is necessary to assess the degree to which a practice is unique to an organization and is not therefore transferable in its present form);
- analysing published data or information from professional/employer's organizations;
- deciding what action needs to be taken on the basis of the information obtained.

When comparing policies, practices and procedures it is essential to establish the extent to which they can be transferred in their present or a modified form. The information can be used to check on the degree to which proposed innovations within the organization are proceeding along the right lines and to amend proposals to take account of the lessons learned elsewhere. Something that works well in one organization may not work well in another because of differences in such areas as organizational culture and structure, management style, technology and customer base. Remember that there is often as much to be learned from the failures and bad practices of comparator organizations as there is from their successes. Even if the best ingredients are taken from a number of different sources, the real skill lies in knowing how to mix the ingredients properly.

When comparing published data, it is necessary to ensure that, so far as possible, like is being compared with like; in other words, that the data is relevant in terms of the functions and operations of the organizations.

BENEFITS

Benchmarking ensures that organizations are aware of best practice elsewhere and/or know how well they are doing in comparison with other similar firms. It provides the basis for ensuring that improvements can be made that are based on successful practice elsewhere, as long as care is taken to ensure that the practice fits the culture, structure and technology of the organization.

122

Business Process Re-engineering

Business process re-engineering is concerned with the systematic analysis and redesign of business processes in order to achieve significant improvement in performance in terms of quality, service, speed and cost. It focuses on processes rather than functions or tasks as the basis for the design and management of business activities. It can involve fundamental rethinking, radical streamlining or the total redesign of a process from its beginning within the organization to its end with the customer.

A process is defined as a sequence of activities that are carried out to deliver a product or service to an internal or external customer. Typical processes are fulfilling a customer order, issuing a new insurance policy, developing a new product and setting up a new retail outlet. Processes link activities within functions so that the end result required by the customer is produced.

AIMS

The overall aims of business process re-engineering is to streamline and link together business processes so that business performance is improved. Specifically, business process re-engineering aims to ensure that:

- work is organized around outcomes, not tasks;
- work is performed where it makes most sense;

- the steps in the process are performed in a natural order – they are sequenced in terms of what needs to follow what and parallel activities are linked;
- unnecessary activities and tasks are eliminated or combined into one process;
- boundaries between work teams and their activities are eliminated;
- jobs change from simple tasks to multidimensional and therefore multi-skilled work.

METHODOLOGY

The steps required in a business process re-engineering exercise are to:

1. Select the process to be re-engineered.
2. Define the aims of the exercise.
3. Select and brief the process re-engineering team.
4. Critically analyse existing processes in conjunction with the staff concerned. The analysis may use the 'what–how–when–where–why?'
5. Diagnose problems and issues, again in conjunction with staff.
6. Define the scope for redesign and the results to be achieved.
7. Redesign the process, setting out the sequence involved, the activities carried out and the roles of those involved in introducing and managing the new process. Again, it is vital to involve those concerned with the process in the redesign so that they 'own' the results. It is essential at this stage to identify any problems that might arise for the people concerned because their roles will change or because new skills will be required. If the programme should result in fewer or radically changed jobs, the consequences for people must be recognized so that steps may be taken to alleviate the problems.
8. Plan the actions required to implement the new process, recognizing that this is a change management issue and that steps must be taken to communicate to and involve the staff affected and to provide help and training.
9. Implement the new process.
10. Monitor the implementation and amend or improve arrangements as required.

BENEFITS

If re-engineering is done well it can deliver worthwhile gains in speed, productivity and performance. It can, however, be difficult to manage effectively and it will fail if it does not take account of the people implications, including the opinions and feelings of those concerned.

FURTHER READING

Hammer, P, *Beyond Re-engineering*, HarperCollins, Oxford 1997.
Hammer, P and Champy, J, *Re-engineering the Corporation*, Harper Business, Oxford 1993.

123

Ratio Analysis

DEFINITION

Ratio analysis studies and compares financial ratios which identify relationships between quantifiable aspects of a company's activities. The object is to reveal factors and trends affecting performance so that action can be taken.

TYPES OF RATIOS

Ratios cover the following areas:

1. profitability;
2. performance;
3. cost;
4. liquidity;
5. capital structure;
6. financial risk;
7. efficiency – debtors, creditors, inventory;
8. productivity.

PROFITABILITY

The profitability ratios are as follows:

1. *Return on equity*

$$\frac{\text{Profit after interest and dividends but before tax and extraordinary items}}{\text{Average ordinary share capital, reserves and retained profit for the period}}$$

2. *Return on capital employed*

$$\frac{\text{Trading or operating profit}}{\text{Total assets (fixed assets and current assets)}}$$

or

$$\frac{\text{Trading or operating profit}}{\text{Net total assets (fixed and current assets − current liabilities)}}$$

3. *Earnings per share*

$$\frac{\text{Profit after interest, taxation and ordinary dividends but before extraordinary items}}{\text{Number of ordinary shares issued by the company}}$$

4. *Price/earnings (P/E) ratio*

$$\frac{\text{Market price of ordinary shares}}{\text{Earnings per share}}$$

5. *Economic value added (EVA)* is post-tax operating profit minus the cost of the capital invested in the business.

PERFORMANCE

The main performance ratios are as follows:

1. *Return on sales or profit margin ratio*

$$\frac{\text{Trading or operating profit}}{\text{Total sales}} \times 100$$

2. *Asset turnover ratio*

$$\frac{\text{Total sales}}{\text{Assets}}$$

These two ratios are discussed in Chapter 62.

The asset turnover ratio can be divided into:

1. $\dfrac{\text{Sales}}{\text{Fixed assets}}$ which is subdivided into:

(a) $\dfrac{\text{Sales}}{\text{Land and buildings}}$

(b) $\dfrac{\text{Sales}}{\text{Plant and machinery}}$

(c) $\dfrac{\text{Sales}}{\text{Vehicles}}$

2. $\dfrac{\text{Sales}}{\text{Current assets}}$ which is subdivided into:

(a) $\dfrac{\text{Sales}}{\text{Material Stocks}}$

(b) $\dfrac{\text{Sales}}{\text{Work-in-progress}}$

(c) $\dfrac{\text{Sales}}{\text{Finished stocks}}$

(d) $\dfrac{\text{Sales}}{\text{Debtors}}$

COST

Overheads

The key overall cost ratio is:

$$\frac{\text{Overheads}}{\text{Sales}} \times 100$$

Functional or departmental cost ratios

The main functional or departmental cost ratios are:

1. $\dfrac{\text{Production cost of sales}}{\text{Sales}} \times 100$ which is subdivided into:

(a) $\dfrac{\text{Cost of materials}}{\text{Sales value of production}} \times 100$

(b) $\dfrac{\text{Works labour cost}}{\text{Sales value of production}} \times 100$

(c) $\dfrac{\text{Other production costs}}{\text{Sales value of production}} \times 100$

2. $\dfrac{\text{Distribution and marketing costs}}{\text{Sales}} \times 100$

3. $\dfrac{\text{Administration costs}}{\text{Sales}} \times 100$

4. $\dfrac{\text{Payroll costs}}{\text{Sales}} \times 100$

Cost per unit of output

Where it is possible to measure outputs in units, the cost per unit of output provides a long measure of productivity as well as cost control.

The formula is:

$$\frac{\text{Production costs}}{\text{Output in units}}$$

The relationships between the profitability, performance and cost ratios referred to above are shown in Figure 123.1.

LIQUIDITY

The two main liquidity ratios, which establish that the company has sufficient cash resources to meet its obligations, are as follows:

1. *The working capital ratio (current ratio)*

$$\frac{\text{Current assets}}{\text{Current liabilities}}$$

2. *The quick ratio (acid-test ratio)*

$$\frac{\text{Current assets minus stocks}}{\text{Current liabilities}}$$

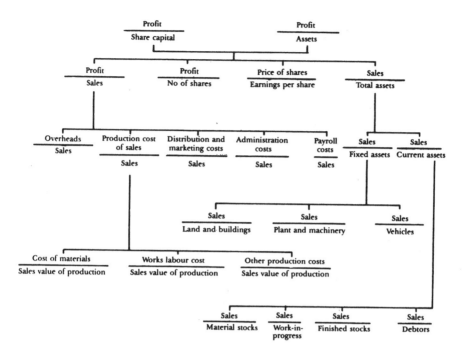

Figure 123.1 *Relationship between ratios*

CAPITAL STRUCTURE

The key capital structure ratios are as follows:

1. *Long-term debt to equity ratio (the gearing ratio)*

$$\frac{\text{Long-term loans plus preference shares}}{\text{Ordinary shareholders' funds}} \times 100$$

2. *Long-term debt to long-term finance ratio*

$$\frac{\text{Long-term loans plus preference shares}}{\text{Long-term loans plus preference shares plus ordinary shareholders' funds}} \times 100$$

3. *Total debt to total assets ratio*

$$\frac{\text{Long-term loans plus short-term loans}}{\text{Total assets}}$$

The liquidity and capital structure ratios referred to above are examined in more detail in Chapter 61.

FINANCIAL RISK

Financial risk ratios measure, primarily for the benefit of shareholders and investors, the risk of dividends or interest payments not being adequately covered by the earnings of the company.

The main risk ratios are as follows:

1. *Interest cover.* Interest cover ratios focus attention on the relationship between interest payment liabilities and the profits or cash flow available for making these payments, thus providing an alternative way of analysing gearing. They show the number of times interest is 'covered' by profits or cash flow and therefore indicate the risk of non-payment of interest.

    Interest cover ratios exist in two forms:

    (a) $\dfrac{\text{Profit before interest and tax}}{\text{Gross interest payable}}$

    (b) $\dfrac{\text{Cash-flow operations before interest and tax}}{\text{Gross interest payable}}$

Profit provides the overall measure of ability to pay, but as interest has to be paid out of cash, the cash-flow ratio is perhaps more significant.

There are no optimum ratios which are generally applicable. It depends on the circumstances of the company, although any company would be in a really bad way if it could not cover interest by profits or even cash. The more profits or cash flows fluctuate, the higher the ratio should be. For profits, a two times cover is fairly satisfactory in stable conditions. For cash flows, a four times cover is quite healthy.

2. *Dividend cover.* The dividend cover ratio examines the amount by which profits could fall before leading to a reduction in the current level of dividends. The dividends ratio is calculated as:

$$\frac{\text{Profits available for paying ordinary dividends}}{\text{Ordinary dividends}}$$

If ordinary dividends are covered, say, three times (a reasonably safe position), this means that profits could be three times less than they are before there would be insufficient current profits to pay the dividend.

EFFICIENCY

Debtors

The three main debtor ratios are as follows:

1. *Debtor turnover*, which measures whether the amount of resources tied up in debtors is reasonable and whether the company has been efficient in converting debtors into cash. The formula is:

$$\frac{\text{Sales}}{\text{Debtors}}$$

The higher the ratio the better.
2. *Average collection period*, which measures how long it takes to collect amounts from debtors. The formula is:

$$\text{Average collection period in days} = \frac{\text{Debtors}}{\text{Sales}} \times 365$$

The actual collection period can be compared with the stated credit terms of the company. If it is longer than those terms, then this indicates some inefficiency in the procedures for collecting debts.
3. *Bad debt*, which measures the proportion of bad debts to sales:

$$\frac{\text{Bad debts}}{\text{Sales}}$$

This ratio indicates the efficiency of the credit control procedures of the company. Its level will depend on the type of business. Mail-order companies have to accept a fairly high level of bad debts, while retailing organizations should maintain very low levels or, if they do not allow credit accounts, none at all. The actual ratio is compared with the target or norm to decide whether or not it is acceptable.

Creditors

The measurement of the creditor turnover period shows the average time taken to pay for goods and services purchased by the company. The formula is:

$$\text{Creditor turnover period in days} = \frac{\text{Creditors}}{\text{Purchases}} \times 365$$

In general the longer the credit period achieved the better, because delays in payment mean that the operations of the company are being financed interest free by suppliers' funds. But there will be a point beyond which delays in payment will damage relationships with suppliers which, if they are operating in a seller's market, may harm the company. If too long a period is taken to pay creditors, the credit rating of the company may suffer, thereby making it more difficult to obtain suppliers in the future.

Inventory

A considerable amount of a company's capital may be tied up in the financing of raw materials, work-in-progress and finished goods. It is important to ensure that the level of stocks is kept as low as possible, consistent with the need to fulfil customers' orders in time.

The two stock turnover ratios are:

1. *Stock turnover rate*

$$\frac{\text{Cost of sales}}{\text{Stock}}$$

2. *Stock turnover period*

$$\frac{\text{Sales}}{\text{Cost of sales}} \times 365$$

The higher the stock turnover rate or the lower the stock turnover period the better, although the ratios will vary between companies. For example, the stock turnover rate in a food retailing company must be higher than the rate in a manufacturing concern.

The level of inventory in a company may be assessed by the use of the *inventory ratio*, which measures how much has been tied up in inventory. The formula is:

$$\frac{\text{Inventory}}{\text{Current assets}}$$

PRODUCTIVITY

Productivity ratios measure how efficiently the company is using its workforce. The main ratios are as follows:

1. *Profits per employee*

$$\frac{\text{Trading profit}}{\text{Number of employees}}$$

2. *Sales per employee*

$$\frac{\text{Sales}}{\text{Number of employees}}$$

3. *Output per employee*

$$\frac{\text{Units produced or processed}}{\text{Number of employees}}$$

4. *Added value per employee*

$$\frac{\text{Added value (sales revenue minus cost of sales)}}{\text{Number of employees}}$$

USE OF RATIOS

Ratios by themselves mean nothing. They must always be compared with:

- a norm or a target;
- previous ratios in order to assess trends; and
- the ratios achieved in other comparable companies (intercompany comparisons).

Caution has to be exercised in using ratios. The following limitations must be taken into account:

1. Ratios are calculated from financial statements which are affected by the financial bases and policies adopted on such matters as depreciation and the valuation of stocks.
2. Financial statements do not represent a complete picture of the business, but merely a collection of facts which can be expressed in monetary terms. These may not refer to other factors which affect performance.
3. Overuse of ratios as controls on managers could be dangerous in that management might concentrate more on simply improving the ratio than on dealing with the significant issues. For example, the return on capital employed can be improved by reducing assets rather than increasing profits.
4. A ratio is a comparison of two figures, a numerator and a denominator. In comparing ratios it may be difficult to determine whether differences are due to changes in the numerator, or in the denominator or in both.
5. Ratios, as Figure 123.1 demonstrates, are interconnected. They should not be treated in isolation. The effective use of ratios therefore depends on being aware of all these limitations and ensuring that, following comparative analysis, they are used as a trigger point for investigation and corrective action rather than being treated as meaningful in themselves.

BENEFITS

The analysis of management ratios clarifies trends and weaknesses in performance as a guide to action as long as proper comparisons are made and the reasons for adverse trends or deviations from the norm are investigated thoroughly.

FURTHER READING

Pendlebury, M and Groves, R, *Company Accounts* (2nd edition), Unwin Hyman, London 1990.

124

Productivity Planning

DEFINITION

Productivity planning is the use of the technique of a productivity audit to prepare productivity improvement programmes.

Productivity is the relationship between the input and output of a good or service. The productivity index can be formulated as a series of ratios:

$$\text{Productivity index} = \frac{\text{Output obtained}}{\text{Input expected}} = \frac{\text{Performance achieved}}{\text{Resources consumed}} = \frac{\text{Effectiveness}}{\text{Efficiency}}$$

High productivity reflects the full (ie effective and efficient) use of resources.

MEASURING PRODUCTIVITY

Productivity is not simply performance and not simply the economic use of resources, but a combination of both. Its measurement is carried out by means of ratios which cover:

1. *input variables* – payroll costs, the associated costs of employment, the number of people employed and the number of hours worked or time taken; and
2. *output variables* – units produced, products sold, tasks completed, revenues obtained, value added, responsibilities met and standards reached (including standard hours produced).

A wide variety of productivity ratios can be derived from these input and output variables and these can be analysed and added to under the following headings:

1. *Output ratios*

   (a) $\dfrac{\text{Units produced or processed}}{\text{Number of employees}}$

   (b) $\dfrac{\text{Sales turnover}}{\text{Number of employees}}$

   (c) $\dfrac{\text{Added value}}{\text{Number of employees}}$

   (d) $\dfrac{\text{Standard hours produced}}{\text{Number of employees}}$

2. *Cost ratios*

   (a) $\dfrac{\text{Wages cost}}{\text{Units produced}}$

   (b) $\dfrac{\text{Sales turnover}}{\text{Payroll/employment costs}}$

   (c) $\dfrac{\text{Added value}}{\text{Payroll/employment costs}}$

   (d) $\dfrac{\text{Actual labour cost per standard hour}}{\text{Target cost per standard hour}}$

   (e) $\dfrac{\text{Standard hours produced}}{\text{Labour costs}}$

3. *Performance ratios*

   (a) $\dfrac{\text{Standard hours produced}}{\text{Actual hours worked}}$

   (b) $\dfrac{\text{Actual performance}}{\text{Target performance}}$

The choice is ample and one or more ratios can be selected to suit individual circumstances. There are very few occasions, however, when the basic index of:

$$\frac{\text{Results}}{\text{Resources}} \text{ ie } \frac{\text{Sales}}{\text{Employees}}$$

will not prove to be the most useful of all.

THE PRODUCTIVITY AUDIT

The productivity audit examines performance as revealed by the productivity ratios. It considers, first of all, actual performance compared with company standards and trends and what other organizations achieve. It then explores the reasons for unsatisfactory performance with the help of checklists under the following headings:

- Poor planning, budgeting and control procedures.
- Inefficient methods or systems of work.
- Inadequate use of work measurement.
- Insufficient mechanization or inadequate plant and machinery.
- Poor management.
- Poorly motivated employees.
- Badly paid employees.
- Too many restrictive practices.
- Inadequate training.
- Excessive waste.

THE PRODUCTIVITY PLAN

The productivity plan incorporates improvement programmes in one or more of the following areas:

1. *Work simplification*. Eliminating unnecessary operations, movements and paperwork.
2. *Mechanization*. Introducing new tools or equipment to speed up processing.
3. *Automation*. Replacing human labour with machines or electronic equipment.
4. *Facilities improvement*. Providing more efficient services; improving the availability of materials, manufactured parts, small tools; improving the working environment through better layouts and ergonomic studies.
5. *The more effective use of human resources*. Employing fewer but more highly qualified or trained people; improving the skills of existing staff; improving the quality of management and supervision.

6. *Better planning and scheduling of work.*
7. *Productivity bargaining.* Negotiating with unions to get their agreement to changes in working practices which will improve productivity as a quid pro quo for a pay increase.

BENEFITS

Improvements in productivity do not just happen. They have to be worked for. Productivity plans based upon a systematic audit provide the foundation for successful productivity improvement campaigns.

125

Method Study

DEFINITION

Method study is the systematic recording and critical examination of existing and proposed ways of doing work as a means of developing and applying easier and more effective methods and reducing costs.

Method study and work measurement are the two main branches of work study.

TECHNIQUES

Flow processing

The sequence of activities carried out by individuals can be recorded by flow process charts. The standard ASME (American Society of Mechanical Engineers) symbols are:

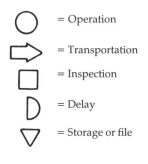

= Operation

= Transportation

= Inspection

= Delay

= Storage or file

Flow charts (see Figure 125.1) are prepared as follows:

1. *Main sequence of activity.* Each activity is described in terms of one of the ASME symbols. The sequence of activities is shown by setting out these symbols vertically in the order of their occurrence and joining them by a vertical line.
2. *Subsidiary activities or alternative routes.* The main sequence is shown on the right-hand side. Subsidiary activities or alternative routes are

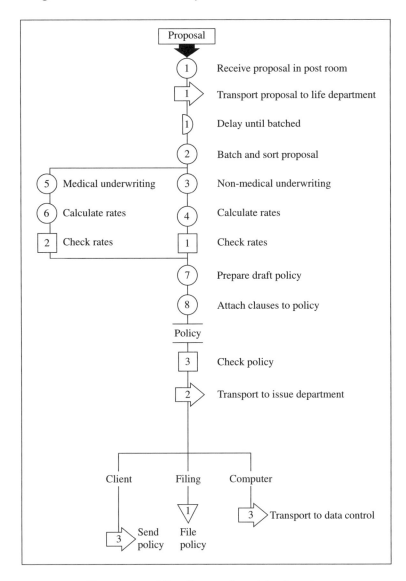

Figure 125.1 *Life policy – underwriting flow chart*

represented on the left as a vertical sequence of activities joined to the main stream by a horizontal line at the appropriate place.

3. *Reference numbers.* Each activity symbol is numbered separately so that a reference can be made when conducting the critical examination. Numbering starts at the head of the main sequence, continues to the entry of a subsidiary activity, then to the top of the subsidiary, and back to the main sequence to the foot of the chart.

4. *Repeats and changes.* Shown by breaking the chart with a double horizontal line immediately below the activity to be repeated or the point when the article being processed changes significantly.

5. *Identification.* Data are included on the chart to identify the method or the job, when the process starts and finishes and who did the charting. A summary of the activities charted may also be included.

Individual work analysis

An individual's work can be analysed by the use of therblig charts (see Figure 125.2). Each therblig is identified by a symbol, a name, a definition, an abbreviation and a colour for charting purposes. The sequence of operations, activities or events are charted vertically. Therblig charts are only used when highly detailed studies are required.

Procedure charting

Procedure charting uses the same symbols and conventions as individual activity charting. The documents are identified in boxes at the beginning of each sequence and their distribution is shown in the same way as alternative routes in process charting (see Figure 125.1).

Recording group activities

Group activities can be recorded by multiple activity charts which show the activities of each member of a group linked to a timescale (see Figure 125.3).

Recording movements

The main techniques for recording movements round a workshop, office, room or site are as follows:

1. *String diagrams*, which record the movements of an operator by tracing them with a reel of cotton routed round pins placed on a plan at the points where there is a change of direction. String diagrams give a vivid picture of how movements take place and can quickly reveal unnecessary, unnecessarily long or duplicated movements.

SYMBOL	NAME	COLOUR CODING
⌒⊙	search	black
⊙	find	grey
→	select	light grey
∩	grasp	red
⌴	hold	gold ochre
◡	transport load	green
9	position	blue
#	assemble	violet
U	use	purple
#	disassemble	light violet
( )	inspect	burnt ochre
↓	pre-position	pale blue
◠	release load	carmine red
◡	transport empty	olive green
℗	rest for overcoming fatigue	orange
⌂	unavoidable delay	yellow
⌐	avoidable delay	lemon yellow
℗	plan	brown

Figure 125.2 *Therblig symbols*

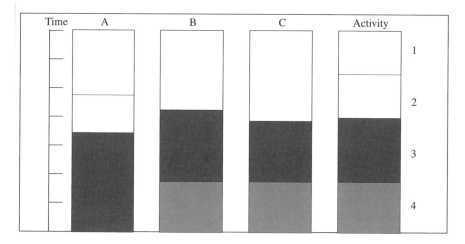

Figure 125.3 *Multiple activity chart*

2. *Flow diagrams*, which are a representation of a flow chart on a plan so that the physical movements are traced by a line between the different activities.

Critical examination

Critical examination uses the questioning approach to find out what, how, when, where and, most importantly, why an activity is carried out, and who does it. From this analysis two fundamental questions are posed:

1. Does the activity need to be done at all? If so:
2. Are there any better ways of doing it?

The questioning approach is set out in more detail in Figure 125.4.

BENEFITS

The main benefits resulting from method study are:

1. work simplification – eliminating unnecessary operations, movements and paperwork;
2. facilities improvement – providing more efficient transportation and procurement services, speeding up the flow of paperwork and materials, speeding up processing activities;
3. the more effective use of the workforce; and
4. better planning and scheduling of work.

	Current facts	Reasons	Possible alternatives	Review purpose
WHAT?	What is done now?	Why is it done?	What *else* could be done?	What *should* be done?
HOW?	How is it done?	Why in that way?	How *else* could it be done?	How *should* it be done?
WHEN?	When is it done?	Why at that time?	When *else* could it be done?	When *should* it be done?
WHERE?	Where is it done?	Why in that place?	Who *should* do it?	Where *should* it be done?
WHO?	Who does it?	Why that person(s)?	Who *else* could do it?	Who *should* do it?

Figure 125.4 *Questioning approach*

126

Work Measurement

DEFINITION

Work measurement is the application of techniques designed to establish the work content of a specified task and the time for a qualified worker to carry out that job at a defined level of performance.

Work measurement and method study are the two main branches of work study.

USES

The uses of work measurement are to:

1. *Provide the basis for incentive schemes* which relate pay to performance as measured by the ratio between standard and actual hours.
2. *Monitor performance* – by providing the common denominator of standard hours, work measurement enables the performance of different units and a single unit over time to be compared. Actuals can be compared with targets to indicate where corrective action may be required.
3. *Assist in budget preparation.* The time standards can be used to convert forecast volumes into the total number of working hours required, which can in turn be converted by the application of hourly rates into the cost of labour.
4. *Determine current workforce levels.* By objectively providing an indication of 'should take' time, work measurement gives management the ability

to compare the amount of time actually spent with the amount of time that should have been spent. When current workforce levels are in excess of what time standards show to be required, reductions can be achieved. When the reverse applies, the current level can be increased.

5. *Determine future workforce needs.* By defining the time required to perform specific tasks, work measurement makes it possible to translate forecast activity levels into anticipated workforce requirements.

TECHNIQUES

Time study

Time study employs stopwatches to determine the standard time for completing a job. The process starts by analysing the job into its basic elements. This stage permits the critical appraisal of the method of performing the job and then the improvement of the method wherever possible.

The next stage is to time each element of the revised procedure so that the time for the total job is built up.

Finally, a rating adjustment is made to take account of the speed and effectiveness of the operator, and a relaxation allowance is calculated to provide for the effect of fatigue over a longer period. The relaxation allowance varies according to the job, but is typically 10 to 15 per cent.

The end result is the time for the task defined in standard minutes, which is the time the experienced worker of average ability should take to do the task while taking the normal amount of rest from fatigue and for personal needs. Such a worker should produce at an average rate of 60 standard minutes per 60 clock minutes over the whole day or shift without undue strain or fatigue. On the British Standards Institute scale this is called a 100 rating (ie $60/60 \times 100$) and is referred to as standard performance. A worker who takes 80 clock minutes to do 60 standard minutes' work will be working at a 75 rating, ie $60/80 \times 100$.

Synthesis

Synthesis is used by work study departments, which over the years have built up a library of 'synthetics', ie standard times for doing common tasks which can be applied to any of these tasks as they exist in a job. The use of synthetics saves repetitive timing, leaving the time study engineer only the unusual elements to measure with his or her stopwatch.

Predetermined motion time systems (PMTS)

Predetermined motion time systems (PMTS) are libraries of standard synthetics which are based on the concept that human work of a physical kind consists of combinations of basic motions of the hands, arms, trunk, legs, head and eyes. The time required to perform each basic motion differs only in the smallest degree between different workers, so that by studying a series of basic motions a sufficient number of times, tables of standard performance times can be prepared for each motion pattern. Standard times for a task can then be calculated by adding up the PMTS times for each motion, and these standards can be used for planning and control purposes in exactly the same way as those resulting from time studies. PMTS systems are also used in *clerical work measurement programmes*.

Analytical estimating

Analytical estimating builds up standard times partly from synthetics and partly on values estimated by experienced workers who have been trained in rating. It is not as accurate as the other two systems and is generally used when the non-routine nature of the job makes it difficult to prepare time-studied data, as in maintenance work.

DEFINING WORK STANDARDS

Work measurement produces standard times for each job expressed in standard minutes. For rated work, a standard of 100 is expected when there is an individual incentive scheme. If there is no incentive scheme, a standard of 83 is expected from experienced and reasonably well-motivated workers.

Individual performance

Individual performance is measured by the number of standard minutes of work produced, expressed as a percentage of the actual time taken to produce them. The number of standard minutes of work produced is calculated by multiplying the number of units produced by the standard minute value per unit. Actual production time is the time spent on measured work excluding lost time (diverted and waiting time). The formula is therefore:

$$\frac{\text{Number of units produced} \times \text{standard minute values per unit}}{\text{Time taken to produce the units in minutes}} \times 100$$

Thus, if the number of standard minutes per unit is 15 and in 360 minutes an operator produces 20 units, his or her individual performance will be:

$$\frac{20 \text{ units} \times 15 \text{ standard minutes per unit}}{360 \text{ minutes on measured work}} \times 100 = 83$$

Overall performance

Individual performance measures the rate of working while actually doing the job. The rate of working for the whole period while the operator is at work (attendance hours/minutes) is termed overall performance. It is measured by the following formula:

$$\frac{\text{Number of standard minutes of work produced}}{\text{Total attendance time in minutes}} \times 100$$

Overall performance is usually about 10 units below individual operator performance. It is useful to monitor the difference between individual and overall performance as this is directly controlled by supervision through minimizing lost time, especially waiting time.

USING WORK STANDARDS

Workforce budgeting

Workforce budgets can be built up from the overall performance figures as follows:

- Calculate number of standard minutes to be produced by multiplying output required (say 430 units a day) by standard minutes per unit (say 15) = 6,450.
- Take overall performance rate (say 80) and calculate attendance minutes required to achieve this rate given the standard minutes to be produced.

$$\frac{\text{Standard minutes of work produced (6,450)}}{\text{Attendance minutes (8,100)}} \times 100 = 80$$

- Divide attendance minutes by minutes attended per person per day (say 450) to give number of staff: 8100/450 = 18.

Workforce costs

Standard labour costs can be calculated by multiplying the standard minutes per unit (assuming 100 performance where an incentive scheme operates) by the hourly rate at 100 performance. The actual cost per standard hour will be the gross wages divided by the number of standard hours worked.

Workforce controls

The control information supplied by work standards will be:

- actual individual performance: planned individual performance;
- actual overall performance: planned overall performance;
- actual individual performance: planned overall performance; and
- planned cost per standard hour: actual cost per standard hour.

In addition to comparing actuals with planned performance, this control information can be used to compare trends between different periods of time. Adverse variances can then be picked up and analysed.

BENEFITS

Work measurement provides an analytical basis for incentive schemes, for budgeting and controlling workforce costs and for increasing productivity by providing standards against which performance can be planned, monitored and improved.

FURTHER READING

Barnes, R, *Motion and Time Study*, Wiley, New York 1969; London 1980.
Currie, R M, *Work Study*, Pitman, London 1977.

127

Value Analysis

DEFINITION

Value analysis is a cost reduction technique which uses organized procedures for the identification of unnecessary cost elements in a component or product by the analysis of its function (function being defined as that property of the product which makes it work or sell) and design.

Value can be classified as either *use value* (the ability of the item to achieve its function) or *esteem value* (the status or regard associated with ownership). For value analysis purposes, value is the sum of these two, use value normally being the principal component.

The objective of value analysis is to improve the value–cost relationship, which means a product which provides the necessary function with the essential qualities at minimum cost.

METHOD

Value analysis is carried out in the following stages:

1. *Select the products to be analysed.* Those that give the greatest return for the costs incurred in the analysis itself. Criteria for choice include:

   ■ a multiplicity of parts;
   ■ a large usage;
   ■ a small difference between use value and cost value;
   ■ a long-designed product.

2. *Define the function of the product.* This means answering the following questions:

- What is its purpose?
- What does it do?
- What do customers expect from it?

The function is best described in two words, a verb and a noun, for example: 'supports weight' for a beam; 'transmits force' for a shaft.

3. *Record the number of components.* The more there are, the greater the chance of cost reduction.

4. *Extract existing costs.* The actual or marginal cost of making each component and the product as a whole.

5. *Develop alternatives.* These will include changes in design, specification or manufacturing methods which will reduce costs without affecting the function of the product. The fundamental questions to be answered are as follows:

- Is this component needed? If so:
- Why is it manufactured this way?
- Is there a cost-effective substitute or alternative method of making it?

These questions may be dealt with by using brainstorming techniques (the generation of ideas by groups) which are eventually distilled into a list of practical suggestions. The aim of this key stage is to identify the scope to:

(a) eliminate or simplify parts or operations;
(b) substitute alternative materials;
(c) use standard parts;
(d) eliminate unnecessary design features;
(e) substitute low-cost manufacturing processes;
(f) change design to facilitate manufacture;
(g) buy rather than make, if this is cheaper; and
(h) relax manufacturing tolerances.

6. *Evaluate alternatives.* The ideas generated are evaluated from the point of view of the cost savings they will achieve and the extent to which this can be done without seriously affecting the ability of the product to fulfil its function and retain its value in use and esteem value. Recommendations for implementation are then made.

BENEFITS

Value analysis is a common-sense but systematic method of reducing costs by taking each part of the product and looking in detail at its function. It ensures that every feature, tolerance, hole, degree of finish, piece of material or part of the service is vetted to ensure that none of these is adding to the total cost without serving a necessary purpose.

128

Variety Reduction

DEFINITION

Variety reduction is the analysis of the range of products or components manufactured by a company with a view to minimizing the variety of products, parts, materials or processes.

AIMS

The overall aims of variety reduction are to increase efficiency and reduce costs. To achieve these aims, variety reduction:

1. *simplifies* – reduces unnecessary variety;
2. *standardizes* – controls necessary variety; and
3. *specializes* – concentrates effort on undertakings where special expertise or resources are available.

METHODS

Product variety reduction

Product variety reduction is conducted in four stages:

1. *Product analysis*. Products are listed in order of sales turnover or contribution (ie selling price less variable costs). Following Pareto's law, it

might well be the case that 20 per cent of the products account for 80 per cent of the turnover or total contribution. This is known as the 80/20 rule.

2. *Trend analysis*. The relative performance of the items generating less income are scrutinized to check recent trends in turnover.

3. *Action plan*. Any lower-income items for which sales are static or declining are examined in more detail to see if their contribution can be increased by such actions as reducing variable costs and/or increasing the selling price.

4. *Final decision*. The final decision on whether or not to phase out a product for which the action plan has not improved its performance will be affected by two considerations. The first will be the opportunity costs of concentrating on other, more profitable, products, ie what would be gained by transferring production to them. The second will be the economies that would result from discontinuing the product. If, in the short term, they are less than the contribution made by the product, it might be worth retaining it until it can be replaced by an improved version.

Component variety reduction

Component variety reduction examines every component in the final production to find out if there is any scope for standardization, amalgamation or eliminating unnecessary items. If a new component becomes necessary, an effective coding system for existing components will indicate if one is already available. Rather than making the component, it might be more economical to buy it from an outside supplier.

BENEFITS

1. Production runs will be longer and ancillary time for setting up and breaking down will be reduced.
2. Inventory levels will be reduced.
3. Planning and production control will be simplified.
4. Potential savings will be achieved in plant and equipment requirements.
5. Activity can be concentrated more in development and design, marketing and sales, and after-sales service.

Index

NB: page numbers in *italic* indicate figures or tables